THE COURTHOUSES
OF EARLY VIRGINIA

Colonial Williamsburg Studies in Chesapeake History and Culture

CARY CARSON, EDITOR

CARL R. LOUNSBURY

THE COURTHOUSES
OF EARLY VIRGINIA

An Architectural History

UNIVERSITY OF VIRGINIA PRESS
CHARLOTTESVILLE AND LONDON

University of Virginia Press

© 2005 by the Rector and Visitors of the University of Virginia

All rights reserved

Printed in the United States of America on acid-free paper

First published 2005

9 8 7 6 5 4 3 2 1

LIBRARY OF CONGRESS CATALOGING-IN-PUBLICATION DATA

Lounsbury, Carl.

    The courthouses of early Virginia : an architectural history / Carl R. Lounsbury.

      p. cm. — (Colonial Williamsburg studies in Chesapeake history and culture)

    Includes bibliographical references and index.

    ISBN 0-8139-2301-8 (cloth : alk. paper)

1. Courthouses—Virginia—History—17th century. 2. Courthouses—Virginia—History—18th century. 3. Public architecture—Virginia—17th century. 4. Public architecture—Virginia—18th century. 5. Architecture, Colonial—Virginia. 6. Architecture and state—Virginia—History—17th century. 7. Architecture and state—Virginia—History—18th century. 8. Virginia—Social life and customs—To 1775. I. Title. II. Series.

    NA4472.V8L68 2004

    725'.15'0975509033—dc22
                                       2004005183

To the memory of
my father, Tracy McKnight Lounsbury, Jr.,
and for
my mother, Mary Elizabeth Reavis Lounsbury

CONTENTS

ILLUSTRATIONS

All illustrations are from the Colonial Williamsburg Foundation unless otherwise noted.

Drafting conventions for measured drawings

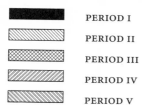

PERIOD I

PERIOD II

PERIOD III

PERIOD IV

PERIOD V

TABLES

PREFACE

THIS WORK BEGAN IN THE EARLY 1980s when the Colonial Williamsburg Foundation decided to restore the interior of the Williamsburg and James City County courthouse, a T-shaped brick building erected on Market Square in the early 1770s. The original fittings had disappeared long ago, and after a fire in 1911, little except the exterior brick walls survived from the colonial period. No documents concerning its design and construction existed. Early court records, which may have provided such information, were destroyed on April 3, 1865, when a warehouse in Richmond in which they were stored, along with thousands of documents from other counties as well, burned with the Confederate evacuation of the capital.

Shorn of its documentary evidence and with few clues left in the original fabric, the Williamsburg courthouse could only be restored to an eighteenth-century appearance based on analogous material from other county court records and other extant buildings. Over the course of three years in the mid-1980s, I examined all the surviving colonial court record books from Virginia counties, teasing out information about the construction, repair, and function of public buildings in the seventeenth and eighteenth centuries. This systematic sweep through hundreds of minute books of Virginia's county courts allowed me to trace the development of the courthouse, prison, and clerk's office as building types, ones that evolved distinctive characteristics shared across the colony and commonwealth between 1650 and 1800. Of particular benefit were the half dozen or so contemporary plans used by magistrates in the eighteenth century in their design deliberations. Once part of a far larger body of drawings, the few that have survived in the county records illustrate courtroom layouts that varied little from the second quarter of the eighteenth century through the first quarter of the nineteenth century.

While documentary sources provided much of the information needed for developing the design proposals for reconstructing the fittings in the Williamsburg courthouse, extensive fieldwork proved to be the key in turning a two-dimensional understanding of the form and function of Virginia's early public buildings into actual working drawings. A number of my colleagues at Colonial Williamsburg and I recorded all the surviving colonial Virginia courthouses, prisons, and clerks' offices in drawings, photographs, and written descriptions. This was not the Herculean task it might seem, for only a little more than a half dozen courthouses remain from the eighteenth century. Like the Williamsburg courthouse, these buildings, too, have lost most if not all of their early fittings to fires and renovations. Yet the fragments of wooden trim found in the Charles City County courthouse, the original sand bed for paving stones found beneath the present floor in the King and Queen County courthouse, and the ghost marks discovered when the walls of the King William County courthouse were stripped of their modern plaster revealed much about the spatial configuration and level of ornamentation in early Virginia courtrooms. A chance discovery of some courthouse sketches at Gunston Hall led to the partial excavation of the Prince William County courthouse in Dumfries, whose plan proved to be an interesting fusion of academic ideas and traditional design.

The fieldwork soon extended beyond the boundaries of the Old Dominion to include early courthouses and other public buildings along the eastern seaboard from South Carolina to Maine. The courtroom in the Chowan County courthouse in Edenton, North Carolina, proved to be particularly useful because it retained as much of its eighteenth-century fabric as any in the country. Along with these forays beyond tidewater Virginia, the opportunity to examine more than two dozen seventeenth- and eighteenth-century courtrooms in England allowed me to put the material that I had found in Virginia into a broader perspective, distinguishing architectural variants and regional manifestations in the Anglo-American legal system. The courtrooms of colonial Virginia shared many of the same features as those found in the Beverley guildhall in the East Riding of Yorkshire, the town hall in Bishop's Castle, Shropshire, and the courthouse in Chester, Pennsylvania, but differences in the arrangement of the magistrates' platform, clerk's table, and lawyers' bar testify to the impact of regional or provincial practices on a common legal culture.

This documentary research and fieldwork informed the restoration of the Williamsburg courthouse, which opened to the public in June 1991. Since that time, additional research in archives and the investigation of other public buildings, particularly the courthouses in Edenton, North Carolina, and Charleston, South Carolina, refined many of the conclusions reached earlier. All of this material forms the basis of this book.

A project of this magnitude and duration naturally accumulated a large debt of gratitude owed to a number of people and institutions. From the custodians who kept a courtroom open long after closing time so that we could record its fittings to the county clerks who gladly searched trunks and muniment rooms for old record books, I have encountered an extraordinary number of people who have been more than willing to help hold the other end of a tape measure or decipher cryptic accounts. The initial research was made possible by grants from the National Endowment for the Humanities, the Richard Gwathmey and Caroline T. Gwathmey Memorial Trust, the Dyson Foundation, the C. M. and M. D. Grant Foundation, the Pew Charitable Trusts, the L. J. and Mary C. Skaggs Foundation, and the Bank of America.

At Colonial Williamsburg, I was able to build upon the work done by my predecessors, especially Paul Buchanan, Catherine Schlesinger, and Marcus Whiffen, whose files I inherited. My colleagues in the Architectural Research Department provided an extraordinary amount of help with this project. Doug Taylor was an industrious draftsman during the first phase of the fieldwork and produced many of the measured drawings that have been used as illustrations. Mark R. Wenger, Willie Graham, Edward Chappell, Peter Sandbeck, and Cary Carson contributed their expertise to the recording process, taking measurements, photographs, and notes, discovering evidence, and providing useful insights into seventeenth- and eighteenth-century building practices and the nature of colonial society. I am especially thankful to Willie Graham for contributing most of the better photographs that illustrate this work. As my research in the field of early American and British architecture has stretched from years to decades, I have grown to appreciate my coworkers' ability to decipher many enigmatic buildings. From Chignal Smealey to Pompion Hill and in many places in between, they have made fieldwork immeasurably fun. I have learned much from them.

I am also grateful to Diane Murphy, Marty Miller, Gwen Miller, Inge Flester, Pam Mendoza Miller, Helen Tate, Ethel Hawkins, Janet Murray, and Wendy Sumerlin for their administrative support. Vanessa Patrick, a former member of the Architectural Research Department, and Susan Lounsbury contributed to the research and spelled my weary eyes by keeping me company at the Library of Virginia and by reading a number of microfilm reels. David Konig of Washington University in St. Louis spent two years at Colonial Williamsburg as the legal scholar in residence. During that time he aided me beyond measure in sorting out the structure and complexities of the colonial legal system. Jeremy Fried, Tom Hay, and other members of the Williamsburg courthouse interpretative staff answered many questions concerning court procedure and have made the eighteenth-century legal system a surprisingly lively topic for those who visit their courtroom. Alfredo Maul and Carrie Alblinger provided much needed technical wizardry that turned words and drawings on paper into electronic files.

In gathering illustrations, Marilyn Melchor pulled together material from a variety of files in my office and across the Colonial Williamsburg Foundation.

I would also like to recognize the efforts of our library staff in supplying research material and illustrations for this project. Susan Berg, Mary Keeling, Liz Ackert, Del Moore, Juleigh Clark, John Ingram, Gail Greve, George Yetter, Marianne Martin, Cathy Grosfils, Laura Arnette, Kathy Rose, Mary Norment, and Lael White happily chased down interlibrary loans and produced photographs from our collections.

I would like to thank those who patiently waited for this book to appear. Far too many years intervened from its inception to its publication, but this lag has in no way diminished my appreciation of the encouragement and support of many scholars, archivists, associates, and friends. I have benefited from the assistance of William H. Adams, Stephen Alexandrowicz, Laura Barry, Barbara Batson, John Beattie, John Bernard, Catherine Bishir, Susan Borchardt, Michael Bourne, Bill Bushong, Marley Brown, Charles Brownell, Linda Baumgarten, Hamilton Bryson, Jeanne Calhoun, Barbara Carson, Allen Chambers, Abbott Lowell Cummings, Claire Dempsey, Patricia Gibbs, Bryan Green, Doug Harnsberger, Noel Harrison, John Hemphill, Bernard Herman, Graham Hood, Carter Hudgins, Quattro Hubbard, Ron Hurst, Rhys Isaac, Audrey Johnson, Stanley Katz, Kevin Kelly, John Larson, Betty Leviner, Ann Carter Lee, Calder Loth, Lori Cousins Macintire, Martha McCartney, Turk McCleskey, Travis McDonald, Martha McNamara, Barbara Mooney, Alan Morledge, W. Brown Morton III, Dean Nelson, Louis Nelson, Nicholas Pappas, Janet Parks, John Pearce, John Peters, Jonathan Poston, Lou Powers, Ellie Reichlin, Selden Richardson, Orlando Ridout V, Linda Rowe, Robert St. George, Paul Shelton, Lee Shepherd, Sarah Shields, Pam Simpson, Gary Stanton, Garry Wheeler Stone, Jane Sundburg, Kevin Sweeney, Thad Tate, Robert Tittler, Dell Upton, Lorena Walsh, Donna Ware, Camille Wells, Frank Welsh, Richard Guy Wilson, and Gibson Worsham. In addition to these individuals, I would like to thank the many members of the Library of Virginia, the Virginia Historical Society, and the Museum of Early Southern Decorative Arts for their support over the past two decades.

As my fieldwork took me across Virginia, I found local officials, clerks of courts, historians, and other individuals more than willing answer my queries and to share their knowledge of their counties' public buildings. Among those were: Gladys Lee Hamilton, Accomack County; Dawn Smith, Amelia County; Iona Adkins, Matthew Carr, Fred Darden, and Lloyd Jones, Charles City County; Nancy Carter Crump, Chesterfield County; James B. Slaughter and Augusta Wilkerson, Essex County; Constance K. Ring, Fairfax County; Gail H. Barb, Fauquier County; Edwin Watson, Fredericksburg; Clementine Bowman, Sue Grow, Wesley Jones, and Carol Steele, Gloucester County; Kathleen Cabell, Louise Parrish, and Don Swofford, Goochland County; J. C. Sizemore, Halifax County; Bruce and Virginia English, Nancy Kilgore, Lois Wickham, Williams

C. Wickham, and Allan Williams, Hanover County; Ann Carter Lee, Henry County; Dick Austin and Diane Howard, Isle of Wight County; Cary C. Hall and Martle Owen, King and Queen County; Alonzo Dill, Emmett M. Upshaw, Charles Waddell, and David Whitlow, King William County; W. R. Moore, Lunenburg County; Patricia Hobbs, Lynchburg; Frank Pleva, Mathews County; John Verrill, Northampton County; Carolyn Jett and Robert McKinney, Northumberland County; Ann Miller, Orange County; John Rothert, Powhatan County; James Bishop, Stephen Bodolay, Lorraine Dow, and Lee Lansing, Prince William County; Gary Williams, Sussex County; John Quarstein, Warwick County.

For buildings investigated outside Virginia, I would like to thank Kay Mahoney, Tolland, Connecticut; Ann Fulmer, New Castle, Delaware; Thomas Parker, Boston; David Miller, Mount Holly, New Jersey; Linda Eure, Al Honeycutt, Ross Ingliss, Don Jordan, Peter Sandbeck, Paul Stephens, and Mitch Wilds, Edenton, North Carolina; Gerald Yoder, Bedford, Pennsylvania; M. K. Toanone, Chester, Pennsylvania; Gloria J. Maize, New Berlin, Pennsylvania; Penelope Batcheler, Philadelphia; Al Benson, York, Pennsylvania; Charlotte Schoonover, Kingston, Rhode Island; John Lauth, Newport, Rhode Island; Ted Sanderson, Providence, Rhode Island; and Jonathan Poston, Charleston, South Carolina.

In the mid-1980s when there were no fax machines, electronic mail, or a decent British telephone system, I was fortunate to have a number of colleagues in the United Kingdom who kindly took the time to notify county archivists and local officials of my interest in courtrooms in England, Scotland, and Wales. Bob Machin of the University of Bristol wrote dozens of letters on my behalf, became a clearinghouse for the project, and participated in the fieldwork. J. T. Smith opened the resources of the Royal Commission on Historical Monuments (England). Howard Colvin of St. John's College, Oxford, and John Harris of the RIBA Library offered sage advice about research sources. A number of individuals took time to show us buildings in their areas including: Roger Evans, Buckinghamshire; D. G. Penrose, Suffolk; Geoffrey Pink, Surrey; and Pam Slocombe, Wiltshire. I would also like to thank the following county archivists, magistrates, clerks of court, curators, mayors, and other officials who graciously permitted us to investigate courtrooms or provided information about individual buildings: H. A. Hanley, Buckinghamshire; Hugh Jacques, Dorset; J. A. Murphy, Hertfordshire; John Fisher, Guildhall Library, London; W. W. S. Breem, Inner Temple, London; R. L. Lambourn, Abingdon; W. Turner, Barnstaple; Einion Wyn Thomas, Beaumaris; Roy Gregory, Beverley; Stanley Angel and James Whalley, Bishop's Castle; C. C. Wheatcroft, Brackley; P. A. Butler, Bridnorth; G. Y. Strawson, Bridport; P. G. Rendall, Burford; Julia Atkins, Clun; D. S. Erskine, Edinburgh; Matthew Alexander, Guildford; John

Crawley and Arthur Jewell, Haslemere; John J. Crawley, Hedon; Peter Walne, Hertford; Ivan Sparkes, High Wycombe; Robert Walker, Huntingdon; G. Davies, Lancaster; Cecil Clarke, Langport; G. C. Parkes, Leicester; R. E. Taylor, Lincoln; G. S. Stephens, Ludlow; Ron Daws, Maldon; Michael Moad, Rochester; W. J. D. Shellabear, Salisbury; C. Wanostrocht, Sandwich; P. G. W. Smith, Shrewsbury; Michael Turner, Slaidburn; Laurence Cramp, Somerton; R. W. Dunning, Taunton; I. A. Crompton, Wallingford; and W. Heatherington, Witney.

Cary Carson, David Konig, Susan Kern, Catherine Bishir, and two readers for the University of Virginia Press kindly read the manuscript. Their comments were invaluable and improved the book immeasurably. I would especially like to thank Susan Kern for taming much of the wild prose that stampeded through earlier drafts. I am grateful to the Society of Architectural Historians for granting me permission to republish parts of two articles of mine that appeared in the *Journal of the Society of Architectural Historians*: "'An Elegant and Commodious Building': William Buckland and the Design of the Prince William County Courthouse," *JSAH* 46 (Sept. 1987): 228–40, and "Beaux-Arts Ideals and Colonial Reality: The Reconstruction of Williamsburg's Capitol, 1928–1934," *JSAH* 49 (Dec. 1990): 373–89.

Penelope Kaiserlian, Mary MacNeil, and others at the University of Virginia Press efficiently negotiated the manuscript through production and publication. I appreciate their professional guidance.

Finally, Susan, Reavis, and Anne have made the end of this long court session a joy to celebrate.

THE COURTHOUSES
OF EARLY VIRGINIA

FIGURE 1. The seat of county government for nearly three hundred years, King William County courthouse retains its rural setting.

INTRODUCTION:
THE STRUCTURE OF JUSTICE

Prologue: Court Day

COURT DAY IN EARLY Virginia transformed many small crossroad villages into bustling rural forums. For one, two, or three days of each month, hundreds of inhabitants set out from their farms on familiar paths and well-worn roads that converged near the center of the county at a clearing commonly called the courthouse grounds (fig. 1). The local gentry who presided over the county court and a few itinerant lawyers and merchants journeyed on horseback across a countryside covered with fields of tobacco and corn interspersed by wide tracts of forests and underbrush. Numerous broad creeks and rivers bisected the terrain, isolating farmsteads and plantations. Rain sometimes turned the roads into muddy morasses and swelled the rivers to impassable depths, making the trip to the courthouse an arduous affair. More often than not, severe weather—torrential downpours or deep snows—postponed court or other public activities until the "next fair day." High water or poor ferry service added further travel delays. Those who rode to the courthouse left their horses in the care of tavern keepers, who provided pasture and provender, or simply tied them up to the post-and-rail fences that sometimes lined the grounds. Some counties built stables for their magistrates and other officials, though they provided little security for personal property, as the Westmoreland justices discovered in 1691 when their saddles were stolen while they were deliberating in the courtroom.[1]

Far more people had the opportunity to examine this rural landscape in greater detail as they traversed on foot the two, three, or dozen miles from their homes to the courthouse grounds. Walking a considerable distance on hot summer mornings often produced a thirst that could only be quenched by several hours over a keg of cider or brandy provided by local tavern keepers or unlicensed vendors at their destination. A few lucky citizens who lived in small courthouse villages or provincial towns such as Williamsburg, Norfolk, and Alexandria had the public business at their doorsteps. Convenience sometimes had its price as trustworthy local freeholders found themselves seconded to

FIGURE 2. Court day, Warsaw, Richmond County, 1909. (Courtesy of The Library of Virginia)

FIGURE 3. Court day, Harrisonburg, Rockingham County, before 1897. (Loaned by Mr. Julius Ritchie, The Library of Virginia)

jury duty and other court assignments with no remuneration for their time or service.

By midmorning, scores if not several hundred men along with a few women and children had reached the courthouse grounds, adding their voices to the cacophony of musical instruments and animals that pierced the air (fig. 2). Maria Carr, who grew up in Harrisonburg in the early nineteenth century, recalled that court day in Rockingham County

> was looked upon as a great event, every one that could leave home was on hand. It was a day of great interest, farmers coming in with their produce—such as butter, eggs, and other articles which they exchanged for groceries & dry-goods. The streets around the Court House were thronged with all sorts of men—others on horse back riding up and down trying to sell their horses. Men in home made clothes, old rusty hats that had seen several generations, coarse shoes and no stockings, some without coats or vests, with only shirts and pants. I have seen a rich man come in from his country home, riding a fine horse. The man was dressed in home made linen shirt and pants, coarse shoes, no stockings, and an old slouch or straw hat. He had a large yellow silk bandana handkerchief under his arm, with the two ends tied over his shoulders. He made money by buying deeds and other papers or loaning money on notes—this was called shaving paper, and many men got rich by this business. This was also a day to settle all grudges—when a man got too much whisky, he was very quarrelsome and wanted to fight—others would follow suit & go in pellmell. It was a dreadful sight to see them beat one another, I used to run off and hide. It was a great day for ginger bread and molasses beer—the cake sellers had the front of the Court House spread with white cloths, with cakes piled high upon them and kegs of beer near by. I have seen the jurymen let their hats down from the window above, get them filled with ginger-bread, and a jug of beer sent up by a rope [fig. 3].[2]

As this recollection of court day in Harrisonburg suggests, the event provided an opportunity for most segments of county society to gather to transact personal business, renew acquaintances, and participate in both the great and small events that affected the community.[3] Court day was a leveling event in this deferential society; visitors were often struck by "the perfect familiarity with which all ranks were mingling in conversation" and commercial transactions.[4] Displaying goods imported from England and other colonies as well as local manufacture, country vendors and traveling peddlers set up temporary booths to cater to the hunger, thirst, and pocketbooks of the crowd (fig. 4). The grounds and shops often had the appearance of a bazaar where stands displayed

FIGURE 4. Woman selling geese. From W. H. Pyne, *Microcosm* (London, 1802).

items that many locals had never encountered (fig. 5). An itinerant merchant who set up his wares on the grounds of the Henry courthouse found that he and his fellow peddlers "exposed our Goods, not to sell, but to be Gazed on, there being none as I suppose able to purchase. Many Enquiries respecting Prices and even their use."[5]

In the cold winter months, fires set about the courthouse grounds kept small groups warm against the morning chill. The fear of fires being built too close to the county buildings prompted Accomack justices to allow them only at a safe distance across the road from the courthouse and prison.[6] At tables inside the taverns and in the corners of courthouse arcades, a handful of lawyers went about their work, going over cases with clients and drumming up new business with farmers and artisans who were scheduled to appear in court later in the day. Small planters and merchants nervously glanced at legal papers, quietly rehearsing for their brief moments before the bench. Others walked over to the courthouse to read the various legal notices and personal announcements nailed to the front door. Undersheriffs scurried about the grounds impaneling prominent freeholders to serve on petit juries.

By late morning many wondered if enough magistrates had shown up to conduct the county's business or whether their long trip to the courthouse would turn out to be a waste of time. Frequently, the ten o'clock scheduled opening passed by with the doors of the courthouse still closed. In a letter to the editor of the *Virginia Gazette* in 1770, "C. R.," a justice of peace himself, complained that delays in court business were not infrequently brought about by the dawdling of court officials. He observed that

> the usual hour of adjournment from court day is to ten o'clock, the court in course; but perhaps if those who constitute and should attend the courts, meet by one o'clock, it may be called, through the colony, a very early meeting; and as two hours are generally spent in *how do you's,* and seeing *who and who are together,* this brings almost the constant setting of the courts down to three or four o'clock. . . . Some justices live too far off to be there by ten, and for that reason perhaps seldom set off before ten; others, though convenient enough, conclude they need not get there sooner than they do, because the rest of the Justices will not be there; and what is very extraordinary, Lawyers, clerks, and Sheriffs, although they are the only persons who *get money* by the business, will be complaisant

FIGURE 5. Temporary stands jostle with more permanent booths in a German market-place, c. 1750. Print based on a drawing by Daniel Chodowiecki.

enough to accommodate their expectations to the general time of meeting, rather than to the time of adjournment; so that each person concerned, by a species of laziness, contributes his full proportion to compleat this delay.[7]

Goochland magistrates set the opening time for court in the winter months at 11:00. In the summer months, in order to take advantage of the coolness of the morning and the extra daylight, they set their opening time back an hour. The records do not reveal how successful they were in keeping to this schedule.[8]

Finally, if a quorum of magistrates appeared, the court crier came out of the courthouse, called for the attention of the crowd, and begged those who had business before the court to step inside. Many entered the courthouse to watch the proceedings or attend to their public business on the docket, but others remained outside as numerous diversions kept them occupied on the courthouse grounds and surrounding buildings. Some pursued private business discussions; others headed for shops or temporary stands to examine newly imported goods, purchase staples, or arrange for the repair of a valuable farm implement. Carpenters and other craftsmen, who may have come to court to bid on public projects, often found private clients eager for their services and settled on terms on the courthouse steps. There was always an eager number who sauntered off to the neighboring tavern for a drink. Finally, a few joined in impromptu games and other amusing distractions to pass the time. Fast horses always drew crowds, and court day proved a convenient time to settle arguments about the merits of various racehorses.[9] Until the Frederick County magistrates put a stop to the practice in 1747, horsemen daringly raced their animals past the court-house through the streets of Winchester. No doubt, court-day gamblers bet on the outcome of these sprints.[10] As Mrs. Carr's reminiscences of Harrisonburg suggest, court-day entertainment sometimes turned violent. In scenes repeated countless times across the colony, rowdy men fought one another to win the approbation of intoxicated bystanders as eyes were gouged and ears were bitten off in frenzied brawls.[11] Goaded by the taunts of a crowd and fueled by alcohol, an overenthusiastic John Sanford bit off Owen Wynn's left ear in one such fight in front of Johnson's ordinary at Westmoreland courthouse in the spring of 1741. An observant onlooker later retrieved the severed appendage and returned it to its owner. An itinerant peddler who hawked his wares at courthouse towns across the state in the early nineteenth century often found his business thrived in this tumultuous atmosphere. However, temperance tended to restrain buying impulses, as he discovered at Bedford on court day in November 1807, where there was "a very Poor Court, no fighting or Gouging, very few Drunken people."[12]

Even as the magistrates were deliberating, young men took advantage of the solidity of the brick walls of the courthouse to play fives and other ball-games. The thump of a ball against the wall sometimes intruded in the most dramatic way, as Gloucester court participants discovered in April 1776. In what was seen as an omen during the heightened tensions of the American Revolution, the Gloucester sheriff formally opened the court proceedings to try a man of Tory sympathies. "As usual, he was going to conclude with God Save the King, when, just as he was about pronouncing the words, a five's ball, struck by a soldier of the 7th regiment, entered the window, and knocked him in the mouth, which prevented him from being guilty of so much impiety." The noise created by the game, the disrespect shown toward the court in session, and the annoyance of broken windows and chipped brickwork and mortar forced several counties to crack down on unauthorized fives playing. In 1763 Accomack magistrates ordered the sheriff to "take any person into his custody who shall hereafter presume to play at fives or any other Game against the Court House and bring them before the Court to answer the same." In a similar effort to keep the courthouse free of fives players, the sheriff of Westmoreland County was ordered in 1791 to report the names of all those who violated the prohibition.[13] Frequent repairs to damaged windows suggest that similar prohibitions in other counties had little effect as justices continued to suffer the impertinence of court-day crowds not easily cowed by magisterial authority.

Playground for the young, public arena for rough-and-tumble brawling, social center for a sprawling rural community, marketplace for itinerant peddlers and local tradesmen, and administrative and judicial seat of county government, the courthouse grounds hosted many activities and contained a wide array of public and private buildings. Most structures were indistinguishable in form and materials from the kind found on the farms inhabited by those who gathered on court day during the colonial and early national periods. Small frame buildings that served as woodsheds, privies, stables, offices, dwellings, stores, and trade shops spread in irregular groupings on the urban lots or the two acres of rural land specifically set aside for the public business. On closer inspection a handful of these buildings had unusual features: a small building with one or two thickly barred windows or a stone office with a vaulted ceiling and tile floor. In the middle of this agglomeration stood the county courthouse, a brick building that had achieved some measure of architectural pretension in many tidewater counties by the late eighteenth century.

This is a study of the public buildings that formed the nucleus of the courthouse grounds—the courthouse, clerk's office, prison, and instruments of punishment—and important private buildings, especially the taverns, that grew up around them. In 1650 few of these structures existed as distinct building types. By 1800 they had developed into specialized structures with particular plans, fittings, and construction details. These architectural forms responded to changes in the legal system and the structure of county government, the maturation and growing wealth of an agricultural society that became wedded to slave labor, and the interplay between local building practices and academic design principles. The chapters that follow chart this transformation in some detail as they trace the pedigree of building types, document the introduction of particular construction details, and explore the design process from committee room to construction site over the course of the first two centuries of county government in Virginia.

The opening chapter describes the role of the county court and its officers in the legal, social, and economic affairs of Virginians in the colonial and early national periods and provides the cultural context for understanding the function and changing perception of public buildings. It is an overview that is informed by a variety of historical scholarship. Students of early Virginia have long recognized the centrality of county government as the skeletal structure that bound colonial society. In their histories of Virginia, contemporaries such as Robert Beverley and Thomas Jefferson described the basic duties of the county courts, which were codified with the publication of colonial laws in the early nineteenth century by legal scholars such as William Waller Hening and Benjamin Leigh. Philip A. Bruce furthered the study of the origins of the county courts in his careful reading of county court order books, which culminated in 1910 with a history of the legal system and other institutions in seventeenth-century Virginia. In 1952 Charles Sydnor animated the action of the county courts, describing in vivid vignettes, including the alcoholic splurges that enlivened court and election days, the social climate in which the magistrates and leaders of colonial Virginia operated. In recent decades scholars such as Rhys

Isaac have examined the cultural context of the county courts, using the devise of theatrical dramaturgy to read meaning in the activities and interactions of individuals and groups on court day. Viewed as a complex set of public performances, the county court, in Isaac's estimation, "served not only to make the community a witness to important decisions and transactions but also to teach men the very nature and forms of government." In his study of the rise of the legal profession in the eighteenth and early nineteenth centuries, A. G. Roeber also interprets the social interactions of court day as dramatic play that "informed Virginians where they stood in society."[14] More recent scholarship has warned against taking theatrical dramaturgy too literally, as the activities and actions that came before the court were about as exciting as standing in line to renew a driver's license. Confrontation was rare, ceremonial oaths at the start of court day were as tedious as reading the fine print of a contract, and the court docket was enveloped in a monotonous litany of procedural motions uttered before a distracted audience that could barely hear or care.[15]

If not the place where a composite audience of gentlemen justices, small freeholders, widows, children, servants, and slaves dramatically reprised the various roles historians have assigned them, the court did indeed play an integral part in the lives of most inhabitants of a county. It was charged with defining and clarifying their status, rights, and obligations and arbitrating civil and criminal disputes that arose among them and with outsiders. While interpretations of the structure and role of the legal system have varied, few scholars have closely examined the stage where both the quotidian and the occasional drama occurred. The first chapter turns, then, to a description of the physical setting of court day in one community: Yorktown, a small port laid out in the late seventeenth century, which became the York County seat in 1697. Here, within sight of the county courthouse, York inhabitants and visitors gathered in taverns to drink toasts to the success of British armies engaged in wars across the globe, stepped into well-stocked shops to purchase the latest fashions from London unloaded from the wharves along the river, learned the latest gossip about neighbors in conversations struck up on the main street, or witnessed the whipping of a slave who dared to transgress laws interpreted by tobacco planters and merchants who acted as justices of the peace sworn to uphold the king's peace. Finally, the last section of this opening chapter looks at one incident in the long history of public building in early Virginia: the process of constructing a new courthouse in Yorktown in the early 1730s. The building was one of the first structures in the colony that self-consciously used academic architectural forms to assert the corporate identity of the county authorities. That story broaches a number of issues concerning the integration of outside ideas into local practices, a theme explored in greater detail in subsequent chapters.

The second and third chapters document the emergence of the courthouse as a distinctive building type from its first appearance in the middle of the seventeenth century to its conceptual reinterpretation by Thomas Jefferson and his followers in the opening decades of the nineteenth century. They are divided chronologically into two very distinct periods and focus in some detail on the specific social and legal forces that shaped the development of the courthouse. As Dell Upton has argued in his study of the architecture of Anglican churches in colonial Virginia, buildings can be read as products of specific social landscapes.[16] In early Virginia the form, plans, and finishes of dwellings, churches, and courthouses offer insights into the manner in which colonists perceived and ordered their domestic and public lives. The second chapter examines the seventeenth century, a period when Virginians created civic institutions in novel circumstances. In the absence of towns and with comparatively few people living on scattered farms within large county boundaries, inhabitants wrestled with the problem of finding a commonly acceptable principle for situating public institutions. Gradually the notion of geographic centrality became the established norm for permanently seating the court. Many of the English attributes of civic architecture—bell towers, arcades, and places of parade that worked well in an urban environment—had to be discarded or redefined in the rural setting of most courthouse grounds. Chesapeake building practices too worked against the replication of English forms. The exigencies of an unstable plantation society fostered the use of impermanent earthfast carpentry, which became the standard method for building most structures in the seventeenth century. The first clapboarded courthouses were domestic in scale and had few of the characteristics associated with public buildings in English towns.

The third chapter focuses on the architectural transformation of the courthouse in the late colonial period. The rise of a gentry-dominated bench initiated the construction of buildings of greater pretensions. Upton contends that the gentry refashioned the architectural landscape in their own image. The brick walls, large sash windows, raised platforms, panel wainscoting, and painted woodwork specified by the gentlemen justices for eighteenth-century courthouses also appeared or had their equivalents in the Anglican churches where they worshiped and the great houses they inhabited. These materials, forms, and finishes were far from common in colonial Virginia, and their use in buildings associated with the planter elite epitomized the predominance of that oligarchy of families in the affairs of state, church, and society. In the minds of the gentry, Upton contends, "the ideal order and the existing social order were one." Well aware of their position in Virginia society, the magistrates also used architectural symbols to assert their place in the British imperium. The use of bell turrets, arcades, and seats of honor indicated the desire of the gentlemen justices to reach beyond local architectural standards to appropriate metropolitan forms as part of an effort to be seen, as Cary Carson has argued, as informed participants in a genteel society that spanned the transatlantic world.[17]

Inside the eighteenth-century courtroom, the form of the fittings was determined as much by the changing nature of the legal system as by the rise of gentry culture. Roeber asserts that the late colonial period witnessed an increasing movement toward specialized knowledge of the law based on print culture, which "spread throughout a formerly oral and largely nonliterate plantation society."[18] In the seventeenth century a few tables were all that was required for the orderly functioning of a courtroom where many of the activities took place in face-to-face encounters between litigants, magistrates, and witnesses and paperwork remained an optional way of pursuing legal redress among a large illiterate population. By the second quarter of the eighteenth century, a courtroom could scarcely function without a host of specialized fittings required to accommodate a number of court officials and participants. The growing bureaucratization of the law and legal proceedings can be seen in the different types of seats, tables, chairs, and balustraded bars with attached bookshelves arrayed throughout late colonial courtrooms. The degree of elaboration of these fittings mirrored the social and legal hierarchy of the courtroom. Those in charge—the gentlemen justices—got the best seats, while those with fewer claims to deferential authority received sparer versions or none at all. The detailed attention paid in chapter 3 to the form of the courtroom fittings reflects the careful consideration that magistrates paid to their design.

Traditional architectural histories of early America trace the growth of forms from English and European precedents and seek to attribute the design of buildings to the self-conscious work of individual architects. Fiske Kimball's broad overview of American design in *Domestic Architecture of the American Colonies and of the Early Republic* (1922) and Thomas Waterman's more tightly focused study of gentry houses in *The Mansions of Virginia, 1706–1776* (1946) described the flow of architectural design ideas in an east-to-west, transatlantic direction. Kimball saw architectural books published in England as the catalyst for the transfer of ideas, while Waterman cited individual buildings in Britain as prototypes for American builders. In their reading of colonial architecture, deviance from British or Continental models could be attributed to the rudeness of colonial culture and the undeveloped nature of its economy, the shortcomings of trained craftsmen, or the lack of sophistication on the part of colonists in interpreting the original forms. In contrast to the premise that provincial architecture was in some way a diminished version of metropolitan ideals, the fourth chapter, on the design of public buildings, takes a different tack. Colonists were not insecure rustics hovering on the fringe of empire, overawed by the monuments of London. British and European precedents did indeed provide a cultural benchmark for public building design in Virginia, but a different climate and different social and economic conditions played a pivotal role in determining the appropriate form and finishes of courthouses, prisons, clerks' offices, and other public structures. Cognizant of their peculiar circumstances, colonial builders selectively drew upon local practices as well as academic sources to meet their peculiar needs and aspirations. There was a far greater interplay between outside ideas and homegrown customs than previous scholarship has acknowledged. Virginians devised an aesthetically satisfying one-story, T-shaped, arcaded brick courthouse capped by a hipped roof that had no direct parallels, though arcades, hipped roofs, and Flemish bond walls with glazed headers could be found in dozens of eighteenth-century public buildings in Great Britain. It was the combination of these familiar elements in different ways that distinguished the architecture of colonial Virginia, responsive to but by no means subservient to British prototypes.

Another premise in chapter 4 that differentiates it from most scholarship is the fact that architectural design in colonial America was a collaborative affair: the hands of many individuals were involved from the conception to the completion of a public building. No architect in colonial Virginia worked in the manner that is familiar to modern practitioners, and attempting to attribute the design of a building to the hand of an individual person is problematic if not anachronistic as it distorts the way in which buildings were planned and executed. In *Mansions of Virginia*, Waterman provided a classic example of this misreading of the design process in colonial Virginia by identifying John Ariss as the designer of more than a dozen great gentry houses based on their stylistic similarities. Subsequent research has failed to sustain Waterman's claim for Ariss's authorship or involvement in many of the projects or even to identify others who might have fulfilled a similar role.[19] The design of the county courthouse was a corporate affair, devised by a committee and executed by a host of individual craftsmen who had the ability and were expected to shape many aspects of the building's appearance, from its plan to the bonding pattern of its brick walls.[20] Drawings were few, providing rudimentary guidance to the gentlemen justices who developed the basic layout of their buildings. Specifications generally detailed the size and placement of various elements and the quality of the workmanship and materials but left the shaping of specific features to the skills of individual craftsmen. Tradition rather than innovation governed the thinking of most clients and builders, ensuring the continuity of forms over a long period of time.

The final two chapters examine the ancillary buildings and other structures scattered around the courthouse grounds that were an integral part of the legal system and court day. Prisons, stocks, pillories, whipping posts, and gallows stood as powerful reminders of the authority of the county court to punish those who violated the law. Despite their symbolic significance as deterrents and their everyday role in maintaining order in a community, Virginians rarely considered these structures as anything more than necessary but impermanent expedients, appropriating as little money as possible on their upkeep. As a result, stocks and pillories rotted, and poorly constructed prisons provided clever inmates with plenty of chances to escape. Chapter 5 opens with a brief consideration of the nature of crime, attitudes toward punishment, and the manner that it was meted out according to race and class. It then traces the architectural transformation of prisons from flimsy, one-room lockups to well-secured, multicelled spaces. As with courtroom fittings, few scholars have addressed this topic in any detail. Here too, changing social sensibilities shaped architectural solutions. As the composition of the prison population changed, Virginia justices responded to the growing presence of slaves and transported English convicts and the plight of debtors by segregating prisoners into different cells or buildings, separating men from women, blacks from whites, and debtors from criminals.

The last chapter documents the history of two building types: the courthouse tavern, which was often the largest structure on the grounds and an essential element in court-day affairs, and the clerk's office, a small repository of public records that rarely appeared before the end of the eighteenth century. While much literature has been written about the impact of alehouses on English and early American social behavior and their role as a venue for political discourse, little attention has been given to the tavern as a building type.[21] Chapter 6 opens with a discussion of the function of the courthouse tavern and describes the level of comfort and service found in such establishments. Although a number of high-minded people railed against the iniquities of taverns, they were an integral part of court day, serving as a more relaxed forum for the conduct of personal and community business. By the late colonial period, the courthouse tavern also became a formal venue for more polite entertainments, as Richard Bushman has observed in his study of refinement in early America.[22] Fashionable balls, dinners, and concerts required specialized spaces, and tavern keepers in many parts of Virginia, especially in towns such as Alexandria, Williamsburg, Norfolk, and Fredericksburg, erected ballrooms, dining rooms, and cardrooms in order to attract and accommodate genteel society. The chapter ends with an account of the storage of public records. Despite the central role that documents played in keeping track of litigation, the transfer of real and personal property, and as a collective record of local law and custom, most county courts treated this written testimony with shameful neglect through the colonial period. Long before the wanton destruction unleashed by the Civil War, fires, dampness, and rats took their toll on early records. By the

FIGURE 6. Courthouse boys, Williamsburg–James City County courthouse, in c. 1901 photograph

end of the eighteenth century, legislation finally prompted magistrates in each county to build fireproof offices for their records.

An epilogue following chapter 6 serves as a foil to the court-day prologue in this introduction. It briefly follows the evolution of the courthouse grounds from their knockabout appearance in the colonial period to more formal public squares in the nineteenth and early twentieth centuries. New aesthetic sensibilities repudiated much of the legacy of the colonial landscape, and new attitudes about public behavior circumscribed or banned many traditional court-day activities, from the consumption of alcohol and peddling of goods to the discharging of firearms and grazing of animals. As a social phenomenon, court day suffered a precipitous decline between the Civil War and World War II. By the time of the Great Depression, the "courthouse boys" were reduced to sitting on benches beneath the courthouse portico, telling stories of the past to one another (fig. 6). Today, no one has the time or is encouraged to lounge about the courthouse doors. They might set off the security alarms.

THE COUNTY COURT
IN EARLY VIRGINIA

The Role of the County Court in Colonial Society

L AW AND AUTHORITY in colonial Virginia were rooted in local experience and inherited traditions. The cohesive force that defined the rights and rules of rural Virginia communities was the county court. Neither a remote authority nor an abstract ideal, it was central to the lives of all free men, women, and children and the chattel slaves they possessed. In the mid-1750s Landon Carter, a justice of the peace in Richmond County, addressed a group of freeholders called to court as members of a grand jury on their solemn duty, a responsibility that the magistrate called part of "our most glorious Constitution." Carter and those neighbors who had assembled at the county courthouse firmly believed that the rules that governed local society derived from the English constitution, a vast and sometimes contradictory set of principles and laws that had evolved over several hundred years. "The Laws of *England*," declared one Virginian, "are our best Inheritance, the Ties of harmonious Society, and Defence of Life, Liberty, and Property, against arbitrary Power, Tyranny, and Oppression."[1]

Although novel social and economic circumstances had transformed many familiar English institutions in the years since first settlement, Virginians in Carter's day insisted that their fundamental rights as Englishmen remained unchanged. The core of that inheritance was the common law. They thought of it as a comprehensive body of precepts and practices that regulated relationships among people and mediated disputes of all kinds. It extended beyond the narrow limits of statutes to encompass traditional notions of justice practiced from time out of mind and procedural forms that guaranteed the security of person and property. In the broadest sense the law embraced both the judicial and political aspects of society and was thus inextricably woven into the fabric of local government. Virginians claimed the common law as their inheritance, but its concern with individual rights and principles of due process was not a clear blueprint for an orderly structure of government. When the common law went against their own interests, the Chesapeake colonists did not hesitate to cast it aside, as in the case of slavery, which had no legal precedent but was essential to their economic welfare. The common law did provide, however, the general context in which to exercise authority.

From the outset of settlement in Virginia, colonial officials recognized the necessity of imposing a legal framework for governing in a remote and wild land. The early attempt to keep the colony from foundering led to a series of stringent regulations that combined military and civilian legal practices. The introduction of martial law by Sir Thomas Gates and Sir Thomas Dale secured the colony's existence in the early 1610s but came to be seen as too restrictive in better times. In order to promote the "good government of the people," the Virginia Company tried to clarify the legal nature of its enterprise by stipulating that the laws of the colony should be "as neer to the common lawes of England and the equity thereof as may be." Without the benefit of such instruments, the colonists were bound to sink to the level of the savages. Such an assumption was rooted in seventeenth-century political theory, which maintained that some form of government was necessary for the orderly functioning of society and the protection of an individual's civil liberties. John Locke argued that the enjoyment of an individual's rights was insecure in a state of nature. The unrestricted freedom of natural liberty was dangerous because it quickly led to the dominion of some men over others. Without restraints, men grasped for power, which by its very nature was aggressive and tended to expand beyond legitimate boundaries. The natural prey of power was individual rights. Consequently, it was necessary for individuals to join together in a system of government "for the mutual protection of their lives, liberties, and estates," which Locke called by the general name "property." Government's chief function, therefore, was the preservation of property. Those moralists who subscribed to Locke's theory stressed that the preservation of property was best served in an orderly society, one that recognized and fully accepted a harmonious arrangement of human affairs, clear patterns of authority, and a shared set of values. This ideal order of society was divinely inspired with a coherent hierarchical structure of social relationships and moral values based on deference and authority that eliminated the possibility of social conflict. Believing that they could "live quietly and peaceably together," the founders of Exeter, New Hampshire, willingly bound themselves to a government based on "such Godly and christian laws as are established in the realm of England." Yet as the New England Puritans who tried to establish such utopian societies based on Christian communalism quickly realized, not all men were willing to subscribe to such a system of order.[2] The ideal order was based on a static view of society; in reality, society in seventeenth-century England and its American dominions was constantly adjusting to new political, social, and economic conditions.

As an ideology, the idealized concept of order had a powerful appeal. Even in Virginia where the turbulent period of early settlement had only gradually given way to a more stable society in the eighteenth century, men like Landon Carter could still speak of the possibility of a harmonious community tied together by "Duties" to God, Sovereign, and fellow citizens.[3] However, the primary concern for order in the affairs of local communities in England and in its American colonies was not so much maintaining a harmony between God and man, or even between the monarch and his people, but between individuals within local society in their daily relationships and face-to-face activities. Order was less an idealized state of society than the management of local relationships that conformed to a set of loosely prescribed local customs and laws.

The nucleated settlements that had developed along the James River in the 1610s and 1620s had matured by the end of the century into an agrarian colony that stretched across hundreds of miles of forests, fields, and rivers. Hand in hand with the growth of the colony emerged the county court as the primary instrument for administering the law to the thousands of planters and indentured servants and the ever-growing number of African slaves who inhabited this vast territory. The peculiar economic, social, and demographic circumstances of colonial society created an institution that had no exact jurisdictional counterpart in England. Many of the offices of county government had familiar English names—justice of the peace, sheriff, clerk, and constable—but the roles and the types of men who filled them sometimes varied dramatically from English custom.

As it developed from its first appearance in the 1630s, the Virginia county court became the central mechanism for maintaining the peace, administering the county's business, and adjudicating civil and criminal disputes. It served as an executive and judicial body. In the early nineteenth century, Virginia jurist Benjamin Watkins Leigh declared that "as it is the most ancient, so it has ever been one of the most important of our institutions, not only in respect to the administration of justice, but for police and economy." Leigh argued that since the 1660s the court's functions had "been so important, that their institution may well be considered as part of the constitution, both of the colonial and present government. No material change was introduced by the revolution in their jurisdiction, or general powers and duties of any kind. . . . It would perhaps be impossible for any man, to estimate the character and utility of this system, without actual experience of its operation."[4]

The principal officers of the court were appointed by the governor to a "commission of the peace" that granted them powers to act as justices of the peace within the county of their residence. From the late seventeenth century until the early nineteenth century, the larger planters and prominent merchants in each county dominated the office of justice of the peace. Before that time, the social status of some members of the bench occasionally appeared suspect, as new men were appointed who seemed little better than small free-holders. In 1662 William Hatton accused the magistrates of York County of being nothing more than "Coopers, Hogg trough makers, Pedlars, Cobblers, tailors, [and] weavers" who were not fit "to sit where they doe sit."[5] Some indeed may have had short-tailed and undistinguished pedigrees. Once the population of counties became more settled, disparities in the ownership of land and slaves created an unbridgeable gulf between great planters and small operators, and marriages bound successful planters and merchants into a more cohesive social group, fractious challenges such as Hatton's to the appropriateness of men appointed to the bench all but disappeared. By the 1720s few men rose from humble ranks to take their place among the grandees.

The number of justices appointed to the commission varied from county to county. In the seventeenth century statute law set the number at eight, but the size of the commission swelled with time due to pressure among the magistrates and gentry families to find places for younger sons and nephews. By the early eighteenth century, most counties had anywhere from one to two dozen men enumerated on commissions of the peace, although fewer than half actively took part in county affairs. Many lived far away from the county courthouse and found it inconvenient and troublesome to travel several miles to attend their duties. A number of Prince William County magistrates simply did not bother to "burthen themselves with the expence of attending court as so great a distance from home." In the wintertime many magistrates faced the task of traveling over impassable roads and crossing swollen streams, making the journey to the courthouse nearly impossible. Time and time again two or three dutiful magistrates showed up on court day only to find that there were too few of them to conduct the county's business. Some justices sought to remedy the lack of zeal shown by fellow magistrates by enlarging the commission. In 1715 Henrico magistrates, concerned that the "business of this court is very often delayed for want of a sufficient number of Justices," proposed to the governor that nine more men be added to the commission. Goochland court likewise desired to remedy the shortage of bench members by adding three more individuals to its ranks in 1729.[6]

Although inclusion in the commission of the peace was a requisite for any man intending to make his mark in politics and local society, the task of carrying out the county's business without remuneration deterred some from taking the oath of office. Four men nominated to the York County bench in 1724 were so slow in accepting their appointments that the sheriff was ordered to approach them and ask "whether they will accept or refuse to Act as Justices pursuant to the said Commission." The four, Henry Tyler, John Blair, Graves Pack, and Mathew Pierce, had all served previously. Perhaps their hesitancy to accept the appointment resulted from health or other business concerns. In the end they all resumed their place on the bench after renewing their oaths of office. In an uncharacteristic case of reluctance, William Fauntleroy of Richmond County refused the commission of peace in 1716 because he "did not think himself capable." More typical were the responses of John Bushrod, George Eskridge, and Daniel McCarty of Westmoreland County when they were called to serve again in 1716. Bushrod complained that old age and infirmity prevented him from taking the oath. Eskridge and McCarty argued that the responsibilities of business affairs kept them from serving the public; Eskridge did not want to give up his lucrative legal practice. A younger county resident, the politically ambitious Thomas Lee, declined to become a member of the commission because he was planning a long voyage. He did promise to reconsider on his return, and by 1720 he was on the bench.[7]

In a two-year period between 1731 and 1732, thirteen men held commissions of the peace for York County. As in all counties by this time, they were the elite members of their community, which also encompassed part of the city of Williamsburg. Typical too was their lack of formal legal training. Most magistrates appointed to a county commission gained their knowledge of the law only after their appointment, learning through observation and participation in the courtroom. Although amateurs in the law, they brought to the bench the practical experience of managing a plantation or a mercantile business and a knowledge of their community. Merchants Richard Ambler, John Buckner, Thomas Nelson, and William Stack lived in Yorktown, as did Lawrence Smith, son of the surveyor who laid out the town in 1691. Williamsburg merchant Archibald Blair, who also had served on the James City County bench, his son John, and John Holloway, the Speaker of the House of Burgesses, served the interests of those who resided in the capital. Robert Armistead was a planter whose primary residence was in neighboring Elizabeth City County but who held estates in York County. Tobacco planters Francis Hayward, Mathew Pierce, Edward Tabb, and Samuel Timson represented various parts of the county at the Yorktown court sessions. A number of the older magistrates—Richard Ambler, Archibald Blair, Thomas Nelson, and John Holloway—had been born in Britain, while the rest were native to the area. Six members had been or were to be elected members of the House of Burgesses. John Blair progressed from this provincial body to take his place on the Governor's Council in the early 1740s and served until his death in 1771. Wealthy planters, merchants, or provincial officials, these York justices were also well connected socially and assumed positions upon the bench because of their family connections. Six justices had fathers who had served as magistrates before them, and several would pass on their positions to their sons or nephews. The Blairs sat together as father and son, while Tabb and Hayward were brothers-in-law.

By the early 1730s only a few men reached the top rungs of the county court system by dint of their hard labor and good fortune. William Stark was something of a self-made man, since he inherited neither a fortune or social standing, being the son of a York County physician. Stark established his credentials as a moderately successful businessman in the competitive mercantile world of Yorktown. Before he was appointed to the bench in 1722, he proved his capabilities in minor offices such as constable and jury foreman. Although similar men sometimes served as magistrates in other counties, by the 1730s the York County court was already assuming the air of a closed shop where family connections and wealth were the preeminent requirements for service at the top of the judicial system.[8]

The York County court convened a dozen times in 1731 and the same number the following year. Unlike later years when a lengthy court docket required most courts to meet over the course of two and even three days, the York magistrates dispensed with their business in a single day. On the day before, known as "rules" day, the clerk of the county often set up a temporary office in one of the rooms of the courthouse if his own office was not nearby. People appeared before the clerk to have their motions entered upon the docket, to make oaths, and to post bonds for the performance of some court-appointed task. More than any other official, the clerk set the agenda for the county magistrates to undertake the following day, including anywhere from thirty to one hundred items of business. Some actions were routine and took no more than a few minutes, while others, such as cases brought to trial, could last for a number of hours. On four occasions in 1731–32, York magistrates returned for a second day to finish old business, lay the county levy and settle public accounts, or meet as a special oyer and terminer court to try a slave. They did not meet in April or October, presumably because planting and harvesting kept many away and a number of the justices participated in provincial meetings or "public times" in Williamsburg when the General Court and the House of Burgesses met in the capital. Over this two-year period, two-thirds of the York magistrates attended at least half of the county court sessions. In most cases five or six magistrates presided over each session, with John Holloway in the chair as the chief magistrate or, in his absence, Yorktown resident Lawrence Smith, who had been a member of the commission since 1704. Smith had perfect attendance in 1731 and 1732, followed closely by fellow townsman John Buckner and planter Francis Hayward, who in his early thirties was one of the youngest members of the commission. Thomas Nelson attended eight sessions in 1731 and six the following year, a pattern that was common to most magistrates. Planters Robert Armistead, Samuel Timson, and Mathew Pierce made far fewer appearances, sitting only three, four, and five times, respectively, over this two-year period.

Perhaps plantation affairs and bad roads kept them from the courthouse more often than not. Or possibly they accepted the honor of the office without assuming the responsibilities.[9]

Empowered to "keepe the peace" of their community, these county magistrates were expected to enforce "all ordinances, statutes, & Acts of Assembly set forth for the conservation of the Peace and good rule & government of the people." They had the authority to "punish or chastise" those who disobeyed or broke the laws or "threaten or assault any of the Ma[jes]ties liege people, either in their bodies or burning their houses." In order to prevent and discourage breaches of the peace and maintain order and harmony in local society, magistrates were granted the power to imprison troublesome individuals unless or until they could provide bonds and sureties for their good behavior.[10] Recognizance bonds for "good behavior" helped reduce the risk of future misconduct by the threat of substantial monetary penalties for repeat offenders.

As keepers of the social order, justices of the peace also had the authority to raise a "hue and cry," which called on neighbors to join in the pursuit of felons or runaway slaves. As Landon Carter recognized, the maintenance of "the constitution" required the vigilance and active participation of the community. Without a paid police force to enforce its will, the strength of magisterial authority rested upon the good opinion of the public. Effective government needed the widespread cooperation of the community, for it required the services of many individuals. For example, justices depended upon a small unpaid and untrained band of constables to police neighborhoods, enforce local bylaws, and report "all manner of felonyes, witchcrafte, forestallinge & extorsions . . . and of all and singular other misdeeds, and offenses."[11]

Of all the positions in county government, that of constable was one of the lowest ranking and least prestigious ways of serving the public. Every county had a number of constables who served for no more than a year or two, with one assigned to each section or precinct in a county. These were the eyes and ears of the community, the men who maintained the peace and aided in the enforcement of the law. Most commonly, appointment to the position of constable was the first public-service job held by a freeholder who aspired to roles of leadership. Men who filled the position generally were small landowners or tradesmen who had few connections to the ruling families. Albrighton Wagstaff, the constable for upper Yorkhampton Parish in York County in 1733 and 1734, conforms to the standard. In the years before becoming a constable, he made a few court appearances as a litigant in minor debt cases, a witness to deeds, and a provider of evidence to the court in a case against a woman for "curseing and reviling" the king. He appraised a few estates of his neighbors in the upper part of York County and served as the executor of his father's estate. Aside from serving on several juries during his two-year tenure as constable,

Wagstaff filled no other public duties and presumably spent most of his time tending his tobacco crop on his plantation with the aid of his six slaves. When he died in the summer of 1735, the former constable had an estate valued at £190, which placed him solidly in the small planter class of freeholders.[12]

The effectiveness of many laws and ordinances passed by the assembly and the local court was only as good as the diligence of men like Wagstaff who were enlisted to enforce them. Their duties varied widely, from acting as members of search parties and patrols and overseeing punishments at the public whipping post to "view[ing] and cutting up [tobacco] suckers."[13] Thus inhabitants had some limited power to determine local norms. A disorderly round of drinking at Moody's Tavern in Yorktown might go unreported to the magistrates if Wagstaff, the neighborhood constable, decided it was boisterous but innocuous fellowship.[14]

Another means of bringing criminal offenses to the attention of the court was through the "presentments" made by grand juries. Called twice yearly to inquire into any violations of the laws, twenty-four prominent freeholders were asked to look into charges known to them personally or brought to their attention by the court or parish churchwardens. Presentments made by the grand jury to the court generally divided into two types: moral offenses that violated Christian behavior and civil offenses that ranged from the dereliction of public duties to the disruption of the orderly functioning of the community. Church-wardens provided information about the moral lapses of their neighbors such as sabbath breaking, failure to attend church, adultery, fornication, and profane swearing. For the most part the grand jury was extremely cautious in returning a "true bill" to the court, which provided the bench the power to prosecute suspected individuals. For example, in 1731–32 grand juries in York County presented only six men for failing to attend church. Not that the inhabitants of York County were particularly God fearing, but those presented must have been particularly conspicuous in their absence. Four of them were presented again the following year. When John Pate of Yorktown finally did attend divine service, he so misbehaved in church that he was presented once again for his irreverent antics.[15] The grand jury also looked into secular failings. Those men derelict in their communal duty to maintain the roads in their neighborhoods found themselves under investigation by their peers in the courthouse. Like the constable, members of the grand jury helped shape the norms of community behavior by their discretionary interpretation of the law when they considered public shortcomings, moral failings, and sexual misconduct of their neighbors.

In its judicial capacity the court was empowered to "hear & determine all" suits, "snits and Controverseys between party & party as neare as may be According to the Law of England and Lawes & customs of this Countrey."[16] In some instances justice was often swift, with cases decided in a few moments of open court discussion among the magistrates. Yet it was not capricious. One of the hallmarks of the Virginia legal system in the eighteenth century was its adherence to the notion of due process, a course of legal proceedings carried out regularly and in accordance with established rules and principles. Each court had a professional who understood these rules and principles. The county clerk, who had gained a thorough education in legal procedures from an apprenticeship in the secretary of the colony's office in Williamsburg before taking up his post, provided guidance to untrained magistrates and citizens alike in the nuances of the law. Motions were made, oaths taken, and the proper type of writs served according to English legal precedents as they were interpreted and modified by Virginia experience. In complex cases justices took depositions and examined witnesses to determine the validity of arguments. Others sometimes appeared to move through the legal process at a slow pace as contending parties exercised tactical maneuvers, pleading and counterpleading in ways that delayed their outcome for months or even years. Though some members of the legal profession, especially those trained at the Inns of Court in London and others who practiced in the General Court, occasionally bemoaned the informality of county court practices, few saw blatant abuses of the system.

Those who tried to circumvent or deviate from accepted practices generally were stymied in their effort, as Lawrence Smith of York County learned in 1722 when he clashed with Deputy Clerk Daniel Fisher. A York County magistrate with nearly twenty years of experience, Smith, who had been drinking in one of Yorktown's taverns one Saturday night, sent for Fisher and tried to persuade the clerk to issue a writ against a certain person and to backdate it so that it could be presented in court the following Monday with less than the required three days' notice. When the deputy clerk pointed out the impropriety of the action, the justice alleged "that such things had been done" before by people of higher rank than the clerk. Fisher recounted that when he again refused to comply with Smith's demands, the justice "struck me with his cane, but I being a younger man than he took hold of his collar with one hand and his cane with the other, laid him on the floor and his cane by him . . . it was said he broke Two of his ribs in falling on the Hilt of his sword." Smith was later found guilty of "menaceing, beating, and wounding" Fisher, but his fellow magistrates exacted a light punishment, fining him only six pence. Although Smith's social standing probably tempered the judgment of his fellow magistrates, in the end he did not get away with stretching the legality of his actions. "For colonial Virginians," legal historian David Konig has argued, "the way in which justice was obtained stood central in their jurisprudence." An anonymous writer in the *Virginia Gazette* in 1745 observed that "Law is a dead Letter, and lives only in the due Administration thereof."[17]

On the criminal side of its jurisdiction, the county court heard misdemeanors and minor infractions such as drunkenness, disturbing the peace, and petty theft that disrupted the harmony of community relations. It also served as the first court to hear more serious cases involving assault and battery, unlawful entry, and theft. The county court could not try felonious crimes committed by white inhabitants that were punishable by the loss of life or limb. Cases involving free persons arraigned for such felonies as murder were within the purview of the General Court, sitting first in Jamestown in the seventeenth century and then in Williamsburg until 1780. Composed of the governor and council members, the General Court also heard civil cases involving substantial sums of money and served as the appellate court for the inferior county courts. In contrast, by the late seventeenth century, slaves had little legal recourse to the superior court but were tried locally for major offenses in specially called courts of oyer and terminer convened by the county justices.

The court often acted as an economic forum, working to secure the protection of private property. Invariably in the money-short economy of colonial Virginia, cases of debt flooded the courts' dockets. Creditors and debtors waged constant procedural battles to speed up or slow down the progress of their cases. When cases finally came to trial, either the magistrates or a petit jury determined whether the terms of a bond had been met and if not, how much money was owed the plaintiff. From small loans from planter to neighboring farmer to sizable investments by British merchants in the local tobacco economy, the court became involved in the tangled web of personal finances and obligations that linked the community together. Sometimes magistrates found themselves in embarrassing situations, being sued in their own court by creditors for long-standing debt. At other times they sued to recover debts, and their presence upon the bench no doubt affected the decisions of their fellow magistrates.

The court was deeply involved in many aspects of the community's welfare, both corporate and individual, which meant a widespread involvement of county inhabitants in the legal system. It granted licenses each year to individuals like Ishmael Moody of Yorktown to operate taverns and set the amount that Moody and other hostelers could charge for a meal, a drink, and provender. The court kept a standard set of weights and measures that were used to settle trade disputes and to gauge accuracy in the marketplace and in main street shops (fig. 7).[18] In towns where markets developed, the authorities appointed a clerk of the market to enforce market regulations, which set the hours of operation, forbade forestallers and engrossers, and controlled the general prices of staples such as beef, eggs, cheese, and butter.[19] Magistrates also assigned men from various precincts to oversee the maintenance of public high-

FIGURE 7. Fairfax County weights and measures, 1744. (Courtesy of The Library of Virginia)

ways. The justices raised money to build bridges and granted licenses to individuals to operate ferries. They ordered the construction of tobacco inspection stations and appointed men to judge the quality of the crop shipped from designated wharves (fig. 8). Perhaps most importantly, the justices appointed individuals to compile for tax purposes a list of tithables, which consisted of white males over the age of sixteen and all blacks above that age. Planters brought their slaves before magistrates to certify their age for tax purposes. For example, in York County court in July 1731, "Rachel a Negro girl belonging to Thomas Hawkins" was reckoned "to be twelve years of age."[20]

They also relieved the burden of taxation of those poor and aged freeholders who showed just cause for their plight. Justices laid the yearly levy, deciding how much to tax freeholders to pay for public expenses that ranged from salaries for county officials such as the clerk, king's attorney, and constables to the payment of bounties offered on predatory wild animals such as wolves. That amount varied each year, sometimes more than doubling over a previous year when county expenses were unusually high. The construction of a new public building such as a brick courthouse would drive the tax rate up for two or three years in a row before it decreased again. Freeholders contributed to the payment of the annual levy based on the number of tithables in their households, the larger planters paying a greater proportion because of their larger slave labor force.

Death brought private lives and family matters into public scrutiny. The county court was the vehicle that ensured the orderly transfer of wealth from one generation to the next. Relatives or trusted friends submitted a will to the court, where it was probated or authenticated as the binding instructions for the disposition of the deceased's estate. Those who had witnessed the signing of the will by the testator appeared before the clerk to verify the document's validity. Any challenges to the will were aired before the local magistrates. The bench appointed an administrator for those who died intestate or for those who failed to name an executor in their will. It also appointed two or three friends and neighbors of the deceased to make an itemized inventory and establish the value of all the goods and chattels in the estate. The administrator

FIGURE 8. The shipment of tobacco, the economic lifeblood of the colony, was regulated at inspection warehouses established by the counties in the early eighteenth century. Cartouche, Fry-Jefferson map, 1751 (London, 1754).

was responsible for gathering together the estate, paying debts held against it, and distributing any remaining assets to the heirs. To assure an accurate and fair discharge of these duties, an account of these affairs was submitted to the court for approval. Even at the poorest level of white society, the court played an important role when a death occurred. The mortal remains of indigents who died with little or no estate often became the responsibility of the court because carpenters and parish sextons had to be paid for making coffins and digging graves.

For the survivors, justices approved the selection of guardians to oversee an orphan's estate and required that accounts of their management be examined periodically in court to protect helpless children from unscrupulous individuals who might plunder their holdings for personal gain. At the instigation of churchwardens or a poor widowed mother, magistrates placed orphans or indigent children in the care of planters or tradesmen so that they might learn a useful skill and not become a burden to the parish. The court also provided a means for resolving disputes that arose between apprentices and their masters, inquiring into the treatment of the young and making sure that both parties adhered to the provisions of the indenture.

From the birth of bastards to the death of the decrepit, the county court engaged the inhabitants within its jurisdiction in a host of matters that made private travails a matter of public record. Above all else, the court was a local institution, led by the leading citizens but run by a myriad of people in a variety of capacities that made them responsible for their own welfare and that of their neighbors and those most vulnerable to the vagaries of life. This diffusion of judicial authority from members of the bench into the hands of other officials such as clerks, constables, jurymen, and individual freeholders meant that the English common law and equity were subtly shaped to conform to local ideals. Some magistrates abused their positions on the bench to settle personal vendettas, while others knew how to manipulate a bewildering array of procedures to use the court to enhance their own pockets at the expense of the dull-witted and poor. Although there were always those who would take advantage of their positions or flaws in the process, what is most striking about the legal system is that so few challenged its authority. Most white Virginians in the late colonial period accepted the power of the county court to regulate their lives in part because they saw that they had a stake in its orderly functioning.

The Social World of Court Day in Yorktown

The physical setting for court day can be re-created in some detail in Yorktown where the scale of the town and some of the buildings from the period of its greatest prosperity in the mid-eighteenth century have not only survived but have been thoroughly studied and partially restored by the National Park Service (fig. 9). Where buildings have disappeared, a full complement of colonial court records provides detailed accounts of people, activities, and buildings in this small town standing on 50-foot high bluffs overlooking the York River. Established in 1691 by an act of the General Assembly, the town was laid out at an advantageous location along the river where it narrowed from two to three miles in width to about a half mile. Jutting out into the river opposite Yorktown is a peninsula known in 1691 as Tindall's Point and later as Gloucester Point. Ferries plied this narrow stretch in the river by the second half of the seventeenth century, and an ordinary had been established on the York side to take advantage of the trade. In 1700 the ferry cost six pence for a person and one shilling for a rider and his horse.[21] Yet another advantage of this site was the deep channel of the river that ran close to the York side of the shore, making it unnecessary to build long expensive wharves from the beach. A number of broad ravines cut through the bluffs, linking the waterside to the main part of town above. By the 1730s town authorities annexed the area under the hill to the town.[22] Overland communications were by way of a good road leading to Hampton from the eastern end of town and to Williamsburg from the west. A short distance beyond the western limits of Yorktown, the road to Williamsburg went past a merchant windmill that dominated a point above a small creek flowing into the river.

The fifty-acre tract on the plain at the edge of the bluff was laid out to form a rectangle whose long northern side ran parallel to the river. The town was di-

FIGURE 9. *A View of the Town of York, Virginia, from the River,* watercolor, John Gauntlett, 1755. The large house on the right belonged to William Lightfoot. Thomas Nelson Sr.'s house is the five-bay, two-story dwelling left of center. The parish church and county courthouse are obscured in the cluster of buildings just to the left of the flagpole. (The Mariners' Museum, Newport News, Va.)

vided into eighty-five half-acre lots (fig. 10). The surveyor, Lawrence Smith, created a broad main street that ran parallel to the water longitudinally nearly east to west and roughly bisected the town. Northern cross streets ran down through natural ravines in the bluff to the waterfront, while those on the south side of town simply stopped at the boundary line three or four lots back from the main street. Though laid out in a grid typical of most colonial towns in Virginia, the plan did take advantage of the natural topography and divided the town into distinct zones of activity. In the opening decades of the eighteenth century, the port attracted merchants such as Philip Lightfoot, Thomas Nelson, and Richard Ambler, who developed much of the waterfront area, where they built wharves and warehouses to handle ships that brought British consumer goods from Bristol, Liverpool, Whitehaven, Glasgow, and London.[23] In this maritime district "under the hill," seamen found hospitality and shelter in the ordinaries and lodging houses spread in a haphazard fashion along the shore. On the plain above, merchants built their residences and stores, craftsmen erected trade shops, and tavern keepers operated ordinaries on the main street. Also standing in the center of town were the public buildings: the local Angli-

FIGURE 10. Plan of Yorktown based on documentary and archaeological evidence compiled by research historians, Colonial National Park, 1940. The buildings are in approximate locations and not scaled to size. Not all colonial structures are indicated on this map. *A:* York County courthouse; *B:* church; *C:* Philip Lightfoot house (first); *D:* Philip Lightfoot house (second); *E:* Thomas Nelson house; *F:* William Nelson house; *G:* Secretary Thomas Nelson house; *H:* Ambler's store; *I:* Robert Ballard house; *J:* Swan Tavern; *K:* Powers/Moody tavern; *L:* Reynolds house and store.

can church and the county courthouse. The vestry of Yorkhampton Parish erected a small, rectangular stone church in 1697, built from the porous native marlstone on a lot just back from the main street overlooking the river. As was typical in the Anglican tradition, the church was precisely oriented in an east-west direction, skewing it from the town's grid. In the same year the county court selected the town as its permanent venue and erected a modest wooden courthouse on the north side of the main street on lot 24, a block west of the church. This lot was first owned by Thomas Jefferson, the third president's great-grandfather, who apparently forfeited his title to it by not building on the site.[24] Finally, there was a third zone of development located on the back lots along the southern edge of town away from the water. Tradesmen such as carpenters, bricklayers, barbers, tailors, and shop clerks rented or owned modest-sized dwellings, built shops, or ran ordinaries in the parcels on these back cross streets.

Trade made Yorktown one of the wealthiest and most cosmopolitan ports in Virginia in the first half of the eighteenth century, and nowhere was this more evident than along its main street. The town filled with native-born merchants, tradesmen, shopkeepers, tavern keepers, river pilots, and mariners, immigrant British merchants and sea captains, and African and Virginia-born slaves who were employed as skilled craftsmen, stevedores, laborers, and servants. Merchants and prosperous tradesmen built substantial dwelling houses, stores, and taverns that catered to a growing clientele who aspired to a more refined manner of living. Though Yorktown had its rough edges, a French visitor observed that the town was "inhabited by some of the genteelest people In virginia, who have some very pretty buildings here."[25] An English traveler in the 1730s found the port

> tho' but stragglingly built, yet makes no inconsiderable Figure. You perceive a great Air of Opulence amongst the Inhabitants, who have some of them built themselves Houses, equal in Magnificence to many of our superb ones at St. James's [in Westminster near Piccadilly, London]; as those of Mr. Lightfoot, Nelson, &c. . . . The most considerable Houses are of Brick; some handsome ones of Wood, all built in the modern Taste; and the lesser Sort, of Plaister. There are some very pretty Garden Spots in the Town; and the Avenues leading to Williamsburgh, Norfolk, &c., are prodigiously agreeable.[26]

Perhaps the leading merchant in Yorktown in the first half of the eighteenth century was Philip Lightfoot, a second-generation Virginian. He purchased nearly a dozen lots in town, owned a warehouse and landing on the waterfront, and built two large dwellings in an enclave off the north side of the main street with a dramatic view overlooking the bluffs. Besides his business interests, Lightfoot served the county as the clerk of court from 1707 until 1733 when he was elevated to the Governor's Council, an honor that recognized his wealth and power. Sometime after 1724 he purchased additional lots just behind the courthouse grounds opposite his original house and erected a brick dwelling where he lived until his death in 1748. Some saw the economic clout Lightfoot wielded as a detriment to the growth of the town. Francis Jerdone, a Scottish merchant who settled in Yorktown in the late 1740s, believed that Lightfoot's "great riches while he continued in health deterred everybody from settling there, none being of ability to vie with him but Mr. Nelson, who always had an equal share of the trade with him."[27]

As Jerdone observed, Lightfoot's only rival in business was Thomas Nelson,

FIGURE 11. Thomas Nelson Sr. house, Yorktown, 1729

FIGURE 12. Secretary
Thomas Nelson
house, Yorktown,
c. 1765, showing the
damage suffered
during the 1781 siege
of the town. Drawing
by B. H. Latrobe,
1796. (The Maryland
Historical Society,
Baltimore)

a native of Penrith in the north of England who settled in Yorktown around 1705. His interests expanded to include most aspects of the town's economy. He built a storehouse and wharf on the beachfront, established a store to vend his imported goods on the north side of the main street, and in 1729 erected a large brick dwelling house that still stands on the opposite side of the street (fig. 11). Trimmed with imported and native stones, this double-pile dwelling with its carved brick frontispiece rivaled the Governor's Palace in Williamsburg in its scale and elaboration.[28]

Two of Nelson's sons added even greater luster to the family name. His eldest son, William, continued the family mercantile business, became sole owner of the Swan Tavern, and inherited much

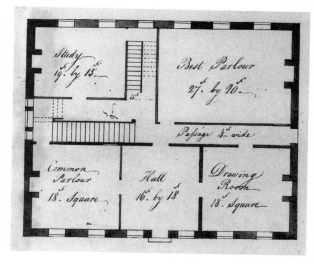

FIGURE 13. Plan, Secretary Thomas Nelson house, Yorktown. Drawing by Thomas Hunt, 1765. (RIBA Library Drawings Collection)

of his father's property. In the 1740s he erected a large brick house on the north side of the main street near the family storehouse and opposite the dwelling built by his father. By 1765 Nelson had more than doubled the size of the house to form an H-shaped configuration similar in plan to Tuckahoe in Goochland County (this house was destroyed in a fire that swept through the central part of Yorktown in 1814). In politics William rose to the top posts in the colonial government. He was elevated to the Governor's Council and later acted as its president in 1770–71 after the death of the governor, Norborne Berkeley, baron de Botetourt. William's younger brother Thomas also held high provincial office, serving as the secretary of state for the colony from 1743 until 1776. Thomas, too, made his mark on the Yorktown landscape, building sometime between 1744 and 1765 on the eastern edge of town a two-story brick house which measured 56 by 48 feet, making it larger than the original footprint of the Governor's Palace (figs. 12, 13).[29] The front of the house faced the main road coming in from the south and the rear elevation was enframed by a large garden and commanded a "fine Prospect of York River."[30] In 1781 the marquis de Chastellux described Secretary Nelson's dwelling as "a very handsome house, from which neither European taste nor luxury was excluded; a chimney-piece and some bass reliefs of very fine marble, exquisitely sculptured."[31] Covered by a distinctive M roof, the house suffered great damage during the siege of Yorktown and was left in ruins following the war.

Large merchant houses with attached garden plots appeared along the main street, giving the town a verdant if straggling appearance.[32] In many ways Yorktown followed the pattern of growth found in other southern ports such as Annapolis, the capital of Maryland, where large private estates punctuated the densely built fabric of shops, stores, taverns, dwellings, and tenements. Merchants, provincial officials, and prosperous professionals consolidated a group of lots in which they erected large brick dwellings surrounded by pleasure gardens. Often next door to these urban compounds stood a number of smaller commercial buildings—shops, stores, and taverns—crammed together in a manner more characteristic of urban growth. Even in its period of most intensive development in the middle of the eighteenth century, Yorktown never lost its sylvan appearance, replaced by contiguous buildings jammed together in minutely subdivided parcels. It was simply too small to be anything more than a large village.

With storehouses lining the main street and at the river's edge, Yorktown thrived as an entrepôt where exotic and essential merchandise enticed the appetite of a growing consumer society. Among the more successful of these emporiums was Richard Ambler's storehouse located on the south side of the main street next to his residence. Known rather confusingly today as the Custom House because of Ambler's position as collector of customs, the two-story brick building had the specialized features characteristic of mid-eighteenth-century

FIGURE 14. Ambler store (Custom House), Yorktown, c. 1725–50

stores in Virginia. Its plan and brickwork suggest that it was constructed between the 1730s and the 1760s (fig. 14). A wooden sign attached to the front wall or projecting on an iron bracket advertised the place of business. With the short side of the store turned toward the street, customers entered through a centrally placed doorway flanked by two large windows (fig. 15). Its eighteenth-century fittings have disappeared, but Ambler's storehouse was arranged in the standard manner.[33] It had a large front room where imported European and domestic goods ranging from crockery, books, and confectioneries to nails, paint, and glass would have been on display or in containers on shelves that lined both sides and perhaps the back wall separating the salesroom from the counting room. Because shelves often extended the full length and height of these long walls, there were few side apertures. Merchants depended upon the two front windows as the primary source of illumination of their salesroom and sometimes artfully placed goods there to attract customers. Counters just in front of the shelves allowed clerks to display items to interested customers (fig. 16). A door in the back of the salesroom led a stair passage to the upper floor, which may have been used for the storage of goods, as was the cellar. A second-story door with a winch above allowed goods to be hauled up for storage. If not devoted entirely to storage, the second story in Virginia stores sometimes contained accommodations for clerks or others who worked on the premises. At the back of the ground floor, a small heated room equipped with a desk and

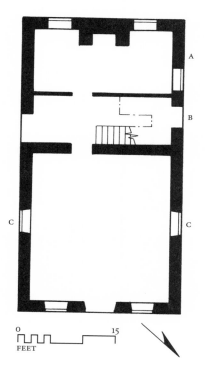

FIGURE 15. Plan, Ambler store, Yorktown. *A:* cellar entrance below; *B:* door added in twentieth century; *C:* window added in twentieth century.

FIGURE 16. London draper's shop. English engraving, eighteenth-century. Shelves and counters where goods were displayed and examined by customers appeared in specially built stores in the Chesapeake by the early eighteenth century.

chair served as a counting room where Ambler kept account books for his storehouse as well as the books recording the clearance of customs in the port. The merchant could enter this room either through the passage from his salesroom or from an exterior door on the side of the building, which allowed him private access.

The most intensely developed area of the upper town stood clustered around the courthouse grounds on the main street where there were a number of dwellings, stores, shops, and ordinaries. "The taverns," an English traveler noted in 1736, "are many here, and much frequented, and an unbounded Licentiousness seems to taint the Morals of the young Gentlemen of this Place. . . . Schemes of Gain, or Parties of Gaming and Pleasure, muddy too much their Souls."[34] When the York County court convened on the third Thursday of every month at the courthouse, the area around it came alive with scores of people gathering in the neighboring taverns and shops as well as participating in the impromptu entertainments found on the courthouse grounds. In the second quarter of the eighteenth century, lots 12 and 18 to the east of the courthouse on the north side of the street contained a dwelling and store. Carpenter Robert Ballard lived catty-corner to the courthouse on lot 19 and may have had his shop next door on lot 13 if it was not leased as commercial space. On the south side of the main street just opposite the courthouse on lot 25 stood the leading hostelry in the town, the Swan Tavern, a wooden one-story structure. Jointly owned by Thomas Nelson and fellow merchant Joseph Walker, it operated as the social center of town, the place where merchants made deals, mariners related shipping information and recounted the latest news from Europe, and locals gathered to bid at auctions of land, slaves, and goods from estate sales. The Nelson family also owned lot 31 next door to the Swan. At least two shops may have been located here in the first half of the century. In the early

1770s William Reynolds, a merchant who had received his training in the offices of the London merchant firm of John Norton and Sons, purchased the property and erected a brick storehouse and dwelling.[35]

A tavern on the north side of the main street dominated the block that contained the courthouse. Several generations of innkeepers operated this establishment on lot 30. Its location just east of the courthouse made it one of the busiest and most lucrative ordinaries in Yorktown, catering especially to the court-day trade. In the 1710s Edward Powers owned the property and built up a thriving business before his death in 1719. An inventory of his estate describes a rambling complex with at least one addition already made to a one-story frame building. Powers and his wife Elizabeth lived in part of the house, while the hall was used as the entertaining room of the tavern, replete with punch bowls, decanters, tables, leather chairs, money scales, backgammon board, tea kettle, coffeepot, and a speaking trumpet either left behind by a sea captain or provided for the hard of hearing. Guests slept in a room above the hall that contained four beds and suitable bed furniture. Two white servant boys and an indentured white woman labored for the innkeeper.[36] After Powers's death, the tavern descended to Elizabeth's children from a previous marriage. Her son Ishmael Moody expanded the tavern, adding new specialized rooms that were coming into fashion in Virginia in the second quarter of the eighteenth century, including a barroom and a billiards room, and increasing the number of beds and bedchambers. At his death in 1748, Moody's property contained a house at the rear where guests found a sitting room and bedchambers. The space designated the "ordinary" contained three bedchambers abovestairs, public sitting rooms on the ground floor, a billiards room, and the barroom, the heart of the tavern's operations, which housed china punch bowls, decanters, bottles, tables, chairs, a money scale, and an inkstand. Moody stored ample stocks of domestic and imported liquors and the old speaking trumpet in the cellar under this section of the sprawling property. In addition, there were rooms in other spaces, which may have been physically separated from the ordinary. Domestic furnishings in the "new house," the large room and smaller room of the "lower house," and in upstairs bedchambers suggest that the family inhabited these spaces as their private apartment. Yet the presence of a large amount of dining equipage and chairs argues that some of these rooms may have served as additional entertaining rooms for the public. The cellar under the lower house contained bottles of Yorkshire ale and porter, as well as old pewter. To run such a large establishment, Moody had several outbuildings, including a kitchen, two dairies, and a meat house and kept an assortment of livestock including cows, pigs, and horses. He owned ten slaves, who cooked, laundered, cleaned, and waited upon guests and family members.[37]

With court day each month, Moody's Tavern brimmed with activity as lawyers and their clients gathered in the public rooms to discuss legal strategy, planters talked of crops over drinks of porter, and idlers found diversions at the backgammon table or in the billiards room. Busybodies quizzed strangers about news from distant places and then turned to more personal questions concerning their religious and political views. Some walked next door to the courthouse to watch the proceedings or converse with their neighbors. After warming themselves by the fire in the entertaining room, others headed down the street to Nelson's or Ambler's store to purchase a bolt of cloth, a pound of coffee, or a keg of nails. On their way they could have been enticed to haggle with country people at their temporary stands where they sold produce or handmade goods such as baskets. As the course of the court's docket slowed, many of those who had traveled a long distance and still had business before the magistrates scrambled to secure lodgings for the night, perhaps finding that they were to share a bed with courtroom adversaries they would meet again the following morning. Although Yorktown provided more opportunities for dissipation and shopping than most rural settings, court-day activities and rituals repeated themselves across the colony in the same familiar pattern.[38] Punctuating the isolated routine of rural life, court day was a great social event, providing the opportunity for members of local society to renew ties of friendship over a drink in the tavern or to participate in harmless amusements. Court day was also a time of reckoning when county inhabitants examined the workings of their community and sought to address some of the serious problems that arose regarding their families, their livelihood, and their fundamental beliefs. Frivolity and solemnity shared the day.

York County Builds a New Courthouse

In 1732 York County magistrates replaced an undistinguished old wooden courthouse with a brick structure, heralding the start of an era of self-conscious public building in Virginia. The new building replaced a small wooden structure that had served the county for thirty-five years. In 1697 the county court agreed with Henry Cary—a local undertaker or building contractor who in a few years would be hired to build a number of the public buildings in Williamsburg—to erect a wooden courthouse on lot 24 in Yorktown. Paid 28,000 pounds of tobacco (the typical medium of currency used throughout most of Virginia in the colonial period), Cary finished the frame structure by the end of the year.[39] Given its relatively inexpensive cost, the building had few embellishments inside or out. It probably resembled other courthouses of the period, with the exterior sheathed in clapboards and the few windows lit by wooden casements. But it may have had one improvement over the earthfast courthouses: that no substantial repairs were made to the building between its construction in 1697 and its demolition in 1732 or 1733 suggests it had masonry foundations, perhaps the local marlstone used in building the church.[40] The courtroom probably had a raised platform at one end with a table and benches for the magistrates. The rest of the room was devoid of any furniture except a few benches for other court officials and a balustrade or bar that separated the public from court officials.

This unremarkable courthouse served the nascent port for ten years before any changes were made to the building. In 1708 Major William Buckner, one of the magistrates, agreed to add a 7-foot-square enclosed entrance porch to the courthouse and also built a detached clerk's office on the public lot for the new clerk, Philip Lightfoot. Three years later Buckner hired a laborer to coat the courthouse exterior with tar, a material commonly used in the colonial period to preserve the fabric of the building. In 1713 Buckner made unspecified alterations and additions to the courthouse, mended the windows, and tarred the exterior of the new work. Because he was paid 15,120 pounds of tobacco, more than half of the original cost of construction, the work must have been substantial.[41] After this, the courthouse underwent only minor repairs to the windows and door over the next twenty years. With the growth of Yorktown as a prosperous port in the 1710s and 1720s, an increasingly critical audience of court officials and town inhabitants viewed the small tarred courthouse as an outmoded relic of the early years. After two additions, the building probably had a rambling appearance, and the interior fittings seemed cramped and no longer suitable to the growing demands of a busy court. The success of the town no doubt generated the desire to replace the building with a more commodious and pretentious one that matched the ambitions of its successful merchants, sea captains, and neighboring tobacco planters.

The idea of building a new courthouse surfaced in the late 1720s when York magistrates began to raise money for its construction. In 1728 they agreed to levy 8,640 pounds of tobacco that would then be sold at public auction "for building the courthouse." Although no county levy was laid in 1729 for any outstanding public expenses, the following year the magistrates set aside 23,460 pounds of tobacco for building the courthouse.[42] With more than 30,000 pounds of tobacco in reserve to pay for the initial costs of construction, York officials began to plan the design of their new building. Building contracts in colonial Virginia usually required a client, whether county justices, parish vestry, or individuals, to pay a certain portion of the building's total cost to the undertaker on the signing of the agreement. Generally this meant as much as a third of the total amount. This down payment allowed the builder to purchase or pay for the manufacture of materials such as bricks and mortar and to secure the services of craftsmen and laborers. Most undertakers, especially those who operated in the early eighteenth century, rarely had the financial wherewithal to begin constructing a sizable brick parish church, county courthouse, or two-story gentry house without an initial payment. Indeed, in an era before the mechanic's lien, few builders were willing to stake what capital they had in costly investments in materials that they might not be able to recoup should disaster such as a fire strike the building site. A second round of payments went to the builder after the successful completion of a major portion of the work such as raising the walls or closing in the building. A further payment went to the builder once all the obligations laid out in the contract were fulfilled and the building was officially turned over to the client. The builder was then released from the performance bond that he had posted—usually amounting to twice the cost of the project—at the signing of the contract.

On December 21, 1730, a month after the second levy of money for the new courthouse, the York magistrates appointed a small committee of its members to proceed with the project by entertaining "Proposals from proper workmen to undertake the erecting a new Courthouse."[43] Typically, the county bench as a group decided upon the basic size, form, and materials of a new structure and left it to a smaller building subcommittee to develop more detailed specifications, sometimes in consultation with leading craftsmen. Because they had already raised more money than had been expended on the original Yorktown courthouse and they intended to expand the building budget in subsequent years, it seems quite likely that the magistrates had determined from the very beginning to erect a brick courthouse. By the 1730s a new attitude was beginning to prevail about public building, and the county wanted to keep pace with other jurisdictions in the region that were striving to overcome the longstanding predilection to build in a shoddy, impermanent manner.

Two months later, when the building committee had done nothing, a new committee of justices composed of Lawrence Smith, Thomas Nelson, and Richard Ambler was appointed to push the project forward. This time the bench instructed them to receive proposals from workmen "for erecting a brick Courthouse forty eight feet long and Twenty four feet wide in the clear."[44] If the brick walls showed a commitment to raising the level of public architecture, the rectangular plan reflected a conservative choice of a familiar courthouse form. Since the late seventeenth century, courthouses of similar size had been built throughout the colony. Most buildings of this configuration had side entrances near the middle of the two long walls, with the magistrates' platform located at one end and a pair of jury rooms partitioned off at the other end. Occasionally some courthouses had stairs to garret rooms that may have been fitted out as a clerk's office or additional jury rooms.

Within a month Smith, Nelson, and Ambler had set aside this traditional plan in favor of one that incorporated popular English civic forms. On March 15, 1731, the committee reported that it had devised "a new draught" for the courthouse and had contracted to have it built for £600.[45] The building that carpenter Robert Ballard, a Yorktown neighbor of the three members of the committee, erected over the course of the next two years was unlike other Virginia courthouses. Instead of a rectangular plan with two side entrances, the York County courthouse was built in a T-shaped configuration with a principal entrance through a central arcade or piazza at the crossbar of the T, which faced the main street squarely (fig. 17). One or two jury rooms and a clerk's office flanked the central arcade at either end of this upper section. The central doorway led into the courtroom, which was arranged longitudinally to form the stem of the T. Dramatically placed at the end opposite the entrance stood the raised magistrates' platform, so that all eyes were drawn immediately to the magistrates upon their seats of honor. The arcade and single entrance gave the courthouse a distinct front facade that had been absent from earlier courthouses.

The question arises as to the source of this novel design. Rather than a copy from a published drawing or a particular building, in all likelihood the design derived from the amalgamation of traditional English public building features applied to the particular needs and purses of county government in colonial Virginia. Hugh Grove, an English visitor to Yorktown in 1732, noted that "they are just finishing a Court house or Town hall of Brick with a Piazza before it (which is) very handsom and Convenient."[46] Grove recognized the arcade as a telltale sign of the building's public nature because many town halls and market houses in England had been built with such features in the seventeenth and early eighteenth centuries (fig. 18). Richard Ambler and Thomas Nelson, two

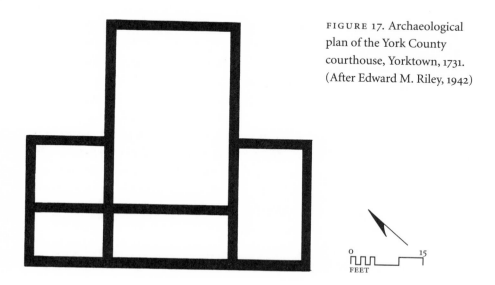

FIGURE 17. Archaeological plan of the York County courthouse, Yorktown, 1731. (After Edward M. Riley, 1942)

FIGURE 18. Town hall, Reigate, Surrey, 1728

members on the building committee who were intimately involved in shaping the plan of the building, were English immigrants to Virginia. Ambler had come from York, the ancient provincial city of the north, while Nelson was from the Cumberland market town of Penrith. Both were well acquainted with the arcaded town halls and markets that stood in countless towns across England. The strength of memory may have shaped their ideas for the new courthouse in Yorktown. Closer to home, the magistrates had to travel no farther than Williamsburg to see public buildings that borrowed English civic forms. The Capitol and the College of William and Mary had arcades used to link different sections of these large structures (fig. 19). Cupolas capped their rooflines, drawing further attention to their special nature. The Capitol, the magazine, and Bruton Parish Church featured rounded or compass-headed windows. All of these features replicated forms that had become second nature in English public building design by the 1730s.

If the English debt is transparent in the arcaded facade of the York County courthouse, the plan is more a product of local circumstances elegantly fashioned to provide a dramatic effect. By moving the jury rooms from the traditional location at the lower end of the courtroom to the sides, the builders created an axial progression that was terminated at the upper end of the courtroom by the raised platform of the magistrates' bench. Who was responsible for the inspired piece of design is impossible to say. Smith, Ambler, and Nelson may have worked it out themselves one evening over a bottle of wine or bowl of punch at the Swan Tavern. They may have developed the plan in conjunction with Ballard the undertaker, a second-generation native of Yorktown who had worked previously with the magistrates to repair the old courthouse. Ballard's father had been one of the original trustees of the port and had served on the county bench. Although Robert Ballard was a reliable neighbor with known skills, no evidence appears to suggest that he had special design experience outside the usual craftsman's competence or had worked on any other major public buildings. It is unlikely that he had traveled in England, and few imported architectural books were circulating in the colony to provide inspiration for such a structure. Yet Ballard's practical knowledge of building may have been invaluable to the committee. He may have demonstrated to them the structural logic and geometric clarity of a building whose front range of jury rooms and arcade was the same width as the rear courtroom wing. The 28-foot widths of both elements made the roof construction easier because all the rafters could be cut the same length and thus would provide a ridgeline of uniform height with hip angles of the same slope.

FIGURE 19. Arcade, College of William and Mary, Williamsburg, 1695–97, restored 1928–31

Was the T-shaped Yorktown courthouse the first of its kind in Virginia? The question is not easily answered because so much has disappeared from the colonial landscape. Many buildings that may have been built before the experiment in Yorktown have long since disappeared, replaced in later generations by larger structures.[47] A few T-shaped buildings of the Yorktown vintage survive but have not been precisely dated. In planning their courthouse in 1731, the York justices may have seen or been aware of a building of similar form farther west in King William County where an arcaded brick courthouse still remains in active use (figs. 20, 21). A traditional date of 1725 has been assigned to the

FIGURE 20. King William County courthouse, c. 1730, in c. 1900 photograph. (Valentine Richmond History Center)

FIGURE 21. Plan, King William County courthouse.

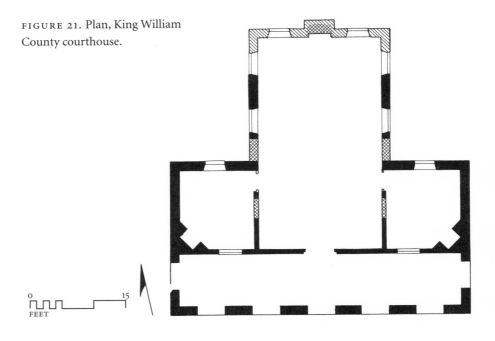

King William courthouse, but because the county has lost its colonial records, the date cannot be verified. If the King William courthouse was built in the mid-1720s, it has one of the earliest king-post roof truss systems in Virginia. The glazed header brickwork, rubbed-and-gauged jack arches, beveled water table, and other surviving features offer little diagnostic help, for they fit comfortably into the patterns found from 1725 through 1775.

If its status as the progenitor of a distinctive Virginia public building form cannot be affirmed, the Yorktown courthouse was still among the first wave of self-conscious public buildings that appeared in Virginia in the 1730s and 1740s. The final cost of the York courthouse when it was completed in 1733 was more than 122,650 pounds of tobacco, or close to £1,022 Virginia currency, an amount well over the £600 estimated by its building committee and more than four times the cost of the old wooden courthouse built in 1697.[48] Furnishing the building with tables, chairs, bookpresses, and other essential items added to the overall price over the next few years. One final element appeared in 1739 when the court asked Thomas Nelson and his son William to "send to England for Stone to lay the floor of the Court House and of the two offices," which they did and were paid £40 sterling for their effort.[49] Prestige had its price, and York magistrates were willing to raise county taxes substantially over a four-year period. The cost of building the new courthouse may have seemed considerable, but it was a reasonable sum when compared to British public building prices. Though exact comparison is difficult because the scale of buildings varied widely, as did the number of people who were called upon to underwrite their cost, town halls and courthouses built in Britain ranged from just under £1,000 sterling to several thousand pounds.[50] For example, the two-story shire hall built in Monmouth in 1724 cost the ratepayers of Monmouthshire £1,700 (fig. 22). Substantially larger than the York County courthouse, the shire hall was sheathed in ashlar Bath stone festooned with giant Ionic pilasters and contained courtrooms above an arcaded ground floor used as market space.[51]

The fact that no York County freeholder openly complained or refused to pay the increased burden suggests that they were willing participants and saw the courthouse as a source of community pride. Visitors immedi-

FIGURE 22. Shire hall, Monmouth, Wales. Lithograph, c. 1850.

FIGURE 23. York County courthouse, Yorktown, 1814, in c. 1862 photograph. (Library of Congress)

ately took notice. An Englishman in 1736 observed that "the Court-House is the only considerable publick Building" in Yorktown "and is no unhandsome Structure," a sentiment rarely expressed about Virginia courthouses built in the seventeenth and early eighteenth centuries.[52]

The York magistrates must have been proud of their achievement, believing that they had built something worthy of their ambitions and of lasting significance. In the long run fate cheated them as the building survived for less than a century, and no known drawing was made of it that would have preserved its image for later generations. Though no doubt influential in raising the level of civic design in Virginia in the late colonial period, the building suffered substantial damage in 1781 during the battle that guaranteed the independence of the new American nation. Refurbished at great cost at the end of the 1780s, the courthouse fell victim to a fire that destroyed much of the town in 1814. The new courthouse that was built over its ruins lasted only half a century before it was violently blown apart in an explosion of Federal munitions stored in it during the Civil War (fig. 23). Though other county courthouses suffered less dramatic endings, most of the public buildings erected by Virginia's colonial magistrates gradually disappeared, replaced by larger structures that met changing civic aspirations and aesthetic predilections of succeeding generations.

FIGURE 24. Market house, Chipping Camden, Gloucestershire, 1627

FIGURE 25. Market-day activities. Frontispiece, Richard Bradley, *The Riches of a Hop-Garden Explain'd,* 2d ed. (London, 1733), vol. 3, no. 1. (Courtesy of The Library of Virginia)

THE EARLY COURTHOUSES
1650–1725

Introduction

THE FAILURE TO DEVELOP TOWNS in seventeenth-century Virginia had a profound influence on the county courts. Without towns there were few natural or commonly accepted centers of economic or political activity. For Englishmen, towns were not only centers of trade but also the natural place for governmental institutions. Town halls, market houses, and courthouses stood in the center of English towns and cities (fig. 24). Municipal bells, hung in turrets and bell cotes, summoned inhabitants to meetings, announced great events, and tolled the hours. Covered space enclosed by an arcade or colonnade provided shelter for the civic market, a gathering place for town folk, and often housed the lockup, pump, and fire engine (fig. 25). Coats of arms and statues placed in prominent positions on the facades of these buildings informed viewers of the patronage of grand families that underwrote their construction or proclaimed the loyalty of the inhabitants to their sovereign (fig. 26). The provincial town provided the stage for the ceremonial display of power. A parade of horsemen and coaches through the high street and marketplace marked the opening of assize courts. Trumpeters and liveried servants heralded the arrival of circuit-riding justices from the King's Bench in London, who were accompanied by the local gentry, court officials, and the high sheriff of the county (fig. 27). This display was followed by a sumptuous banquet hosted by the county elite for the magistrates and sermons delivered in the parish church that reminded hearers of the moral duty of court officials and inhabitants.

In early Virginia no such stage existed for municipal spectacles. There were no processional routes, hardly any roads. Without an urban population, there were few to be impressed by a parade of ranking officials, scarcely anyone within earshot to hear the striking of the municipal bell, and no sheltered space to market goods and produce. There were no robed judges adorned with civic regalia. Without the panoply of power, emblems of authority, and symbols of royal sovereignty, colonists along the tobacco coast faced the task of replicating English institutions under novel circumstances and creating civic architecture

FIGURE 26. Royal arms, statue of Justice, arms of the city of Warwick, courthouse, Warwick, Warwickshire, c. 1751

in rural settings. The public buildings erected in Virginia in the seventeenth century were profoundly shaped by the nature of the plantation society that grew up along the broad estuaries of the Chesapeake Bay.

In the ninety years that separated the first English settlement at Jamestown and the establishment of the royal capital at Williamsburg, the colony of Virginia developed in a manner quite unforeseen by its seventeenth-century promoters and much lamented by its early eighteenth-century chroniclers. John Smith and other explorers of the New World praised the natural fecundity of Virginia, with its temperate climate, its fertile soils, its broad bay well-watered by many deep rivers, and its great forests teeming with abundant game. With all these natural advantages, they believed it only a matter of time before industrious settlers would transform the wilderness into a colony that would match its mother country in productivity and wealth. Substantial and well-ordered towns, replete with public buildings constructed of brick, would spring from virgin sites and grow to rival provincial English cities such as Bristol, Norwich, and Newcastle.[1]

Somewhere in those years between 1607 and 1699 something went wrong. James City, Elizabeth City, and Charles City, the names given to the first settlements in Virginia, were by the end of the seventeenth century ironic reminders of unfulfilled schemes.[2] Scattered across hundreds of miles stood isolated plantations worked by planters, indentured servants, and black slaves. In the midst of unkempt agricultural fields were poorly constructed frame houses half falling to ruin, surrounded by rude slave and servant quarters no better than the shelters provided for animals on many English farms. That the colony was not living up to its expectations was painfully evident to many thoughtful Virginians at the turn of the century. Some considered the inhabitants indolent, depending "upon the Liberality of Nature, without endeavoring to improve its Gifts, by Art or Industry."[3] Compared to the newer colonies in the Delaware Valley or even to New England, which had far fewer natural advantages than the Chesapeake, Virginia showed few signs of material progress. Henry Hartwell and his fellow authors James Blair and Edward Chilton observed of Virginia in 1697 that "if

FIGURE 27. Procession of judges before the opening of the quarter session courts in Chelmsford, Essex, 1762. Engraving after a painting by David Ogborne.

we enquire for well built Towns, for convenient Ports and Markets, for Plenty of Ships and Seamen, for well improv'd Trades and Manufactures, for well educated Children, for an industrious and thriving People, or for an happy Government in Church and State, and in short for all the other Advantages of human Improvements, it is certainly, for all these Things, one of the poorest, miserablest, and worst Countries in all America."[4]

It was not too difficult to see why Virginia had fallen so short of its promise. Like many before them, Hartwell, Blair, and Chilton placed the blame on the destructive effects of tobacco, which "swallows up all other Things."[5] The road to stagnation had been charted early. After a decade of floundering for lack of quick riches, the settlers at Jamestown finally discovered in tobacco a commodity that had an overseas market. In the 1620s England could not get enough of it. Tobacco's high price precipitated a boom in its production in the roughly cleared fields along the James and brought an influx of new planters hoping to make their fortunes. By 1623 many of these planters had moved away from nucleated, particular plantations, such as Jamestown, Henrico, and

THE EARLY COURTHOUSES, 1650–1725   51

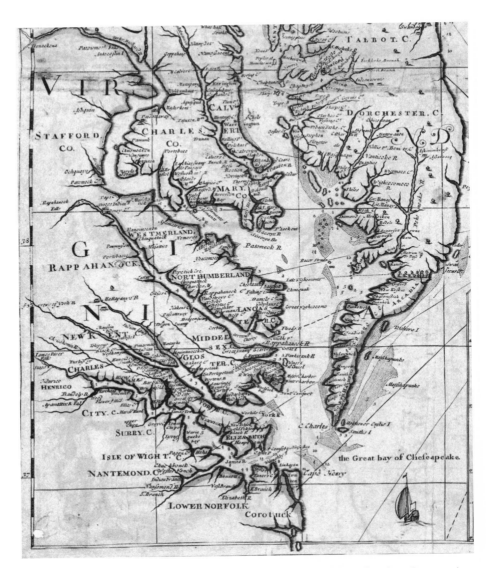

FIGURE 28. Detail of *A Mapp of Virginia*, John Thornton, cartographer (London, 1679). Twenty counties had been established by this time.

FIGURE 29. South elevation of structure 144, row house, Jamestown, as it appeared in the late seventeenth century. Drawing by William Graham Jr.

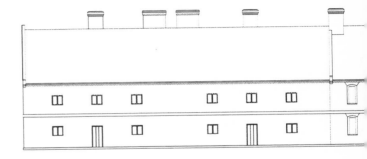

Wolstenholme Towne, to live "farr asunder" on "diverse small plantacions . . . scattered one from another."[6] Although the boom collapsed by 1630, people still flocked to Virginia, spreading out in a thin line of settlement along the river's edge. Finding the land along the James taken up, later immigrants patented tracts farther inland or northward along the York and Rappahannock Rivers (fig. 28). By 1700 perhaps 60,000 inhabitants occupied widely dispersed tobacco plantations that stretched from the south side of the James to the Potomac River.[7]

One of the harshest indictments of the colony was its failure to nurture the growth of towns. The capital at Jamestown never developed to more than a straggling collection of a few dozen houses; Henrico, Wolstenholme, and other early towns had become fields, woods, or long-forgotten sites by the end of the century.[8] In the eyes of Englishmen, only cities and towns could foster the growth of trade and material wealth, both seen as necessary to the development of civil behavior. Governor Thomas Culpeper, second Baron Culpeper of Thoresway, believed that "noe other nation ever begunne a plantacion, or any yet thrived" without them. Even some Virginians recognized "that our present necessities and too much doubted future miseries are much heightened by our wild and Rambling way of living [and] therefore are desirous of cohabitation."[9]

From the 1660s onward, several governors tried to correct this deviation from acceptable settlement patterns by sponsoring legislation and promoting schemes to create towns and ports, only to find themselves faced with the inertia of established custom or an open unwillingness on the part of some colonists to give up their tobacco production for other economic pursuits and trades.[10] With official prodding, Jamestown showed some signs of progress toward urbanization and urbanity. By the time Nathaniel Bacon's followers burned the capital in 1676, it boasted at least three sets of substantial brick row houses (fig. 29). The builders of the three units, designated as structure 17 by archaeologists, selected a plan as up-to-date as any constructed in London at midcentury. Two rooms deep with a central chimney heating both rooms and a winding staircase enclosed within the space between the stack and the passage between the two rooms, the plan of these brick dwellings exemplifies the

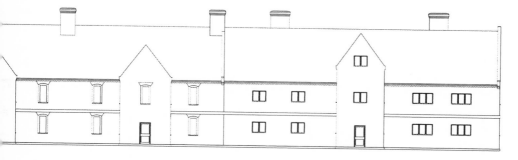

familiarity that Virginians had with contemporary English urban planning.[11] However, this distinctly urban form as well as the two sets of four lobby-entrance row houses were not to be replicated in Jamestown or elsewhere in Virginia for more than a century. Instead, their failure to match the economic and social circumstances of the colony was yet another indication of the rejection of English practices. Outside of Jamestown, halfhearted attempts to urbanize the landscape shared a similar fate. A few tobacco ports such as Yorktown developed some of the functional services associated with towns, but these never grew into sizable entrepôts.[12] Building civic institutions in rural surroundings therefore took a different course from English prototypes.

The Selection of Court Locations

In lieu of towns, Virginians turned to the concept of the geographic center to establish the physical location of government buildings. Within the boundaries of large political jurisdictions with no towns or heavily concentrated centers of populations, colonists gradually came to build their public structures on land in or near the geographic middle of the area encompassed by the county. This method of selection often meant constructing civic structures in the middle of nowhere, at a place that was equidistant from all corners of the county. This novel approach took more than half a century to become embedded in the thinking of colonial Virginians. By the time settlement moved beyond the tidewater and new counties were established in the Southside and piedmont in the early eighteenth century, the idea was firmly rooted. As a result, courts generally agreed to hold their sessions "at the most Centrical and convenient place" within their jurisdictions.[13] Among the first tasks for a newly constituted court was to assign a surveyor to draw a plat of the county boundaries in order to locate its geographic center.[14] Eventually, this concept became a part of American thinking about the political division of the physical landscape, making it seem logical to divide huge swaths of frontier into equal units regardless of topographical features, with the center reserved for the location of political and cultural institutions, a practice that shaped the division of the Northwest Territory and the designation of state capitals, for example.[15]

Before geographic centrality became ingrained, seventeenth-century Virginians struggled to find the most equitable means of establishing a public institution among a dispersed rural population. The division of Virginia into eight counties in 1634 did not mark the beginning of local government in the colony but signaled official recognition of a trend toward the devolution of authority from Jamestown that had already begun. Local courts had been established at several locations under the leadership of commissioners at least a decade previously. With the transfer of many of the powers of the provincial government into the hands of local commissioners and then county magistrates, it became increasingly important to inhabitants in these new jurisdictions to have unencumbered access to the local court. Having the court sitting conveniently nearby gave many individuals an advantage in pressing legal claims or influencing the course of public action over those citizens living on distant plantations. However, rarely in the first half of the century were there men or families whose power and authority could persuade or bully the local court into sitting permanently in an area particularly advantageous to their interests. In most counties local factions were too weak or too unorganized to pressure the courts into settling on a permanent home. Through most of the seventeenth century, county courts generally led a peripatetic existence.

The decision to hold court in a particular place was a highly localized issue with many factors coming to the fore when county justices debated the subject. The constraints of travel meant that geography played a major role in many deliberations. Smaller counties with natural water routes had a far easier time of deciding locations than larger ones with poor lines of communication. Counties with dispersed populations might give magistrates trouble in trying to find a demographically central place for court meetings, but in counties with concentrated areas of population, more often than not, different areas of settlement competed against one another for the right to hold court in their locality. Such feuds often erupted at the magisterial level, tearing the court apart and reducing its effectiveness in solving countywide issues. A bench that was continually plagued by turnover in its membership found it even harder to take the necessary steps to settle factional disputes. The debates over the location and construction of public buildings demonstrate that some Virginia counties operated quite smoothly throughout the seventeenth century while others suffered grievously from the instability of local governance.[16]

County governments labored for many years to overcome the decentralizing effects of wide geographic boundaries, poor means of communication, and a small, dispersed population. Most of the twenty-three counties that had come into existence by 1700 had followed several different paths in an effort to find suitable locations for the holding of monthly courts. In 1642 the governor gained the right, on advice from the council, to appoint the place where each county was to keep its court.[17] Before that time the responsibility of selecting the appropriate site was probably in the hands of the commanders of the various settlements and later the county commissioners. Direction from the provincial government was rarely a high-handed attempt to impose an unpopular location upon an unwilling populace but generally a de facto recognition of the wishes of the county. Most county commissioners probably desired as little interference as possible from the outside in such an important decision.

Only when local bickering blocked any acceptable solution did the governor and council actively take part in deciding where the courts should be kept.

In 1656 inhabitants living on the south side of the James River in what was then part of Charles City County petitioned the governor and assembly to have the local court moved from its location on the north side of the river to a site on the southern shore. Colonel Abraham Wood, Anthony Wyatt, and other prominent residents on the south side of the river apparently convinced the General Assembly of the sincerity of their plight, because it ordered that henceforth "the place of keeping courts for the said county shall be on the south side of the river, at such place as the commissioners or the major part of them shall find most convenient for the ease and benefitt of the inhabitants." However, their victory was short-lived. Two years later the inhabitants on the north side of the river caught the ear of the governor and assembly, which passed an act intended to satisfy both sides in this feud. Instead of dividing the county in two as might have been expected when such differences arose, the assembly decided that the county should maintain two courts, one on each side of the river, with sessions presided over by members from both shores. This agreement eventually broke down, much to the detriment of the inhabitants on the south side; by 1673 the only court being held was at Colonel Edward Hill's plantation on the northern shore.[18]

Although not without some enmity on occasion, most county courts did not suffer the long and rending dispute that befell Charles City County in the 1650s. Court commissioners considered several factors in their search for the most "convenient" locations, using the adjective in its now obsolete meaning of "suitable" or "proper."[19] Foremost, they recognized that despite the dispersed nature of most settlements, some areas were more thickly populated than others; accordingly, they tried to find a place close to the majority of the inhabitants. They also knew that water offered the only practical means of communicating with the world beyond their isolated farmsteads. The James, York, Rappahannock, and Potomac, the four major rivers that divided the tidewater into distinct peninsulas or necks, were the economic lifelines that connected the planters along their shores with their neighbors and to English ports and tobacco markets. Dense forests, deep ravines, swift streams, and tidal marshes impeded overland travel from one isolated farmstead to the next. The early scarcity of horses and the absence of well-maintained and clearly marked paths and roads further retarded movement through the countryside. Because most inhabitants still clung to the edge of the rivers and streams, commissioners favored sites along the shores. They had little incentive to establish the court in the geographic center of the county, which, in larger counties might often lie in the thinly populated and impenetrable interior dozens of miles from navigable rivers.

As the example of Charles City County demonstrates, it was particularly difficult to choose an acceptable location when many of the early counties extended across both banks of a major river. Though basic to communication, river travel was far from ideal. The river might act more like a barrier, a broad expanse more hazardous to cross in a canoe or flatboat than to coast in a small ship. At some crossings ferry service could be irregular, unavailable, or too costly for many travelers. Along with Charles City County, James City and Elizabeth City Counties spanned the James River until new counties were established at various times on its south side. For nearly twenty years York County took in both sides of its eponymously named river before Gloucester was created on the north shore. Farther north, Northumberland County encompassed all lands watered by the Rappahannock until it was subdivided into Lancaster, Westmoreland, and Rappahannock Counties in the 1650s. As settlement spread upriver to the fall line in the last half of the century and frontier counties such as Henrico and New Kent extended their jurisdiction many miles into the thinly settled interior, pressure grew to move the courts farther inland.

Finally, court officials considered the particular benefits of a site. They looked for farmsteads that contained freshwater creeks and springs so that the court could be well supplied with an adequate source of drinking water. They also took into account the type of accommodation in which they would be quartered, for it was not until the 1650s that structures specifically intended to house the public business began to be erected. Before that time, and long afterward in many counties, courts sat in makeshift quarters such as private dwellings, taverns, and tobacco houses. Some individuals allowed the courts to meet on their plantations for one or two days, six to nine times a year. The routine of the tenant or owner of the house was, therefore, only disrupted for a few days out of the year when scores of men and some women gathered to settle their disputes and to administer the county's affairs. Sometimes a man actively solicited the court's business by promising the county the benefit of his house without charge. John Cole, a tavern keeper in Accomack County, did not have just the public welfare in mind when he gave the county "free Liberty to keep Court at my house" in the 1670s. His business profited substantially from the dozens of people who descended upon his tavern at Pungoteague requiring food, shelter, and spirituous beverages. Desperate not to lose this lucrative trade, he became concerned over the court's decision to move its monthly sessions to a new location in 1677. To maintain his monopoly, he offered the county yet another site free of charge as well as the building materials to construct a courthouse.[20]

Court officials, too, could mix public weal with private gain. From the 1670s through the early 1690s, Richard Robinson, a justice for Middlesex County, had few excuses for missing court because it took place in the hall of his own house. This lengthy stay in one spot was unusual for the period and might have stemmed from the fact that Middlesex was a relatively small county that had few boundary readjustments. Robinson's house was located near the middle of the county just off the main county road and close by one of the creeks that fed into the Rappahannock River. For his troubles, Robinson was handsomely remunerated 3,800 to 6,500 pounds of tobacco annually.[21]

For many years York County court customarily held sessions at the house of one of its justices. However, unlike Middlesex, the court of this large county was frequently on the move, never settling on a permanent site but meeting at various locations throughout its jurisdiction. In the 1630s justices met at more than a dozen different plantations, which eventually led to the practice of having each member host the court on a rotating basis at his house.[22] The commissioners may have received some payment for the use of their houses and for at least one or two months out of the year were also saved the trouble and expense of having to attend a distantly held court for a few days. After Gloucester and New Kent Counties had been created by the partition of York in the 1650s, the justices of the much truncated parent county finally decided to establish a permanent site for their monthly court. In 1658 they rented Captain Robert Baldrey's house on Wormeley's Creek for 1,000 pounds of tobacco a year, which gradually rose to an annual payment of 4,000 pounds within a decade.[23] The York court continued to meet at Baldrey's house for a number of years, but by 1677 it found itself "destitute of a house to keepe Court in." The governor then granted the court permission to use the house of Thomas Hansford, who had forfeited his estate by his treasonous participation in Bacon's Rebellion. This order was later disallowed, forcing the court once again to meet in various private houses. In 1681 the court purchased a house at the French Ordinary in the center of the county and fitted it out for its sessions.[24]

As in York County, courts in many large counties were forced to move about from one location to another. In the 1680s the justices in the frontier county of Henrico constantly changed the site of meetings from magistrates' houses, rented dwellings, and taverns. In July 1683 they met in the house of William Byrd at the falls of the James near the county's western boundary. The next month they moved eastward and conducted business in the tavern owned by Thomas Cocke. Northumberland justices met at the house or tavern of James Magregor in the late 1650s but later shifted their meetings to the houses of two of their members. By the late 1670s they had settled on a permanent location at John Hughlett's old Indian field where they met for some time in a tobacco house.[25]

Other counties made it a policy to alternate between established sites in widely scattered locations. The commissioners of Norfolk County recognized that two distinct settlements existed within its borders by the 1640s, one along the Elizabeth River in the west and another farther east clustered around Lynnhaven Bay. The court reasoned that favoring one area at the expense of the other would create ill feelings. Weighing the relative density of population in each region, the court decided in 1642 that it would have twice as many meetings at Will Shipp's ordinary in the Elizabeth River settlement as it would have at Lynnhaven.[26]

Some counties eventually began to follow this pattern of alternating court locations on a regular basis. This was particularly true of counties whose boundaries extended across major rivers or those where inhabitants continually complained of the difficulty in attending distant courts. In 1646 James City County established a separate court on the south side of the river "for the ease of the inhabitants," which had the same power as the parent court on the north shore. The court was to be conducted by commissioners who lived on the south shore, and the county clerk and sheriff were to attend. In 1652 the residents of Bristol Parish, which encompassed the remote frontier area of both Charles City and Henrico Counties, were allowed the privilege of maintaining their own court with the provision that all decisions made by this subcourt could be appealed to monthly courts in either county. Because of their size, Isle of Wight, Lancaster, Rappahannock, and Northampton Counties all maintained at least two permanent court locations for some part of the century.[27]

The idea of such an arrangement was not new, since the quarter session courts in a number of English counties had long rotated in an established circuit among market towns, making attendance accessible to all regions.[28] Both in England and in Virginia, the division of the court's venue sometimes exacerbated rather than ameliorated the problem it was intended to resolve. In some Virginia counties the court's business tended to become confined to whatever concerned the area in which it was held, and few magistrates, constables, and jurors residing outside the immediate vicinity found it useful to attend. Some suits might be prosecuted in one region, and those living elsewhere who were affected by them would suffer from their ignorance of the court's proceedings. By the 1680s Norfolk County was for all practical purposes two distinct jurisdictions. Residents in the western section of the county were not answerable to suits instigated in the court held for the eastern settlements, and those inhabitants of Lynnhaven Bay in the east did not need to answer to the court at Elizabeth River.[29] Elsewhere, justices who chose not to attend one session because of its distant location would, at the next convenient court, be poorly informed about what transpired in the previous court. As in Charles City in the 1650s, justices in one part of the county might be openly antagonistic and work against the interests of other areas. The inefficiency inherent in dispersed jurisdictional authority made it difficult for justices to act in concert for the benefit of the entire county on a variety of shared matters that ranged from the maintenance of roads to the construction of public buildings.

Growing out of the bitterness of their experience during this period, Virginians gradually began to accept the concept of geographic centrality as the fairest and principal means of determining the location of the county seat. This does not imply that squabbles never punctuated the early sessions of new county courts in the eighteenth century, but these were generally over the peculiar qualities of one core location compared to another equally central place. The basic principle, however, was by now unchallenged.

The Early Courthouses

The fracturing of authority and the concomitant effect it had on determining the location of the court was but one difficulty that retarded the emergence of the first purpose-built public buildings. Perhaps a far greater impediment stemmed from the fact that few colonists perceived any need for them. During the first half of the seventeenth century, when courts met so infrequently and for such short periods of time, it must have seemed extravagant to build a structure solely for public business. The notion that minor courts should be housed in a specialized space, much less a separate building, held little currency in English or colonial society. In provincial towns across England, scores of Tudor and early Stuart market houses and guildhalls could be found, but these structures generally contained large open assembly halls used for a variety of civic activities including, at times, local courts. Yet for every courtroom above a market house, scores of makeshift courtrooms were set up in large inns in county towns. At Chelmsford in Essex county magistrates met in the Black Boy Tavern in the seventeenth century. Farther south in Maidstone a room known as the Justice Chamber at the Star Inn on the High Street served as the venue for the Kent assizes as early as the 1630s.[30] Undoubtedly, no small number of Virginia immigrants could well recall standing before English magistrates in the improvised surroundings of a tavern, guildhall, or great hall of a manor house.

The first years of the colonial government in Jamestown offered no source of inspiration for county magistrates either. Until the middle of the 1660s, the General Court and General Assembly paid great sums of money to tightfisted tavern keepers for the privilege of conducting affairs of state in their ordinaries. Dissatisfied at the expense of such arrangements and a little embarrassed by the fact that "all our laws [are] being made and our judgments given in alehouses," colonial officials, responding to the active prodding of Governor Sir William Berkeley, finally undertook the construction of a statehouse in the mid-1660s.[31] Even then, the government may have encased in brick and refitted an old earth-fast structure rather than construct a new building.[32]

After the restoration of royal authority in Virginia in 1660, Governor Berkeley renewed his efforts to steer the colony away from its dependence on tobacco. Like others before him, he stressed that one of the ways to overcome this problem was for settlers to gather in towns where new economic opportunities could flourish. In order to promote urban development, public buildings were to be constructed to attract town dwellers and centralized trade.[33] Throughout the decade the provincial government encouraged their construction through a series of acts. In 1663 it offered to finance the building of county courthouses out of funds raised in the public levy. The law authorized the Speaker of the House of Burgesses to contract with workmen to build at least four courthouses per year until every county was provided with one. Two years later, in an attempt to foster "cohabitation," the General Assembly passed a law that urged each county to select one or two places "where the whole trade of the Countie shall bee and that the Church and ministers house, the Court house Records and clerks residence the Sheriffs, & officers and Bayliffs the prison and ordinaries, and what else shall be thought fitting, shall be established there." Finally, in 1667 it authorized each county to purchase and hold in trust two acres of land on which to erect public buildings.[34]

The first two laws proved to be ineffectual; the third achieved a more lasting success. The public building scheme and the plan for cohabitation failed because the provincial government lacked the financial wherewithal and organizational resources to underwrite and oversee this massive public works program and because the local jurisdictions found it in their interest to work against them. On the surface the offer to build county courthouses from the provincial revenues seemed a generous one, but the inferior courts ignored this bold scheme probably out of a fear that any direct control by the Speaker and governor over such an important local issue might diminish the magistrates' own jealously guarded authority. As most justices were well aware, only a few years earlier the county courts had defeated the provincial government's attempt to have members of the council sit officially in their monthly sessions. The last enacted law, providing the counties with the authority to purchase with public funds two acres of land on which to build courthouses, posed no outward threat to county government and disposed of any legal problems that might have arisen about public building on private land.

Blunting initiatives from outside for fear of losing some of their autonomy, the county justices eventually found it in their interest to build courthouses for reasons not unlike those given for erecting the first statehouse in Jamestown. The magistrates of Middlesex County, having finally grown tired of paying the "great yearly charge for the rent" of Richard Robinson's house, decided in 1685 that it would be "the great advantage and conveniency of all his Maj Subjects" to invest the county's money in "a good strong convenient & sufficient" brick courthouse. Other counties thought that the dignity of the court might be enhanced by the construction of "suitable buildings." The "Gentlemen of the court" of Accomack believed it absolutely necessary that a "decent and convenient accomodation" be erected for their proper carrying out of the public's business. Toward the end of the century, justices in new counties often were eager to build courthouses as visible manifestations of their new corporate identity. When Richmond County was formed in 1692 from the northern part of Rappahannock County, the magistrates in the new county quickly vacated the farmhouse where court had previously been held for the old county because it was "seated in a neck of land far from the main road." Starting afresh, they built a permanent courthouse and located it "in the middle of the county."[35]

The first buildings specifically erected to house county courts appeared in the third quarter of the seventeenth century. Among the earliest was the one built by Major John Carter, father of Robert "King" Carter, on his land at Corotoman for the lower half of Lancaster County in 1655. This marked the beginning of the involvement of three generations of this influential family in courthouse construction in the Northern Neck. Responding to the act of assembly providing for the establishment of court sessions on the south side of the James, Charles City magistrate Anthony Wyatt, along with other justices, supervised carpenter Thomas Tanner's construction of a courthouse in 1657 at the settlement known as Merchants Hope.[36] Across the river Colonel Edward Hill worked with fellow magistrate John Stith to supplant the influence of the south shore by completing the construction of a rival courthouse at Westover in the late 1650s.[37] Lieutenant Colonel William Waters, a member of the House of Burgesses for Northampton County, undertook the erection of that Eastern Shore county's first court building in 1664. Norfolk County, too, may have had a separate structure by the mid-1660s.[38] At the close of the century, courthouses stood in the counties of Essex, Gloucester, Henrico, King and Queen, Northumberland, Princess Anne, Rappahannock, Richmond, Stafford, Warwick, Westmoreland, and York. Justices in Accomack, Elizabeth City, and Isle of Wight Counties may have been sitting in their own buildings by this time as well.

Despite their specialized purpose, the construction of these early courthouses neither marked the appearance of a distinctive new form nor heralded the replication of English public building prototypes. Nearly all of them were simply fashioned frame buildings whose structure, size, and configuration differed little from neighboring farmhouses. With divergent attitudes that would mark the discourse on civic architecture for the next three centuries, those leaders who desired better or more imposing accommodations often found themselves frustrated by other factions within the county who were just as adamant for personal or geographic reasons to spend as little public money as possible. The elite in most counties had not yet developed a social and corporate sense of identity that would make them stick together on issues affecting the entire community. In many areas the magistracy suffered a constant turnover in membership due to the high mortality rate that plagued the colony. For many years this instability retarded the emergence of a stable ruling class bound together in a common outlook by the ties of kinship and mutual obligations.[39] In the search for the aggrandizement of political or economic power, one great planter might work to undermine the efforts of another. When the magistrates of Middlesex County wanted to build a "good Strong, Substantiall" courthouse in 1692 on land laid off for a town on Rosegill Creek, the local magnate, Ralph Wormeley, stymied their efforts by physically hindering the construction of the building and, more importantly, by refusing to deed the land to court-appointed trustees. Wormeley apparently preferred a proprietary interest in the project and was unwilling for members of the court to exercise exclusive authority.[40]

Except in a few instances of private benefaction (generally by a tavern keeper who hoped to profit from public business by building a courthouse on his land), public building was publicly financed by the county freeholders through an annual levy of tobacco on all tithables. In counties where the bench stood split on many issues, there was little political will to tax the inhabitants heavily for more substantial structures.[41] In 1689 the justices in the relatively populous but demographically divided county of Norfolk proposed to build two courthouses in different parts of their jurisdiction. The building at the proposed townsite on the Elizabeth River was to be constructed of brick, while the one that was to be built near the chapel of ease at Lynnhaven was to be constructed of wood. After receiving several petitions against the measure, the Norfolk magistrates concluded that the cost of building in brick would have been "too burthensome to the inhabitants" and decided instead to construct a cheaper wooden courthouse on the town land.[42]

The reluctance to lavish money on public building projects certainly limited the capacity to build well, but such parsimony had little influence on the physical arrangement of the first courthouses. If interest existed to create a distinctive civic architecture, local government buildings in England provided only the most general guidance for Virginians to emulate. The most common public building, the two-story market houses and town halls found in most sizable market towns, served a variety of purposes far different from Virginia courthouses. The open arcade provided a dry and shaded space where butchers could hang their sides of meat and farmers vend their fruits, vegetables, eggs, and cheese to an urban population dependent upon their wares. Above the smells and sounds of the produce market stood a large room where corporate or manorial officials met to regulate the affairs of the town and market and to settle disputes that arose among the inhabitants. Well designed for the diverse functions of court, corporation, and market, the urban form of the two-story arcaded or colonnaded public building such as those in Faringdon, Oxford-

FIGURE 30. Market hall, Faringdon, Oxfordshire (formerly Berkshire), late seventeenth century. The space above the market served a number of civic functions.

shire (formerly Berkshire, late seventeenth century; fig. 30); Ross on Wye, Herefordshire (1660–74); Amersham, Buckinghamshire (1682; see fig. 65); and Abingdon, Oxfordshire (formerly Berkshire, 1678–82), proved unnecessary and unadaptable to the Arcadian wilderness of the Chesapeake (figs. 31, 32).[43]

The planters of rural Virginia had little need for food markets or municipal gatherings. The business of the court required only a modest amount of space, no more than a few undifferentiated rooms. Unlike churches or English town halls that were planned for the meeting of a body of religious worshipers or active citizens, courtrooms were never intended for sizable audiences. One large room, domestic in scale, could accommodate the half dozen or so attending justices, clerk, sheriff, and subordinate officials sitting in open court. The public stood in the corners and at the back of the courtroom. Other than one or two smaller rooms, which were necessary for the private consultations of juries and magistrates, the court needed no other space. Because the court's functions could easily fit within the ground-floor space found in many Virginia houses of the period, there seemed little need to experiment with new arrangements. As a result, the plan of most early courthouses followed the same rectangular form of domestic structures. Occasionally a shed room was added to the main block, or an enclosed porch was extended from one of the long walls in a manner common to contemporary farmhouses. In 1704 the Middlesex County courthouse specifications called for a "twelve foot square room on the back side for a Jury room." A few years later York County magistrates ordered the construction of "a porch to the Court house Door of Seven foot Square to joyn to the House."[44] By the middle of the eighteenth century, the courthouse that had been built in Gloucester County in the 1680s had a central porch with an arched opening (see fig. A14).

Most courthouses were simply modified houses that contained courts. However, the absence of distinguishing features did not prevent Virginians from thinking of these buildings as public structures. In their search for the appropriate terminology to describe their courthouses, they borrowed from the one established public building form they knew. Many of the same men who

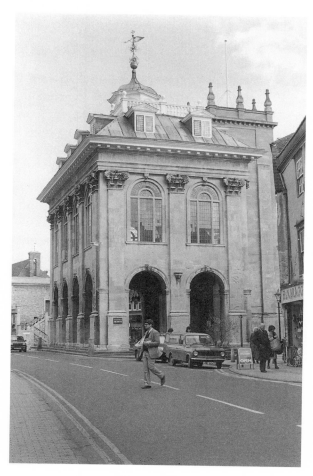

FIGURE 31. County hall, Abingdon, Oxfordshire (formerly Berkshire), 1678–82.

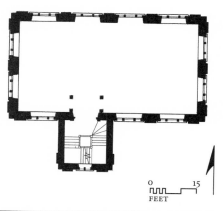

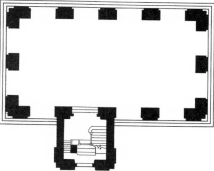

FIGURE 32. Plan, county hall, Abingdon, Oxfordshire. A purpose-built courtroom used for the county assizes was located in the upper floor *(top)* above the open arcaded market *(bottom)*.

built the first courthouses belonged to the vestries overseeing the construction of the early parish churches. A common religious heritage and the rituals prescribed in the Anglican prayer book provided most settlers with a basic understanding of the symbolic significance of church architecture. They appropriated familiar ecclesiastical terms to give meaning and order to their secular surroundings. This perspective required no great leap of imagination in a society where the difference between secular and religious authority often blurred. Justices of the peace believed that their authority derived from both common law and biblical law. They passed judgment on those who broke the laws of Moses as well as those who violated the laws of England. Thus it seemed entirely natural for magistrates to orient their buildings, both figuratively and literally, on an east-west axis and to describe the upper end where they sat as the "east end."[45] Below this place of authority stood the "congregation" of petitioners, litigants, and spectators.[46] Gradually, courthouses began to shed their domestic appearance in favor of the stylistic and structural features employed in churches. Northumberland County justices patterned the arched ceiling in their 1681 courthouse after one found in the neighboring Fairfield Church.[47] In a later generation of structures, king-post roofs, compass-headed windows,

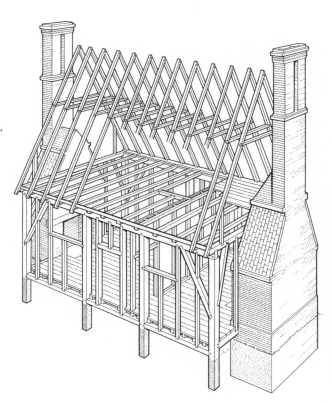

FIGURE 33. Post-in-the-ground framing, Matthew Jones house, Warwick County (now part of Newport News), early eighteenth century. Drawing by Allan Adams.

freestanding interior balustrades, and stone pavers passed from ecclesiastical usage into the widening public building vocabulary of Virginia courthouses.

Nearly all late seventeenth-century courthouses used inferior materials and methods of construction commonly employed in the region's domestic architecture.[48] County magistrates quite knowingly ordered the construction of structures that would seldom survive more than one or two decades without substantial repairs. In 1692 justices in Middlesex County proposed to erect a 30-by-20-foot courthouse in the manner of a "Virg[ini]a Built house," a shorthand reference to describe a flimsy wooden framing system in which several of the principal timbers stood directly on the ground or embedded in postholes (fig. 33). In contrast to the elaborate carpentry of a "good English frame," which sat off the ground on masonry foundations, Virginia builders developed a variety of cheap framing techniques that lessened the need for expensive labor-intensive joinery.[49] To reduce the cost of preparing materials, carpenters rived the smaller framing members such as the studs and rafters, roughly hewed the larger posts, sills, and plates, and secured them together with simple mortise and tenon or lap joints. Riven clapboards provided the necessary structural rigidity for the wall and roof frames.

Many courthouses, such as the one intended for the town land in Middlesex, had hole-set posts anchored 3 or 4 feet in the ground. Instead of posts sitting on top of sills, as in English framed buildings, these structures had sills framed into the sides of the posts. These interrupted sills made possible the installation of a wooden floor. In an effort to slow the decay of these members and ground-laid sills, carpenters selected durable species such as cedar or locust. Specifications for the Northumberland courthouse in 1681 called for locust posts and sills, while those for the Norfolk courthouse built eight years later stipulated cedar ones. Even so, buildings required regular replacement of their "earthfast" members. Within a few years of its construction, the Charles City courthouse at Westover needed new locust posts in 1659. The Henrico courthouse had fallen into such disrepair by 1688 that carpenter John Fail had to rebuild most of it to keep it from collapsing on its occupants. He took down the roof to replace the rotten false plates, wind beams, and rafters and later added new shingles. He also removed decayed ground sills and girders, replaced deteriorated floorboards, and underpinned the new timbers with wooden blocks. The space between the interrupted sills and ground and other sections of the wall received new clapboards. The magistrates paid Fail more than 7,000 pounds of tobacco, a substantial sum that would have gone a long way in paying for the cost of a new structure.[50]

Far more expensive and far rarer were brick courthouses. One of the earliest stood in the populous and prosperous county of Gloucester located between the York and Piankatank Rivers. By the mid-1680s Gloucester magistrates met in a brick-walled structure that had quickly become the envy of neighboring counties. In 1685 Middlesex justices planned to build a structure "at least of equall goodness and Dimentions with the Brick Courthouse lately built in Gloucester County," but nothing came of this proposal. In yet another attempt to build a courthouse seven years later, the Middlesex justices specified that there should be "one Door at the End & another at the side like Gloucester Court house."[51] The Gloucester building served the county for more than eighty years until it was replaced in 1766 by another brick structure that still survives. By 1691 the magistrates of Warwick County had erected a brick building for their sessions at the nascent village of Warwick Town on Deep Creek, but little is known of its appearance and configuration.[52] The only other well-documented brick courthouse erected in the seventeenth century was the one undertaken by Robert "King" Carter for Lancaster County in the late 1690s. As in several other counties, the magistrates decided to locate the courthouse in a newly established town in order to promote its growth. In 1698 they instructed Carter to build both a courthouse and prison on public lots laid off in the port of Queenstown on the optimistically named Town Creek.[53] Measuring 33 by 23 feet with a 10-foot-square porch, the building cost more than 40,000 pounds of tobacco, a sum that easily surpassed that paid for earlier courthouses. This courthouse served the county for forty years before the desire for a larger structure in a more central location away from the decayed village led to its replacement.[54]

The Plan and Furnishings of Early Courthouses, 1650–1725

When justices of the peace sat down to discuss the plans of their courthouses, they thought primarily of the arrangement of courtroom space. If considered at all, subsidiary meeting rooms and offices were relegated to the attic or a small partitioned area at the end of the courtroom. Unlike their counterparts in Maryland, rarely did Virginia magistrates combine court requirements with some other function. A few seventeenth-century Maryland courthouses stood two stories with a garret and contained apartments above the ground-floor courtroom where magistrates could lodge while conducting their business (fig. 34).[55] Justices in Virginia designed their courtrooms to be roughly 20 feet square or, in some cases, 5 to 10 feet longer than they were wide. This provided enough room for the magistrates to gather around a table with some space left over for litigants and petitioners. Few courthouses extended more than 23 feet in width, which eliminated the necessity to devise elaborate and costly roofing systems to carry longer spans. In length, buildings ranged from 25 feet in both the 1687 Northampton County and the 1693 Essex County courthouses to 46 feet in the 1678 Westmoreland County courthouse. Most structures, such as the ones planned for Charles City (1687), Norfolk (1689),

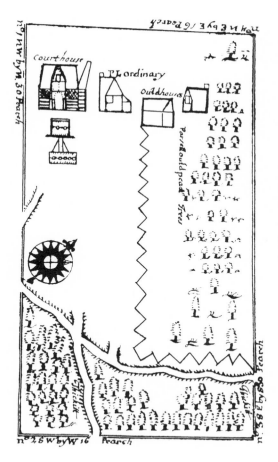

FIGURE 34. Plat of the Charles County, Maryland, courthouse grounds, 1697. The courthouse provided accommodations in its second-floor rooms, and next door was an ordinary that provided additional rooms as well as food and a variety of beverages. Just in front of the courthouse are the instruments of punishment: the stocks and pillory. (Charles Co., Md., Court Book 5, 277, Sept. 16, 1697, courtesy of Maryland State Archives)

Middlesex (1692), Richmond (1692), and Princess Anne (1692), measured no more than 30 to 35 feet long. Unlike some two-story Maryland courthouses, Virginia buildings, following domestic precedent, had only one main floor with a usable loft lit by dormers and gable-end windows. The height of this ground-floor courtroom between the floor and the ceiling varied from a low 7½ feet in the 1693 Essex courthouse to a pitch of 11 feet in the brick Lancaster courthouse.[56]

The court used subsidiary space for meetings of juries, magistrates, and minor officials. In some structures builders floored over part of the courtroom ceiling joists to provide an enclosed jury chamber. Specifications for an early Westmoreland courthouse outlined such an arrangement that also included a raised 5-foot gallery across the back of the courtroom.[57] Staircases to these garret rooms generally rose in one of the corners of the front gable end. In some buildings the entire ceiling was floored over and the attic subdivided into two or three roughly finished jury and storage rooms. Magistrates spent little money in finishing these spaces in any elaborate manner. Rooms measured from 10 to 12 feet square, a few were heated by fireplaces, and almost all either had exposed framing or were covered with riven clapboards and whitewashed. They required nothing in the way of furniture except forms or backless benches and perhaps a stretcher table. Less rudely fashioned rooms could be found in early courthouses in Charles City and Westmoreland Counties, each of which had "a fair closett or office for the clerk" abovestairs. In the latter the office was lined with planks and provided with a bench, a table, and shelves for the clerk's use.[58]

A second but less popular alternative to attic rooms was ground-floor chambers partitioned off at one end of the courthouse. In order to do this and provide enough space for the courtroom, the buildings had to be extended an extra 10 or 15 feet, making their overall form an elongated and ungainly rectangle, which may account for their relative scarcity in early specifications for earthfast structures. In 1678 the magistrates of Westmoreland laid off 21 feet at one end of a 46-foot-long structure for two meeting rooms, with the remaining 25 feet taken up by the courtroom. The Northumberland courthouse had two rooms opposite the justices' end of the building; one room was set aside for juries and the other for witnesses. In the 1690s Norfolk County magistrates retired to a ground-floor "withdrawing room," while a decade earlier their counterparts in York County met in the privacy of a shed room attached to the back of the makeshift courthouse.[59]

Some courts erected structures without ancillary rooms but gradually realized the necessity for such spaces. In the early eighteenth century, several counties constructed additions or separate structures near their cramped courthouses. Annoyed by not having a "private room for Juryes to consult in" and a place for their own "Convenient Retirement," Richmond County magistrates in 1703 ordered the building of a 20-by-16-foot "room" adjoining the courthouse to house the deliberations of justices and juries. Westmoreland officials found that they too required an additional room for the "recess of her Majesties's Justices upon *advisare volum* or otherwise as occasion may require." In 1705 they agreed to erect a 15-foot-square building adjoining the courthouse that would have a heated withdrawing room for the magistrates and an "upper room for the retirement & consultation of the several juries."[60] During the next half century a few other counties, particularly those in the Northern Neck, followed this pattern of erecting separate justices' or jury houses rather than incorporating these functions in the body of the courthouse.

Court officials and the public alike entered most early courthouses either through a set of double doors at one gable end or a door in or near the center of each of the long walls (fig. 35). A third arrangement found in some buildings such as the brick Gloucester courthouse had an entrance on one of the long walls and another on one of the gable ends. One or two large casement windows, subdivided by transoms and mullions and placed on each of the two long walls, provided light and air for the proceedings. Windows on one of the gable-end walls enabled the magistrates, clerk, and sheriff sitting below them to have ample light to read, take notes, and question witnesses, litigants, and lawyers. The advantage of having many apertures sometimes disappeared on cold or rainy days in buildings like the Westmoreland courthouse, where officials often suffered through winter sessions because the windows had no glass or shutters.[61]

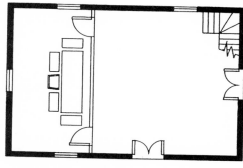

FIGURE 35. Conjectural plan of Middlesex County courthouse, 1692. (From specifications, Middlesex Co. Deed Book 1687–1750, 10, Apr. 4, 1692)

The litigant who came to court to prosecute his case found himself wedged in at the back of the courthouse to wait with dozens of others for his few minutes before the judges in the front of the room. In an act of deference to the court, the tactful spectator removed his hat and tamped his pipe and then listened as the court crier periodically called out cases on the docket.[62] He was expected to follow certain standards of orderly decorum. For those who could read, rules of etiquette and procedure sometimes were transcribed on a piece of paper and nailed to the courtroom wall. In 1671 the magistrates of Lancaster County drew up a set of "rules and orders" that were to be

> duely observed of all mannr of persons, whose occasions shall now, or att any tyme hereafter require their attendance at this Court:
> 1. That noe person presume to move the Court, for any thing, but by petition.
> 2. That noe person presume to smoake tobacco, or to be covered in the Face of this Court; upon the penaltie of lying in the stocks one houre, or paying 100 lbs of tobacco to be disposed off by the further order of Court.
> 3. That no person presume to speake to any business in Court, wherein hee is not duely called, & concerned, or permitted by the Court.
> 4. That noe petition be presented to this Court, but in a faire and legible hand, otherwise the petition to be [rejected].

The magistrates ordered the clerk to post these rules in a "conspicuous place for the view of all persons that none pretend ignorance." Even with such rules in

FIGURE 36. Courtroom with magistrates seated around a table. From Johann Amos Comenius, *Orbis sensualium pictus* (London, 1685).

plain view, a number of courts were less than orderly forums of decorum. The magistrates in Rappahannock County established a fine for the "Rude & uncivelized Custom of Smoaking Tobaco in this County Court house during the Sessions of Court."[63]

Standing quietly in the crowd near the back of the room, a court visitor could just catch glances of the magistrates huddled over their business at a large table (fig. 36). On cold days an inviting fire emanating from the courtroom hearth that appeared in a few buildings may have competed for the attention of the spectators if the heat carried beyond the immediate vicinity of the justices' table.

Contemporary English courtrooms served as precedent for early Virginia courts both in decorum and arrangement. Whether in a market house, town hall, "or in some open or common place," most major English courtrooms by the middle of the seventeenth century had "a tribunall or place of judgement made aloft upon the highest bench" where the most ranking judges sat "according to their estate and degree [fig. 37]. On a lower bench before them, the rest of the Justices of the peace, and some other gentlemen or their clarkes" occupied seats. "Before these Judges and Justices, there is a table set beneath, at which sitteth the *Custos rotulorum*, or keeper of writtes, Thexchetor, the undershirife, and such clarkes as doe write. At the end of that table, there is a barre made with a space for thenquestes and xij men to come in when they are called, behind that space another barre, and there stand the prisoners which be brought thither by the gaoler all chained one to another." At the opening of the session, the court crier "commaundeth silence." Then "one of the Judges briefly telleth the cause of their coming, and giveth a good lesson to the people."[64] This description of a criminal case before a quarter sessions court describes the most common features in mid-seventeenth-century English courtrooms. The most senior magistrates sat on a raised platform according to their status and seniority in the commission. Just below them junior members of the bench were arranged. Before this group, seated around a large table that provided a writing surface for the clerk of the court, sat other minor officials of the court. At one end of the table, a railed enclosure defined the place where jurymen stood or occasionally sat to hear a case. Another bar separated the officials from the public, and just inside this barrier space was allotted to prisoners to stand before the magistrates to plead their cases.

A number of seventeenth-century English courtrooms preserve these elements. At the most humble level, the second-story courtroom in the c. 1540

FIGURE 37. Magistrates' bench, 1604, Guildhall, Beverley, East Yorkshire

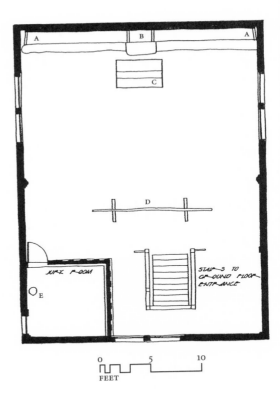

FIGURE 38. Plan of court-
room, town hall, Fordwich, Kent.
A: magistrates' bench; *B:* chief
magistrate's chair; *C:* magistrates'
table; *D:* bar; *E:* privy hole.

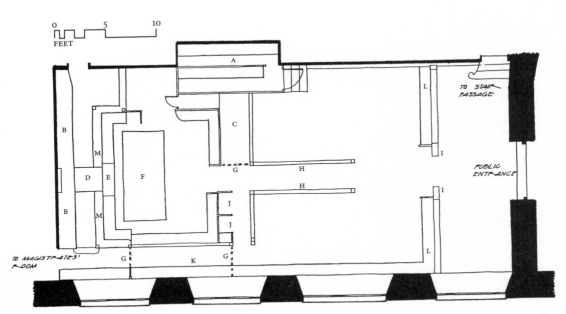

FIGURE 39. Plan of courtroom, guildhall, Sandwich, Kent. *A:* jury seats; *B:* magistrates'
bench; *C:* prisoner's dock; *D:* chief magistrate's chair; *E:* clerk's seat; *F:* table; *G:* drop gate;
H: bar; *I:* outer bar; *J:* witness box; *K:* press; *L:* bench; *M:* shelf.

town hall in Fordwich, Kent, has raised paneling with hollow and round shadow moldings at the magistrates' end (fig. 38). A long justices' bench stretches across the entire width of the building in the center of which is the chief magistrate's chair raised above the bench and enclosed with arms. A movable stretcher table stands in front of this seat of honor and provided a work surface for the chief magistrate and others. Higher courts had more elaborate fixtures. The courtroom in the guildhall in Sandwich, Kent, was fitted with paneling early in the seventeenth century and then refurbished in a similar manner in the 1690s when the magistrates' platform was rearranged (fig. 39).[65] As at Fordwich, the magistrates sat on a raised bench that stretched across the end of the courtroom. In the center was a seat for the principal justice. Below an arcaded balustrade was a bench where the clerk and other court officials sat around a 3½-by-8½-foot table. On the other side of the table, facing the magistrates' platform, were additional benches used by lawyers. Beyond on one side of the courtroom was a paneled box reserved for petit juries. Finally, a railing separated members of the court from the public.

If the 1690s woodwork of the Sandwich courtroom repeated typical seventeenth-century forms, the fittings in the courtrooms in the guildhall in Rochester, Kent (1687), and the town hall in Hedon, East Yorkshire (1693), clearly

FIGURE 40. Magistrates' platform, courtroom, guildhall, Rochester, Kent, c. 1695, in an early twentieth-century photograph. (Guildhall Museum, Rochester, Kent, England)

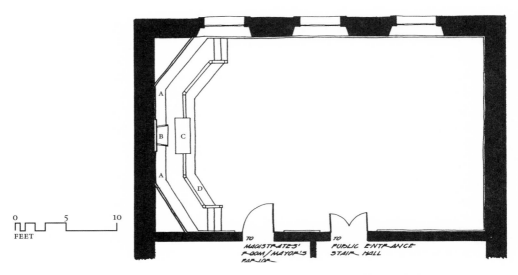

FIGURE 41. Segmental magistrates' bench configuration in the late seventeenth-century courtroom, town hall, Hedon, East Yorkshire. *A:* magistrates' bench; *B:* chief magistrate's chair; *C:* desk; *D:* jury bench.

mark the beginnings of a new style with their ovolo and cyma moldings, raised paneling, and classically inspired balusters (figs. 40, 41). Although the rest of the fixtures in these two courtrooms have been removed, both retain their raised magistrates' platforms. The balustraded platform at Rochester is curved, while the one at Hedon is faceted. The former has lost its bench, but the latter retains its associate magistrates' bench and chief magistrate's chair with its arms and pedimented cap.

As was true of minor English courts such as Fordwich, most seventeenth-century Virginia magistrates conducted their business on benches around a long table at the far end of the building. The tables, benches, and armchairs used by court officials were no different from the type of furniture found in the houses of the wealthier planters. Their arrangement in the front of the room also had domestic antecedents. In the great hall of many English manor houses, a long bench was located on a dais at the upper end of the room. At this great table sat the lord of the manor and privileged guests during meals and ceremonial feasts with servants and lower-ranking guests in attendance at the lower end of the hall. Here too sat the bailiff, steward, and other manorial officials to hear and try cases within their ancient jurisdictions. In the less formal setting of a seventeenth-century Virginia planter's hall, members of the household sat according to rank and privilege as well. As an acknowledgment of his authority, the head of the household generally sat in an armchair at the head of the table while members of his family deferentially sat on forms or benches. By clearing away other furniture and rearranging the hall table, great chair, and benches, this domestic furniture easily served the needs of many early Virginia courts when they met at various private dwellings.

When courthouses began to be built, magistrates simply appropriated familiar furnishings with their easily understood associations of status and authority. Typical of many early courthouses were the fittings provided in 1685 for Rappahannock County court, which consisted of a table for the justices with a "Bench of Plank sufficient to sitt upon" and "a Chaire for the President of the Court at the upper end of the Table." York County magistrates ordered for their use in 1692 a new 10-foot-long "tennant" table with two equally long forms and a shorter one 3 feet in length. In 1682 the "Seat of judicature" in the Charles County, Maryland, courthouse had a 6-by-8-foot table.[66] A surviving seventeenth-century magistrates' table in the Yelde Hall (guildhall) in Chippenham, Wiltshire, measures 12 by 2½ feet and separates into two pieces; the longest section extends more than 8 feet. Other than size, courthouse tables were no different from domestic or ecclesiastical ones. Most probably resembled the seventeenth-century one that survives in the town hall at Fordwich, Kent, or the early eighteenth-century Virginia-made communion table in Yeocomico Church in Westmoreland County (fig. 42). They are joined tables with rectilinear tops and turned legs connected by plain stretchers. Undistinguished

FIGURE 42. Communion table, Yeocomico Church, Westmoreland County, in a 1930s photograph

in their own right, they were often covered with cloth like communion tables.[67] In 1678 the justices of Surry County enhanced the dignity of their courtroom by purchasing a "carpitt for the courthouse table." Likewise, magistrates in Somerset County, Maryland, sat in seats that announced their status. They occupied a set of chairs carved with the coat of arms of the proprietor, Lord Baltimore.[68]

Some late seventeenth-century courts followed the practice of elevating the magistrates' seats above the courtroom floor to emphasize the sitters' authority. Such seats of honor were long familiar to English custom where rigidly defined protocol dictated that the royal throne, bishop's cathedra, or high table in a manor house or collegiate hall be raised above all others.[69] Although relaxed and simplified by English standards, notions of status and rules of precedence governed the thinking of a number of Virginia magistrates as they planned the arrangement of their courtrooms. Officials in Northumberland County specified that their courthouse was to have "a place decently made with some assent for the magistrats to sit in"; in Westmoreland County justices sat on a 10-by-15-foot platform raised 3 feet off the ground at the upper end of the courtroom.[70]

The same pattern appeared in Maryland courtrooms. In 1682 the justices in Charles County upgraded their courthouse by lengthening it an additional 10 feet with "a seat of Judicature with turned wood [balusters] as at the Provintiall Court" in the ground-floor room of the statehouse in St. Mary's City. They also requested the builder to make a convenient place on the platform to hang Lord Baltimore's coat of arms. Dorchester County magistrates instructed builder Anthony Dawson in 1686 to install "a Judges Chair going up two or three steps with rails and Banisters" in front of the bench. A quarter century later the judges' seat in the 1710 Baltimore County courthouse in Joppa was to be 4 feet off the courtroom floor, 4 feet deep, and reached by a set of stairs at each end of the platform against the side walls of the courtroom.[71]

Sometimes justices chose to emphasize the east end of the courtroom even further through variations in wall, ceiling, and flooring materials and finishes. Many buildings such as the Northumberland courthouse were "lathed, filled and white limed or filled and sealed as farre as the Rayles goe at the session end of the house on both sides." In the area beyond the magistrates' end, the wall framing was often left exposed. While many courtrooms had plastered walls, sometimes clapboards were used to cover part or all of the framing. In 1692 Princess Anne magistrates intended the area behind their seat to be enclosed with half-inch thick planks from the floor to about 2 feet above their seated heads with the rest of the wall left open to the framing. Like the 1681 Northumberland courthouse, the ceiling over the magistrates' end in this posthole courthouse was to be arched and covered with thin clapboards.[72]

Floors, too, were treated differently, with the justices' end generally laid with plank while the public space in the other end of the building was paved with a variety of materials. In 1665 the courtroom in Northumberland County was "to be sealed over the Table & floored with boards underfoot, under & about the Table" where the magistrates sat. Presumably, this was the only area raised off the ground. This division of the courtroom by flooring material also appears in the 1704 specifications for the framed Middlesex County courthouse where the space for the "congregation" was to have a "good even clay floor" while the area within the bar was to be laid with grooved planks. In 1715 the Northampton County court also specified "an earthen flower except where the justices is to sitt," which was to be covered with pine plank. Spectators in the brick Lancaster County courthouse stood on paving stones, a durable but expensive material.[73]

The architectural demarcation between the dispensers and the seekers of justice was clearly drawn. Railings had long been used in European and English society to restrict access to important places in palaces and churches. State bedchambers often would have a balustrade in front of the bed to separate the area around the bed from the rest of the room and keep all but the most favored at a distance. Similarly, Anglican reforms in the late sixteenth and early seventeenth centuries required the communion table to be surrounded by a railing in the east end of parish churches in order to protect it from rude abuses and provide it with a greater sense of dignity, a canon followed in seventeenth-century Virginia churches.[74]

The notion of restricted space was also an integral part of English legal tradition with the employment of a "bar" to physically separate judges from the judged. Bars ranged from simple movable barriers consisting of no more than a railing attached to posts, such as the early seventeenth-century one in the town hall in Fordwich, Kent, to elaborately turned balustrades such as the one in the guildhall in Rochester, Kent, dating from the late seventeenth century (fig. 43). Early court records in Virginia suggest that magistrates preferred a fixed balustrade of turned banisters. Such a bar ran across the width of the 1673 Westmoreland courthouse at a distance of 10 feet from the back wall. Although a bar was a powerful reminder of authority and a useful means of separating the court from the public, not all seventeenth-century courtrooms had one, as the 1671 minutes of Northumberland County court make clear. "For

FIGURE 43. Courtroom bar. Detail, English engraving depicting the deposition of Titus Oates, 1679.

THE EARLY COURTHOUSES, 1650–1725   79

want of a Barr," crowds of people disrupted a number of sessions by pushing their way forward toward the justices' table. By contrast, the 1710 courthouse in Joppa, Maryland, had two bars, one 8 feet in front of the magistrates' platform that enclosed the space reserved for court officials and another 15 feet from the platform that separated bystanders from those with business before the court. Lawyers, litigants, witnesses, and minor officials such as a constable no doubt sat or stood in the area between the two bars.[75]

Justices may have dominated the proceedings of the small courtrooms, but they were far from being the only officials active in the monthly sessions. The clerk, sheriff, crier, undersheriffs, constables, juries, and lawyers all played important parts in the court routine but through most of the seventeenth century had no specialized place or fittings set aside for their use. The clerk's responsibilities during court sessions consisted of keeping track of the voluminous paperwork that accumulated for each case as well as taking minutes of the court's deliberations. Strangely, the clerk seldom was fit into the planning schemes of the magistrates, although he was an essential member of the judicial process. The first reference to a seat for the clerk appears in the 1688 specifications for the repair of the courthouse in Somerset County, Maryland, which noted that there was to be a railed-in area near the magistrates' table with a table and seat for the clerk. Not until 1696 was any mention made in Virginia's county order books about accommodating this official in the courtroom. In that year Essex County justices ordered a table and chair for their clerk. Not long afterward counties such as Warwick and Middlesex followed suit.[76] Presumably, through the earlier part of the century the clerk either sat at the same table with the magistrates or, more likely, sat nearby at a table or desk that he may have provided for himself and was thus not part of the county furniture.

Early court records are also mute about fittings for the sheriff and his subordinates. A former colleague of the members on the bench, the sheriff was the court's chief executive officer. In order to carry out his courtroom duties, the sheriff needed to sit close to both the magistrates and the clerk so that he could inform and follow the court's proceedings as well as pass papers back and forth to other officials. In the absence of any seventeenth-century references to a special chair or box for the sheriff, it seems likely that he too probably sat at the magistrate's table or on a bench nearby. Presumably undersheriffs, constables, and criers remained standing around the periphery of the courtroom when they were not engaged in their duties, although it is reasonable to believe that the crier stood close to or inside the bar where he could be in communication with the clerk.

Until the very late seventeenth century, no place was specifically set aside for petit juries in the courtroom. Jury trials occurred infrequently: between 1681 and 1686 only two cases went before a jury in Lancaster County, while in the older and more populous county of York, juries sat for only thirteen trials over a similar five-year period.[77] Months passed in many counties between jury trials, so that there was little incentive to provide the twelve freeholders who comprised a trial jury with a permanent and substantial space in an already crowded courtroom. When a jury was selected to hear a case, its members gathered in the courtroom and stood close by the magistrates' table to hear the arguments in the case. Most cases could be tried in a matter of a few minutes, after which the jury retired to a room at the far end of the courtroom or abovestairs to pass judgment on the facts presented.[78]

Like the custom in some English courts, Virginia juries did not necessarily have to leave the courtroom for their deliberations. In straightforward cases they may have simply gathered around the foreman at the bar to decide their verdict.[79] The seventeenth-century courtroom fittings in the guildhall in Sandwich, Kent, include a jury box provided with ceiling-hung panels that could be lowered around it to sequester the jury from the rest of the room. Gradually, Virginia courts began to partition off part of the courtroom for juries. In 1691 the Westmoreland court supplied a railing for the jury to stand behind during a trial. Other counties such as Essex in 1702 and Middlesex in 1704 followed suit by building an enclosed "place for the jury."[80] These accommodations were nothing more than a segregated stall for the jurymen to stand in, for it was still many years before they were given a place to sit.

Lawyers gained a tenuous acceptance of their profession in the county courts. Through the seventeenth century they endured an uneasy relationship with the magistracy; at various periods the provincial government either banned them outright from practicing in the lower courts or severely limited the amount of money this small cadre of "mercenary" pleaders could exact from their clients.[81] Lawyers deplored the inadequacies of an untrained bench and challenged its authority. In turn, those who argued their cases on the strength of precedent and points of procedure frequently faced an independent-minded or hidebound body of magistrates who either ignored learned arguments or treated them with contempt. In the early 1680s the governor, Lord Culpeper, tried to stop the increasing formality of the law in Virginia courts, an effort that earned him the approval of the historian Robert Beverley in 1705.[82] Rather than hiring attorneys at law, many clients, particularly those who resided outside a court's jurisdiction, elected to appoint an untrained friend, relative, or business associate as an attorney in fact to represent them in court. This may have worked for some, but at other times "impertinent discourse of many busy and ignorant men who will pretend to assist their friend in his business and to cleare the matter more plainly to the court" did the client little good, instead provoking the ire of the magistrates. By 1680 the General Assembly decreed that anyone who pleaded a case in court had to be licensed by the governor.[83]

In the courtroom when the crier called their cases, both professional and surrogate advocates stepped before the bar separating them from the magistrates' table to plead or enter their motions. In Richmond County court and perhaps elsewhere, people created great disturbances by crowding around the lawyers when they came before the bar. After each case lawyers stepped unceremoniously back into the undifferentiated mass of spectators. Not until 1709 do county records mention any type of accommodation for attorneys. In that year the Middlesex court ordered that a bench be set up within the bar. Other counties eventually followed suit over the next quarter century, but seating was by no means adequate, much less comfortable. Respect was hard won. As late as 1723 lawyers in King George County crammed uneasily together on a narrow plank seat.[84]

Summary

By the end of the century, Virginia county courthouses stood as poor advertisements for the material achievement of colonial culture. Rarely the inspiration of a community or the pride of their builders, most were cheaply constructed, ill treated, and poorly maintained, giving them a shabbiness characteristic of the seventeenth-century Chesapeake landscape. Contemporary observers such as Hartwell, Blair, and Chilton viewed them as symptomatic of the colony's many shortcomings. However, the architectural insignificance of these buildings belies the fact that they served as a vital rural forum for many contending factions of local society. Believing the county court to be one of the few places where their grievances could be openly aired, small freeholders, landless laborers, and indentured servants seem to have been far more willing to challenge the authority of the magistrates who presided in rough and cramped courtrooms than were their descendants a century later who cautiously entered imposing brick edifices. As the Lancaster County justices discovered in 1666 when they were forced to make a hasty courtroom departure in the face of an angry crowd upset over one of their rulings, contentious debate and confrontations among individuals and social classes flourished in a relatively humble surrounding.[85]

Only with the growth in stability, wealth, and power of the gentry in the early eighteenth century did attitudes toward public building begin to change. This new respect in part reflected the changing nature of courtroom activities. The increasing professionalization of the law, the growth in the bureaucratic routine of court day, and a concerted effort by magistrates to establish an atmosphere of propriety during their sessions reduced the incidents of fractious behavior in late colonial courtrooms.[86] Yet that process was well under way by the last quarter of the seventeenth century. If the exterior of these buildings showed little distinctiveness, the appropriation of ecclesiastical elements such as arched ceilings and compass-headed windows and the introduction of hierarchical ornamentation and division of fittings and finishes according to court status set a pattern that would be further elaborated during the next century. Well-built and well-furnished courthouses, heralded by Robert "King" Carter's brick building in Lancaster County, gradually displaced makeshift structures. Purpose-built courthouses became as important an expression of the new social order as the appearance of great houses and parish churches.

3

COURTHOUSES
1725–1815

Introduction

I N THE SECOND QUARTER of the eighteenth century, the consolidation of county government in the hands of an elite coterie of planters, the maturation of the legal process, and shifting attitudes toward public building combined to reshape the architectural form of Virginia's county courthouses. In a number of long-established tidewater counties, justices replaced their old earthfast courthouses with larger brick buildings whose form and fittings reflected the primacy of a small but powerful class of wealthy planters in the affairs of local society. These men were proud of their accomplishments, jealous of their status, and increasingly saw the public buildings of the courthouse grounds as symbolic manifestations of their authority, conflating in that vision public weal with oligarchic identity.

One of the earliest chroniclers to describe the attitudes of this gentry class was Robert Beverley. In 1705 he published *The History and Present State of Virginia,* a detailed study of the colony's first century of development. No panegyric but a thoughtful account of the deeds and misfortunes of the English and Indians in the Chesapeake expressed in a concise if not sparing style, Beverley's history differed from earlier English travel journals and colorful narratives such as John Smith's *General History* in that it was written from the point of view of a "Native and Inhabitant of the Place." Beverley was born in Virginia in 1673; married Ursula Byrd, the daughter of leading merchant and officeholder William Byrd; held a number of offices in the provincial government; and had witnessed the progress of the tobacco colony and its institutions in the last decades of the seventeenth century. Although Beverley upbraided his fellow countrymen for the colony's economic shortcomings and lack of improvements, he expressed a great fondness for the natural beauty and bounty of the landscape and respected the social and political traditions that Virginians had created. Cognizant of the shabby appearance of the dispersed tobacco plantations coupled with the absence of industrious towns, he observed that "this Part of Virginia now inhabited, if we consider the Improvements in the Hands of the

English, it cannot upon that Score be commended; but if we consider its natural Aptitude to be improv'd, it may with Justice be accounted, one of the finest Countries in the World."[1]

Although Beverley was not the first and would not be the last to sound the discordant note between the liberality of nature and the dismal appearance of the settlement, his constructive criticisms of his fellow countrymen were indicative of a shift in Virginian's attitudes toward the places they lived. While acknowledging the limitations posed by an overwhelming reliance upon a staple crop, second- and third-generation Virginians saw possibilities in this colonial culture. By the beginning of the eighteenth century, many planters actively sought to reshape their physical surroundings and cast them in a more enduring and orderly manner. Foremost was the transformation of their attitudes toward buildings. Even as *The History and Present State of Virginia* was being published in London, the first concerted effort to build substantial and architecturally sophisticated government buildings was coming to fruition in the new capital of Williamsburg. There the construction of the College of William and Mary, the Capitol, and the governor's house, carefully arranged at strategic points in a spacious plan, heralded a new era in which building matched public expectations (fig. 44).

FIGURE 44. Public and collegiate buildings in Williamsburg. *1:* the Brafferton, 1723; *2:* College of William and Mary, 1695–97; *3:* the President's House, 1732; *4:* the Capitol, 1701–5; *5:* southwest view of the college showing the chapel *(foreground)*, 1732, and the great hall, 1695–97; *6:* the Governor's Palace, 1706–20. Bodleian plate, c. 1737.

FIGURE 45. Rosewell, Gloucester County, c. 1726–38, before the house burned in 1916

With a growing feeling that Virginia and not England was home, these colonists found the modest houses of their forebearers uncomfortable reminders of the long struggle to transform the New World frontier into a provincial version of English society. With the accumulation of wealth and the development of a sense of community forged through bonds of marriage, trade, and social obligations, a small but influential class of emerging gentry pulled down their old wooden houses and replaced them with solid brick structures. By the end of the 1720s, a few houses such as Berkeley and Rosewell matched the scale of minor gentry houses erected in England (fig. 45). Far more dwellings, however, were wooden structures of modest size that nevertheless boasted brick foundations and chimneys, large sash windows, and elaborate woodwork. Well-built dwellings provided a degree of permanency and comfort rarely known in Virginia in previous decades.

Although the plantation—with its great house surrounded by fields of corn and tobacco worked by slave labor—was the basis of the nascent gentry's power, the influence of the large planters stretched beyond their holdings to encompass local and provincial institutions. By the 1720s and 1730s, they dominated most of the parish vestries and local courts. From these bases of power they actively sought to transform the physical surroundings of church and state. On the one hand, it is easy to see in the large parish churches and arcaded brick courthouses that they built the visible manifestations of a deferential social order in colonial Virginia in the second and third quarters of the eighteenth century.[2] Yet their control of this legal and social landscape was less sure than the buildings themselves might at first suggest. The command that a small number of closely linked gentry families exercised over the county court was never absolute but was tempered by circumstances and necessities that required the participation of many freeholders. Unlike English quarter session courts that maintained power in the hands of a small percentage of a county's population, local government in the comparatively sparsely settled counties of Virginia by necessity included a large segment of local society. In the absence of a standing police force, the power of the gentlemen justices to enforce their judicial and administrative decisions depended upon a broad acceptance of the legitimacy of their authority. Freeholders comprised the backbone of county government, supporting the right of the gentry to rule in exchange for some share in shaping the form of local institutions. Small planters, farmers, and craftsmen executed the decrees of the magistrates and sheriffs in their role as constables, highway surveyors, and guardians and mitigated the disputes of their neighbors as jurymen. Without their participation the structure of local government would have foundered.

With this tacit recognition of the right of the gentlemen justices to oversee the direction of local government, the county freeholders expected that the system would not be openly abused by the powerful in a pursuit of personal authority and wealth or be unfairly demanding of their time and money. As the gentlemen justices understood that deference had its obligations. In the matter of public building, magistrates rarely had an open purse that they could draw upon to construct large and costly courthouses, prisons, and clerks' offices. Time and time again, freeholders questioned the need to build new structures, satisfied that old wooden buildings were perfectly sound or could be repaired and made serviceable for another generation. However, in other counties the desire of magistrates and freeholders often coincided, and new brick buildings were erected with little controversy.

Public building in eighteenth-century Virginia was thus marked by strong contrasts. In the fifty years preceding the Revolution, the courthouses, prisons, and clerks' offices erected by magistrates in counties that stretched several hundred miles from the Eastern Shore of the Chesapeake to the Shenandoah Valley varied significantly in size, materials, and elaboration. Yet at no time was there a radical break with past building practices. Construction methods that had become characteristic of Virginia architecture in the first century of settlement continued to influence public building across the colony. The spatial needs of late colonial courts also remained modest in scale. Like their predecessors, eighteenth-century magistrates required only a large courtroom and

FIGURE 46. Hanover County courthouse, c. 1740, in a c. 1899 photograph. (Valentine Richmond History Center)

one or two smaller meeting rooms to conduct their business. In contrast to the new brick churches that often required costly king-post and principal-rafter roofs to enclose broad unencumbered interiors, courtrooms rarely exceeded 24 feet in width and continued to be spanned with simple common-rafter roofs. No new technology, materials, or building systems came into use in county buildings in the eighteenth century. Matters of style and functional needs changed, but construction practices that had passed into a regional building tradition by the last quarter of the seventeenth century became the common language of public building in the next century. Riven clapboards, common-rafter roofs, false plates, wood shingles, and oyster-shell mortar, elements that were standard in the Chesapeake in 1700, continued to be widely employed a century later.

With an eye toward limited county purses, many benches felt no reason to give up the construction of earthfast prisons, stocks, and pillories although their posts soon rotted in the moist and termite-infested soil. As new counties were carved out of older ones on the western frontier, magistrates erected simple frame and log structures to house the public's business. Shifting county boundaries coupled with the undeveloped nature of the building trades worked against the construction of costly permanent buildings during the first generation of western settlement. In terms of size and specialization, they were scarcely different from those erected nearly a century earlier in the tidewater counties.

Just as many county courthouses repeated past conventions, others such as the arcaded York County, King William County, and Hanover County courthouses responded to changing social conditions, aesthetic tastes, and functional needs (fig. 46). A growing number of courthouses and prisons cast off their domestic appearance and acquired the civic attributes and distinctive shapes of public buildings. New brick arcades, bell turrets, and pedimented porticoes were matched by substantial changes in courthouse interiors. The growing sophistication of the legal system coupled with the bureaucratization of local government affected the plan and fittings in the courtroom in a profound manner. Magistrates replaced the domestic furniture of the earlier courtrooms with a set of highly specialized and symbolic fittings that reminded court participants of the structure of local authority.

The county courts transacted business in the name of the king. Magistrates and freeholders had long professed their allegiance to the crown in oaths sworn upon taking office or keeping the king's peace, but in the late colonial period the authority of the crown was accorded greater ceremonial deference. Virginians not only acknowledged the crown's authority in their courtrooms, but they subscribed to a legal fiction that recognized the possibility of the king's real presence in their courts of law. Governor William Gooch stated that because "our Sovereign's Presence is always to be presumed in the Exercise of his Authority," courtrooms required "Decency in their Structure and Forms, as well as Rectitude in the Managers of their Proceedings."[3] Therefore, in deference to the king's majesty, orderly decorum and suitable surroundings were essential elements of a Virginia courtroom. Rude behavior and shabby fittings were as much an affront to His Majesty's person as to his vested authority, no matter how remote the likelihood of his ever appearing in the American colonies or a Virginia courthouse. As many Virginians subscribed to this perspective, attitudes toward public buildings changed. In the last decades of royal rule, fewer incidents of boorish behavior and insubordination among the populace appeared in courtrooms and courthouse grounds where magistrates erected increasing numbers of brick buildings of imposing presence.

No one knew the range of buildings that housed local government institutions better than lawyer John Mercer of Stafford County, whose peripatetic practice took him to dozens of county courthouses from the 1740s through the 1760s. On a circuit that covered more than a thousand miles each year, Mercer frequently spent many hot days in the cool shade of the arcade of the brick courthouse in King William County. He traveled to the growing town of Fredericksburg where he argued points of law with the chief magistrate of Spotsylvania County who sat in a canopied armchair on a raised platform. In neighboring King George County, Mercer walked past a 12-by-12-foot plank prison to reach the tar-covered courthouse built in the 1720s. In the early 1750s he watched the construction of a large new wing to the wooden courthouse in Orange County and saw the completion of many elaborate details in the new double-arcaded brick building undertaken by Landon Carter for the Richmond County court. In April and October of each year, he enjoyed good food, comfortable lodging, and lively entertainment in the taverns of Williamsburg where the lengthy sessions of the General Court kept him extremely busy. After fire destroyed the Capitol in 1747, provincial officials erected a new brick structure on the foundations of the old building in the early 1750s complete with a two-story pedimented portico, a feature that marked the entrance into the General Court on the ground floor and introduced a new form that would transform the appearance of many county courthouses in the following seventy-five years.

Overcrowded courthouse taverns, dark and rotting county prisons, and grandly arcaded courthouses surrounded by muddy paths provided the setting for court-day activities that blended the most mundane of human affairs with those of the greatest moment. As Mercer could well attest, justice in colonial Virginia at midcentury was both rudely and well served by its public buildings.

FIGURE 47. Old Bedford County courthouse, New London, late 1760s. Woodcut from William Howe, *Historical Collections of Virginia* (Charleston, S.C., 1845). Made redundant when the county was divided to create Campbell County in 1782, the courthouse was sold by the magistrates when the county seat was moved to Bedford. This woodcut seems to show that the building was converted into a store at some later date with the addition of a small secondary doorway near the chimney end.

Shortages of funds or disagreements among court officials prolonged the perpetuation of inadequate and often wretched public buildings (fig. 47). Yet the growing wealth of the colony, an increasingly sophisticated legal system, and the cosmopolitan perspective of many of the gentry class who dominated local offices prompted the introduction of academic architectural elements from outside the regional building tradition. As a result of experimentation and the desire to build large brick structures, the architecture of many courthouses assumed a self-conscious air of importance by the end of the eighteenth century.

Structure

Firmly entrenched in the Virginia legal system by the middle of the seventeenth century, the county court retained absolute control over public building within its own jurisdiction until the late nineteenth century. As a result, the vagaries of local politics played an important role in the shaping of courthouse architecture. Local squabbles often delayed the construction of buildings, the lack of money frustrated the attempts of many courts to build enduring structures for many years, and the force of a dominant personality in the design process sometimes meant that a new or idiosyncratic plan was adopted, just as the collective conservatism of other benches signaled the continuation of old patterns.[4]

Despite the strong influence of local circumstances on public building, courthouse architecture followed certain broad patterns of development over two hundred years from the first appearance of such structures in the 1650s through the Civil War. Foremost was the gradual replacement of impermanent wooden structures with larger and more costly masonry ones. When Robert Beverley published his history of Virginia in 1705, no more than three or four of the twenty-five counties in existence could boast a brick courthouse. In the second quarter of the eighteenth century, many courts began to replace their second or third wooden buildings with larger and more imposing brick structures. By the time of the Revolution, this process had been nearly completed in the older established tidewater counties but had scarcely begun in the newer counties to the west. In 1776 slightly more than half the sixty counties had brick courthouses (fig. 48). An itinerant lawyer practicing beyond the fall line would have spent much of his time in frame and log structures on courthouse grounds in the piedmont, the backwoods of the Southside, and the western frontier counties. In his *Notes on the State of Virginia* written in the 1780s, Thomas Jefferson approved of this process as a civilizing one, believing "a country whose buildings are of wood, can never increase in its improvements to any considerable degree. Their duration is highly estimated at 50 years. Every half century then our country becomes a tabula rasa, whereon we have to set out anew, as in the first moment of seating it. Whereas when buildings are of durable mate-

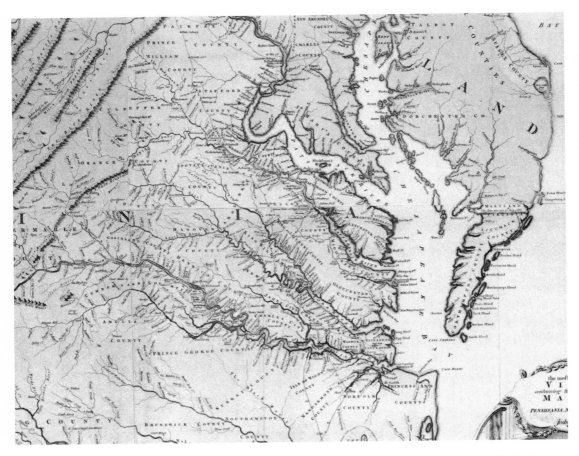

FIGURE 48. Detail of Fry-Jefferson map of Virginia, 1751. Virginia was now divided into forty-four counties.

rials, every new edifice is an actual and permanent acquisition to the state, adding to its value as well as to its ornament."[5] Half a century later, masonry buildings, many of them two stories with imposing pedimented porticoes inspired by Jefferson's ideas, designs, and workmen, had supplanted nearly all the smaller wooden courthouses throughout the Commonwealth.

Although the timing varied significantly from one county to the next, the experience of the Northampton County court is representative of this slow transformation of public architecture. For the first thirty years of its existence, the county court moved about, meeting in houses and taverns. In 1664 the first purpose-built courthouse, a hole-set frame structure, was erected, and it served the county for a number of years before it fell into disrepair and proved to be inconvenient to many of the Eastern Shore inhabitants.[6] The donation of land and a new wooden courthouse by Joseph Godwin, a tavern keeper anxious for increased trade, spurred the court to move in 1690 to its present-day location in Eastville (fig. 49). This second frame building remained open to the roof for a number of years before the ceiling joists were floored over to provide for a jury room. Even so, it gradually proved unsuitable for court activities. In 1715 the court paid William Rabyshaw 7,000 pounds of tobacco to construct its third earthfast building, a 30-by-20-foot frame structure that must have been only marginally better than the previous two structures (fig. 50). Eight feet in height, enclosed with riven pine planks and covered with wood shingles, the courtroom was a dark, crowded space on court day. The magistrates performed their duties on a small wooden platform while spectators stood on an earthen floor. During gray winter days one or two small casement windows and two doors

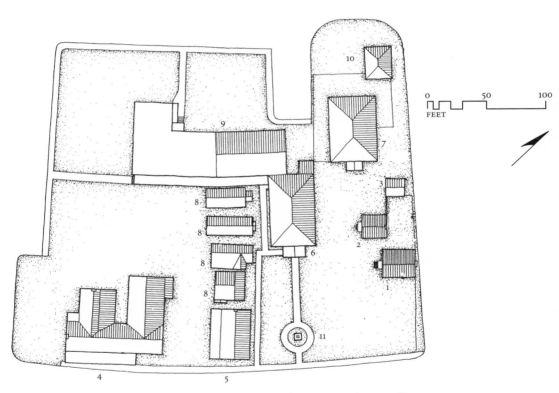

FIGURE 49. Site plan of the Northampton County courthouse grounds, Eastville. *1:* courthouse, 1731, moved to present site 1913; *2:* clerk's office, c. 1810; *3:* prison, c. 1815; *4:* Eastville Inn, late eighteenth century with later additions; *5:* store, c. 1820; *6:* courthouse, 1899; *7:* jail, c. 1900; *8:* law offices, late nineteenth and twentieth centuries; *9:* offices, twentieth century; *10:* shed, early twentieth century; *11:* Confederate monument.

FIGURE 50. Plat of the Northampton County prison bounds, East-ville, 1724, showing the frame courthouse built in 1715. (Deed and Will Book, 1718–25, 209, June 10, 1724, Clerk's Office, Northampton County)

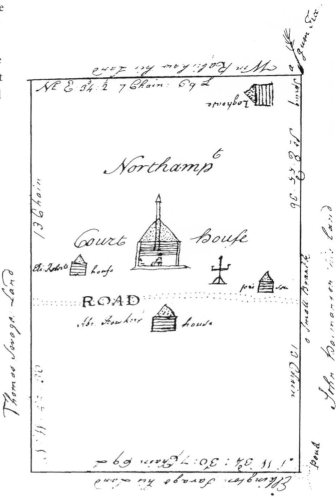

provided what little light illuminated the court's proceedings while a wooden chimney warmed those near the hearth.[7]

This third frame building survived for less than two decades. In 1730 the court noted that the building was "much out of repair and not in a condition for the justices to do county business in," and resolved to build a brick court-house.[8] Erected relatively rapidly the next year, the new courthouse measured 23 feet in width and perhaps 40 feet in length (figs. 51, 52). Although the build-ing scarcely surpassed the size of its wooden predecessor, the solidity of its construction, its increased height, large sash windows, wooden floor, and the provision for an upstairs room marked significant improvements. The cost exceeded by tenfold that of its 1715 predecessor. The new building sported such decorative features as a double cut-molded water table and a chevron-

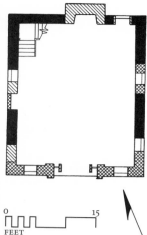

FIGURE 52. Plan, Northampton County courthouse, Eastville, 1731, after the 1913 restoration by the APVA

FIGURE 51. Northampton County courthouse, Eastville, 1731, showing the large nineteenth-century addition made to the front of the building so that it could serve as a storehouse and later as a tavern. In 1913 the Association for the Preservation of Virginia Antiquities (APVA) removed this section, added a new gable facade, patched the walls, and installed new interior woodwork. (Virginia Historical Society)

patterned gable end that echoed the trend in the use of decorative brickwork in a few rich planters' houses such as the Mason house in neighboring Accomack County. Still, there was little on the outside of this building that would distinguish its public function.

This first brick courthouse served the county for more than sixty years and is still standing, though it has been through many changes. In 1795 a larger rectangular courthouse was built (fig. 53). This new brick structure contained a larger courtroom and two heated jury rooms on the ground floor opposite the magistrates' bench, all of which were lit by large windows. Although one story, the courtroom stood five steps above the ground and was entered through two large folding doors in the center of one of the long walls of the building. A short squat cupola rose above the apex of the roof at one end of the building, signifying the public nature of the building. After many changes in the legal system in the nineteenth century and corresponding alterations to the building and fittings, the local court demolished the 1795 courthouse and moved into a new two-story brick building in 1899 (fig. 54). The county is still using this building although it was enlarged in the 1970s, reflecting the increasing role of local gov-

FIGURE 53. Northampton County courthouse, Eastville, 1795, demolished 1899. (Virginia Historical Society)

FIGURE 54. Northampton County courthouse grounds, Eastville. Behind the Confederate monument stands the present courthouse, built in 1899. To the right of the courthouse are *(left to right)* the jail, clerk's office, and 1731 courthouse.

ernment in the daily affairs of Northampton County citizens. In the course of more than three hundred years in Eastville, the county constructed five courthouses on or near the same site. After replacing its last frame building in 1731, each new brick structure was a little more substantial and lasted longer than the previous one.

The gradual displacement of wooden buildings with masonry ones has obscured the importance of frame and log courthouses in early Virginia. Because of their modest size and lack of pretension, these frame and log structures exhibited the same construction techniques employed in domestic architecture. For this reason, magistrates and undertakers rarely troubled themselves to specify in any detail the framing methods or size of timbers to be used in a new courthouse, leaving such details to the practical experience of the carpenters. Occasionally, justices did note the desired quality of materials and construction. Anxious to guard against costly repairs in the future, the Amelia County court in 1791 ordered the framing members of its new building to be "made from heart lumber," rather than inferior sapwood that was prone to decay. Halifax magistrates required that the structure of their new courthouse be "a good and sufficient sawed frame," not a far more economical riven and hewn one.[9]

At the other end of the scale, in 1727 the Essex court wanted to erect a cheap wooden structure for a temporary home while it awaited the completion of its new brick courthouse. The terse specifications called for the structure to be "of common clapboard work," suggesting that it was an earthfast building with roughly fashioned framing members.[10] This is one of the last recorded examples of a court relying upon a building technique long used in the Chesapeake. By the second quarter of the eighteenth century, magistrates no longer favored earthfast construction for new courthouses. The use of hole-set posts, ground-laid sills, and other non–masonry foundation construction techniques provided little stability for larger and more complex buildings that required multilevel floors, sizable stairs, and plastered or tightly sheathed walls and ceilings.

Instead of impermanent building practices, county courts turned to a more substantial framing system referred to by Virginians as an "English frame." Despite its name, the primary elements of this framing system derived from the laborsaving practices that had developed in the Chesapeake in the previous century. As in earthfast construction, Virginia carpenters reduced the size of the major framing members and eliminated much of the complicated joinery associated with English framing. This Virginia hybrid consisted of a boxed skeletal frame of large posts, plates, and sills with smaller secondary members such as studs and braces, all of which were secured by mortise and tenon or nailed lap joints and raised on a masonry foundation. Although they varied slightly from one building to another, the dimensions specified for the framing members in the 1759 Johnston County, North Carolina, courthouse are typical of those found in standing colonial structures throughout the upper South. The sills, which rested on brick foundations, measured 12 by 10 inches; the principal posts, which were mortised into the sills, were 8 by 4 inches; and the plates that sat atop the 12-foot-high posts were 12 by 4 inches. Smaller 3-by-4-inch studs filled in the wall frame and provided support for exterior weatherboards and interior sheathing and plaster laths. The 1792 specifications for a framed courthouse in Amelia County, Virginia, required a similar range of sizes for scantling.[11]

The advantage of this box framing system over an earthfast one lay in the use of a continuous sill raised off the ground. Angled-down braces tied the sill to corner and door posts and prevented lateral racking. Because many monthly courts regularly had large numbers of people crowded into the courtroom, some building committees hoped to strengthen the floors of their new buildings by inserting one or two large transverse summer beams between the sills. Such concern led Amelia County magistrates in 1766 to order the installation of "a hued timber a foot Square to go a Cross the middle of the house to bear up the Sleepers."[12] These beams provided greater structural rigidity by reducing the span of the smaller sleepers or floor joists, thus taking much of the springiness out of the courtroom floor. With less movement in the frame, plaster walls were less likely to crack, thus allowing magistrates to finish their courtrooms in a more imposing fashion without the risk of plaster falling down on them. Structural decay from dry rot and termites decreased significantly when the lower part of the frame was elevated above the ground on brick walls and piers. Added to this structural advantage was the ability to raise the courthouse 2 to 4 feet above ground level, thus giving the building with its ascending stairs an air of importance that was missing from those that hugged the ground.

Log courthouses gained a tenuous hold on the western frontier of Virginia in the late colonial period. Although horizontal log construction appeared in the Chesapeake in the third quarter of the seventeenth century, public officials in the tidewater and piedmont rarely used it except to erect prisons. Prisons of carefully sawn horizontal planks, measuring from 2 to 4 inches in width and secured with interlocking dovetail corner notches, provided strength and security far superior to frame construction. As early as 1677 a small 10-by-10-foot prison constructed in such a manner confined political troublemakers in Pasquotank County, North Carolina, just south of the Virginia border.[13] Magistrates erected similar structures in the two Eastern Shore counties, Accomack and Northampton, by 1690 and in Princess Anne County in 1692.[14] This technique was ideal for small prisons and spread throughout Virginia in the eighteenth century, but it was never used for larger courthouses until the settlement of the Shenandoah Valley.

On the western frontier settlers migrating south from Pennsylvania and Maryland employed log construction for almost all their building needs. For more than a generation, they erected log houses, outbuildings, and barns that varied in quality from the precision of plank building to the cheaper method of roughly notching partially hewn logs at the corners and filling in the wide interstices with clay, wood, and brick. As was true of the seventeenth-century courthouses in the tidewater counties, the early public buildings in Augusta, Botetourt, Montgomery, Henry, Rockingham, and Russell Counties followed local building practices. Measuring 38 by 18 feet, the first courthouse built in Augusta County in the late 1740s showed few signs of craftsmanship. With large gaps in the log walls, no glass in two small windows, and no seating for the magistrates, the dark, cold interior provided little comfort for court participants and showed no expression of its civic function. This pattern was repeated nearly a quarter century later when Botetourt County was carved out of the southern part of Augusta. In 1770 the magistrates of the new county ordered the construction of a 24-by-20-foot "log cabbin" with a clapboard roof for their first seat of government. The building also had two small shed spaces for jury rooms at each end. The first courts in new counties created in Virginia's northwestern frontier at the time of the Revolution met in similar undistinguished accommodations. In the mid-1770s both the Yohogania and Ohio County magistrates ordered buildings to be fabricated out of round logs. The 24-by-16-foot structure in Yohogania County served a double capacity; the gaol was housed on the ground floor while the courts were held above. Those people attending court climbed exterior stairs to a courtroom with walls that were just 5 feet high at the eaves. A low cabin roof did little to mitigate the diminutive, dark space.[15]

A concern for a more durable form of log construction probably motivated the magistrates in Henry County in the southwest frontier to build their new courthouse out of "hewed or sawed loggs." This was almost certainly the case in Rockingham County where the magistrates stipulated that their building was to be built of square logs with diamond corner notching.[16] Despite their better construction, these buildings and others like them erected in the transmontane counties created after the Revolution rarely survived more than twenty years. Invariably, they repeated the pattern that became common throughout Virginia, as log buildings were supplanted by brick and stone structures toward the turn of the century. Augusta County erected a stone courthouse in Staunton in 1788, and Shenandoah County followed with an imposing two-story building with an ashlar facade. Anthony Mustoe, the builder of the Augusta County

FIGURE 55. Russell County courthouse, 1799, with later brick section added when the building was converted into a dwelling

courthouse, also constructed one for Bath County in 1796;and Russell County built its modest structure in 1799 (fig. 55).[17]

The absence of substantial outcroppings of building stone in the tidewater made brick the prestigious building material through the early nineteenth century. Just as Chesapeake craftsmen devised a regional timber-framing tradition, the builders of early courthouses experimented with the visual subtleties and structural flexibility inherent in masonry construction to produce a distinctive building type. Yet Virginians devised no new language of brick building but used a narrow range of common features that, when combined and repeated over and over again, created a novel form whose symbolic meaning was well understood within this provincial society. Many elements in these courthouses shared the same stylistic details characteristic of Georgian architecture in Great Britain and other regions of America. The use of Flemish bond, gauged jack arches, and molded water-table bricks provided a visual coherence to an international style that shaped speculative row housing in the West End estates of London, prominent churches and meetinghouses in the American colonies, and the houses of Caribbean planters. Out of this commonly understood but flexible vocabulary of sources, Virginians subtly manipulated and combined a few elements—compass-headed windows, arcades, pediments, and paved flooring—to develop a public building form that conveyed a sense of civic dignity and regional identity.

As a building material, brick provided resourceful craftsmen with an almost infinite variety of design choices. Georgian builders in Great Britain and America molded bricks into different sizes and shapes; inconsistent kilns produced bricks of uneven colors, shapes, and density; and rubbing, carving, and cutting fired bricks added to the profusion of textures and shapes. By bonding these bricks in different patterns with mortar joints of varying sizes, colors, and finishes, eighteenth-century craftsmen erected buildings contrasting greatly in appearance: from richly articulated country houses of stunning elegance and sophistication to humble utilitarian structures of rudimentary workmanship. Despite these variables, chronological and regional patterns provided a visual coherence in masonry architecture. Brick building skills, which were passed from one generation of masons to the next through apprenticeships, tended to reduce experimentation in favor of tried and true methods. Clients in a conservative culture who wished to emulate their betters preferred to copy prominent standing buildings rather than introduce novel ideas that would need clear and precise instruction.

Changing aesthetics slowly transformed the appearance of brickwork over time. The fashion for vigorously cut and molded brickwork with projecting window and door surrounds, cavetto and ovolo brick mullions, pilastered corners, and curvilinear gables produced a style of brickwork known as artisan mannerism that flourished in England through much of the seventeenth century.[18] Elements of this style appeared in the brick buildings erected by Chesapeake planters during the same period. A rare and celebrated survivor of this style in Virginia, Bacon's Castle (1665), features twin curvilinear gable parapets with diagonally set chimney stacks, projecting window surrounds, and the remnants of a rudimentary pedimented frontispiece surrounding the front door (fig. 56). In public building a number of Anglican parish churches erected from the 1670s through the 1710s displayed similar embellishments. Stepped or curvilinear gables adorned Newport Parish Church in Isle of Wight County (c. 1682), the second Bruton Parish Church in James City County (1683), St. Peter's Parish Church in New Kent County (1703), and possibly the present Bruton Parish Church in Williamsburg (1711–15) (fig. 57).[19] Newport Parish Church and Yeocomico Church in Westmoreland County (1706) have decorative pedimented entrance porches (fig. 58).[20] A decorative frontispiece may have adorned the parish church in Jamestown in the late 1670s before the surviving tower was erected at the end of the seventeenth century, for in 1901 members of the APVA excavated the church ruins and discovered a cut-molded torus and cavetto pilaster base reused as floor paving in the aisle of the church. The Catholic chapel erected in St. Mary's City, Maryland, in the late 1660s and

FIGURE 56. Bacon's Castle, Surry County, 1665

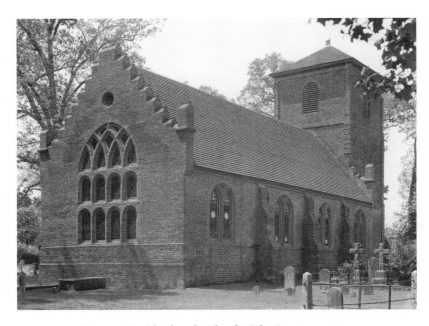

FIGURE 57. Newport Parish Church, Isle of Wight County, c. 1682

the last church erected in Jamestown had brick cavetto mullions.[21] Although such decorative brickwork was not itemized in courthouse specifications, perhaps some of the early ones such as Gloucester courthouse (before 1685) or Lancaster courthouse (1699) may have followed the prevailing patterns.

By the 1730s when brick courthouses were being erected in greater numbers, the artisan mannerist style of decorative brickwork had lost favor. Few brick houses and churches that date from the second quarter of the eighteenth century display any embellishments except pilastered and pedimented frontispieces that derived from standard classical details (fig. 59). The brickwork in the handful of surviving colonial courthouses exhibits none of the decorative flourishes of the earlier period. Instead, it follows a more restrained style that became fashionable in England and many parts of America, especially Virginia, under the influence of a Palladian aesthetic that preferred chasteness and classically correct ornamentation to the vigorous enthusiasms of the artisan mannerist style. Virginians sometimes referred to this new aesthetic in the shorthand terminology of "neat and plain."

With the disappearance of three-dimensional ornamentation, surface decoration provided the primary means of embellishing brick buildings. Since the late seventeenth century, Virginia bricklayers had taken advantage of the wide range of colors produced by unevenly heated kilns to construct walls with bricks that were glazed, rubbed, gauged, and bonded in different patterns.[22]

FIGURE 58. Yeocomico Church, Westmoreland County, 1706

FIGURE 59. Lower Church, Christ Church Parish, Middlesex County, 1714, one of the earliest examples of the more restrained style of brick decoration

The bond of the exterior brickwork shaped the most conspicuous of these patterns. Solid brick walls measuring anywhere from 12 inches to 2 feet in thickness were bonded together in various ways to ensure stability of construction. Colonial bricklayers carefully laid the outside facing bricks in a lime and sand mortar in one of two bonds. The exterior face of English bond walls contained courses of long bricks, or stretchers, alternating with courses of short bricks, or headers. In contrast, Flemish bond walls had an alternating pattern of headers and stretchers in the same course. This latter bond became standard in courthouse construction by the second quarter of the eighteenth century and remained the preferred choice on primary courthouse facades in Virginia through the 1840s, long after so-called common bond and other types of bonding had supplanted it in other regions. Despite the predominance of Flemish bond, some builders combined it with English bond foundations. In the Essex (1729), Hanover (c. 1740), Williamsburg–James City (1771), and Warwick (1810) courthouses, English bond plinths supported Flemish bond walls above the water table. Builders emphasized this break between the thicker foundation walls and the rest of the building by a band of molded water-table bricks. While most courthouses had simple beveled water tables, the ones at Northampton County (1731) and Charles City County (c. 1757) had a two-course water table. At the former, bricklayers roughly cut-molded the bricks in the top two courses of the water table in the shape of ovolos. In a much more refined piece of workmanship at Charles City, the double water table consisted of molded cavetto stretchers paired with a lower course of ovolo stretchers (fig. 60).

Craftsmen often enlivened surfaces with glazed bricks. Burned to glasslike density and smoothness, glazed bricks had long been used in English brickwork in a variety of decorative patterns. In colonial Virginia chevrons, diamonds, and other more idiosyncratic patterns glistened in the sun on chimneys and walls of houses, churches, and occasionally courthouses. The north gable end of the Northampton County courthouse has the remnants of a chevron of glazed headers. More common, however, was the use of glazed bricks as headers to accentuate the checkered or diapered pattern inherent in Flemish bond. In Essex, King William (c. 1730), Hanover, Accomack (1758), and King and Queen courthouses, craftsmen selected those bricks whose short ends had been glazed to a bluish-green hue and inserted them repetitively over the entire exterior wall surface, creating a glimmering contrast to the darker stretchers. Elsewhere, the formula was not rigidly adhered to as many buildings only received random glazing. For example, the walls of the Williamsburg–James City County and Richmond County (1750) courthouses display no deliberate patterning of glazing but have glazed headers and partially glazed stretchers interspersed throughout the building.

Far subtler but no less distinctive, rubbed bricks surrounded windows, doors, and arcade openings and accentuated the corners of facades. These bricks were rubbed with a stone, brush, or an abrasive tool to produce a smooth surface whose uniform color reflected light almost as well as glazed bricks. The practice appeared in domestic and ecclesiastical architecture by the last two decades of the seventeenth century and probably was incorporated into courthouse construction shortly thereafter. The 1736 specifications for the arcaded Spotsylvania County courthouse in Fredericksburg called for the "corners of the building round the Doors and Windows to be made of good Rubbed Brick." Four years later the Lancaster County magistrates had the same decorative effect in mind when they ordered the "jams and returnes" of their new courthouses to be rubbed brick.[23] The brickwork of these long-demolished buildings must have resembled that at the King

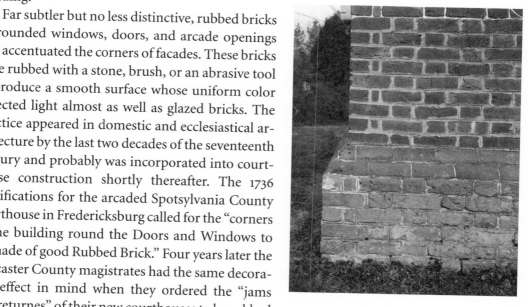

FIGURE 60. Plinth and water table, Charles City County courthouse, c. 1757

William County courthouse. In contrast to the bright glazing of the Flemish bond headers, each course terminates at the corners in either a rubbed stretcher or a rubbed header and closer brick, creating a solid, uniform band of color. Although the flat jack arches above the windows have been rebuilt, the original wedge-shaped or gauged bricks were rubbed as well. Rubbed bricks the width of a stretcher accentuate the sides of the window openings as well. The most dramatic and skilled use of rubbed bricks occurs in the front arcade where gauged and rubbed bricks are tightly bonded and secured by thin lime putty joints in the semicircular arches above the projecting impost blocks (fig. 61). In some colonial buildings a coat of red wash was applied over these joints, which added to the illusion of regularity in these virtuoso displays of the bricklayer's

FIGURE 61. Rubbed brickwork around the arches and jambs, King William County courthouse, c. 1730

FIGURE 62. Rubbed and gauged brickwork of the Hanover County courthouse arcade, c. 1740

art. Evidence of red wash survives on the frontispiece of the Thomas Nelson house in Yorktown and the frontispieces on Christ Church, Lancaster County, and Abingdon Church, Gloucester County. Rubbed bricks laid in regular mortar extend below the King William courthouse's impost blocks and terminate at the beveled water table. A similar decorative scheme was followed at neighboring Hanover courthouse (fig. 62).

By the end of the eighteenth century, variegated brickwork lost much of its appeal, replaced by a new aesthetic that valued machinelike regularity and uniformity of color. Harbinger of the new style in Virginia were gentry houses such as Blandfield built in Essex County in the early 1770s, whose carefully laid brick walls show slight variation in color. Although glazed header brickwork continued to appear on a few public buildings such as the Lancaster County clerk's office (1795–98; see fig. 192), most structures had only random glazing or no glazing at all. At Fairfax courthouse (1800), random glazing appears on one long side and the rear of this two-story building. In contrast, the two front or "public" sides of the courthouse, which face a pair of cross streets, have no glazed bricks at all. This demotion of glazing to secondary facades is best illustrated in the Warwick courthouse. In 1810 masons T. R. Dunn and R. Ratcliffe laid the side and back walls of this diminutive T-shaped building with glazed headers but deliberately left them out of the front facade (see fig. 217).

Two decades later, with improvements in brickmaking and the growing influence of new design principles eschewing the irregularities of colonial brickwork, evenly shaped and uniformly colored bricks with very little if any glazing dominated public building practices. With their sharp corners, consistent size, and similar deep red coloring and bonded together with thin mortar joints, the bricks employed by the masons at Cumberland courthouse (1818) and Charlotte courthouse (1824) varied significantly from their colonial predecessors, being the forerunners of mechanized standardization that irrevocably transformed the brickmakers' trade in the middle and late nineteenth century. The power of this new aesthetic prompted a number of county courts to bring older buildings into conformity. Some colonial structures were given a coat of red paint and penciled with lime-white mortar joints by the end of the eighteenth century. Wanting a new brick wing to harmonize with an earlier section of the courthouse built in Flemish bond with glazed headers, the magistrates of Chesterfield County in 1805 specified that "the walls of both the old and new Parts of the building . . . be painted & penciled."[24] Evidence of this aesthetic predilection still survives at the Charles City courthouse, where the 1750s brickwork was periodically painted red and the joints made more regular by penciling with lime in the half century after the Civil War.

What distinguished the brick courthouses of Virginia as public structures was not their bonding patterns and decorative ornamentation, which fit comfortably into the local building idiom, but the use of compass-headed windows, large-scale openings, arcaded piazzas, and by the end of the eighteenth century, pedimented porticoes. These features marked these structures as public because they were rarely employed in domestic architecture. Although arched or compass-headed windows frequently appeared in England in the late seventeenth and eighteenth centuries in fashionable houses and public buildings and in stair towers and passages of a few New England and Charleston dwellings, Chesapeake builders invariably limited their use to public structures. Like most ambitious building forms that flourished in colonial Virginia, semicircular and segmentally arched openings first appeared in late seventeenth-century Anglican parish churches. All the window, door, and tower openings in the Newport Parish Church (c. 1682) in Isle of Wight County, for example, are arched, though many are subdivided by brick mullion tracery. The semicircular openings with rubbed arch bricks at Middle Church (1712) and Lower Chapel (1714) in Christ Church Parish, Middlesex County, are precursors of the form and treatment employed in a number of courthouses built from the 1720s through the 1780s.

A second and perhaps equally influential source for the use of compass-headed openings appeared in the first decade of the eighteenth century in the Capitol in Williamsburg. The semicircular arches that crowned the principal door and window openings on the ground floor of the Capitol suggest that the designers were inspired not only by the emerging parish church architecture of the tobacco colony but by English civic architecture as well.[25] Such windows appear in the town hall in Abingdon, Oxfordshire (formerly Berkshire), erected between 1678 and 1682 and are commonly found in early eighteenth-century shire halls and market houses. The circular or ox-eye windows of the twin apsidal ends of the Capitol also had their counterparts in Virginia ecclesiastical and English civic architecture at the turn of the century. The Norfolk County magistrates took their inspiration directly from the Capitol when they constructed their courthouse in 1726, for not only were the interior fittings modeled directly on those in the General Courtroom, but the building featured an oval window above the magistrates' platform in the center of the apse. Although oval windows seem to have passed out of fashion by the middle of the century, as late as 1787 the magistrates of Charlotte County ordered the construction of one over the door of their new courthouse.[26]

Because of the modest amount of money levied on county freeholders for public building expenses, the costly use of compass-headed windows grew slowly in courthouse construction. Although a few now-destroyed early eighteenth-century courthouses may have had such windows, the number of buildings that had them rose significantly after 1730. The arcaded courthouse built in Yorktown in the early 1730s and destroyed by fire in 1814 had compass-headed windows that were mentioned in the repairs made to the building after English troops ransacked it during the siege of Yorktown in 1781.[27] Completed by John Moore in 1729, the Essex County courthouse in Tappahannock is perhaps the earliest surviving county courthouse with arched window heads (fig. 63). Whereas the arches of the Essex courthouse windows are defined by a single band of headers, in later buildings such as the Richmond County (1750) and Gloucester County (1766) courthouses, the arched openings are decorated with rubbed and gauged stretchers. A more formal but relatively unusual treatment appears in the Williamsburg–James City County courthouse where projecting impost blocks mark the springing of the arched windows and glazed headers alternate with rubbed stretchers to accentuate the top of the openings. This treatment of the arched opening appeared in Virginia as early as the 1690s in the tower of the Jamestown church and the ground-floor apertures at the College of William and Mary. It also appears in the present Bruton Parish Church.

By manipulating the scale of the buildings, designers and workmen estab-

FIGURE 63. Compass-headed Essex County courthouse windows, Tappahannock, 1729. The central window was originally an entrance. The window on the left was converted to a door when wings were added for jury rooms in the early nineteenth century.

lished a second and subtler way of distinguishing the public nature of county courthouses. Although the courthouse standing on Market Square in Williamsburg reads as a one-story building, the brick walls extend nearly 21 feet from the ground to the modillion cornice. They stand between 7 and 9 feet taller than the wall pitch of neighboring one-story dwellings and are only slightly shorter than the walls of two-story dwellings such as the Peyton Randolph House. The deceptive appearance of the courthouse derives from the scale of its openings. In Williamsburg dwellings ground-floor window openings range in width from 2 feet 10 inches to 4 feet and in height from 5 feet 8 inches to 7 feet 8 inches. Public buildings generally maintained this 1:2 ratio, but the sizes of the openings were increased proportionally. The brick openings of the Williamsburg courthouse windows are 4 feet 11 inches wide and stand 10 feet 6 inches high.

Although colonial builders never employed an elaborate comprehensive proportioning system to guide the design of their structures, they generally followed the English practice of establishing a proportional relationship of various individual parts to the whole.[28] Thus elements such as door and window openings, cornices, framing members, and roof trusses were scaled to fit the overall size of a structure. As early as the last quarter of the seventeenth century, such a system was at work in public building, for in 1685 Rappahannock County magistrates ordered that the windows of their new courthouse should be 4 feet long and "of a proportionable wideness." Most specifications remained mute or were so vague that it was left to builders to work out the proportions appropriate for a courthouse. In 1741 magistrates in Bertie County, North Carolina, understood that their new courthouse should be scaled in such a way as to express its public nature, but they noted only that the doors, windows, and other elements should be "otherways in Proportion" to the 24-by-32-foot building.[29]

Along with this abstract aesthetic concern for proportion, colonial craftsmen manipulated the size of many architectural elements to meet such anticipated structural requirements. They fabricated larger floor joists for broader spans or thicker corner posts for two-story frame structures. However, with few detailed guides or rule books that stated precise measurements or systems of proportioning, most craftsmen operated from practical experience. In 1793 magistrates of Henry County specified that the frame of their new courthouse was "to be the proper size in proportion to the size of the house," leaving it to skilled craftsmen to work out the appropriate dimensions based upon their intuitive knowledge. In laying out the specifications for a new church in 1769, the vestry of Truro Parish noted that the scantling was "to be of a size and proper proportion to the building."[30]

Similarly, brickmasons followed a rule of thumb based on the size of an individual brick in deciding proper wall thicknesses. Brick walls for most one-story domestic structures standing 10 or 11 feet high were generally 12 to 13 inches wide or 1½ bricks thick above the water table. For taller structures such as courthouses, masons increased the wall thickness above the water table to 16 inches or the length of two stretchers placed end to end.[31] Yet this pattern was not rigidly adhered to, for exceptions can be readily found in colonial articles of agreement. Unusually tall at 26 feet in height, the walls of the 1726 Norfolk County courthouse were only 1½ bricks thick from the water table to the eaves.[32] In contrast to the Norfolk example, the height of most early eighteenth-century courthouse walls remained domestic in scale, reaching no more than 8 to 12 feet in pitch. Gradually, by the middle decades of the century, wall heights increased. The ceiling in the 1740 Lancaster courthouse stood 14 feet above the floor. By the end of the colonial period, even this generous height was surpassed in a number of modest-sized buildings, a trend that presaged the emergence of fully articulated two-story courthouses in the closing years of the century. The 1785 specifications for the Rockbridge County courthouse called for 18-foot walls of two bricks' width with large windows of twenty-four lights to correspond to the increased wall surface, setting the building apart from the domestic scale of surrounding dwellings in Lexington. The stone walls of the two-story Shenandoah County courthouse constructed in 1795 in the town of Woodstock measure 2 feet in thickness on the first floor and 18 inches on the second floor. As in the Rockbridge courthouse, the large ground-floor windows originally consisted of twenty-four panes of 8-by-10-inch glass. The spaciousness of these openings (4 feet by 7 feet 2 inches) not only called attention to the public nature of the building but also accentuated the importance of the ground-floor courtroom. In keeping with general Palladian theories of visual hierarchy, the smaller second-floor windows, which lit subservient office spaces, were only twenty lights in size.[33] Thus proportioning derived from increments of basic modules—the size of a brick, the size of a standard pane of glass—that dictated the dimensioning of most elements of Virginia's early dwellings and public buildings.

The one innovation in brick building forms that established the Virginia courthouse as a distinctive regional building type was the arcade. Although the arcade, colonnade, and covered piazza appeared in a variety of English public buildings from the Renaissance onward, Virginians used these forms in slightly different ways. In seventeenth-century England arcaded spaces could be found on buildings ranging from the Royal Exchange in London, where merchants gathered around a covered walk surrounding an open courtyard to transact business, to market houses in cities and towns, where tradesmen sold their wares from beneath the sheltered space enclosed by arched openings. In the late seventeenth and early eighteenth centuries, architects and builders occasionally

FIGURE 64. Canterbury Quadrangle, St. John's College, Oxford, 1631–36

incorporated arcaded spaces in almshouses, where covered walks linked rows of rooms together. A two-story brick arcade decorated with glazed headers and rubbed arch bricks extends along both sides of a central porch tower in the Brick Alley Almshouses in Abingdon built in 1718–20. The earlier and more modest one-story Geering Almshouses (1715) at Harwell, Oxfordshire, makes use of the arcade for the same purposes: as a linking corridor contained within a unifying architectural element. Arcades and colonnades also provided cloistered walks in a number of Oxford and Cambridge colleges, such as the Canterbury Quadrangle at St. John's College, Oxford, completed with much classical detailing in 1636 (fig. 64).[34] In Christopher Wren's chapel wing at Emmanuel College, Cambridge, dating from the late 1660s, two five-bay wings with open ground-floor arcading flank a central pedimented chapel and provide a screen that closes off one end of the central courtyard. His slightly later library at nearby Trinity College, Cambridge, was raised on a blind arcade that opened only onto the inner side of a quadrangle of buildings. The other wings of Nevile's Court at Trinity College already had arcaded walks. Wren explained that his design would continue this arrangement and would be "according to the manner of the ancients who made double walks . . . about the forum."[35]

The inward-looking arcades of English colleges, almshouses, and the Royal Exchange served primarily as a circulation space as well as a place to gather for conversation. In contrast, the arcades and colonnades of market houses and town halls erected by corporations in cities and market towns served an entirely different purpose. Supported by piers and columns, at least three—and often all four—sides of the ground floor of these buildings stood open and operated as a magnet for trade and the distribution of goods. Raised one or two steps above the surrounding marketplace, the enclosed area housed butcher stalls with spikes and railings fastened into the arcade piers to support the weight of sides of beef, mutton, pork, and game. Above the smells of butchered meat and the sounds of tradesmen hawking their wares, many public buildings had one or more rooms reserved for the clerk of the court, the mayor and aldermen, and the corporation courts. Generally, most two-story market houses or town halls had at least one large space that served either as a court or a place of public assembly where dances, concerts, and other social and political meetings could be held.[36]

Late medieval in origin, market halls became increasingly prominent fixtures in market towns in the Tudor period as stone and brick structures replaced earlier timber ones. The arcaded stone market houses in Rothwell, Northamptonshire (1578), and Shrewsbury, Shropshire (1596), are two good late sixteenth-century examples of this form.[37] Following the Restoration, renewed civic pride and rivalry led a number of towns to construct costly and fairly grand structures. Such was the case of Abingdon, a town that faced strong

FIGURE 65. Elevation, town hall, Amersham, Buckinghamshire, 1682. (Drake Papers, D/DR/4/20/1, Centre for Buckinghamshire Studies)

competition from Reading for recognition as the county seat. In a costly effort to retain the county assize court and gaol, borough officials expended nearly £3,000 to erect a grand two-story stone market house with Composite order pilasters extending two stories above the paved floor of the market arcade.[38] The contemporaneous brick town hall in Amersham, Buckinghamshire (1682), is typical of the less ambitious structures built in successful market towns (fig. 65). Two bays wide and six bays long, the ground-floor area provided ample space for butchers' stalls and other temporary trading stands while the large room abovestairs served as a place for public meeting. Some corporations chose not to erect such freestanding structures but instead constructed market buildings that stood in a contiguous block of buildings on one side of the marketplace. Enclosed by solid walls on either side, the arcaded three-bay front of the 1732 market house in Langport, Somerset, provided light and ventilation for the stalls that were set up on the paved stone floor (figs. 66, 67). Far grander is the two-story stone-faced market house in Blandford Forum in Dorset, erected in 1734 by the local architects John and William Bastard three years after fire had destroyed the center of the town. The three-bay facade has an

FIGURE 66. Town hall, Langport, Somerset, 1732.

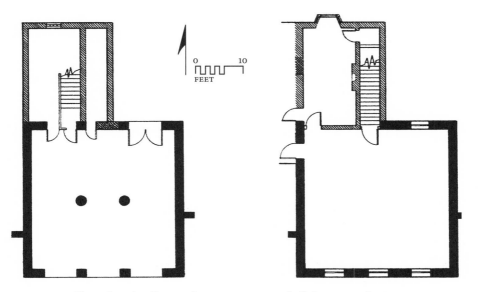

FIGURE 67. Plan of market floor and courtroom, town hall, Langport, Somerset

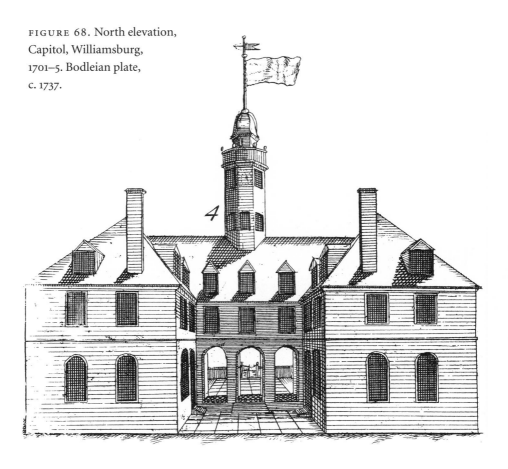

FIGURE 68. North elevation, Capitol, Williamsburg, 1701–5. Bodleian plate, c. 1737.

arcaded market space on the ground floor, a courtroom above, and is surmounted by a pedimented entablature.

If the arcade could be used for a number of functions in a wide variety of English public buildings, colonial builders in Virginia were just as imaginative in their use of this form. It first appeared in Virginia in the mid-1690s in the College of William and Mary, which followed the collegiate tradition with the construction of an open piazza on the west side of the principal floor. Here, the arcade served as a transverse circulation corridor linking rooms from one end of the building to the other and to the north hall wing (see fig. 19).[39]

With the establishment of the new capital of Williamsburg at Middle Plantation in 1699, another important public building with an arcade soon appeared. Under the dynamic but contentious leadership of Governor Francis Nicholson, the General Assembly quite self-consciously resurrected a classical image when it chose to call the new statehouse in Williamsburg the "capitol." Erected at the opposite end of the Duke of Gloucester Street from the College between 1701 and 1705, the Capitol consisted of two two-story brick buildings connected in the middle by a 30-foot-square arcade or "piazza" (fig. 68). As was true of many Virginia building types, the Capitol had a mixed pedigree. Part oversized courthouse, part self-conscious provincial statehouse, the Capitol was a jumbled amalgam of a variety of influences that incorporated regional design precedents and English public building forms.[40] For the first time in the history of the colony, the Capitol provided room for all major provincial offices under one roof. The statehouse erected in Jamestown in the late 1660s and reconstructed following the torching of the town in 1676 contained only the General Assembly, General Court, and secretary of the colony. The governor and council were more peripatetic, meeting in rented rooms, on distant plantations, and occasionally appropriating spaces in public buildings such as the James City County courthouse. Part of the awkwardness of the Capitol plan was the result of the novelty of accommodating such a large number of public offices in a single structure.

The architectural importance of this building on later county courthouse design was powerful and abiding. Not only did the Capitol house the highest court in the colony, but it was a building that many Virginians knew quite well from personal experience. Each year influential citizens from across the colony entered the building to sit as burgesses, petition the council, and act as jurors or argue their cases before the governor and members of his council who presided over the General Court. The semiannual meeting of this latter body brought prominent lawyers, law students, county sheriffs, and others involved in the provincial legal system crowding into the ground-floor courtroom in the west wing of the Capitol.

Typical of county courthouses of the period, entrance into the General Courtroom was through the double doors that opened on each of the two long side walls of the west wing (figs. 69, 70). Accentuated by a semicircular colonnaded porch, the west doors faced the Duke of Gloucester Street and the main part of the city; the east doors opened into the broad arcaded space connecting to the east wing of the building.[41] This arcade served not only as a sheltered link between the two wings but more importantly as a gathering place for lawyers and their clients as well as a covered area for spectators, witnesses, and others to pass idle moments during court days.

By its prestige and familiarity to a large cross section of colonial society, the Capitol eventually had a profound impact on public building in tidewater counties in the early eighteenth century. The distinctive apsidal projection gave visible manifestation to the corporate nature of the judicial authority of the governor and council, the courtroom fittings carefully delineated the roles and status of those who occupied them, and the arched windows and doors and arcaded piazza became part of the architectural iconography of county courthouses.

FIGURE 69. West or principal
elevation, Capitol, Williamsburg, 1701–5

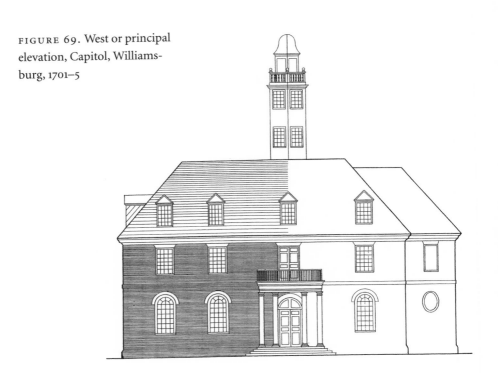

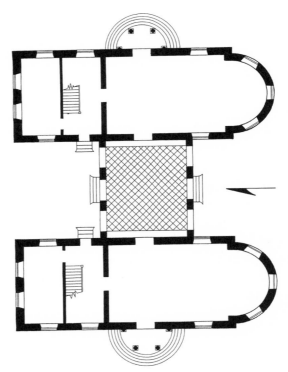

FIGURE 70. Plan, Capitol, Williamsburg, 1701–5

However, more than two decades passed before these features became integral elements of public building on the courthouse grounds of tidewater counties. Although some buildings such as the James City County courthouse, built in Williamsburg when the court moved from Jamestown by 1715, may have had arcades, the first documented reference to an arcaded courthouse occurred in 1732 when York County magistrates built its "Court house or Town hall of Brick with a Piazza before it."[42] A few years later the Spotsylvania County court specified that its new building in the town of Fredericksburg was to "have Eight Arches or Piazas in the outside wall frunting the Courte."[43] The exact configuration of the arcades of these long vanished structures cannot be accurately reconstructed, but they must have been very similar to the ones that still survive in neighboring counties. The Spotsylvania design may have resembled the double-sided arcade built a few years later by Landon Carter in Richmond County. The "piazzas" of the T-shaped courthouses in King William, Hanover, Isle of Wight (1751, rebuilt in 1960), and Charles City (c. 1757, enclosed in the late nineteenth century) are remarkably similar in form (figs. 71, 72). Five bays in length and composed of nearly equal-sized openings and wall piers, these arcades are incorporated beneath the front slope of a hip roof. The depth of this space varies between 8 and 10 feet. The return of the arcade features a single arched opening that terminates flush with the ends of the courthouse walls. At King William, Hanover, and Charles City courthouses, stucco covered the interior faces of the arcades, providing a clean white contrast to the brickwork of the exterior walls.[44]

As was true of many English market houses and town halls, the floors of these spaces were laid with brick tiles or imported stone pavers. Richmond County courthouse had brick pavers in its two side arcades.[45] Other buildings had more costly materials. The use of stone paving in public buildings in the Chesapeake began in the late seventeenth century in Anglican churches where aisles were covered with "Bristol stone," or Portland stone, white and cream-colored limestone slabs imported from quarries in the south of England in Dorset and the area southeast of Bristol. As with many elements of public architecture in Virginia, this pattern soon passed into secular use, so that by the end of the century magistrates began specifying the use of stone for the floors of courtrooms and porches. In 1699 the Lancaster County court ordered that the floor and porch of the new courthouse were to be laid with paving stones.[46] In the arcade at King William courthouse, the original 18-inch-square paving stones, which survive beneath the present 1983 surface, are thin slabs of subarkose or subgraywacke, a conglomerate of Silurian grit rock consisting of rounded pebbles and sand, probably quarried in England and imported into the colony when the courthouse was built around 1730 (fig. 73). The stone

FIGURE 71. Charles City County courthouse, c. 1757.

FIGURE 72. Charles City County courthouse arcade before it was enclosed, in a June 13, 1864, photograph. (Library of Congress)

FIGURE 73. Arcade paving, King William County courthouse, c. 1730.
The paving was covered following renovations in 1983.

paving of the open arcade often continued inside the courtroom where it extended forward as far as the lawyers' bar, covering the back of the room where the public stood.

With the large, double front doors standing open during the summer sessions, the paved arcade became a cooler, exposed outer zone of the courtroom, reminiscent of English courts such as the Old Bailey in London and a number of other courts that had no entrance wall but opened directly into the out-of-doors or sheltered space, expressing literally the cherished English notion of a court system conducted fairly and openly before the public (fig. 74). In Virginia

FIGURE 74. *Justice Hall in the Old Bail[e]y.* Engraving, London, c. 1740. (Guildhall Library, Corporation of London)

these arched open spaces, like the Capitol's arcade, provided a place for people to gather in bad weather or to find shade from the hot summer sun and served as an open anteroom in which clients and their counsel reviewed their cases and mapped out last-minute strategies. A constantly changing crowd of people assembled upon the paving stones or brick tiles to await their business in court or to catch up on the latest news of neighbors and acquaintances and converse with local artisans seeking work. Cognizant of the constant use these sheltered spaces received, the Richmond County court in 1750 ordered four benches "of a Convenient hight and Breadth for people to sit on" to be placed in each of the two side "piazzo's" of Landon Carter's new courthouse, a rare example of the concern for the welfare and accommodation of the public.[47]

Because of the expense of construction, the arcade never dominated courthouse architecture in colonial Virginia. Most courthouses did not have such costly entrances but only a set of wooden, brick, or stone steps leading to unsheltered doorways. However, the form remained a part of courthouse design for more than half a century following the Revolution. Just before the outbreak of the war, the magistrates of Berkeley County (now West Virginia) contracted to construct a courthouse in Martinsburg that was to have a two-story, five-bay arcade across its entrance facade (fig. 75). Delays and changes in the plan prevented completion the project until the late 1770s, but when finished the courthouse was perhaps the most ambitious public structure in the western part of the state. The T-shaped plan with a curved back wall reflected the shape of the magistrates' bench and the double tier of windows in the front wall beneath the tall arcade lit the courtroom. Surmounting the hipped roof, which encompassed the arcade and side jury rooms, was a cupola, an increasingly important element in urban courthouses.[48]

Virginians continued to incorporate the arcade in courthouse designs even as the plan of these buildings changed in the early national period in part because it was so adaptable. As the preference for rectangular, two-story buildings with entrances on the shorter gable ends grew, the arcade was used to define the formal entrance on these fronts. The open arcade extended three, four, or five bays below an upper tier of jury-room windows. The 1791 design of the Rockingham County courthouse may have had a 10-foot-deep arcade.[49] Completed by 1800, the Fairfax County courthouse is the same width as the one specified in the Rockingham County plan. Thirty-two feet across, the three-bay arcade is of a similar 10-foot depth. Following the pattern established by earlier Virginia courthouses, the arcade is a single bay wide on each side. Other arcaded courthouses followed these prototypes. In 1809 the magistrates in the newly formed western county of Nelson deliberated over a variety of plans, some of which had partially arcaded fronts, before deciding upon a five-bay arcade that stretched across the front gable-end entrance (see figs. 118, A37).[50] The central

FIGURE 75. Berkeley County courthouse, Martinsburg, now W.Va., 1773–78. Woodcut from William Howe, *Historical Collections of Virginia* (Charleston, S.C., 1845).

FIGURE 76. Madison County courthouse, 1828–30

bay is slightly wider than the flanking ones and the two side, or return, arches. This feature was unusual. Subsequent arcaded buildings, such as the central three bays of the Sussex County courthouse (1828); the four-bay, pedimented courthouses in Madison County (1830), Page County (1833), and Caroline County (1835); and a relatively late example, the three-bay Middlesex County courthouse (1852) in Saluda, have evenly spaced arcade openings (fig. 76).

If the arcade helped define the image of civic architecture in Virginia in the late colonial and early national periods, another element gradually challenged its primacy. Porches had long been a part of courthouse architecture. The courthouse built by Anthony Dawson in Dorchester County, Maryland, in 1686 had "a large Porch att the end of the house with rails and Banisters about it." The 1699 courthouse in Lancaster County had an enclosed 10-by-10-foot brick porch.[51] For the next half century, the principal entrance of many public buildings and dwellings had similar porches, squarish in plan, which served as lobby spaces enclosed to varying degrees by walls with windows or balustraded apertures. However, in the same year that Robert Carter undertook the construction of the Lancaster County courthouse, specifications for the new Capitol in Williamsburg called for an open, 15-foot-wide, semicircular porch supported by cedar posts and surmounted by an iron railing.[52] This porch marked the entrance into the General Court on the west side of the building. Curiously, unlike other novel design elements in the Capitol, this early example of an open porch or portico had little influence on county courthouse architecture over the next fifty years. There are no unambiguous references to columned porticoes attached to courthouses before the third quarter of the century.

After fire destroyed the Capitol in 1747, a second building was constructed in the early 1750s on the foundations of the earlier one. Once again, the principal entrance into the General Court was dominated by a sheltered appendage. This one was a much grander two-story pedimented portico, marking the first time such an element appeared in public architecture in Virginia (fig. 77). The double-tiered tetrastyle portico spanned the central bays of the west front facing the Duke of Gloucester Street and contained within the broad space of its tympanum the carved and gilded coat of arms of the monarch. Although monumental in scale, the execution of the design was less than successful to the critical eye of Thomas Jefferson, who noted that the lower order, "being Doric, is tolerably just in its proportions and ornaments, save only that the intercolumnations are too large. The upper Ionic is much too small for that on which it is mounted, its ornaments not proper to the order, nor proportioned within themselves. It is crowned with a pediment, which is too large for its span." Despite these shortcomings, Jefferson thought the Capitol "the most pleasing piece of architecture we have."[53]

Like so many other aspects of design in early Virginia, this innovative ele-

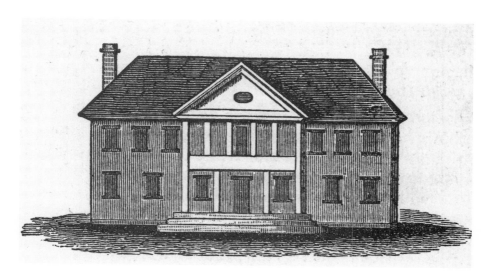

FIGURE 77. West elevation, Second Capitol, Williamsburg, 1751–53, James Skelton, undertaker. Woodcut from William Howe, *Historical Collections of Virginia* (Charleston, S.C., 1845).

FIGURE 78. Williamsburg–James City County courthouse, 1770–71

FIGURE 79. Capitol, Richmond, 1785–89. Engraving by William Goodacre, 1831. (Library of Congress)

ment had little immediate effect. Nearly two decades passed before the precedent set by the Capitol found a response, not surprisingly, in a building no more than a few short blocks down the street. In 1770 the magistrates of the Williamsburg hustings court and the James City County court agreed to undertake jointly the construction of a new courthouse on Market Square in the heart of the city. Completed the following year with an entrance raised four steps above the surrounding square, this T-shaped brick building had a one-story pedimented portico of the Ionic order spanning the central three bays of the five-bay front facade (fig. 78). Like the Martinsburg courthouse in Berkeley County, it had a short cupola crowned by a vane at the intersection of the apex of the two hipped rooflines. Extending at least 8 feet from the front wall, this pedimented porch projected like a pent over the entrance platform without columns. Before the fire that gutted the building in 1911, the portico had no columns to support it but was structurally cantilevered to carry its own weight (see fig. 6). When the courthouse was completed in 1771, it may have had four Ionic columns to match the pulvinated frieze of the entablature, but if so, they were gone by 1796 when architect Benjamin Henry Latrobe noticed their absence.[54]

What little influence the second Capitol may have had on courthouse design was eclipsed in 1780 when the capital moved from Williamsburg to Richmond and new public buildings were constructed. When completed in 1789, Thomas Jefferson's Capitol charted a new course in public building imagery for Virginia and much of the nation (fig. 79). Whereas the old Capitol in Williamsburg had been based on a combination of classical elements—the cupola, piazza, and portico—the design of the new Capitol in Richmond derived from a single, unified source: an ancient classical temple. Jefferson patterned his building after a Roman temple of the first century A.D., the Maison Carrée, in Nîmes, in the south of France, which he considered "the most perfect model existing of what may be called Cubic architecture." Although the plan of the building followed the layout of the old Capitol in Williamsburg in many respects, the exterior was strikingly different, especially the massive hexastyle pedimented portico executed in the Ionic order that terminated the southwest facade overlooking the James River.[55] Unlike the Williamsburg Capitol, this portico was not the principal entrance into the building but served as a terrace; the main entrances remained on the longer sides of the building until new wings were added there in the renovations of 1904–6 and steps were built in front of the portico.

Jefferson's porticoed temple challenged traditional thinking about public building design. With its singular-block massing unified under a shallow roofline, the imposing scale of its double tier of windows and two-story columns rising above a plinth, and its conspicuous placement standing majestically isolated on Shockoe Hill above the shops, dwellings, and warehouses of the city below, the Capitol boldly repudiated all the lingering domestic qualities that still imbued the public architecture of late eighteenth-century Virginia. It took more than two decades for county magistrates in the Old Dominion to appreciate fully the implications of this transformation. As two-story pedimented temples became the model for new courthouse design in the first quarter of the nineteenth century, officials had to reconsider the scale and relationship of courtroom, jury room, and office spaces.

The Plan and Furnishings of Courthouses after 1730

From the 1730s through the adoption of the Jeffersonian temple design a century later, the plan of Virginia courthouses became increasingly sophisticated. The introduction of public building elements, such as arcades and changes in fashion, slowly transformed their appearance. Yet during this period, for every building that showed any refinement in the scale and arrangement of courtroom and office spaces, dozens continued to follow the patterns established in the previous century. Numerous county benches chose to erect rectangular structures measuring between 20 and 24 feet in width and from between 30 and 48 feet in length, which contained a large open courtroom at one end with one or a pair of jury rooms at the other end or abovestairs in one gable end. The brick courthouse in Accomack County completed by Severn Guthrey in 1758 measured 25 by 45 feet and contained a single heated jury room and staircase at the lower end of the courtroom (fig. 80). The staircase rose in the corner to a clerk's office lit by dormer windows in the garret (see fig. 132). This arrangement followed some seventeenth-century plans where the lofted space above contained rooms for the clerk, juries, and storage. The seventeenth-century courthouses in Charles City and Westmoreland Counties each had a clerk's office above the courtroom.

FIGURE 80. Plan, Accomack County courthouse, Accomac, c. 1755. Redrawing of the original in Accomack Co. Loose Papers, The Library of Virginia; see fig. 131.

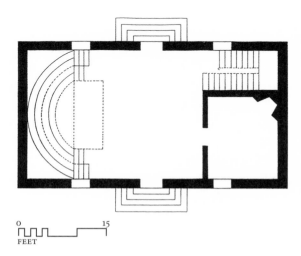

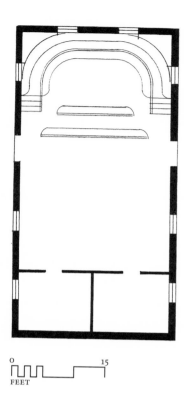

FIGURE 81. Plan, Amelia County courthouse, 1767. Redrawing of the original in Loose Papers, Clerk's Office, Amelia Courthouse; see fig. 116.

0   15
FEET

The traditional rectangular plan continued to be used through the late colonial period. In 1772 the magistrates in the piedmont county of Prince Edward saw little reason to experiment with new forms and agreed to replace their old rectangular frame structure with a new one of the same plan. They contracted with Christopher Ford, builder of a similar-sized courthouse in neighboring Amelia County, to erect a building that was "to be 46 feet long 24 feet wide and 12 feet pitch with two jury rooms 12 feet square with a fireplace in each room, the roof to be hipped" (fig. 81). Except for the hipped roof and the use of sash windows, little distinguished the Prince Edward courthouse from the one specified nearly a century earlier in 1678 by justices in Westmoreland County. Of the same dimensions, both were to have a ground-floor courtroom at one end of the building with entrances on each of the two longer walls. The other end of both buildings was partitioned off for jury rooms. Even the 12-foot pitch of the Prince Edward courthouse walls was the same height as the Westmoreland building. The only difference in plan was that the Westmoreland courthouse was to have a room finished in the gabled attic for a clerk's office. In 1767 a separate building was constructed on the courthouse grounds for the use of Prince Edward's clerk of court five years before the new courthouse was undertaken.[56]

While the Westmoreland plan was perhaps the largest one devised in the late seventeenth century, the 46-by-24-foot dimensions of the Prince Edward courthouse were fairly standard by the end of the colonial period. During that time the number of square feet in courthouses had slowly increased. Seventeenth- and early eighteenth-century courthouses contained between 600 and 800 square feet. By the time of the Revolution, the average Virginia courthouse measured between 1,100 and 1,500 square feet. Much of this expansion occurred through an increase in the width of the building. Most early earthfast structures spanned between 16 to 20 feet in width. Later buildings constructed on masonry foundations with good "English-framed" walls and roofs were more spacious. Specifications for a 24-foot width became standard because a common-rafter roof truss could still span the distance quite easily.[57] A few late colonial courthouses, especially brick structures, measured from 2 to 6 feet wider than this norm, although the thickness of the brick walls accounted for some of this increase. Broader courthouses extending between 30 and 40 feet came into fashion with the introduction of two-story arcaded and templed buildings in the very late eighteenth and early nineteenth centuries. For example, the Fairfax County courthouse (1800) is 32 feet wide, Nelson County courthouse (1809) 40 feet, Lunenburg County courthouse (1823) 40 feet, Goochland County courthouse (1826) 36 feet, and Madison County courthouse (1830) 40 feet (see figs. A9, A10, A37, and 76). The increased width of these buildings was necessary to achieve the proper spacing for the tetrastyle porticoes and arcade bays.

If the tradition of the rectangular courthouse with side entrances continued well into the late colonial period, a concomitant desire arose for a plan that contained a single primary entrance on the wall opposite the magistrates' bench. In order to do this, jury and other ancillary rooms had to be shifted from their standard position at that end of the courthouse. Some early courthouses had resolved this problem by maintaining the jury rooms abovestairs, but for the most part these jury and clerk spaces were wedged in tiny garret rooms lit only by gable-end windows or dormers because until the end of the eighteenth century Virginians were reluctant to erect full two-story public buildings. But the advent of the fashion for flatter hipped roofs left little attic space for such offices. In some areas magistrates had moved jury rooms and magistrates' meeting rooms out of the courthouse into smaller structures erected nearby, much in the manner of domestic service buildings, which came into fashion in the last quarter of the seventeenth century, or vestry houses erected in churchyards. In 1735 in the Northern Neck, an area with a history of dispersing court functions into several buildings, the magistrates of Westmoreland County thought it useful to have "a small room . . . built with a brick chimney adjoining to this Court house for the reception of the magistrates and officers of this

Court at such time and times as they shall have occasion to be therein and more especially in cold weather to have the conveniency and use of the fire to warm themselves att." Similarly, justices in neighboring Richmond County in the same year ordered the construction of "a room . . . adjoyning to the courthouse brick walls thirty two foot in length, twelve foot pitch, sixteen foot wide, with an inside chimney" which no doubt was to be used as a private meeting place for magistrates and court officials.[58] Detached buildings such as these provided deliberative space for magistrates and juries and office space for court clerks and for the most part freed one end of the courtroom of subsidiary rooms.

Another solution that appeared by the 1730s was the shift of these deliberative rooms to the sides of the courtroom, forming a T-shaped configuration with the magistrates' bench located at the bottom end of the stem of the T and the entrance situated directly opposite at the top. The placement of these rooms in two wings flanking the courtroom provided a more integrated courthouse plan, one that allowed all court activities to occur under one roof, albeit with a much more complex roof structure. The imposing view of the justices' bench rising on the opposite wall from the central entrance with the king's coat of arms directly above the chief magistrate's chair would have been made all the more dramatic by the mediating presence of the formal arcade found in many of these buildings. At York, King William, Hanover, Isle of Wight, Stafford, and Charles City Counties, the width of the top of the T, or the front section of jury room and arcade combined, matched or came within a few feet of equaling the width of the courtroom stem (fig. 82). At the Hanover courthouse, the outside width of the courtroom stem is 26 feet; the side wall of the jury room wing is 16 feet, which when combined with the 12-foot width of the arcade equals 28 feet, a span 2 feet wider than the stem (fig. 83). Following a pattern established in Virginia Anglican church roofs, the approximately equal width of the two intersecting blocks created two arms of a similar slope and rafter length that made the hipped-roof frame easier to construct. For courthouse plans that eschewed the arcade in favor of a portico or porch such as those at King and Queen, Gloucester, Williamsburg–James City, and Buckingham Counties, the pattern remains the same, the only difference being that the side walls of the jury rooms were increased in size from around 16 feet to more than 20 feet. The King and Queen County courthouse had jury rooms 15 by 22 feet, and the original ones at Gloucester County courthouse measured 20 by 23 feet. The width of the courtroom section of the Williamsburg–James City County courthouse is 27 feet, which is the same as the width of the two jury-room wings. Indeed, the wings are so wide that each was subdivided into two rooms of unequal size (fig. 84). The front rooms of these wings were heated, while the two smaller back rooms remained unheated and probably were used for storage by the two jurisdictions that shared the courthouse.

FIGURE 82. Present plan, Hanover
County courthouse, c. 1740

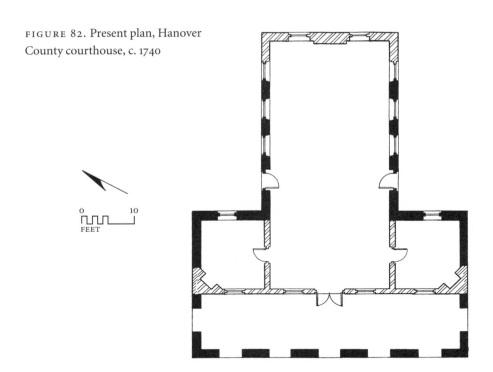

FIGURE 83. Side view of the Hanover County courthouse. The rear bay was added in the
nineteenth century and refaced to match the Flemish bond of the original section in the
mid-1950s.

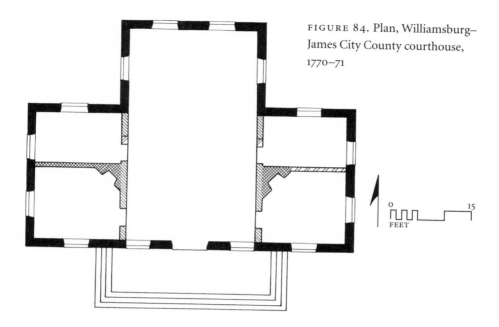

FIGURE 84. Plan, Williamsburg–James City County courthouse, 1770–71

The jury room was, of course, reserved first and foremost for the meeting of juries (fig. 85). Grand juries that numbered up to twenty-four members sat twice a year and presumably retired to a jury room to review the bills of indictment brought before them. Petit jurors, who sat on a bench below the magistrates, filed out of the courtroom and were closeted in a room for deliberations. Because jury trials occurred infrequently in colonial Virginia, many court sessions passed between trials decided by a petit jury in the seventeenth century. Although there was variation from county to county, by the end of the colonial period, the number of cases heard before a jury had risen but was still only a handful, generally no more than two or three per court session. Considering that court sessions lasted from two to four days and sometimes one of these days was set aside for hearing all the jury trials, then the amount of time a jury room was being used by juries was quite small. In the many courthouses with more than one jury room, it is likely that some of the rooms were used only rarely for their ostensible purpose.

Why, then, did eighteenth-century Virginians go to so much trouble to build rooms that would see only limited use by juries? After all, the main variable in the planning of courthouses was in deciding the placement of these ancillary spaces. By contrast, English town halls and market houses were rarely built with prominent jury rooms opening directly off the courtroom. What warranted their conspicuous inclusion in the colonial courthouse of Virginia?

FIGURE 85. Southwest jury room of the Williamsburg–James City County courthouse. Fittings reproduced 1990–91.

If infrequently occupied by juries, jury rooms were nonetheless essential to orderly workings of the county courts. The growing complexity of court procedure in Virginia in the late colonial period probably expedited the movement of jury rooms to the more accessible ground-floor space, whether at the end of a rectangular courthouse, in a separate building, or in flanking spaces of a T-shaped building. The increasing number of cases, petitions, and actions brought before the courts required that matters be handled in a more formal and systematized manner than in the past. Court after court required that such petitions and other documents be submitted in advance so that a schedule could be developed. On rules day preceding the monthly court session, the clerk needed a space to certify warrants, coordinate the schedule of the court, and satisfy the questions of individual litigants. Clerks had previously been wedged in an unheated upstairs chamber at best. Until the very end of the eighteenth century, most did not have any formal office space on the courthouse grounds but kept the public records at their dwellings, many of which were miles away. With the creation of larger jury and deliberative rooms on the ground floor of courthouses, clerks and an increasing number of assistants turned these spaces into offices filled with lawbooks and collections of statutes, as well as active and obsolete court papers stored in trunks and bookpresses. Plaintiffs, defendants, witnesses, constables, and undersheriffs sought out the clerk or his deputy to file papers, check on the status of pending cases, and answer summonses. The long legal process that each case engendered as it made its way through the court docket often started in these rooms as petitioners received the paperwork needed to bring the matter to the court's attention. Besides the clerk, minor court officials may have also used periodically the room to carry out their duties. With the rise of professional lawyers, often hired on the spot, the client and his advocate needed a place to discuss their case in private and line up witnesses before they were scheduled to appear in court. Although many client and lawyer conferences took place in the arcade or a tavern, jury rooms provided a much more secluded place to work out private and complex arguments.

Justices also required the services of a private room in order to set the agenda of the court's business, discuss the issues of a particularly difficult case, and socialize at the court's rising. During the winter months a small, warm room, where the justices could retire to deal with many administrative matters, was much preferred over an unheated courtroom. Yet important county issues such as the laying of the tax levy or the placement and construction of new public buildings were discussed and decided primarily behind closed doors, and the justices thus risked the censure of irate freeholders. In the late 1670s petitioners from Surry County noted that "it has been the custome of County Courts att the laying of the levy to withdraw into a private Roome by wch meanes the poore people not knowing for what they paid their levy did allways admire how their taxes could be so high." They requested that "for the future the County levy may be laid publickly in the Court house."[59] Prudent magistrates were more circumspect and chose to deal with county expenditures in the open under the scrutiny of the public eye, but few courts chose to give up the comfort of a private meeting space.

These ancillary spaces provided the only heated, multipurpose rooms in the courthouse for private conferences and deliberations. Because they were intended for such wide and indiscriminate uses, they were finished in a very plain manner. Like their seventeenth-century predecessors, most of the later jury rooms were sheathed with planks or plastered and had simple architraves and plain chimneypieces. From the early eighteenth century through the first quarter of the nineteenth century, jurymen generally sat around a large table in the middle of the room on backless benches (fig. 86). Chairs became increasingly common during the antebellum period.

By contrast, fittings for the rooms used exclusively for justices' deliberations showed some distinction from those found in common jury rooms. Although none of these spaces was paneled, they may have contained more elaborate chimneypieces, and the seating furniture and tables were of a better quality than those supplied for the jury. Chairs replaced benches, and well-

FIGURE 86. Late eighteenth-century jury table, Chowan County courthouse, Edenton, N.C.

FIGURE 87. New England side chair, a type popular in the Chesapeake in the early and mid-eighteenth century and probably found in a number of jury rooms in Virginia courthouses

wrought tables took the place of roughly made ones (fig. 87). Richmond County justices sat in Russian leather chairs, as did the magistrates of Spotsylvania County. The Spotsylvania officials wanted a handsome oval table to go with their new seating furniture but later settled for a square black walnut one. The justices' room in Westmoreland County was furnished with twelve flag, or rush-bottomed, chairs and a large strong table so that the magistrates could dine in privacy during court sessions.[60] Such a practice was akin to the custom of holding suppers and feasts in the mayor's parlor in English town halls. Fine candlesticks, portraits, and tablecloths further distinguished some magistrates' withdrawing rooms from the plainer jury rooms. They often contained better andirons and fireplace tools while jurymen had to make do with simpler forms.

The early eighteenth century proved to be an important watershed in the development of the Virginia courtroom as many of the older haphazard arrangements were deemed inadequate and were replaced by new specialized fittings. So comprehensive was this transformation that by the 1730s the inside of the county courthouse could be mistaken for nothing else (fig. 88). It was as distinct as the interior of an Anglican church, a store, or a great planter's dining room. By the turn of the century, many courtrooms already had begun to shed their domestic and makeshift appearance in favor of interiors customized for the increasingly complex routine of court business. Magistrates borrowed a number of the furnishings and architectural details from domestic and ecclesiastical contexts as well as from English custom in order to invest their courtrooms with symbolic meaning. Commonly understood symbols such as balustrade railings and elevated platforms had been incorporated in early plans to express the concepts of restricted access and places of deferential honor. However plain, the objects in these early courtrooms were wrought with social meaning. The chairs, benches, and tables were expressions of the power and status of those who used them. To late seventeenth-century society, a canopied armchair with a cushioned seat raised on a platform and a backless bench were not merely two different forms of seating; the former was viewed as a seat of honor, the latter as a seat of commonality. Placed in the same setting, the implications were that the occupant of the simple bench was in a subservient position and as a matter of course would defer to the occupant of the chair.

With the symbolic significance of court fittings established by the late seventeenth century, the years between the erection of the first Capitol in Williamsburg from 1701 to 1705 and the construction of a significant number of brick courthouses some three decades later marked the period of greatest experimentation and elaboration in the arrangement of courtroom fittings. During this thirty-year period, the magistrates' bench was transformed and for the first time specific fittings were developed for other court officials. This intricate subdivision of the courtroom into specific places for the court participants—

FIGURE 88. Courtroom, Williamsburg–James City County courthouse, 1770–71. Fittings reconstructed 1990–91.

judges, lawyers, sheriffs, clerks, and the public—can be attributed to two basic causes. First, by the middle of the eighteenth century the routine and procedures of the Virginia legal system had become more bureaucratized. There were more rules and regulations to follow in all legal matters, and this systemization affected what transpired in the courtroom. More than ever, individuals needed the help of a lawyer to shepherd a case through the intricacies of the court system. As integral members of the court routine, lawyers required a prominent place in the courtroom to follow the court's actions. As the number of cases that went before a jury increased, the need arose for a permanent place for jurymen to sit in the courtroom as well. The makeshift furnishings of the earlier period were deemed inadequate and insufficient for the court's proper functioning.

Second, during the same period that court business and procedures were becoming more regularized, a consumer-oriented society burgeoned in England and America. Economic prosperity allowed an ever-increasing number of people to purchase a wide range of consumer goods never before available.[61] More and more objects with specialized uses appeared in an expanding market. As Cary Carson has observed, Virginians in the late seventeenth and early eighteenth centuries filled their houses with new types of ceramics, textiles, and furniture.[62] The taste for new and more specialized forms of seating furniture was carried over by county justices in equipping their courtrooms. No longer did simple backless benches suffice for magistrates' seating in the courtroom and withdrawing room. Armed chairs and paneled benches softened by cushions as well as leather-bottom side chairs took their place. Specialized furniture even appeared for the storage of papers and books. Uncompartmentalized chests and trunks gave way to bookpresses with subdivided shelves and pigeonholes. As much as the magistrate's house, the appearance of the magistrate's courtroom was a product of the new consumer society.

New design features blended with older ones to create a distinctive courtroom, one that owed as much to English precedent as to Virginia experience. Although the highest courts in Westminster Hall were but indifferently housed until the eighteenth century, English provincial and borough courts proved to be a fertile and influential design source for Virginians. The revival of political stability following the Restoration led to a significant renewal of interest in the construction and refurbishing of town halls, market houses, and shire halls across England.[63] The taproom of taverns no longer seemed a suitable venue for the execution of the law as assize and borough courts moved out of their old quarters to costly new public buildings conspicuously erected in the heart of county and market towns. By the last quarter of the seventeenth century, many of these grand English courtrooms contained fine paneled woodwork, an ornamental principal magistrate's chair surrounded by a curved bench, carved and painted coats of arms of the monarch and corporation, and a balustraded bar enclosing a raised platform. In courtrooms such as the ones in the Rochester guildhall (1687) and the Hedon town hall (1693), the paneled and curved form of the magistrates' bench focused attention upon the entire bench, not just the chief magistrate. It was meant to lend greater dignity to both the local squire who sat in the quarter sessions court and the wealthy merchant who sat on the borough court.

The ceremonial chair of the presiding justice retained its central position and distinctive features, but it now shared its place of honor with the flanking built-in bench of the associate magistrates. The paneled back and occasionally the cushioned armrests marked a significant improvement over the backless benches and forms previously allotted to the junior members of the court. The enhanced status of the elevated bench curving outward from the center chair conveyed an image of corporate power and responsibility shared by an entire class of gentry officeholders. Men did not walk into courtrooms to learn the rules of deference and the social structure of the community, because they experienced them constantly in their daily routines. What they found when they came to court was confirmation of the hierarchical nature of local, county, and royal power.

The seminal conduit for the spread of these new English design ideas was the General Court, the highest court in Virginia, housed in the new Capitol in Williamsburg. Looking to avoid the shabbiness and inconveniences of the old General Court in the Jamestown statehouse, the committee charged with devising plans for the new Capitol clearly had in mind the highly specialized arrangement of fittings found in the latest English borough and assize courts. Reviewing the progress of the courtroom's construction in April 1703, the committee directed:

> That the ffootsteps of the Generall Court house be rais'd two feet from the ffloor, and the seats of benches whereon the court is to sit rais'd a convenient highth above that
> That the circular part thereof be rais'd from the seat up to the windows
> That there be a seat rais'd one step above the bench in the middle of the circular end of the court made chairwise
> That the Queens Arm's be provided to set over it.[64]

Although novel for early eighteenth-century Virginia, these arrangements were straightforward in English terms. Two feet above the courtroom floor stood the magistrates' platform in the semicircular apse.[65] The fixed "Seats of Benches" lined the apsidal wall with the seat of the chief justice (the governor) in the center. This seat was raised a step above the platform and constructed "chairwise" with arms and a tall back capped by a pediment. Above it hung the queen's arms. The back of the semicircular bench was finished with raised paneling up to the lower edge of the three oval windows in the apse, while the rest of the courtroom was plastered.[66]

The architectural influence of the General Court fittings on public building in early eighteenth-century Virginia was profound but delayed by at least twenty years. Although some now-lost courthouse specifications may have described fittings similar to those of the General Court, the first unambiguous reference to their influence appeared in 1726 when the bench in Norfolk County noted that its new courthouse was to be modeled "in the same manner as the General Courthouse." Other examples soon followed, and they conformed to the basic design elements established in the higher courtroom. Gone was the old haphazard arrangement of assorted benches and chairs spread around a large movable justices' table. In its stead, at the far end of the courtroom opposite the entrance, the gentlemen justices sat in session upon a paneled bench raised three or four steps above the courtroom floor. To accommodate the half dozen or so attending magistrates, this long bench curved around the back wall to form a semicircle or quarter circle with steps at either end. Enclosing the platform in a curved balustrade that ran along the edge was the bar, the old symbol of judicial power. Typical of this new pattern was the 1736 Spotsylvania County courthouse with its wainscoted justices' bench raised "a proper height" above the courtroom floor with "a handsome chair for the judge of the court with a canopy over it."[67] By midcentury this design had become so standardized that specifications for new construction rarely went into as much detail as the Spotsylvania example but merely noted that the magistrates' bench should be built "in the usual manner."

Following the earlier pattern, the magistrates' platform was raised above the courtroom floor to give it the requisite dignity for such seats of honor. In a number of late seventeenth-century English courtrooms, the platform stood between 1½ and 2½ feet above the courtroom floor. At Hedon, Blandford Forum, Malmesbury, and Rochester, the magistrates' platforms stand 1½ feet, 2 feet, 2 feet, and 2⅓ feet, respectively, off the courtroom floor. The 1767 platform in the Chowan County courthouse in Edenton, North Carolina, measures 2½ feet high, while joist pockets discovered when stripping the walls in the King William County courthouse indicate that an early nineteenth-century platform was raised about the same height (fig. 89). Evidence from Virginia court

FIGURE 89. Inner apse and framing of magistrates' platform, paneling, and chief magistrate's chair, Chowan County courthouse, Edenton, N.C., 1767–68

order books display a similar range: platforms of 2 feet in the 1702 Essex, 1704 Middlesex, 1726 Norfolk, and 1791 Amelia courthouses; 2½ feet in the 1750 Richmond and 1767 Amelia courthouses; and 3 feet in the 1737 Prince George's County, Maryland, and 1740 Lancaster courthouses.[68] At the Charles City County courthouse (c. 1757), joist pockets located every 2 feet along the back wall indicate that the long demolished platform was of a similar height, about 3 feet. In 1802 Fluvanna magistrates chose a lofty 4 feet for their platform.[69] Many specifications noted only that the platform should be "raised a proper height," which suggests that the platform height during the eighteenth century varied to accommodate individual circumstances.[70]

With few exceptions, all platforms had stairs at each end of the bench. Typical were the 1726 specifications for "a pair of the stairs for the justices seat" in the Norfolk courthouse, which followed the pattern of the General Court in the Williamsburg Capitol.[71] Almost invariably, these stairs rose three or four steps along the two flanking courtroom walls, as can be seen in the c. 1755 plan for the Accomack courthouse and the 1767 plan for the Amelia courthouse (see figs. 80, 81). By the second quarter of the nineteenth century, platform steps sometimes turned from the wall and curved back toward the center of the courtroom. Access to the magistrates' platform was slightly more elaborate in the Edenton courthouse (figs. 90, 91). As in Virginia courtrooms, the stairs were located along the two side walls at the far end of the courtroom. However, after four steps rose against these walls, the railed platform turned ninety degrees and ran parallel with the back wall of the courthouse until it linked up with and followed the circumference of a short curved wall inside the apsidal projection. The narrow radius of the apse made such a design necessary (see fig. 89).

Eighteenth- and early nineteenth-century plans and what little physical evidence survives from standing buildings reflect the correlation between the curve of the platform and the configuration of the bench. The depth of the platform varied to meet two criteria. It had to be deep enough to allow passage for judges to and from their places on the bench but narrow enough to allow them to easily reach their papers, which sometimes rested on a ledge atop the railing that enclosed the platform. To ensure the seated magistrates an unobstructed view of the courtroom, balustrade heights varied between 2½ and 3 feet.

Short tilted shelves perched atop the balustrade railing survive in some English courtrooms, notably those at Hedon, Malmesbury, and Richmond (fig. 92). They were installed to hold court documents and books. Occasionally, these shelves or desks were confined to the space in front of the presiding magistrate, presumably because he was involved in most of the paperwork of the bench. Whether such shelves were a part of the magistrates' bench in colonial Virginia is unknown; at that time magistrates handled little paperwork and probably took few notes. However, by the late eighteenth and early nineteenth

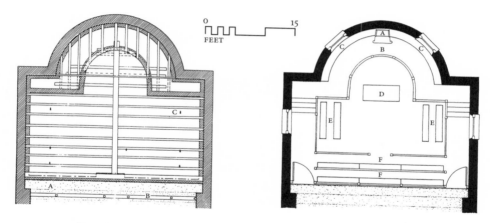

FIGURE 90. Framing and courtroom plan, Chowan County courthouse, Edenton, N.C. *Left:* framing plan. *A:* paving stones; *B:* nosing board; *C:* patched newel mortises. *Right:* courtroom fittings reconstructed. *A:* chief magistrate's chair; *B:* magistrates' platform; *C:* associate magistrates' bench; *D:* clerk's table; *E:* jury benches; *F:* lawyers' bar.

FIGURE 91. Restored elevation of the magistrates' platform, Chowan County courthouse, Edenton, N.C. Drawing by Tim Middleton.

centuries, it is possible that they were becoming more involved in the paper routine of court and perhaps required some type of shelf affixed to the balustrade. An 1806 order for the Richmond County courthouse mentions a "new strong blue or green cloth to be provided for the top railing," which might be interpreted as an indication of a balustrade shelf covered with baize as was

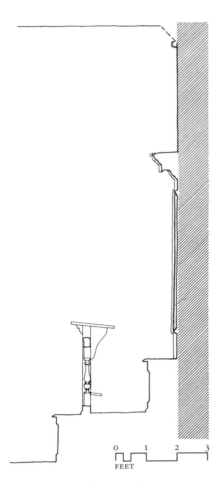

FIGURE 92. Section through magistrates' platform, town hall, Hedon, East Yorkshire, after 1693

typical of some English courts. A more oblique reference a few years later to the "cloth and lining of the banisters on front of the bench" in the neighboring Lancaster County courthouse again might connote the presence of a shelf. In 1816 Southampton County magistrates wanted alterations "made to the front of the banisters so as to make the same more convenient to write upon," but this order may refer to the lawyers' bar rather than the barrier in front of the bench.[72]

As in the General Court in the Capitol, the elevated platform of the magistrates' bench was further distinguished from the rest of the courtroom by the paneled wainscoting that covered the lower part of the wall behind the seat. The plans for the 1767 courthouse in Amelia County called for "Wainscott round the Justices seat 3½ foot high," while the building that succeeded it in 1791 was to be "Wainscoted 6 feet high . . . in a plain neat manner.[73] The wainscot in the Edenton courtroom rises nearly 4½ feet above the bench and is divided into two raised-panel bands of uneven size. As was typical of pew seating in Anglican churches in Virginia, the back edge of the bench of the associate magistrates ran across the paneling and was not specially cut to fit the gap created between the stile-and-rail molding and the raised panel. Sometimes the area below the justices' seats, that is, the lower part of the platform, was "divided wainscott fashion," as in the 1740 Lancaster County courthouse and 1791 Amelia County courthouse.[74] Yet it is clear that not every courtroom had paneled wainscoting behind the magistrates' bench. Many would have been plastered or sheathed with boards. Physical evidence from the Charles City courthouse suggests that the area was plastered with only a washboard marking the juncture of platform floor and rear wall.

The most common, if not universal, seating arrangement for county magistrates in the last two-thirds of the eighteenth century was a curved bench. Sometimes the curvature of the bench was expressed on the exterior of the building. Like the Williamsburg Capitol, a few courthouses had apsidal rear walls: the Norfolk courthouse of 1726 was perhaps the earliest to copy the Capitol, followed by ones in Lancaster County (1740), Isle of Wight (1751), Prince William (1759), and Edenton, North Carolina (1767) (fig. 93; see also figs. 90, 123). In 1809 the magistrates of Nelson County considered but rejected several plans that contained much shallower apsidal walls. However, a similar form was adopted for the rear walls of the templed courthouses built in Lunenburg (1823) and Goochland (1826) Counties (fig. 94).

Whether contained within a flat rear wall or an apsidal one, most benches formed a semicircle. Examples include the 1726 Norfolk County, 1740 Lancaster

FIGURE 93. Apse, old Isle of Wight County courthouse, Smithfield, 1750–51, restored 1960

FIGURE 94. Apse, Lunenburg County courthouse, 1823, in a 1930s photograph before additions

County, 1750 Richmond County, c. 1755 Accomack County, 1758 Loudoun County, 1759 Prince William County, 1767 Chowan County, North Carolina, and 1791 Amelia County courthouses. There were variants of this dominant shape, among them one with a flattened arc in the middle of the semicircle. With the back part of the bench running parallel with the back wall, an elongated semicircle was planned for the 1767 Amelia courthouse, and a very similar arrangement appears in the 1734 town hall in Blandford Forum, Dorset (fig. 95). By flattening out the curve, less dead space was produced in the corners by the side and back walls. The quarter circles specified for the 1766 Bedford and 1779 Rockbridge courthouses also reduced the amount of corner space (fig. 96). In the late seventeenth-century Hedon town hall and in Thomas Jefferson's 1821 plan for the Charlotte County courthouse, the bench stretched polygonally around the back of the room in three segments.[75]

In the center of this curvilinear bench sat the first in the commission or chief magistrate who presided over the proceedings. Other members of the magistracy occupied seats on either side of him according to their rank in county society and seniority in the commission. This closely observed pecking order sometimes could cause friction, as happened in Mecklenburg County in 1771 when Samuel Hopkins refused to take his place on the bench "on Account of Sir Peyton Skipwith's being put higher in the said Commission than himself."[76] Elevated a step above his fellow magistrates, the chief justice sat in a

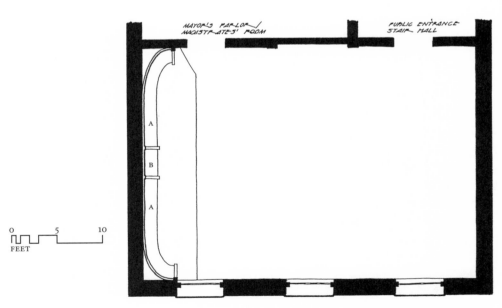

FIGURE 95. Plan, courtroom, town hall, Blandford Forum, Dorset, 1734. *A:* magistrates' bench; *B:* chief magistrate's chair.

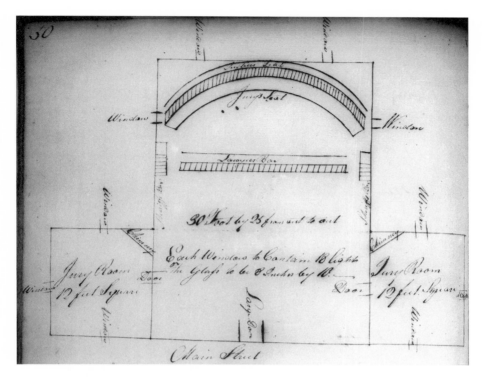

FIGURE 96. Plan, Rockbridge County courthouse, Lexington, 1779. (Rockbridge County Will Book 1, 1778–96, p. 50, The Library of Virginia)

deep-seated armchair of imposing proportions with a canopy or pediment overhead. Befitting the dignity of the office, the presiding justice's chair received the most elaborate ornamentation in order to differentiate it from the seats of his lesser associates. The justices of Spotsylvania County marked this distinction clearly by calling for "a handsom Chair for the Judge of the Court with a Canopy over it" in their new courthouse in 1736.[77] A rare example of this ceremonial chair survives in the 1767 courthouse in Edenton where, standing more than 9 feet tall at the apex of its pediment, it towers over the rest of the magistrates' bench (fig. 97). Unfortunately, none of these chairs have survived in Virginia. Chairs at Blandford Forum, Edenton, and the Speaker's chair in the House of Burgesses were probably typical of the style and degree of ornamentation of the many that were constructed in Virginia courtrooms (figs. 98, 99). Most Virginia ones probably had similar arrangements, with arms and a tall paneled or plain wooden back that was capped by a pediment or canopy. The chief magistrate's chair that was installed in the courthouse in Yorktown in the late 1780s after British troops had destroyed the earlier one during the siege of the town in 1781 fits this description. It was wainscoted, stood 7 feet high and

4 feet wide, and had two pilasters that supported the pediment, which was articulated by a dentilated cornice.[78] These seats of honor were probably deeper
than any other seats in the courtroom; the one in Edenton is nearly 2 inches
deeper than the associates' bench.

County magistrates rested their cumulative wisdom on padded cloth cush-

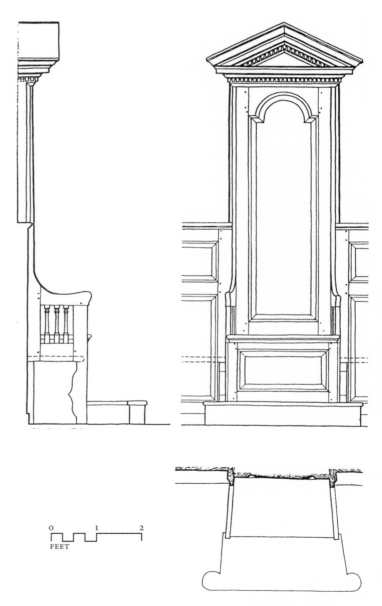

FIGURE 97. Section, elevation, and plan, chief magistrate's chair,
Chowan County courthouse, Edenton, N.C., 1768

FIGURE 98. Chief magistrate's chair, town hall, Blandford Forum, Dorset, 1734

FIGURE 99. Speaker's chair, House of Burgesses, Capitol, Williamsburg, c. 1730

ions, ancient symbols of judicial authority. In the eighteenth century cushions connoted luxury and ease and still bore associations of status and dignity. They were requisite fittings for all ceremonial chairs. A 1703 order called for all the seats in the General Court to be covered with "Green Serge and Stuft with hair." By 1722 the General Court had thirteen green cloth cushions. Cushions also provided some measure of relief from the long hours on the bench, as the magistrates of Richmond County understood when they ordered "one for the chair, six on each side . . . for the convenience of doing business." The thirteen cushions fabricated for the Princess Anne County bench cost more than £11 and were made of "11 yds. Shag or Velveret, 7 yds. Russia Drab, 7 yds. oznabrigs, 24 yds. Binding, Cordage, Thread, and Hair."[79] Although their materials and fabrication cost far less than the textiles and ornaments used to decorate pulpits and altar tables in Anglican parish churches, the cushions were nonetheless visible reminders of the privileged position of those who sat upon them.[80]

FIGURE 100. Royal coat of arms, plaster, guildhall, Beverley, East Yorkshire, 1763

Centrally placed above the chief magistrate's chair hung the arms of the monarch in whose name justice was carried out and to whom each justice reaffirmed his allegiance in the oaths repeated at the beginning of each new commission (fig. 100). A painting of the king's arms appeared in the statehouse in Jamestown in 1684.[81] The earliest reference to this symbol of authority in county courts is in the courthouse built by Robert "King" Carter for Lancaster in 1699. The 1703 specification for the General Court instructed that the arms of Queen Anne be set above the chair of the principal magistrate (the governor). This precedent was followed in the lower courts; Westmoreland court had the queen's arms "fixed in a large handsome frame . . . sett upp over the Justices seat."[82]

The question arises as to the medium employed for depicting the coat of arms. In England dozens of royal arms, dating from the reigns of Charles I to Victoria and painted on wood and canvas, carved in wood, and molded in plaster, survive in town halls and market houses. In Virginia framed paintings (whether on wood or canvas is uncertain) must have been the most prevalent medium (fig. 101). In the late 1730s painter Charles Bridges executed a number of paintings of the king's arms for county courts.[83] Although carved arms appeared in the tympanum of the west portico of the second Williamsburg Capitol, other examples are not known, but this does not preclude the possibility that such carvings existed in the county courts, particularly in the area surrounding Williamsburg where there would have been skilled woodworkers capable of such work.[84] George Cooke's 1830s painting of Patrick Henry arguing the Parson's Cause in the Hanover courtroom in 1763 depicts a carved coat of arms above the justices' bench and suggests that such carved work may have been in existence in the eighteenth century (fig. 102). No matter what medium, none of the royal arms long survived the Revolution. In some courtrooms they were replaced by the coat of arms of the United States.[85]

FIGURE 101. Royal coat of arms, George III. Painting on canvas, English, 1768.

Although the most pronounced changes occurred in the magistrates' bench, the fittings of other court participants underwent similar alterations in the early eighteenth century to conform to their legal and social status. Below the seat of honor, specialized fittings were arranged in close proximity for the benefit of the clerk, sheriff, and lawyers. Directly below the bench of the gentlemen justices, with the same curvilinear form, was a narrower unpaneled bench reserved for the occasional sitting of petit juries (fig. 103). Legal authority may have emanated from the magistrates' bench; however, the close proximity of this less ornate but similar seating arrangement indicated that the jury system provided freeholders of the county with an important instrument for exercising some power in local affairs. Courtroom etiquette dictated that subservient persons stand in the presence of those of higher authority, so during court sessions the public stood at the back of the courtroom, and lawyers at the bar rose to address the seated bench. The seated jurors were treated in the same deferential manner accorded the magistrates, confirming the notion that the jury was a respected part of the judicial system.

The placement of the jury bench below the magistrates' platform, although not unknown in English courtrooms, varied from standard practice in Britain and other American colonies. In most of those eighteenth-century courtrooms, the petit jury was accommodated in a "box" which consisted of two or three rows of benches enclosed by panels or a balustrade. Jury boxes or movable

FIGURE 102. *Patrick Henry Arguing the Parson's Cause*, at the Hanover County court-house in 1763. Painted by George Cooke, c. 1834. Though the handrail and balusters of the magistrates' platform are more appropriate to the 1830s, the general configuration of the bench follows colonial design. The clerk takes notes behind a movable wooden table and just behind him are seated members of the jury. At the bottom of the stair is a raised sheriff's box, occupied here by a number of bystanders. Patrick Henry stands in the second tier of wooden benches of the lawyers' bar, whose rough construction would have been more in keeping with early nineteenth-century designs on the frontier. The exposed ceiling joists are also anachronistic for this tidewater courtroom. Beyond the side doors, which did not exist in the Hanover courthouse at this time, stands the colonial tavern, replaced in the early nineteenth century by the present one. (Virginia Historical Society)

benches stood to one side of the justices' bench, with the jurymen seated at right angles to the justices and the rest of the courtroom. In the courtroom in Edenton, the grand and petit juries probably sat on groups of benches arranged in rows facing one another in the area in front of the clerk's table (see fig. 90). By the late eighteenth century, some courtrooms probably had tiered boxes. The 1801 rearrangement of the fittings in the courthouse in Caroline County, Maryland, probably was typical: there were to be "three benches of seats where the present Jury Boxes are. The first one Eighteen inches high—the others to be raised Eighteen inches above each other, with Bannisters at the South End." This tiered system was repeated in Columbia, Tennessee, in 1808 where the jury boxes were raised 9 and 18 inches.[86]

The fact that Virginia did not follow this pattern might be partially explained by the differences in the legal system as it evolved in the late colonial period. In Pennsylvania, for example, only one or a small handful of magistrates presided over local sessions. Thus the curved justices' bench and the jury bench that replicated it were unnecessary. Elsewhere, in some courts in Britain and other North American colonies, a large table occupied by court officials stood in the area below the magistrates' bench. The crown courtroom in the shire hall in Dorchester, Dorset, has a massive table for clerk and counsel below the magistrates' platform (fig. 104). Jury members in this late eighteenth-century courtroom were seated in a two-tiered gallery off to one side.

Whatever the reason for Virginia's divergence from standard practice, the appearance of a long jury bench that faced the courtroom closely followed the emergence of the curvilinear justices' bench in the early eighteenth century. The first references to a jury sitting in a courtroom appear in 1709 and 1710. Middlesex judges ordered a bench to be set up for the jury in front of the justices' seat, while in the following year Lancaster magistrates purchased two

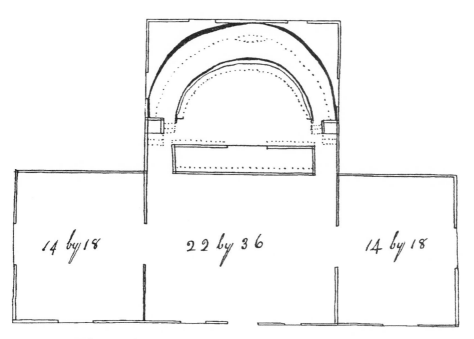

FIGURE 103. Plan, Amelia County courthouse, 1791. (Deed Book, 1789–91, Clerk's Office, Amelia County)

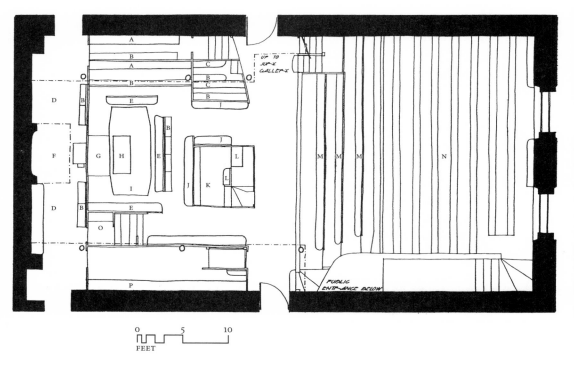

FIGURE 104. Plan, courtroom, shire hall, Dorchester, Dorset, 1797. *A:* jury bench; *B:* shelf; *C:* court officials; *D:* magistrates' bench; *E:* counsel; *F:* chief magistrate's chair; *G:* clerk; *H:* clerk's desk; *I:* table; *J:* bench; *K:* prisoner's dock; *L:* seat; *M:* seating for dignitaries; *N:* public seating; *O:* witness box; *P:* press seats.

forms (backless benches) for the jury. No doubt this marked a significant relief for jurors, who previously stood through long cases. Freestanding benches or forms were used in many Virginia courtrooms through the end of the colonial period, but more and more courts chose, as did the Lancaster court in 1740, to build a curved and fixed "seat for the jury under the justices."[87] All surviving eighteenth- and early nineteenth-century plans show this arrangement, which must have become standard by the time of the Revolution.

Although there are few specifications for jury benches in eighteenth-century court orders, the c. 1755 Accomack plan, the 1767 and 1791 Amelia plans, and the 1779 Rockbridge plan show it following the outline of the magistrates' bench (see figs. 80, 81, 96, and 103). The 1830s painting of Patrick Henry speaking before the justices in 1763 in the Hanover courthouse depicts the jurors sitting on a plain bench in front of the magistrates' platform (see fig. 102). The Accomack courtroom plan has the jury bench raised three steps above the courtroom floor and enclosed by a balustrade in front. In keeping with hierarchical elaboration of furnishings, Fluvanna magistrates specified that the jury bench in the 1802 courtroom was to be 12 inches wide, 2 inches narrower than their own bench. Jury members in the 1826 Goochland courthouse sat upon a curved bench raised a step above the courtroom floor.[88]

Just in front of the jury bench and facing the courtroom stood the table and chair of the county clerk, a man trained and appointed by the secretary of the colony in Williamsburg. Although magistrates assumed the panoply of power, clerks served as the fulcrum that kept the machinery of local government properly functioning. By the middle of the eighteenth century, mastery of the law depended as much on mastering the increasingly complex tangle of legal paperwork as understanding abstract legal principles, and few knew the bureaucratic process better than the county clerk. As the only professionally trained official of the county court, the clerk exercised broad discretionary powers, advising the amateur members of the bench on legal procedures and, to a certain extent, controlling the schedule and flow of business that came to the court's attention. In session, the clerk's chief responsibilities included the swearing of witnesses, presenting papers relevant to each case on the docket, and taking minutes of the court's proceedings. The central location of the clerk within the curved space created by the justices' platform allowed him to be cognizant of the proceedings from the bench, sheriff's box, and lawyers' bar.

The few moments of drama that may have enlivened colonial court cases played themselves out in front of the clerk's table. It was here that prisoners, often bound in manacles and closely watched by a deputy sheriff or constable, stood to be examined by the magistrates, who quizzed them on their movements and motives. Making their way through the crowd that gathered at the back of the courtroom, prisoners and their guards passed through the gates separating the public from court officials, squeezed around the lawyers' bar, and shuffled before the table where the clerk would carefully note their testimony. After deliberations of a jury or the magistrates, prisoners heard their fate pronounced standing before the clerk. Court officers may have branded convicted slaves with a hot iron while at the table. Witnesses, plaintiffs, and defendants in civil cases also would come before the clerk to swear their oaths, offer their versions of events of particular cases, and respond to the questions posed by members of the bench. Eventually, specially designated spaces would be created in nineteenth-century courtrooms in Virginia for prisoners and witnesses to follow proceedings and present their evidence.

Most eighteenth-century references to the clerk's table fail to be very specific about its size or fittings. It is clear from a 1735 order for Prince George's County, Maryland, the 1821 Jefferson courthouse plan, and the illustration of the Hanover courtroom that the clerk was centered directly below the justices and in front of the jury bench.[89] This position corresponds to numerous eighteenth-century English plans as well (figs. 105, 106). It also seems likely that

FIGURE 105. Clerks at a cloth-covered table. Detail from *Hudibras and the Lawyer*, by William Hogarth, 1726.

from the 1750s onward a large percentage of Virginia clerks' tables were enclosed on the front, sides, and occasionally the back by a low balustraded railing. The c. 1755 plan for Accomack courthouse depicts a 5-by-11-foot space for the clerk enclosed by a railing on all four sides (see fig. 80). In the 1773 reference to the Goochland clerk's table, the banisters were to stand 6 inches above the surface of the table. This visual barrier, as well as others, may have been just a rail around the top edge of the table, not reaching all the way down to the floor.[90] Clerks in some English courtrooms shared a large table with counsel and other court officials. The table in the crown courtroom in the Dorchester shire hall measures 5 by 10 feet with benches on three sides for court participants and a chair for the clerk on the side fronting the justices' bench. In Virginia there was a clear separation between clerks and lawyers. Clerks sat alone or with their deputies at a table that stood several feet away from the benches provided for lawyers and litigants.

The earliest reference to accommodations for a sheriff sheds little light on the nature of the seating or its location. In 1704 the Middlesex County court directed that its new courtroom be made with a "convenient place for the sheriff."[91] Not until thirty years later do the next references appear in Virginia court books, and these only cryptically mention benches for the sheriff and his deputies and provide no information about their placement.[92] Whatever the previous arrangements, a significant change had taken place by the 1740s with the introduction of a sheriff's box, an enclosed elevated platform that stood at or near the foot of the steps leading to the magistrates' bench and roughly parallel to the clerk's table. The position of the sheriff's box was devised to allow the court's chief executive officer to perform his various courtroom duties. The proximity of the box to the bench and clerk enabled a stream of papers to flow in a triangular route from sheriff to clerk to magistrates and back again. Its location along the side wall near the gate of the lawyer's bar made it possible for the sheriff to prohibit unauthorized persons from entering into the area within the bar. Advantageously perched on his platform, he could monitor the be-

havior of the public and deal with anyone who disrupted the orderly decorum of
the courtroom. In many respects similar
to a simplified pulpit, the sheriff's box was
a small cubicle, perhaps 3 by 4 feet in di-
mension, ornamented with raised paneling. The only illustration of a sheriff's box
appears in George Cooke's 1830s painting
of the Hanover courtroom in 1763, which
shows a paneled enclosure strikingly similar to the reading desks in the pulpits at
Christ Church in Lancaster County and
Aquia Church in Stafford County. Because
the sheriff dealt with many court papers,
his box had a tilted shelf for their accommodation. The sheriff sat either on a built-
in bench or, if space was sufficient, in a
side chair.

The first extant mention of such an arrangement is in a 1744 Spotsylvania record, but that order noted that it was
"Usuall in Courthouses," which implies a
widespread acceptance by that time.[93]
Certainly after midcentury, the sheriff's
box had become a standard fitting, for no
other type of furnishings for this officer

FIGURE 106. Clerks at a table below
the magistrates, Justice Hall in the
Old Bailey. Detail, engraving,
London, 1794. (Guildhall Library,
Corporation of London)

appears in Virginia records through the middle of the nineteenth century.
Some courtrooms had only one box for the sheriff, but most had another at the
opposite end of the magistrates' platform that was used by the undersheriff or
court crier to announce each case as it came before the court. Excavation of the
1759 Prince William County courthouse revealed that a 9-by-6-foot space was
provided on each side for a sheriff's box at the juncture of the apsidal justices'
platform and the courtroom (see figs. 126, 127). They are also shown in this
same position in the 1779 Rockbridge County plan, the 1791 Amelia County
plan, and three of the 1809 Nelson County plans (see figs. 96, 103, 118). Befitting
his station, the sheriff sat at the same height as his former colleagues on the
bench. In 1789 the reconstructed courtroom in Yorktown had "two boxes for
the Sherifs to sett in wainscoted with three Steps to Each," implying that there
were raised boxes for the sheriff and undersheriff that matched the height and
paneling of the justices' bench.[94] The 1791 Amelia plan shows a similar arrange-

ment with the two boxes raised three steps, the same number as the magistrates' platform.[95] The sheriffs' boxes in the 1802 Fluvanna courtroom were to stand 4 feet in height and be 3 feet square with "convenient writing boards to each & Seats."[96] At the 1832 Fluvanna courthouse, a ledge constructed on the landing of the stairs leading to the upper-story jury rooms may indicate an unusual but useful position for a seat occupied by a deputy sheriff, constable, or court crier to oversee the court's proceedings (fig. 107).

Stretching across the center of the courtroom and separating public space from the area reserved for court officials, the lawyers' bar provided seating for attorneys and perhaps litigants. Consisting of one or two long rows of benches

FIGURE 107. Shelf on staircase for court official, Fluvanna County courthouse, Palmyra, 1832

enclosed by a balustrade, it stood in the noisy courtroom within easy earshot of the magistrates' platform. Small ledges or shelves were built in front of the narrow benches to give the lawyers a place to write or hold their papers. Except for an occasional seat reserved for the king's attorney, the bar was not subdivided or arranged with specific seats for plaintiffs, defendants, or lawyers, forcing members of the legal fraternity to crowd together on very hard and narrow benches. The division of the bar into separate spheres for plaintiffs and defendants and their representatives had not evolved. As legal historian John Langbein has demonstrated, the adversarial system of criminal trials with cross-examination of witnesses and the accused led by opposing lawyers did not reach maturity in the Anglo-American courtroom until the second half of the eighteenth century.[97] Until then, Virginia courtrooms had no need for the division of the lawyers' bar into separate physical spaces that represented competing sides. Throughout the colonial period the magistrates took the lead in the conduct of trials by examining witnesses, plaintiffs, and defendants and commenting on their testimony as it was given.

Some formal or even unwritten rule of seating precedent may have been followed by the attorneys. Such was the case in the early nineteenth century in the superior court of sessions and common pleas in the Charleston, South Carolina, courthouse where "the inner bench of the court [was to] be reserved for the elder practitioners of the bar, the second bench to be occupied by the younger practitioners, and the outer bench by the students at law. The gentlemen of the bar to take their seats according to seniority of the dates of their respective admissions."[98] Lawyers who appeared before the General Court in Williamsburg may have followed a similar custom, but whether this deferential formality extended to the county courts is unknown. Whatever the practice, room was tight. A late eighteenth-century attorney complained to the justices of Lunenburg County about the cramped accommodations that he and his colleagues suffered in their court. While magistrates "loll upon the bench," lawyers were

> Confin'd within a compass three yards long,
> We scarce can stand amidst the brawling throng,
> Wedg'd in by shoulders, outstretch'd arms and knees,
> Each poor Attorney scarce can fairly squeeze
> His carcase to a seat within the bar,
> Or stir his joints, so crouded is he there.[99]

The poem proceeds to gently mock the parsimony of the justices in a suppliant tone of sarcasm, underscoring the fact that through the latter half of the eighteenth century the relationship between the legal profession and county magistracy was still an adversarial one as it had been in the previous century. Veteran magistrate Landon Carter showed little respect for the lawyers who appeared before him in the Richmond County court (fig. 108). After one particularly exasperating session, he declared: "Every Lawyer at the bar seemed quite ignorant how he was engaged in the causes, as they were called, what had been done in them, or upon what point they turned. This was one of the evils of delay that I pointed out to them and they have shown not the least tendency to amend it." As Carter's splenetic diary entry suggests and as historian A. G. Roeber has argued, justices and lawyers tussled over many issues in their struggle to define the nature of legal authority. For the most part, late colonial magistrates still received their legal training on the job. Many started as young men appointed to the commission of peace and learned from watching their elders deal with a variety of questions that arose before the bench. Much lamented upon his death in 1768, longtime magistrate Anthony Walke of Princess Anne County had little formal training for his position but acted "in a publick character" that was "animated by the spirit of an old Roman." He filled his position upon the bench "with a suitable dignity." His obituary noted that "from a slender education, such as a little reading and writing as the times could then afford, he made a wonderful proficiency in true and solid knowledge greatly preferable to a knowledge of words and language."[100] Virginians still valued strength of character over formal education.

By the late colonial period, some magistrates had the opportunity to read legal treatises; others studied manuals, including one by New Kent County justice George Webb, whose book *The Office and Authority of a Justice of Peace* (1736) offered practical advice to magistrates (fig. 109). He noted that "the far greatest Part of our Inhabitants are unfurnish'd with" scholarly texts "or diverted from Reading them, by the necessary Affairs of their Plantations, and by the innocent Pleasures of Country Life," and thus he offered a guide that stressed the nontheoretical side of the law. It was this kind of legal education that Landon Carter experienced in his many years on the bench in Richmond County. When homespun practicality came up against the kind of legal knowledge acquired by

FIGURE 108. Landon Carter (1710–1778) of Sabine Hall, justice of the peace, Richmond County, 1734–78. (Courtesy of Beverley R. Wellford of Sabine Hall)

professional lawyers, it often created tension. In 1772 lawyer Richard Parker, who served as the king's attorney for the county, easily outwitted Carter on several points of law, much to the frustration of the gentleman justice from Sabine Hall. No magistrate came to Carter's rescue. Believing that the court showed more respect for the lawyer than for himself, Carter vowed to quit the bench for good and confided in his diary that he was "the most insulted of any man" in the county.[101]

The tensions inherent in the relation between the bench and the bar naturally found their way into the courtroom fittings. The absence of any reference to seats in the courtroom for lawyers in the seventeenth century only emphasized the ambivalent position that they held for so long in the Virginia legal system. After gaining a tenuous foothold in the early years, more and more men found the law a lucrative means of making a living. As an English traveler in the Chesapeake observed in 1746 that "the Lawyers have an excellent Time here, and if a Man is a clever Fellow, that Way, 'tis sure Step to an Estate." Some lawyers such as John Mercer were accepted into the ranks of the planter elite and counted many members of the bench as their friends. More and more planters also found that practicing law was a useful means of supplementing their incomes, so that the distinction

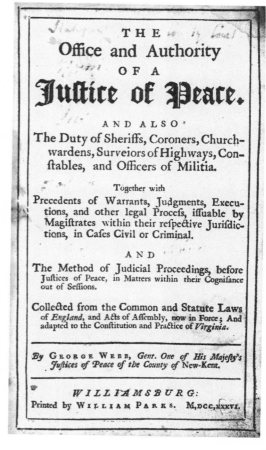

FIGURE 109. Frontispiece, George Webb, *The Office and Authority of a Justice of Peace* (Williamsburg, Va., 1736)

between planter and lawyer was sometimes muted as in the case of Thomas Jefferson. Legal education and the licensing of lawyers slowly improved the level of advocacy in the courts. From the 1670s through the Revolution, as many as sixty Virginians studied law at the Inns of Court in London, but this ancient institution provided almost no practical education, and few colonists who enrolled there argued regularly in the lower courts of Virginia. Far more lawyers gained their legal instruction by more informal means. Most learned by serving as apprentices with practicing lawyers or clerks and by observation in the courtroom.[102] Lawyers and magistrates also had access to a growing body of treatises on the law that were imported into Virginia or published in Williamsburg after a printing press was established in the early 1730s. Whether English trained or locally educated, a few professional lawyers in the late colonial period were even selected to the bench, bringing with them a dose of much-needed professionalism.

With improved fortunes came improved seating. Through the first half of the eighteenth century, lawyers occupied a bench located in front of the clerk's table. By the 1740s and 1750s many courtrooms had a second bar installed behind this bench. The interposition of this additional barrier between public space and the magistrates' bench acknowledged the acceptance and value of lawyers in the Virginia legal system. Whereas in early courtrooms the public was separated from the justices by a single balustrade, the erection of a second one meant that face-to-face proceedings were restricted to only a few. This bar helped prevent what was now seen as the unwanted intrusion of the public in the space immediately in front of the clerk, jury, and magistrates and confirmed the privilege of certified lawyers to pass freely into the area reserved for court officials.

The introduction of the second bar underscores the fact that the public was more dependent than ever on lawyers. Most litigants now appeared before the bench only through the intermediary services of a lawyer. Assured of their entrenched place in the legal system, attorneys demanded and frequently received more elaborate benches as well as shelves or ledges to hold their books and papers. In 1737 Essex County magistrates ordered the construction of "a new barr for the attorneys at this Court within the barr that is now built with a place for them to write upon with six drawers." The 1779 Rockbridge County courthouse plan shows a long bench for the attorneys stretching across the full width of the courtroom with only a narrow space at each end separating it from the two parallel sheriffs' boxes (see fig. 96). This may have been similar to the lawyers' bench in the late eighteenth-century courtroom in York County. Lawyers there had a "Righting Desk at the Bar 15 feet & half Long" to hold their papers. The earlier 1767 Amelia County plan doubled the space for attorneys by providing two rows of benches, each one balustraded along its back (see fig. 81). A more complex arrangement appears in the 1791 Amelia plan where the lawyers' bar consists of two rows of benches, the back one being enclosed on the side and front by a balustrade (see fig. 103). The front row is divided in half in the center, allowing access to the enclosed and undivided back bench. In order to control access to the upper end of the courtroom, Virginia magistrates had gates built at the end of the lawyers' bar. In 1791 Amelia specifications called for "banistered Gates from the sheriffs desks to lawyers bar."[103] Thus access was restricted to two small spaces between the ends of the attorneys' bars and the two sheriffs' boxes and made supervision by the sheriff and undersheriff fairly easy.

Despite improvements and the introduction of specialized fittings, there was still little doubt about the source of courtroom authority. In the event of a strong confrontation between bench and bar, the fittings would suggest that the magistrates still maintained control of the court. The expansive judicial platform stood well above the floor-bound confinement of the lawyers' bar. The cushioned magistrates' bench itself was two or more inches deeper than the attorneys' seats. Cramped narrow seats did little to encourage prolonged occupancy of the bar. Not until the beginning of the nineteenth century did the balance of comfort become more equitable. The new fittings constructed in an 1805 addition to the Chesterfield courthouse contained a two-tiered lawyers' bar with four rows of generously spaced benches (fig. 110). Similarly, two decades later the curved three-tiered bar of the new Goochland courtroom stood well off the floor but not quite as high as the bench. However, it was a spacious affair, occupying more space than the magistrates' platform.[104] As the

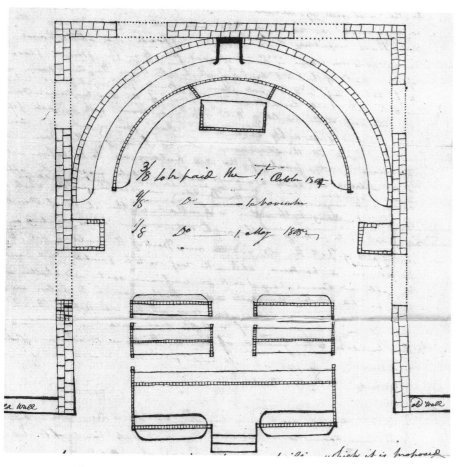

FIGURE 110. Plan, courtroom addition, Chesterfield County courthouse, 1805. (Chesterfield County, Miscellaneous Records, 1805–42, May 15, 1805, The Library of Virginia)

power of the profession expanded in the first quarter of the nineteenth century, lawyers began to see a substantial improvement in their accommodations in most Virginia courtrooms.

Once established in the second quarter of the eighteenth century, the fittings of Virginia courtrooms changed slowly over the next century. Occasionally in the antebellum period, some courts added prisoner boxes and witness stands. Horseshoe-shaped witness stands came into fashion in much of the country in the 1830s, and these portable balustrades may have found their way into Virginia courtrooms sometime afterward.[105] In 1861 a visitor to Fairfax County courtroom reported the presence of an octagonal witness box entered through a gate located near the justices' bench.[106] The plans for Madison County's new courthouse in 1829 specified the fabrication of a criminal box enclosed with turned balusters located at the back of the lawyers' bar.[107] The design for the first Warren County courthouse of 1836 contained a prisoner's box located on one side of the courtroom next to the jury bench. An improvement upon the Madison plan, this position was thought to be the "most convenient and secure; sufficiently near the Court and Jury to make their observations; opposite the clerk and adjacent to the Trial table . . . where the counsel for the prisoners" sat.[108]

These fixed courtroom arrangements with their implicit emphasis on the permanence and prestige of the magistracy were apt expressions of the stability of a social order dominated by a small and powerful set of gentry families. This oligarchy served the county out of a sense of civic responsibility and at the same time gained an important imprimatur of status. Their status was acknowledged and reaffirmed each month as they climbed the steps of the elevated bench to occupy the seats of honor. As long as the squirearchy collectively retained jurisdiction over local affairs, there were few incentives to modify these fittings.

With their specialized and symbolic fittings, the implied judicial power and the deferential social order that these courtrooms embodied also made them targets for those who questioned the fairness or even the legitimacy of the legal system. The disgruntled had the disturbing tendency to torch buildings when the scales of justice tipped in the wrong direction. Less destructive but no less invidious forms of dissent also were devised. In "an Insult of the most Extravagant Nature," someone spread tar and dung upon the magistrates' bench in Richmond County in March 1771. A few years earlier the justices of Loudoun County were outraged to discover that "some evil minded person . . . maliciously and wickedly intending to contemn the court and the Dignity thereof have in manifest violation of the laws and contrary to the peace and good rule of government, lately set up in the courthouse in the chair of the judge . . . a dead and stinking hog with a most scandalous libel in his mouth greatly reflecting on the said court and the officers thereof."[109] Though rising little above such petty but symbolic nuisances, opposition to judicial authority did occasionally strike at any complacency that may have been felt by those who sat in the cushioned seats above the courtroom floor.

The Demise of Traditional Arrangements

Not until the middle of the nineteenth century when the power of the justices of the peace was being slowly curbed by democratic reforms did any noticeable change occur in the arrangement or shape of the magistrates' bench. Whether stemming from an alteration in the system of selecting justices or from a modification in perceptions of comfort and taste, the old monolithic bench was literally broken up in some counties in favor of chairs. The 1849 plans for the new Amelia County courthouse called for a space of 16 feet be left in the center of the bench in order to fit armchairs for the four or five regular justices. Goochland County remodeled its bench in 1857 by removing a sizable section in the center of the apsidal bench in order to install four armchairs. Long-suffering lawyers also benefited from changing standards of comfort, bursting out of their confinement on hard wooden benches within constricted balustraded pens. As early as 1836 those who argued cases in the new Warren County courthouse in Front Royal sat behind a 7-by-3-foot "trial table" in individual chairs, a major concession achieved no doubt by the rising status of lawyers in antebellum Virginia.[110] The era of adversarial lawyers' tables was nearly at hand.

Yet the most drastic transformations in Virginia courtrooms came only after the Civil War when the 1869 Underwood Constitution abolished the system of multiple magistrates in lower courts in favor of a single justice. With ratification of this new constitution, the curved bench stretching across the back wall was rendered superfluous. Boards of county supervisors, which became responsible for the maintenance of the county courthouses, ordered the removal of justices' benches and implemented other improvements to conform to a changed legal system. Over the course of the next decade, county after county came to terms with its outmoded courtroom arrangements. Sometimes the work was slight; at other times the alterations were heavy-handed, as was the case in Richmond County. There the court decided in 1877 to rebuild the interior of Landon Carter's exquisitely quirky double-arcaded courthouse built in 1750. Before the "ancient shape and appearance" of the building was obliterated "by the progressive wants of those who used" it, T. Buckler Ghequiere, a Baltimore architect hired by the court to devise a new courtroom within the old shell, felt compelled to "give the world some record of" the dilapidated courthouse so that it would "not be clean forgot." He drew a plan and elevation of the building and carefully described the plastered blind arches of the side walls and

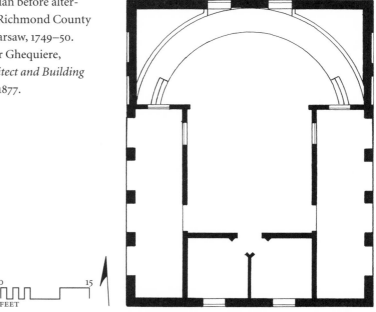

FIGURE 111. Plan before alterations in 1877, Richmond County courthouse, Warsaw, 1749–50. After T. Buckler Ghequiere, *American Architect and Building News*, June 23, 1877.

0   15
FEET

FIGURE 112. Richmond County courthouse, Warsaw

arcade openings, the size and placement of windows, the king-post roof, and the arrangement of the "peculiar" courtroom fittings, including the curved magistrates' bench (fig. 111). Within weeks, all of this was swept away as the exterior walls were raised a few feet in height, the arcade openings enclosed, internal walls removed, and the courtroom was enlarged and reconfigured to meet modern needs (fig. 112). With these dramatic changes wrought in concrete, granite, and factory-produced fittings, the architectural embodiment of a legal tradition, which had spanned more than a century and a quarter, came to an end.[111] Other courts followed the Richmond County example in removing eighteenth-century courtroom fittings and trim. So thorough were the renovations to Virginia's early courtrooms over the next few decades that by the end of the twentieth century little remained except occasional ghost marks of long-removed fittings faintly etched on plaster walls.

4

THE PUBLIC BUILDING PROCESS
IN EARLY VIRGINIA

Introduction

ARCHITECTURAL DESIGN IN EARLY Virginia was a collective endeavor. The planning and construction of public buildings drew a variety of people into a process that developed over many years of experimentation. The parts customarily played by architects, clients, building committees, contractors, and workmen in modern construction were far different in colonial America where the division of responsibilities into discrete and well-defined roles had barely begun. The notion that an architect had the power or even the desire to control each stage of the design process and every component in the construction of a public structure was alien to eighteenth-century Virginians. Design responsibilities were far more diffuse than in modern practice. A modern architect's stamp on working drawings signals the end of the design stage and serves as the blueprint for construction, a distinction that colonial Virginians would have found incomprehensible.

The design and construction of eighteenth-century buildings proceeded in a more ad hoc fashion than modern practices. Most public structures could claim to have a host of creators ranging from gentlemen justices to slave artisans. From the initial decision to build to installation of the last fittings, many individuals had the opportunity and authority to shape general form as well as small details. Design emanated from corporate committees consultations, whose members kept one eye warily on a tight public purse, and continued through a series of compromises and on-site alterations made by the undertaker and his clients and by craftsmen working out structural and finish details.

Building in this pragmatic fashion worked as long as everyone concerned understood and accepted the nature and limits of the local building tradition. Small budgets and mimetic design impulses were common. The conservatism inherent in the design process ensured that immediate and significant change occurred mainly through the intervention of strong-willed personalities or in response to unusual circumstances. In the long run, however, public building did respond to broader changes in colonial society. By the time of the Revolution, Virginians lived in a wealthier and more complex society than that of a century earlier. Because increased wealth supported a greater range of trade specialties, justices could build structures that surpassed simple functional requirements. This situation in turn promoted the rise of entrepreneurial contractors capable of designing and overseeing the construction of sophisticated buildings. At the same time, the growing specialization and standardization of legal procedures coupled with greater concern for symbolic civic features shaped the development of public structures.

The Decision to Build

Initiatives to erect new courthouses, prisons, clerks' offices, and other public structures emanated from the county justices. In contrast to New England, where town freeholders decided at meetings whether to build or repair public structures, Virginia justices of the peace generally acted without consultation in determining whether county business required new buildings.[1] Seventeenth-century magistrates occasionally solicited the views of the public as to whether a new structure was needed, particularly if the cost of such an endeavor might give rise to ill feelings about "burthensome" taxation. In 1677 the benches in both Eastern Shore counties of Accomack and Northampton thought it sensible to put the question of building new courthouses to the freeholders in their respective jurisdictions. Magistrates in the next century showed less regard for the people's concern, only taking into consideration the wishes of the public when pressured to do so by the governor and council who, in turn, had received petitions from disgruntled freeholders. In 1735, for example, inhabitants of the northwestern end of Hanover County went over the heads of their local justices and appealed to the council to stop the erection of a new courthouse, an action that delayed construction for at least two years.[2]

Outside opposition was much easier to deal with than dissension from within the magisterial ranks. A small group of justices might propose the construction of a new building during a monthly meeting, but the decision to build or make substantial alterations and repairs to existing ones was made only after all members of the commission had an opportunity to meet and discuss the matter. If disputes arose among various factions on the bench, a final decision might be postponed for months or even years as justices vacillated or ignored the issue. Some magistrates balked at the necessity of spending money on new construction, while others insisted that justice was shabbily served in old and decrepit structures. Like citizens who felt that their concerns were inadequately considered, judicial factions occasionally presented their respective cases to the governor and council who then intervened to break the impasse.

Magistrates decided to build for a number of reasons. The formation of a new county created the immediate need for a prison and a court. A shift in population exerted pressure to move the courthouse to a more convenient location, or the rearrangement of county boundaries often rendered buildings obsolete and required the construction of new ones. Most public buildings suffered tremendous wear through hard use or neglect, and fires, feloniously set or accidentally ignited, took their toll on flimsy wooden structures. Some courts outgrew earlier, smaller structures, while others simply desired new brick buildings that would lend greater dignity to the proceedings of the magistrates or provide greater security against imaginative criminals.

Although the abuse suffered by most courthouses and prisons made their repair a constant source of concern, the construction of an entirely new building was not a common occurrence. For most magistrates it was a situation that might arise perhaps only once or twice in their long years on the bench. Many of the brick courthouses erected in tidewater counties in the second and third quarters of the eighteenth century lasted for more than a century. The arcaded, T-shaped masonry buildings constructed by Hanover, King William, and Charles City Counties suited court purposes so perfectly that they continued to be used well into the twentieth century (see figs. 20, 46, 71). Prisons, which were generally built of wood, survived for much shorter periods. Solidly constructed log and frame buildings sometimes lasted twenty-five to thirty years before their fabric wore out. However, not all counties chose to build well and therefore faced the task of new construction or major repairs more frequently. Between 1704 and 1770 Essex County erected at least eight flimsy framed structures for the incarceration of prisoners and debtors.[3]

Unlike the cycles of parish church construction, where intense periods of building seemed to have occurred every thirty years, particularly in the 1730s and 1760s, no such pattern can be detected in the erection of courthouses and prisons during the colonial period.[4] The loss of so many late seventeenth- and early eighteenth-century county court order books makes it difficult to determine the overall rate of construction for this period, but surviving documentary evidence suggests a continuum of building activity. After an initial spurt of brick courthouses constructed in the 1720s and 1730s, the erection of permanent structures grew steadily, but no decade outpaced another. The addition of new counties in the piedmont and west and the carving up of older ones in the tidewater set in motion a continuous wave of building across the colony. From 1750 to 1770 the General Assembly created twenty-six new counties, each of them in need of facilities in which to hold court and incarcerate prisoners. During this period craftsmen in different part of the colony started work on three to seven new public buildings per year (table 1). With the political crisis of the 1770s, this level of activity tailed off. Although the Revolution retarded building to some degree, as many courts closed their doors for months or years, a number of counties continued to build throughout the war. Cumberland,

TABLE 1   Public building projects at five-year intervals

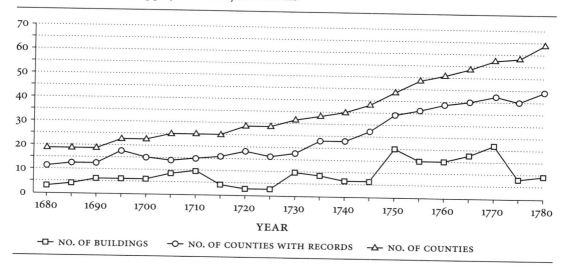

Halifax, Lunenburg, Pittsylvania, Rockbridge, and Spotsylvania Counties all undertook the construction of new courthouses during this period.[5]

Elsewhere, the turbulent military campaigns of 1780–81 proved disastrous to many courthouse grounds. The Frederick County militia housed prisoners of war in their courthouse, much to its detriment; local authorities transformed the Albemarle County courthouse into a hospital; while the James City County courthouse on Market Square in Williamsburg served briefly as a barracks for French troops. The 1750 brick courthouse in Smithfield was repeatedly "damaged by the enemy during their several invasions." The citizens of Chesterfield County saw their new public buildings seized by the militia and used for the storage of matériel for two years, and finally torched by enemy patrols in April 1781 (fig. 113). At Yorktown, the courthouse was systematically damaged, first by English troops who ripped out the wooden furnishings to serve as firewood and later by a barrage of American and French artillery fire.[6] Those buildings that did not suffer directly from military activities deteriorated due to neglect as public moneys, previously spent to maintain them, were siphoned off to sustain the local militia. A spurt of building occurred in the mid-1780s in response to the previous years of neglect and devastation and the addition of several new counties.

Design

Once magistrates decided to build, they immediately took it upon themselves to work out the basic building plans and construction arrangements. Most gentlemen justices not only found it within their purview to devise their

FIGURE 113. Chesterfield County courthouse, c. 1749; repaired after 1781; wing added 1805; demolished 1917. (Valentine Richmond History Center)

own plans, drawings, and specifications for new county buildings but generally considered themselves competent to assess all but the most technical aspects of building. After all, most of them had some experience in supervising the construction of farm buildings on their own plantations and in the erection of churches and chapels in their parishes. A few even had built themselves impressive homes. A visitor to Mount Vernon observed that George Washington "directs everything in the building way condescending even to measure the things himself, that all may be perfectly uniform."[7] A small number of magistrates, such as Larkin Chew of Spotsylvania, Lewis Delony of Lunenburg, Samuel Eskridge of Northumberland, James Skelton of Hanover, and William Walker of Stafford, had been trained as craftsmen and spent much of their lives supervising the construction of buildings.

Through practical management of their estates, widespread travel, education, and contact with colonial officials in Williamsburg, Virginia justices had various understandings of building practices, building precedents, and architectural principles. However, very few of them could be considered "gentlemen architects" in the sense that they had a command of architectural skills gained by practice or a solid understanding of contemporary trends in English and European architecture. The term implies that there was a group of men versed in architectural theory who could discriminate between correct taste and architectural gaucherie. Although some members of the gentry had clear aesthetic preferences, these were seldom rooted in a coherent body of architectural principles. If such a group of men existed within the Virginia gentry, then Thomas Jefferson came closest to meeting this ideal, but his was a rather solitary position.

Although some eighteenth-century planters and merchants owned a handful of costly English, French, and Italian architectural books, handsomely bound and generously illustrated with fine line engravings, few mined these treatises as guides for building. The very few houses that can be directly related to designs published in architectural books include Battersea in Petersburg, Brandon in Prince George County, Mount Airy in Richmond County, and Jefferson's first Monticello in Albemarle County. Not surprisingly, all of these buildings date from the third quarter of the eighteenth century, a period when English and European architectural books became more accessible through booksellers in Williamsburg and other Virginia towns and appear in increasing numbers in gentry inventories. Even then, Virginians plumbed these works for showpiece features such as staircases, mantels, and frontispieces rather than for overall plans of buildings.[8] They may have consulted the more practical and cheaper publications written for builders by William Salmon, William Halfpenny, and Batty Langley for advice on estimating building costs and workmen's wages or the design of small details, but rarely did they browse them like catalogs in search of appropriate plans and elevations. One such example of the practical use Virginia planters made of English architectural books can be found in a letter from John Carter to his brother Charles, who was wrestling with the question of how much to pay his painters and stoneworkers. He advised Charles to refer to the *Builder's Dictionary* as to "the purpose of your charge to the painter," although he expressed doubts about "how much soever you may Rely on the authority of this or the other author."[9] Most of these books, however, were in the possession of professional builders, not planters. Members of the gentry may have understood, for example, the theory of proportion as the basis for the architectural orders, but such knowledge seldom found its way into records or discussions of the construction of public structures. Most building designs were not static but subject to constant changes before they reached their final appearance. When eighteenth-century builders in the colony used terms such as *proportional* or *suitable,* they employed them to refer to smaller standard dimensioning systems used for such items as window glass, bricks, moldings, doors, and windows. The architectural education gained through imported treatises more closely resembled antiquarian scholarship than practical application. It was simply one small part of the curriculum of a gentleman's classical education.

Sometimes, Virginians combined these disparate threads of architectural knowledge in curious ways. Landon Carter, the son of Robert "King" Carter, well-read in the classics, proud owner of Sabine Hall, and longtime member of the Richmond County bench, fancied himself perfectly suited for designing and overseeing the construction of private and public buildings (see fig. 108). His keen if not neurotic concern for plantation and public affairs involved him in many building activities, from overseeing the repair of mud-walled tobacco houses to designing a "Roman arch" for the interior of the Richmond County courthouse, which he undertook to build in 1749. For the construction of a wooden bridge over the Rappahannock River undertaken by local carpenter John Redman, Carter supplied the builder with his version of Julius Caesar's bridge across the Rhine (which had been attributed mistakenly to the Roman architect Vitruvius), a precedent he thought entirely appropriate for the situation. Much to his annoyance, Carter's classical allusion seems to have been mistranslated by the builder who understood little about the precedent but a lot about the more mundane type of bridge construction practiced in the Arcadian world of Richmond County.[10]

The design process for county buildings began with discussions among the magistrates about the overall size, shape, materials, and finish of a proposed structure. When there was consensus, the court sitting en masse might settle quickly on a design and general specifications. Thus after their wooden prison burned, Charles City County magistrates simply ordered the construction of a new building exactly like the old one.[11]

Some courts decided to assign the responsibility of developing the design of a building to an individual justice, the sheriff, or the county clerk. Local political considerations probably influenced some courts, while others recognized the particular design abilities of individuals. In 1777 the Chesterfield court delegated Justice Thomas Worsham to devise a plan for a prison, which he later returned to the court for its approval.[12] A few justices volunteered their own designs, motivated partly by civic responsibility but more often by the lure of profit from undertaking the construction.

Most courts, however, took a longer route by selecting three to five of its members to serve as a building committee. The bench authorized the committee to develop a "suitable and convenient" plan and have it ready for its approbation within a short period, usually by the time of the next session. Commissions often had considerable latitude, as when the Charlotte County court charged the committee members to let the building of a prison "in such manner as they . . . may think necessary." Powhatan County magistrates ordered construction of a courthouse "of the size, plan, & dimensions of Buckingham Court House" but trusted the building committee members to change the plan if they thought it advisable.[13]

The composition of building committees varied from county to county. Some members were chosen because they were senior magistrates or had a reputation for responsibility, and still others for their special knowledge of building. Thomas Jefferson may have been selected to serve on the Albemarle County building committee for a prison in 1771 because of his developing interest in architecture.[14]

Sitting in session in a heated jury room or perhaps in the convivial atmosphere of a private dining room in a courthouse tavern, the county magistrates, either collectively or as a building committee, proposed, discussed, and agreed upon the basic components of each new building. Although little evidence of this initial phase of the design process has survived, it is easy to imagine the spirited give-and-take among the proponents of one scheme or another. Sometimes the merits of one plan might be overshadowed by more personal or political considerations. Occasionally, the support of leading men in the commission swayed other members. Although it is rare to find contentious debate about the architectural merits of various proposals, evidence of friction within the committees occasionally appears in the records, indicating that members took an active interest in architectural matters.

Some building committees devised a complete set of plans and specifications, as did the commissioners charged with the construction of a brick courthouse in Loudoun County in 1758, who fully described every element from the size of the white oak window frames to the dimensions of the flooring tiles. Most committees, however, simply decided on the basic size and materials of a building and left the detailed specifications to workmen who might submit plans for consideration. In July 1766 the Bedford magistrates worked out the general plan and fittings of a 24-by-36-foot frame courthouse. They wanted two 12-foot-square jury rooms heated by fireplaces at one end of the courtroom. Opposite the jury rooms, they planned the magistrates' bench in the form of a quarter circle and then simply listed the other necessary furnishings. After giving some further details concerned with the interior finish, the magistrates agreed that the building committee would work out "any other Matter" once the courthouse was let to workmen. The next month the justices advertised the letting of the wooden building to the lowest bidder at October court day, at which time "the plan" and "conditions of payment" would be made known.[15]

On some occasions, when the court had no clear opinion of what it wanted, the building committee was advised to seek the opinion of experienced craftsmen—typically a prominent local builder—in order to devise a workable plan, gain a better understanding of costs, and receive informal proposals from prospective undertakers. Isle of Wight court directed two of its justices in 1749 to apply to some undertaker to prepare a plan for the new courthouse and prison that were to be erected in Smithfield. They may have applied to William Rand, a carpenter living in the town, to develop a plan. In July 1750 they let the building of the T-shaped brick courthouse to him.[16]

At other times, county courts invited outside advice by announcing their intention to entertain formal proposals submitted to them. Fauquier County magistrates ordered the sheriff to advertise publicly the letting of a contract for a wooden courthouse at their next session, specifying that "who ever is inclinable to undertake it is desired to exhibit a plan or plans of a convenient court house and the terms on which he will undertake the same." Similarly, in November 1748 the Westmoreland magistrates ordered the sheriff to advertise the construction of a prison by publishing notice of the proposal in the neighboring counties of Stafford and Richmond, as well as in public places such as churches and taverns in their own county. They advised workmen to send or bring their plans and estimates for such a structure to their meeting in two months' time. Major William Walker, a justice from Stafford County, a personal friend of Thomas Lee and other Westmoreland magistrates, and the most prominent builder in the Northern Neck, sent in two detailed proposals for two frame prisons complete with cost estimates, which the court accepted without any changes at its January term.[17] At other times courts would consider proposals made to them by prospective undertakers, debate the merits of each, and make changes to suit their needs. Once they had agreed with an undertaker, they might sit down with him to renegotiate the specific construction details,

FIGURE 114. Old Isle of Wight County courthouse, Smithfield, 1750–51, restored 1960. The clerk's office that stands to the left of the arcaded courthouse was built in 1799.

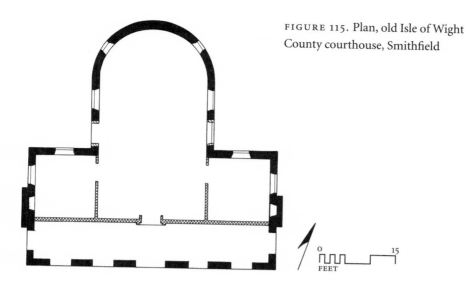

FIGURE 115. Plan, old Isle of Wight County courthouse, Smithfield

which would later be ratified in a written set of specifications so that each party would know precisely its responsibilities. Even with detailed written specifications, considerable potential remained for builders and individual craftsmen to determine how the structure and its many components fit together in a "workmanlike" fashion.

Even after the court had formally accepted a proposal from a bidder or its building committee, the design rarely became a fixed, immutable construction document but was malleable and subject to review and restructuring. As construction proceeded, committee and builder sometimes agreed to make significant revisions. On viewing the considerable progress made on their brick courthouse, Lancaster County officials in 1741 informed their building supervisors to instruct undertaker James Jones to convert two windows at one end of the building into doors and shift the windows on the side elevations closer to the apsidal justices' end of the courtroom. Perhaps their concern for circulation and light had changed since they had approved the plan the previous year, or perhaps they needed the physical reality of brick walls to recognize the inherent shortcomings of the plan as it appeared on paper. Ten years later Isle of Wight court ordered significant changes in the plan of its building (fig. 114). Apparently deciding against unheated jury rooms, they told builder William Rand to add chimneys in the two jury chambers after the walls were well under way (fig. 115). Perhaps believing the rear apse to be too small to accommodate the justices' bench, jury bench, and clerk's table, they had the undertaker make the apse flush with the side wall rather than indented as in the original plan. For his troubles, the justices awarded Rand an extra £20.[18]

An unusually revealing set of records concerning the construction of a courthouse in Amelia County in the 1760s depicts the intertwined involvement of county bench, building committee, and undertaker in the design process. In 1764 the justices concluded that their courthouse was situated in an inconvenient location, partly due to a shift in the county's boundaries and its remoteness from the principal roads. Complaining that the building was so dilapidated that they could not hold court in it during the winter, the justices successfully petitioned the governor to move the court to a more central and accessible spot and immediately began levying money to pay for the construction of new public buildings. By November 1766 the court had appointed an eight-man building committee to contract with workmen for the erection of a 40-by-20-foot frame building to be built on land given by planter and land speculator Nathaniel Harrison. The committee developed a detailed plan for a building that contained two jury rooms abovestairs, courtroom walls sheathed with plank, six small eight-light windows, two conventional six-panel doors for the exterior doorways on the side walls, roughly planed weatherboarding, and wooden block foundations, the whole to be "finished off in a neat plain Manner." They contracted with Christopher Ford, a local builder, to complete the structure by the following August.[19]

Before the undertaker could begin work, some disagreement arose among the justices. Apparently some members thought the structure let by the committee to be a little too "plain" for their tastes and argued for a more "convenient" and ornate building. Perhaps Ford, a man who had more than a decade of experience in Williamsburg during the building boom of the 1750s and early 1760s, urged some of the disgruntled justices to voice their grievances, knowing fully well that he stood to gain a greater profit with a fancier building. In May of the following year, the committee set aside their previous contract and, with the help of Ford, proposed the construction of a larger, better-built structure with more elaborate fittings and woodwork. In the new specifications the committee and undertaker added 10 feet to the length of the building and 4 feet to the width in order to accommodate the two jury rooms, which had been moved downstairs to one end of the rectangular building. They also decided to build the courthouse on brick piers rather than wooden blocks for durability, and they strengthened the framing system by adding a center girder. Rejecting the shabbiness associated with the earlier proposal, they gave the building some architectural pretension. They raised the height of the walls, added a modillion cornice, enlarged the size of the doors to a more public scale, called for the use of larger window glass, specified the construction of paneled shutters, and required the weatherboards to be planed, beaded, and painted. For the inside they ordered a "Neat Chair for the Judge" and "neatly workd" balusters for the bar. They wanted the magistrates' bench to be wainscoted and added such niceties as a simple cornice round the courtroom and raised paneled doors for

the jury rooms. The whole building, Ford estimated, could be built for £210, with the wainscoting alone costing another £14.[20] To help the
full bench membership understand the committee's proposals, Ford sketched a plan of the
courthouse with the position of the openings,
jury rooms, and fittings (fig. 116).

At the May court session, the magistrates
accepted nearly all of the proposed changes
made by the undertaker and building committee. Yet they insisted on such economies as a
cheaper, "plain" cornice and roughly sawn
weatherboards that were to be tarred only. Even
these modest cutbacks apparently were not
enough for the fiscally conservative John Scott,
a member of the building committee, who dis-
sented from accepting the new changes when
they were put to a vote. Although Ford began
construction, the justices continued to meddle,
ordering the installation of different types of
windows and doors and additional courtroom
fittings a year and a half after the approval of
the second set of specifications.[21] Such lengthy
and perhaps contentious debate from initial design through subsequent alterations was not unusual but typical of most Virginia county court
buildings.

What made corporate design possible was
the fact that most magistrates, undertakers, and
craftsmen shared a common understanding of
local building practices. Both the clients' design
considerations and the craftsmen's building
methods were governed by a regional building
tradition that distinguished and limited the
shape and decorative treatment of a building
type to a few predictable forms. Fundamental to the development of design
schemes was the correlation between the quality of a space and its social importance. For those who sat down to plan a tobacco house, dwelling, or public
building, the layout and interrelationship of spaces created an intrinsic logic of
emphasis and detailing. Those buildings or rooms that Virginians considered
symbolically or socially important received more elaborate finishes and fancier

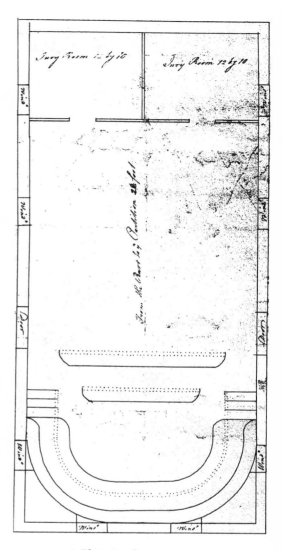

FIGURE 116. Plan, Amelia
County courthouse, 1767.
(Loose Papers, Clerk's Office,
Amelia Courthouse)

woodwork than secondary structures and spaces. Because magistrates regarded a courtroom as more important functionally and symbolically than jury rooms and clerks' offices, it served as the focus around which the plan and architectural detailing developed. The superior status of the courtroom also dictated that it receive a far richer treatment of details compared to the relative simplicity of the subsidiary rooms.

With this spatial hierarchy clearly delineated, designers could make choices about appropriate forms and details in a systematic fashion. Thus if the courtroom was to have a cornice, then the jury rooms would not; or, if both were to have cornices, the one in the courtroom would be modillioned, the one in the ancillary room plain. If the magistrates' bench was to be 14 inches wide, then the lawyers' bench would be a few inches narrower. In many specifications client and builder used shorthand terms such as "plain," "neat," "convenient," "genteel," and "fashionable," which today seem ambiguously cryptic, to convey certain distinctions of quality, fashion, level of craftsmanship, and degree of detail desired in the design and execution of entire buildings or their various parts. Justices serving as public building clients and craftsmen and builders working as undertakers recognized this system and incorporated it either explicitly in their specifications or implicitly in the working out of the details at the site.

The dictates of local precedent shaped and guided most design deliberations. By the early eighteenth century, custom required that courthouses, prisons, and instruments of punishment have certain basic features—an elevated magistrates' bench, the royal coat of arms, iron window bars—that were symbolically or functionally appropriate for different building types. Design was a matter of selecting the appropriate elements and working them into a set of particular forms that suited a county's needs and budget. This disposition resulted in a degree of standardization that enabled justices to agree on the construction of certain features or an entire structure by noting that it should be constructed in the "proper manner for such a building." The specifications for the fittings for the Charlotte County courthouse noted laconically that there should be "the usual lawyers bar and justices bench." However, familiarity of such formulaic brevity could not always be taken for granted. Spotsylvania justices seemed uncertain of the degree of accepted convention when they ordered the construction of a new sheriff's box. They first noted that the box was to be placed "at the End of Justices [bench]," but then crossed through this specific reference to its position, and added the more generalized notation that it should be located "as is Usuall in Court Houses." This confusion may have arisen partly because the sheriff's box was a relatively new feature in the Virginia courtroom when this specification was written in 1744.[22]

In most cases the bench had no desire to depart from past forms and precedent but, as is true of many traditional cultures, sought to replicate buildings that were known to them. Magistrates looked to nearby structures in the design of new buildings because they understood well their functional arrangements. Typical of the age-old English practice of patterning new buildings after neighboring ones, building committees frequently settled their design questions by stipulating that a proposed prison or courthouse was to be "of the same dimensions and in the same form" or of "the exact size and model" as a building in another county.[23] Almost always, the magistrates and building committees confined their horizon to the buildings in contiguous counties (table 2).

Northampton County justices looked no farther than their nearest neighbor on the Eastern Shore in planning their prison in 1690 after the "logg'd Prison by Accomack County Courthouse." Seventy years later Caroline County decided to pattern its new brick courthouse after the one in King and Queen County, its neighbor to the south. More unusual was the decision of the Fauquier County bench to look beyond its own area in northern Virginia for the model of its new courthouse. It ordered the construction of a brick structure "after the same manner of the Courthouse in Lancaster County," a building that was then twenty years old.[24] There may have been some connection between one of the magistrates and Lancaster County that drew the attention of the bench in the northern county, or perhaps the building itself appealed to them for some particular reason such as its solid construction or "convenient" plan.

Altogether at least two dozen examples appear in early Virginia records of such direct copying of one public building after another. In a slow pattern of diffusion, design precedents spread from old counties to newly settled areas: in the late seventeenth century from the lower peninsulas along the James and York Rivers to the Northern Neck and in the next century from the tidewater into the piedmont and Southside. The most common occurrence was for a new county to pattern its public structures after those of its parent county. After years of sitting in familiar surroundings, justices who suddenly found themselves as commissioners in a new county generally favored the repetition of old forms. When they chose to build new buildings based on familiar ones, they knew exactly what they were getting and thus had a fairly good grasp of its cost and peculiar qualities. In 1743 Louisa court ordered the construction of its new courthouse based on the design of the arcaded, T-shaped brick building in its parent county of Hanover. In 1745 Albemarle based the design of its first courthouse and prison on the ones in Goochland. In 1758 the new county of Loudoun stipulated that its prison be built "of the same dimensions" as the one in Fairfax. County courts even elected to copy such ephemeral structures as instru-

TABLE 2　Public building design precedents

Date	Building/Structure	Design precedent
1685	Middlesex County courthouse	† Gloucester County courthouse
1690	Northampton County prison	† Accomack County prison
1702	Essex County courthouse	† King and Queen County Courthouse
1717	Elizabeth City County stocks &c.	Provincial stocks, Wmsbg.
1726	Norfolk County courthouse	Capitol, Williamsburg
1733	Northampton County stocks &c.	† Accomack County stocks &c.
1743	Louisa County courthouse	* Hanover County courthouse
1745	Albemarle County courthouse	* Goochland County courthouse
1746	Brunswick County courthouse	* Prince George County courthouse
1746	Frederick County ducking stool	Fredericksburg ducking stool
1747	Louisa County prison	* Hanover County prison
1747	Louisa County stocks &c.	* Hanover County stocks &c.
1749	Chesterfield County courthouse	* Henrico County courthouse
1752	Halifax County courthouse	* Lunenburg County courthouse
1754	Prince Edward County courthouse	† Cumberland County courthouse
1754	Sussex County courthouse	† Southampton County courthouse
1758	Loudoun County prison	* Fairfax County prison
1760	Caroline County courthouse	* King & Queen County courthouse
1760	Fauquier County courthouse	Lancaster County courthouse
1762	Albemarle County courthouse	Henrico County courthouse
1763	Culpeper County prison	† Spotsylvania County prison
1765	Lunenburg County courthouse	Dinwiddie County courthouse
1767	Pittsylvania County courthouse	* Halifax County courthouse
1772	Charlotte County prison	† Prince Edward County prison
1778	Powhatan County courthouse	Buckingham County courthouse
1792	Henry County courthouse	† Franklin County courthouse
1823	Lunenburg County courthouse	† Charlotte County courthouse
1833	Rappahannock County courthouse	† Page County courthouse

* Parent county.
† Neighboring county.

ments of punishment. In 1717 the Elizabeth City County justices let the construction of stocks, pillory, whipping post, and ducking stool "according to the pattern of them in Williamsburgh."[25]

A standing building served as a general guide for justices and builders, rather than something that had to be exactly replicated down to the last detail. If there were problems with the older buildings or financial restraints to be considered, then magistrates simply altered specifications to suit their own purposes. In sprawling Brunswick County, where boundaries changed frequently through much of the eighteenth century as new counties were carved out of its territory, the location of the courthouse constantly shifted. In 1746, after deciding that they would pattern their new buildings after those in Prince George County, Brunswick magistrates ordered that the courthouse and prison be constructed of wood rather than brick in order to reduce cost, perhaps anticipating that the seat would be moved again within a few years. Less drastic changes were made by the Chesterfield and Albemarle courts, which modeled their new courthouses after the one in Henrico. The 1749 Chesterfield specifications changed the flooring material from stone pavers to wood, and the 1762 Albemarle ones called for 8-inch brick tiles.[26]

Although magistrates generally favored established patterns rather than novel solutions, change did permeate public building practices in eighteenth-century Virginia. No single agent transformed the small, domestic-looking courthouses of the late seventeenth century into the substantial civic structures of a later generation. Many elements converged to give new direction to local vernacular building practices. Indeed, the same loosely organized framework that governed corporate design and generally produced conservative solutions could also serve as the conduit for the introduction of novel ideas. Because so much of the design process depended upon the personal prestige and perceived authority of individual justices, a particularly influential or politically powerful magistrate could sway other members of the bench to his point of view.

When a colonial magnate such as Robert "King" Carter decided to undertake the construction of the Lancaster County courthouse and prison in 1698, few members of the bench had any real power to disagree with him about design matters. After Carter received the contract to undertake the brick courthouse, the court, acting upon his suggestions, decided to enlarge the building, enhance the quality of the interior woodwork, and add the king's arms. Carter's omnipresence in this endeavor had the effect of pushing the Lancaster magistrates toward a more sumptuous and stylish building than they probably had first intended. The power of a leading justice also allowed the introduction of idiosyncratic ideas such as the courthouse design submitted to the Richmond County court by King Carter's son Landon. He produced an unusual plan in which two side arcades flanked the long sides of the courtroom and a "Roman arch" dominated the interior. Of course, the interest of great planters of the Carters' stature did not always mean the introduction of new ideas or even a better building. Ralph Wormeley, for example, placed several obstacles in the way of the Middlesex magistrates when they wanted to build a brick courthouse on his land near Rosegill.[27] But in general, some magistrates or provincial leaders commanded such respect that they had the ability, if so inclined, to introduce novelty in a tradition-oriented design process.

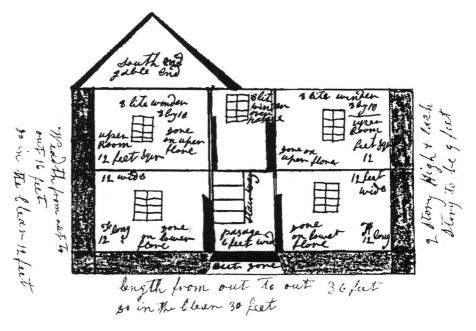

FIGURE 117. Elevation, Westmoreland County jail, 1825. (Loose Papers, May 22, 1826, Clerk's Office, Montross)

One of the tools for shaping new directions in design was the use of architectural drawings. Carpenter Larkin Chew's submission of a "Mapp Platt or Draugh" to convey his proposal for the Essex County courthouse in 1702 is the earliest reference to such drawings for a civic structure in Virginia.[28] It is unclear whether Chew's "platt" and others made at the time marked the beginning of architectural drawings in the colony or a continuation of an existing practice. Nearly all the drawings devised by colonial builders consisted of simple floor plans showing the location of doors, windows, partitions, and courtroom furnishings such as the magistrates' bench, sheriffs' boxes, and lawyers' bar. Although most of the dozen or so plans that survive from the eighteenth and early nineteenth centuries are drawn to scale, a few are rough sketches with the major dimensions written in. Typical of the latter is the sketch for the design of an early nineteenth-century jail in Westmoreland County that depicts the doors, windows, and roof superimposed on top of the plan, a convention frequently employed in both England and the other American colonies (fig. 117). Such drawings were generally used in developing or confirming design decisions and, because of their diagrammatic nature, were not intended as working guides for craftsmen on the site. Carpenters and joiners sometimes produced more detailed and precise working drawings sketched on paper or on a convenient wood surface at the site.[29]

By the second quarter of the eighteenth century, the use of a simple floor plan to convey information about the configuration of the building had become fairly common. Many specifications make reference to a now lost "plan hereto annexed."[30] However, the term *plan* did not always mean a drawing but was often used in the eighteenth century to refer to a set of directions or a method of work. Plans were important but not always present in the work of designers and undertakers.[31]

Virginians seldom depended upon elevation drawings to convey design concepts. When they did appear, they were used to show the size and relationship of openings as well as roof configurations. Accompanying the c. 1755 plan of the Accomack County courthouse is an elevation that shows the position of the ground-floor apertures and dormers. On the reverse, a section was drawn of the roof framing system showing the length of the kick rafters that were to extend beyond the face of the wall to encompass the modillion cornice (see figs. 132–33). The elevation drawing depicts the principal windows as being unusually narrow, the height being more than twice the width. In the constructed building, these dimensions were not followed. Either Severn Guthrey, the builder, ignored the dimensions laid out in the drawing, or the size of the windows was changed in later discussions. The courtroom windows were only twice as long as they were wide, conforming to the more typical proportions. Sometimes elevations or sections were necessary to convey unusual information, especially on elaborate buildings or ones that stepped outside the local building conventions. This may have been the reason that the magistrates of Caroline County, Maryland, in 1774 commissioned architect William Buckland of Annapolis to devise several "plans and elevations" for a two-story brick courthouse they intended to build.[32]

Elevations were also used to clarify structural information, particularly in prison designs where the concern for security often required the employment of many unusual building techniques. The specifications for a prison that was to be built in Dumfries in Prince William County in 1788 depended upon the accompanying plan and elevation to aid in the explanation of planning arrangements. Without them, the several pages of specifications would have been incomprehensible.[33] In 1765 Orange County magistrates depended upon a plan and sectional drawing to illustrate their proposal for the complex construction of triple-thick prison walls and a solid brick roof covered with clapboards (see fig. 149).

Drawings produced by the magistrates themselves or professional contractors such as William Walker and William Buckland provided building committees with the ability to discuss the merits of several schemes simultaneously, opening up the world of design possibilities far beyond their dependence on a limited but familiar range of standing structures. A rare set of surviving design

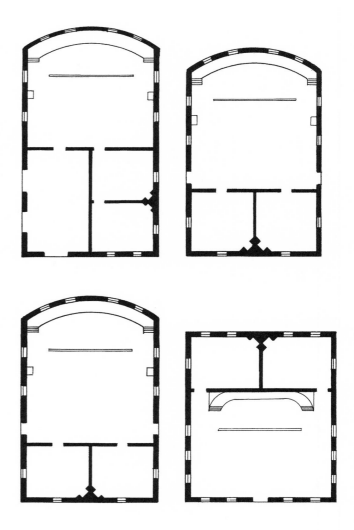

FIGURE 118. Design plans, Nelson County courthouse, Lovingston, 1809. Redrawn from the originals. (Plans for a Courthouse, Massie Family Papers, Virginia Historical Society)

sketches for an early nineteenth-century courthouse in Nelson County reveals four plan variations that were considered by the building committee (fig. 118). Two of these 1809 drawings are similar and were based upon a traditional rectangular plan that had been used in courthouse design since the last quarter of the seventeenth century. The other two mark a departure from contemporary plans. One of these maintains the shape of an elongated rectangle with the courtroom at one end but has an arched piazza in one corner of the other end flanked by a stacked set of jury rooms. The other plan is 40 feet square with two jury rooms placed behind the magistrates' bench in a manner that was to become typical of later antebellum courthouses in Virginia and much of the rest of the nation. Although the four drawings demonstrate that the committee considered both conservative and novel arrangements, the magistrates rejected

FIGURE 119. Gunston Hall, Fairfax County, 1755–59

all of them in favor of a two-story building with second-floor jury rooms placed over a gable-ended arcade (see fig. A37 for first-floor plan). This plan had a long pedigree, being used for detached English market houses, but had only made its way into Virginia public building in the last decade of the eighteenth century. The other plans allowed the magistrates the possibility to explore the implications of their decisions in a way that no verbal presentation could.

The subtle interplay between academic sources and regional traditions can be seen in a set of sketches made in 1759 for the Prince William County courthouse.[34] Found on the back of an interior window frieze at George Mason's home, Gunston Hall, in Fairfax County, ten rough pencil drawings depict schematic plans and elevations for a new courthouse in neighboring Prince William County (figs. 119, 120). Their rough and haphazard appearance belies a skillful fusion of contemporary English fashion with local public building forms and is probably the result of an animated conversation illustrated on the nearest available surface between Mason or one of his Prince William County friends and William Buckland, the young English architect employed by Mason to supervise the completion of his house (fig. 121).

Although the precise connection between Mason, Buckland, and the planning of a courthouse in the port town of Dumfries cannot be clearly reconstructed, the location of the sketches shows that early design discussions took place in one of the half-finished rooms at Gunston Hall. They reveal a sharp

FIGURE 120. Sketches for a courthouse found on the back of an interior window architrave, Gunston Hall, Fairfax County, c. 1759

FIGURE 121. William Buckland (1734–1774). Portrait by Charles Willson Peale. (Yale University Art Gallery, Mabel Brady Garvan Collection)

0   1   2   3
INCHES

departure from traditional courthouse design in Virginia and display an understanding of local building forms coupled with a precocious knowledge of academic sources. Their clear reference to other courthouses in the region suggests the presence of Mason, who had traveled widely on business and, in his capacity as a justice on the Fairfax County bench, was familiar with the routine and requirements of court procedure. However, from his writings it appears that the planter showed no propensity to translate his ideas about building into drawings. He also seems an unlikely conduit for architectural innovation as the few references to building in his papers are mainly concerned with mundane matters. On the other hand, the young and relatively new indentured servant, Buckland, knew less about the special qualities of a county court but had a fertile imagination and the ability to think graphically about architectural ideas.

By midcentury nearly all courthouses built in the colony followed one of two standard plans: a rectangular building with an entrance on one or both of the longer sides or a T-shaped plan with jury rooms at right angles to the courtroom. The Gunston sketches take these two plans as the starting point for a far more sophisticated structure. All the sketch plans incorporate an angled or curved wall to contain the justices' bench, a feature that had become common since the construction of the first Capitol in Williamsburg in the first decade of the eighteenth century.

One of the sketch plans is firmly rooted in Virginia precedent, closely resembling the 1750 Richmond County courthouse built by Landon Carter (fig. 122; see also fig. 111). Two side arcades appear on the long sides of the courtroom with a pair of jury rooms at the lower end, opposite the magistrates' bench. Mason or Buckland may have liked the idea of a double-arcaded building, but they evidently rejected the Janus-like Richmond County plan, which lacked a dominant, centrally positioned entrance. They began to manipulate the Richmond County plan in order to create one that accentuated a single facade. To create a visually satisfying entrance facade on axis with the magistrates' bench, the author of the sketches shifted the position of the jury rooms to the side of the courtroom but kept their outer walls in line with the truncated arcades. This is evident in one of the plans and fully articulated in another. In this latter plan the front of the building is given further prominence by a polygonal projection. The accompanying elevation shows this front projection to be arcaded and the entire facade unified by an unbroken cornice line. One further plan rotates the side jury rooms at a 45-degree angle to the arcaded facade (fig. 123). In the courtroom the angled walls of the two jury rooms match the polygonal form of the magistrates' bench. Buckland and Mason drew two elevations in order to work out the facade and complicated roof configuration of such a scheme.

It is the use of polygonal forms that marks the departure of these sketches from traditional midcentury Virginia design and suggests the hand of William Buckland, who had a penchant for such forms in many of his later designs. Polygonal rooms and faceted facades were coming into widespread use in English architecture by midcentury and were being popularized in the works of Sir Robert Taylor and in architectural books by Robert Morris and Isaac Ware. Buckland probably became familiar with this fashion from plates in English architectural books in his possession in the late 1750s. Morris's *Architecture Improved,* for example, was filled with designs for polygonally shaped pavilions, follies, and other smaller buildings (fig. 124). It would be fruitless to search

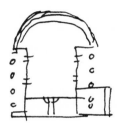

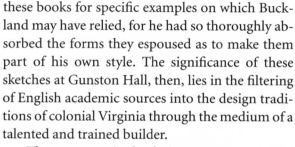

these books for specific examples on which Buckland may have relied, for he had so thoroughly absorbed the forms they espoused as to make them part of his own style. The significance of these sketches at Gunston Hall, then, lies in the filtering of English academic sources into the design traditions of colonial Virginia through the medium of a talented and trained builder.

The next stage in the design process cannot be reconstructed with any certainty. If Buckland prepared designs for the Dumfries courthouse based on the ideas conveyed in the Gunston sketches, no trace of them or his connection with the courthouse project has survived. Whatever the source, the building committee, perhaps influenced by Mason, did settle upon a plan that stretched traditional ideas. Excavation of the courthouse site revealed a building whose plan is fully consonant with the intentions of the Gunston sketches (figs. 125, 126). Although the final design dispensed with

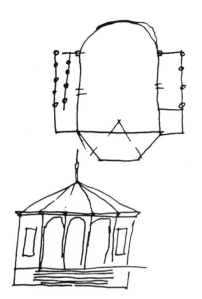

FIGURE 122. Detail from the courthouse sketches, Gunston Hall

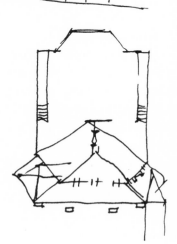

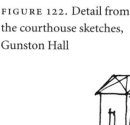

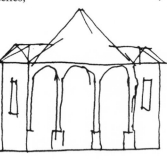

FIGURE 123. Detail from the courthouse sketches, Gunston Hall

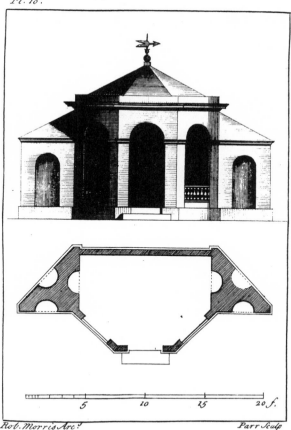

FIGURE 124. Plate 10, Robert Morris, *Architecture Improved* (London, 1755).

exterior polygonal projections and complicated roof forms, it did incorporate the circulation pattern proposed in the sketches. As developed, three entrances opened into the building, two opposite one another on the sides and one on the front (fig. 127). Instead of broad arcades, the entrances formed small loggias. The two smaller side loggias opened into the space inside the bar and were used by court officials, while the slightly larger front loggia led into the space provided for the public. Squeezed between the side and front loggias at the lower end of the building were two small, heated jury rooms. The inside corner in each of these rooms was pared back at an angle in order to eliminate an awkward extension into the courtroom, a solution similar to one proposed in the sketches.

The innovation in the plan of the Dumfries courthouse demonstrates the willingness of a building committee to experiment with new forms only when they seemed to enhance rather than displace design ideas embedded in traditional social and aesthetic preferences. Buckland's imaginative handling of

FIGURE 125. Excavation of 1762 Prince William County courthouse site, Dumfries, 1985

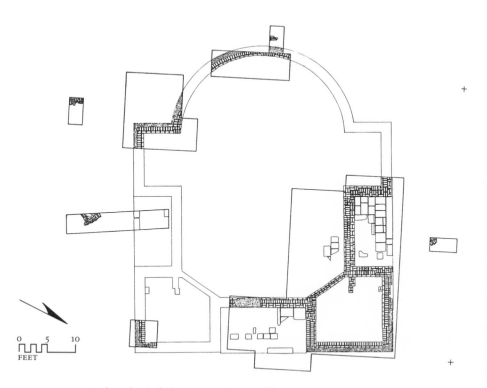

0 5 10
FEET

FIGURE 126. Archaeological plan, 1762 Prince William County courthouse, Dumfries

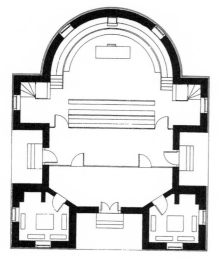

FIGURE 127. Reconstructed plan and elevation, 1762 Prince William County courthouse, Dumfries

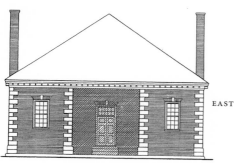

EAST

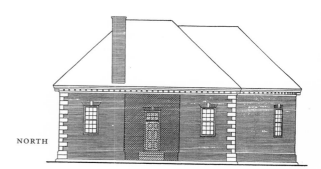

NORTH

polygonal shapes found its way into the final design where it seemed to solve problems of circulation. Otherwise, such forms must have been regarded as unnecessary extravagances. As the architect embarked on his career in the colonies, he was beginning to learn that Virginians welcomed English architectural fashions but employed them on their own terms.

Undertakers

It was the task of the undertaker to translate schematic drawings and terse specifications into finished buildings. The building committee let the construction of a courthouse, prison, privy, stable, or clerk's office to a single individual who would undertake the construction of the project from the gathering of materials to the application of the final coat of whitewash. Other contemporary forms of contracting, either by piecework or by the day, under the general supervision of the building committee rarely occurred in public construction. The undertaker was the clerk of the works, responsible for preparing the site, providing materials, and recruiting and organizing a workforce of skilled artisans and unskilled laborers. He negotiated design changes with the building committee, supervised construction at every stage of the project, and turned over control of the building to the county magistrates when he had satisfactorily completed the terms of his contract. Without his guiding supervision, the construction of large, refined, and specialized public structures would have been difficult if not impossible. The success of the project and the financial reward that he would earn depended directly on the undertaker's understanding of local building practices, the skills and reliability of his labor force, and his ability to organize the construction process in a logical and orderly fashion. Waste of materials, inferior construction practices, and misuse of the time of skilled laborers cut into the profit that the undertaker stood to gain. Undertakers also required tact and a sagacious understanding of local politics to bring their projects to a successful completion.

The undertakers of public buildings were a large and varied group of individuals. Experienced professional builders erected many public buildings in colonial Virginia but never dominated this lucrative trade. In fact, most of the men awarded contracts had no formal training in the building trades. Nearly all contracts went to individuals living within the local jurisdiction or in neighboring counties, whether craftsmen or not; few were awarded to itinerant builders. Strangers with an unfamiliar reputation received little attention from magistrates when buildings were put out for bids, even if they submitted the lowest ones. This reluctance to select outside craftsmen and builders, who might have served as the source for new ideas, only reinforced the insularity of local building practices. Those few outsiders who were awarded contracts either had a colonywide reputation or were connected to one or more of the county justices.

The building committee controlled the procedure for letting important public structures. From the first appearance of public buildings in the 1650s until the first decade of the eighteenth century, they were not put out for open competitive bidding. The bench gave the committee the power to "agree with any person or persons" who would be willing to undertake such a project.[35] Committee members approached or were approached by potential undertakers and settled contracts through private negotiations. Without the opportunity for public scrutiny, this arrangement led to abuses when powerful committee members awarded such lucrative jobs to incompetent cronies, greedy relatives, or themselves. Irate citizens of Charles City County accused Colonel Edward Hill of gouging the county's treasury in the construction of a courthouse tavern in the early 1670s. Crown commissioners appointed to inquire into their grievances in the wake of the disturbances caused by Bacon's Rebellion heard from a number of petitioners how they had "been illegally taxed & forced to pay the sum of 33,322 lb of Tobo. . . . for erecting a small house (wch in the judgmt of knowing workmen might have been done for less than 1,000 lb of Tobo)."[36]

The system that replaced private negotiation served the county taxpayers only slightly better. Whether as an attempt to mitigate the abuses of the closed contract system or as a means to save public money, building committees turned to letting public projects to those who submitted the lowest bid or the "fairest proposal." Once a committee received two or more proposals, it carefully decided which one best suited the county's needs and pocketbook. This did not always mean that the lowest bidder automatically received the contract, as a disgruntled David Harrison learned when his proposal to build the courthouse in Augusta County in 1750 was passed over even though he had submitted the lowest bid. Harrison was a justice of the peace for the county, but his bid may have been passed over because of factional feuds on the bench.[37]

After the decision had been reached to build, the committee, or the sheriff acting on its behalf, published notices at the courthouse and other public places in the county calling for candidates to submit their proposals to the magistrates at an ensuing term. After the mid-1730s, a number of courts used the *Virginia Gazette* in Williamsburg to announce their proposals to a broader audience. Although publication of the notice expanded the potential pool of applicants, in reality the process did little to make the selection any more competitive. Except for a handful of professional builders who worked on a regional basis with a large crew of skilled workmen, few craftsmen could muster the financial and organizational resources necessary to undertake major building projects.

Moreover, public announcements seldom left much time for workmen to prepare estimates. In December 1743 the Elizabeth City County court gave notice that it would treat with workmen at its next session for the building of a new prison. The Stafford court announced in the July 6, 1764, issue of the *Virginia Gazette* that it would let the building of a new prison to the lowest bidder at a meeting within three weeks. Even less time was given builders in Gloucester County. In late September 1769 the magistrates advertised in the newspaper that they would take proposals for two brick prisons the following week. Acting in their other capacity as vestrymen for Ware Parish as well, they also announced that they would be accepting bids for shingling Ware Church. Such short notice primarily benefited builders who had some familiarity with public building and could reasonably and quickly estimate the type of work, the costs, and the logistics of carrying out such an endeavor. William Walker, who had already built at least two county prisons, took less than six weeks to submit detailed proposals and plans for two prisons for the Westmoreland County court after notice had been posted in the surrounding counties.[38]

If professional builders had a leg up on itinerant or even local craftsmen, they still faced a formidable obstacle that prevented them from obtaining most

of the contracts: the magistrates themselves. Despite the formalities of advertising public building projects, in truth, most courthouses, prisons, and clerks'
offices were undertaken by members of the commission themselves or local
members of the colonial elite. The Virginia gentry often thought the public
weal synonymous with their own welfare. Many lined their pockets with the
profits from public building.

Those men who undertook public buildings constituted three distinct
groups (table 3). In the 125 years between 1655 and 1780, well over two hundred
courthouses and prisons were erected in Virginia, and of these, the names of the
undertakers for 175 projects can be identified. More than half of them (the
county officials and the private citizens) had no training in the building trades
but were selected because of their social and political standing. Just over one
quarter of the undertakers were local officials, either justices of the peace,
sheriffs, or county clerks, active in county affairs at the time of the letting of
contract. Nearly all the members of this first group served on the building committee that worked out the design and oversaw the project. Some, like Landon
Carter who had served on the Richmond County bench for nearly fifteen years
when he undertook the construction of a courthouse, were senior members
of the commission and had some familiarity with building. From this vantage,
such men knew precisely the taste and expectations of the bench and could
build accordingly.

The second group of undertakers belonged to the ranks of prominent freeholders who were not officeholders in the local government. Some of them
came from the ranks of the elite such as Robert "King" Carter, while others,
who had previously served on the local bench, represented their county in the
General Assembly. William Clinch of Surry County had been one of the
county's magistrates until his election to the House of Burgesses in 1755. The
next year Clinch agreed with his former colleagues to build a courthouse and
two prisons on his land.[39]

Other prominent residents also obtained coveted building contracts by
offering land for the court's use. William Callaway of Bedford County enticed
the local court to his land by giving them 100 acres near his house and erecting
a frame courthouse and prison. This act of generosity was paid many times over
by the subsequent increase in business that his tavern experienced on court
days. In a further effort to promote trade, Callaway offered the county another
100 acres next to the courthouse land that was to be laid off into lots for the
town of New London.[40]

At least a quarter of the public buildings erected were under the aegis of
men like Callaway and Clinch. Their knowledge of building, like that of their
friends and social acquaintances on the county bench, could neither match the
breadth of a professional builder nor reach the technical level of an experienced

TABLE 3 Public building undertakers, 1655–1780

Type of undertaker	Courthouses	Prisons	Total	%
County official: justice, sheriff, clerk	22	25	47	27
Private citizen: tavern-keeper, gentry, merchant	23	23	46	26
Craftsman: carpenter, bricklayer	27	23	50	29
Unknown occupation or status	13	19	32	18
Total	85	90	175	100

craftsman. However, the lack of expertise mattered little since they generally subcontracted the actual task of building to a craftsman. On occasion an undertaker turned over the task of construction to his slaves. When John Tayloe III of Mount Airy won the contract to make major repairs to the Richmond County courthouse in 1812, and again when he undertook the construction of a brick and stone clerk's office for the county in 1816, he left most of the work in the capable hands of his slave carpenters and masons (figs. 128, 129).[41]

If gentlemen undertakers did not have capable slave craftsmen to call on like Tayloe, they turned to professional builders. Sampson Darrell received the contract from the Stafford County court to erect a new courthouse in 1690 and, with the approbation of the court, was allowed to collect the county levy to pay for the building. With the notion of making a handsome sum as a middleman, he soon entered into a contract with carpenter Ambrose Bayley, who would do the actual construction. Apparently Darrell tried to squeeze out as much profit as he could and for a number of years failed to pay Bayley for his work. The carpenter had to sue to get paid for his work. Most relationships between gentleman undertaker and professional subcontractor were more harmonious, so much so that rarely do records mention the name of the craftsman who acted as site foreman. One such arrangement that does appear in the records is that between planter William Cabell of Albemarle County and bricklayer John Moore for construction of a brick courthouse. In November 1762 Cabell agreed with the county court to build within two years a courthouse "of the exact size and model of the Court-House now in Use in the county of Henrico" for £375.10. Five months later Cabell contracted with Moore "to build and compleat" the courthouse "in the same manner and within the same time" as the undertaker had previously agreed with the court. According to the terms of the second agreement, both men would profit from the project.[42]

The third and last major group of public building undertakers consisted of craftsmen and professional contractors. Almost all of them had been trained in the woodworking or masonry trades, but the nature of their practices varied widely. At one level were two dozen or so men, well connected with local magistrates, who commanded a permanent workforce of slave, convict, and hired artisans and took on many large projects such as churches and gentry houses across a broad region. More typical were those who operated individually or with a few skilled and unskilled laborers within a limited area.

For the most part professional builders seldom had the opportunity to specialize in public buildings. The striking similarity evident in surviving structures, such as the arcaded brick King William, Charles City, and Hanover courthouses, was not the product of the hand of a single architect or designer who traveled across the colony peddling his plans to willing magistrates. Rarely did an individual supply the plans or have the chance to undertake more than one public building. An early exception was Larkin Chew of King and Queen County who erected that county's first courthouse at the turn of the eighteenth century. A few years later, in 1702, he submitted an identical plan of the wooden courthouse to the justices of neighboring Essex County. They accepted his proposal to build a structure of the "Exact dementions and proportions of King and Queene County Court House" in the manner that Chew had "sett downe and portra'ed in a certaine Mapp Platt or draugh." Shortly after signing his

FIGURE 128. Richmond County clerk's office and courthouse, Warsaw, in a c. 1930 photograph

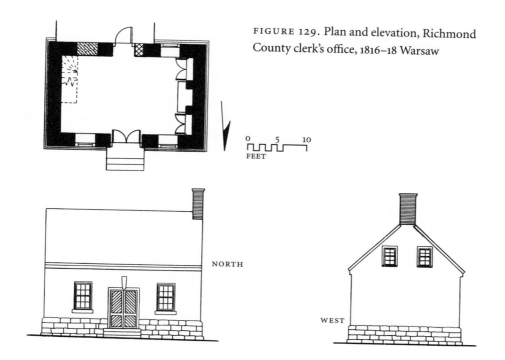

FIGURE 129. Plan and elevation, Richmond County clerk's office, 1816–18 Warsaw

NORTH

WEST

articles of agreement with the court, Chew moved to Essex County where he lived for at least the next half dozen years. He later moved northward to Spotsylvania County where he became a member of the local magistracy and was elected to the House of Burgesses.[43]

Few undertakers could duplicate Chew's success simply because they seldom had the opportunity. Only five other men besides Chew can be identified as having undertaken the construction of public buildings in more than one county before 1780. Christopher Ford built courthouses in Amelia and Prince Edward Counties; Stephen Johnson erected prisons in Essex and Spotsylvania Counties; William Walker constructed prisons in King George and Westmoreland Counties; and Henry Willis undertook the prison and courthouse in Spotsylvania County and a prison in Orange County. All of these men were professional builders in the sense that much of their livelihood was gained from undertaking private and public construction. All of them, with the possible exception of Willis, were trained as craftsmen. The fifth man, John Moore, a brickmaker turned entrepreneurial contractor, ran a far-ranging and busy practice. He undertook dwellings, churches, and public buildings, constructing at least two courthouses in a career that extended from the 1720s to the 1760s. In 1728 he undertook the construction of a rectangular brick courthouse in Tappahannock for the Essex court and in 1763 began building the second Albemarle

County courthouse. He may have participated in developing the design for the first structure, but in the second building he acted strictly as the subcontractor to the gentleman undertaker who received the contract.[44]

All but a handful of the contracts that were awarded to craftsmen went to men such as carpenters Delight Shield of Accomack County, William Rand of Isle of Wight County, and Robert Spilsby Coleman of Essex County, who built houses, repaired outbuildings, and constructed bridges within their own communities. Rand, Coleman, and bricklayer James Jones of King George County, like dozens of other craftsmen, lived near the courthouses, where they operated taverns to supplement their income. Because of their proximity to the courthouse grounds, they were frequently called upon to repair damaged prisons, erect a new gallows, replace broken window glass and patch worn shutters, or construct courtroom tables and benches. Their training and subsequent careers provided them with an opportunity to practice a range of woodworking skills. Most, if not all, of these carpenters and bricklayers were established landowners, filled many minor offices in the county government such as constable and inspector of roads, and had close connections with members of the court.

The career of carpenter Severn Guthrey (or Guttridge) (d. 1777) of Accomack County probably represents that of many successful local craftsmen. Although his origins and early training remain obscure, by the 1740s he had built a house within the courthouse precinct at Drummondtown (now Accomac). He later was granted leave by the magistrates to farm part of the courthouse grounds and build a carpenter's and joiner's shop, which later incorporated a saddler's shop and storehouse as well. Once established at the courthouse, Guthrey became an integral part of the county's public building program for the next quarter century. In 1750 and again in 1754 the court paid him for mending the prison. In the mid-1750s he purchased fifty acres near the courthouse, received a license to keep an ordinary at his house, and took the first of several apprentices. During this same period his professional role shifted from that of a workman to an entrepreneur when he contracted to build a new brick courthouse and log prison (fig. 130). Guthrey may have drawn the plan, elevation, and roof framing detail of the courthouse. These show a modest level of drafting competence. The plan is drawn to scale and depicts the principal courtroom fittings (fig. 131). The elevation is more crudely done with conventions that suggest a frame rather than masonry building (fig. 132). On the backside of the elevational drawing is a sketch depicting the roof framing system, a conventional raftered roof with collar and kick rafter at the eaves (fig. 133). The successful completion of the courthouse and prison enhanced his professional career and social status, for in the 1760s he served on the local parish vestry, trained new apprentices in his expanding carpentry and joinery business, and

FIGURE 130. Accomack County courthouse, Accomac, 1755–58. Around 1807 the ground-floor jury room was removed to create one large courtroom. The central door-way was converted into a window and the doorway shifted to the end bay where it replaced the earlier window. Above the doorway in this late nineteenth-century photograph, the brickwork in the former window opening does not conform to the glazed header pattern of the rest of the wall. Patching also appears on the right jamb of the central window, where the larger original door opening was narrowed when the window was installed. The old stone steps were also moved to the new door location. (Virginia Historical Society)

purchased several slaves. Guthrey undertook the construction of a new parish church in 1763 and was asked to provide plans for a new poorhouse five years later. By the end of his career in the mid-1770s, Guthrey had so gained the respect of the Accomack court that the bench sought his advice on most important public building matters.[45]

Guthrey, like most local carpenters, seldom ventured beyond his parish or county boundary into regions where his reputation was unknown. In this case the physical separation of the Eastern Shore from the rest of the colony by the bay may have restricted the carpenter's field of operations, but throughout Virginia the building process was a local enterprise, and men like Guthrey were its backbone. Successful craftsmen spent much of their professional lives training a younger generation of artisans in traditional building methods and undertaking the construction and repair of numerous houses and outbuildings, as well as a few public buildings. The more successful and ambitious craftsmen controlled a permanent workforce of a few slaves, apprentices, or convict craftsmen; however, most probably worked alone or with a few apprentices, hiring laborers only when necessary. Because of the limited range of their prac-

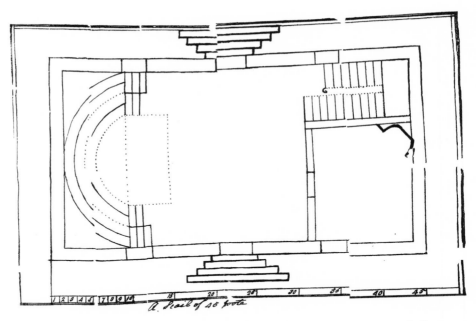

FIGURE 131. Plan, Accomack County courthouse, Accomac, c. 1755. (Accomack County Loose Papers, The Library of Virginia)

tice, they seldom had the opportunity to work on more than one or two major projects in their careers. Such limits provided them with few chances to specialize or sharpen their skills in particular aspects of joinery such as carving but required them to be knowledgeable and competent in many aspects of the woodworking trades.

With their social background rooted in a class of small landowners, these craftsmen rarely had the chance or inclination to introduce new ideas into local building. Unlike William Buckland, Severn Guthrey probably felt no need to explore new design concepts when the Accomack building committee was planning its courthouse or when he was undertaking its construction but instead followed a plan that had been in use for nearly a century. Some craftsmen possessed copies of English carpenters' books that they consulted on technical matters such as devising a complicated roofing system or methods for estimating quantities of materials. When called upon, craftsmen of Guthrey's stature had the basic skills to devise drawings for complicated buildings, but their solutions were almost always rooted in the familiar rather than experimenting with novel forms.

At the top of the building trades stood a small group of regional builders. In the second and third quarters of the eighteenth century, probably no more than two dozen of these professional contractors operated in the entire colony,

FIGURE 132. Elevation, Accomack County courthouse, Accomac, c. 1755. This drawing was severely damaged from its many years stored among the loose papers in the clerk's office. (Accomack County Loose Papers, The Library of Virginia)

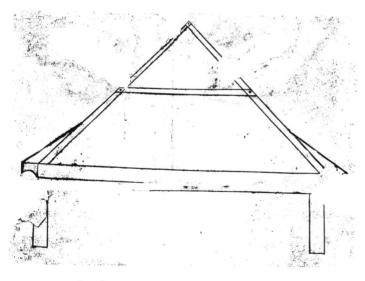

FIGURE 133. Roof truss, Accomack County courthouse, Accomac, c. 1755. (Accomack County Loose Papers, The Library of Virginia)

nearly all of them in the long-settled tidewater counties. In contrast to local craftsmen, they commanded a large and specialized workforce and had the financial resources and managerial skills to take on such sizable and complex projects as the construction of a brick courthouse or parish church. These undertakers required considerable capital because they bore much of the initial cost of construction. Although building committees sometimes handed the undertaker one-fourth or one-third of his total payment at the time of signing the contract, most of this money went into the purchase of materials and labor, leaving the builder with little margin to see him through until the next scheduled payment. Those builders who could afford to put some of their own capital into the project at critical times cushioned themselves from some of the risks inherent in such undertakings. Until a building was accepted by the building committee, it remained the property of the undertaker. When the brick church that Mourning Richards had almost completed for Overwharton Parish burned accidentally in 1754, the undertaker faced economic ruin because he would have to forfeit his security bond or rebuild the church at his own expense. Only by appealing to the provincial government for financial relief did Richards survive this disaster.[46]

By the late 1730s bricklayer James Jones of King George County had moved into the category of building contractor. A decade earlier Jones first appeared as a craftsman in King George County, taking small public jobs such as the repair of the prison. Over the next decade he showed all the signs of success in his field. He took apprentices, purchased indentured British craftsmen, and acquired slaves. By the late 1730s he operated a tavern at the county courthouse, served as a constable, and expanded his building operations into other Northern Neck counties. In 1737, for example, he repaired the windows of the Richmond County courthouse. He also worked for members of the gentry in the region. As early as 1730 his men made bricks for and plastered Marlborough, John Mercer's first Stafford County dwelling by that name. A decade later, Jones was involved in a lawsuit with the irascible Landon Carter of Richmond County over some unspecified work.[47]

Toward the end of his life in the early 1740s, Jones reached the pinnacle of his success. In 1739 Jones, who styled himself as an "Undertaker in Architecture," began the construction of a cruciform brick church in Lancaster County known as St. Mary's White Chapel (fig. 134). The following year he contracted with the magistrates of Lancaster County, a number of whom served on the vestry that had engaged him for St. Mary's, to build a brick courthouse and a prison. This ability to take on three major public buildings at one time, to move his workmen about from project to project in a timely fashion, signaled a scale of operations that not many regional contractors were capable of handling. The successful completion of these projects on time no doubt enhanced Jones's reputation. Shortly after his work in Lancaster, he moved on to other projects, about which little is known, for Lunenburg Parish and for Landon Carter in Richmond County. Jones's involvement in these was cut short with his death in the spring of 1744. The inventory of his estate shows that Jones had under his control an indentured bricklayer, a plasterer, a carpenter, a sawyer, a servant boy with two years left in his apprenticeship, and four slave men who may have been skilled craftsmen, each valued at £35 or £37 apiece.[48]

Through the years some of these crafts-trained contractors accumulated substantial wealth from their profession. A builder of prisons, churches, and bridges for more than forty years in Essex and Spotsylvania Counties, Stephen Johnson owned sixty-nine slaves and left an estate valued at nearly $13,000 when he died in 1801.[49] Because most major undertakers had received their training in the building trades, they rarely became the social equals of the colonial elite, but nonetheless they operated on familiar terms with a wide circle of leading families. Successful undertakers sought to emulate their social superiors by marrying well; purchasing plantations, slaves, and luxury goods; and serving in local parish and county offices. Many of their offspring moved into the ranks of the local gentry when they reached maturity. Henry Cary, who built the 1697 York County courthouse and subsequently supervised the construction of many of the public buildings in the new capital of Williamsburg,

FIGURE 134. St. Mary's White Chapel, Lancaster County, 1739–41. The east and west arms of the original cruciform-shaped church were demolished in the nineteenth century, and the space in between the surviving north and south wings was enclosed.

spawned a family of planters and builders.[50] Second-generation undertakers such as Henry Cary Jr. and Harry Gaines, son of Henry Gaines of King William County, continued in their fathers' professions, though probably without practical training in one of the trowel or woodworking trades. As entrepreneurs, their primary concern was with the business of building rather than the craft of building.

Professional builders filled a specialized function in colonial Virginia. The growth of genteel culture promoted the need for individuals who had the skills to instruct aspirants to polite society in the manners and forms of polished behavior. To improve their taste and personal bearing, gentry families hired dancing masters, music teachers, and Latin tutors. In order to create the proper environment to display their charm and parade their social accomplishments, the ambitious built great houses and substantial public buildings for private and public assemblies.[51] The source of taste in building, like social manners, derived from aristocratic and gentry culture in England. Although some Virginia planters added architecture to their list of accomplishments, most depended upon professional undertakers to guide their taste; and like good dancing masters, professional builders instructed their clients in the proper forms.

Contractors had the ability to translate sometimes vague gentry notions of English taste into reality. Their value derived from two complementary services. First, as professional undertakers, they could oversee the manifold tasks involved in a major project such as the construction of a large brick manor house. As project supervisors, they relieved owners from many hours spent organizing a work schedule, procuring materials, and hiring and supervising skilled laborers. Second, with a firm understanding of the local building process, many were able to bridge its limitations and design structures that suited the growing sophistication of many of their clients. John Ariss, a builder from Westmoreland County, defined the dual services that professional undertakers provided when he advertised in the *Maryland Gazette* in 1751 that he was prepared to supervise construction of "Buildings of all Sorts and Dimensions" as well as devise "Plans, Bills of Scantling, or Bills of Charges, for any Fabric, or Public Edifice." Besides his managerial skills, he advised fashion-conscious gentry that his designs were based on the latest English styles derived from the "Ancient or Modern Order of Gibbs' Architect," that is, James Gibbs's *Book of Architecture*, 1728 (fig. 135).[52]

Professional builders' knowledge of English precedent derived from three sources. A few men had direct experience in England either through training or travel, others hired English craftsmen who immigrated or were deported to the Chesapeake, and most had a vicarious familiarity with English architecture through the many builders' books that became increasingly available in the colony after 1750. Like many craftsmen in towns such as Williamsburg, Norfolk, and Alexandria who sought merchant and gentry patronage, John Ariss noted in his advertisement that he had just returned from Great Britain, thus establishing his credentials as a man in touch with "Modern Taste."[53] It is unclear whether Ariss actually received training in England or merely traveled there. William Buckland, on the other hand, had just finished several years of a joinery apprenticeship in London in 1755 when he was selected by Thomson Mason to oversee the construction of Gunston Hall, the new brick house of Mason's brother in Fairfax County (see figs. 119, 121).[54] Buckland not only brought with him the latest understanding of English shop-joinery styles but a handful of builders' books as well.

The backbone of most master builders' shops of artisans consisted of indentured or convict carpenters, joiners, turners, carvers, bricklayers, and plasterers from Great Britain. Each year ships entered the Chesapeake to unload their human cargo of English, Scottish, Welsh, and Irish craftsmen, hopeful to make a start in the New World or thankful for evading the hangman's noose. While some Virginians worried about the dumping of undesirable convicts in the colony, many in this labor-starved society welcomed the arrival of men with skills, particularly those in the woodworking and trowel trades.[55] Sailing from London in the *Elizabeth*, Captain Leitch piloted his ship filled with "healthy Indentured Servants" up the James River in early March 1774. Within ten days of landing, British blacksmiths, edge-tool makers, bricklayers, plasterers, stonemasons, carpenters, joiners, cabinetmakers, and sawyers found themselves on the auction block in Petersburg, waiting for their services for the next three or four years to be sold to the highest bidder.[56] Standing in the crowd of interested onlookers were the master builders of Virginia or their agents. As his business grew in the early 1770s, William Buckland continually expanded his shop with more than a half dozen skilled woodworkers and masons purchased off the convict ships that landed in the Northern Neck and Maryland. However, he had problems with keeping his convict servants on the job; nearly a dozen of his servants bolted.[57]

Hundreds of convict and indentured laborers filled the Chesapeake building trades each year, enriching the local building tradition with new ideas and

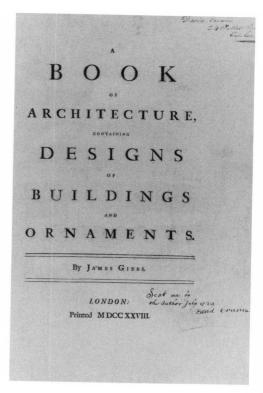

FIGURE 135. Frontispiece, James Gibbs, *A Book of Architecture* (London, 1728)

techniques. Many were young men in their twenties just starting their careers when they ran afoul of the law and found themselves transported to the New World. Others such as bricklayer Arthur Kating, who worked for brickmaker Humphrey Harwood in Williamsburg in the late 1760s, had fifteen to twenty years of experience in England before deciding to immigrate to America.[58] Their reasons for leaving Britain varied, but many craftsmen no doubt looked to Virginia as a place where they could exercise their trades without the restrictions of an entrenched guild system or too much competition. Labor-starved Virginia must have seemed appealing to carpenters and joiners struggling to make a start in London or Bristol, where powerful guilds exercised control over trade practices. Some immigrated for more personal reasons. Carver William Bernard Sears, who spent many years working at Gunston Hall and other places in Fairfax County, was said to have left England for America in the 1750s because he was "tired of the oppression in his own country."[59]

These British craftsmen brought with them varying degrees of mastery of their crafts. Many had training and experience far beyond that which could be obtained in the colony and were purchased for their talents in carving and turning. The finely executed woodwork by Sears at Gunston Hall indicates that the quality their work could be quite high (fig. 136). Undertaker William Rand considered his Irish servant Thomas Field to be "a very good joiner." A New Kent County employer described carpenter Thomas Smith as "an excellent workman." Scottish joiner and carpenter Robert Robinson had considerable experience in his craft before he immigrated to Virginia in 1775. Although only twenty-eight years old when he left Glasgow in the *Friendship,* Robinson already had spent several years working in Edinburgh and Kelso and had supervised the construction of a church in Inverness.[60]

Imported servants occasionally failed to meet their masters' expectations. Some proved to be incompetent; Thomas Bemish was advertised as a bricklayer when sold, but his unfortunate King William County employer soon found out that he knew "nothing of the business." Others simply had no intention of continuing their servitude. The Scottish builder Robert Robinson left his master within three weeks of his purchase. Along the Potomac, Richard Kibble, a convict carpenter fond of drink and tattoos, found it difficult to admire the pleasant surroundings of Mount Vernon and Stratford. Arriving in the Chesapeake in 1738, he soon fled the service of Augustine Washington, returned to England, committed six new felonies, was convicted, and once again was transported to Virginia. Master builder William Walker, who was working at Stratford for Thomas Lee in the summer of 1739, purchased Kibble but had the benefit of his service for only three days before the carpenter paddled off on the Potomac on his way to freedom along with another convict carpenter. As Walker and others were to learn, reliance upon skilled convicts, although a cheap source of labor in the short run, often proved to be more of a risk than it was worth.[61]

Professional builders depended upon architectural books imported from England for rules on correctly detailing elements of the five classical orders, lessons in mensuration, and guidance for working out structural problems. The more ambitious of these books such as Isaac Ware's *A Complete Body of Architecture* and Joshua Kirby's *The Perspective of Architecture* covered theoretical issues. More practical books by Salmon, Langley, Morris, and Abraham Swan provided plate after plate of plans, sections, and elevations for houses, offices, and garden structures and architectural elements such as newel-posts, stairs, chimneys, doors, arches, and moldings. Possession of such books allowed Virginia builders to present a catalog of designs to clients desirous of following English tastes. Mardun Eventon, a cabinetmaker and joiner who wanted to move into the role of a "Superintender, or supervisor, over any reasonable Number of hands, either in Public or Private Buildings," claimed to be well acquainted with the "Theory & Practice in any of the grand branches of the five ancient Orders viz. Ornamental Architects, gothick, chinese, and modern Taste, etc." He had

FIGURE 136. Pilaster capital carved by William Bernard Sears, Gunston Hall, Fairfax County, c. 1759

gained this knowledge through the study of more than a dozen "Books of Architecture, by the latest and best authors in Britain," that he imported from London and Liverpool. For those who wanted to superintend public and private buildings, "from the most elegant and superb, down to the gentleman's plain country seat," the possession of architectural books implied the ability to translate fashion into reality.[62] If the illustrations of buildings and details did not easily fit the architectural aspirations of Virginia planters, many of these books provided useful, albeit cryptic summaries of Palladian theories of proportion that found some limited expression in the scaling of wall heights, openings, and room sizes in the structures erected by colonial builders.[63]

Once in the Chesapeake, William Buckland continued to supplement his collection of architectural books, owning at least fifteen by the time of his death in 1774. Peale's portrait of the architect includes two of those books on the table next to his case of drafting tools, suggesting how integral they had become to his work and his professional identity (see fig. 121).[64] By contrast, bricklayer

James Jones had but two "volumes of Architecture" at his death in 1744, the difference perhaps reflecting the increasing supply of such books circulating in the colonies after 1750.[65] Many builders, such as Christopher Ford who bought Batty Langley's *Builder's Jewel* in 1752, purchased their books from Williamsburg printers who imported them from London. Other books advertised for sale by Williamsburg printers included William Halfpenny, *Rural Architecture in the Chinese Taste;* Robert Morris, *Architecture Improved;* William Salmon, *Palladio Londonensis;* Abraham Swan, *The Carpenter's Complete Instructor in Several Hundred Designs;* and Isaac Ware, *The Four Books of Andrea Palladio's Architecture.*[66] Like English magazines and the front page of the *Virginia Gazette*, these books kept Virginia planters on the fringe of the empire informed about the latest trends at the metropolitan center. For those who wanted to boast of refined tastes, smaller architectural details were sometimes copied, but rarely did Virginians incorporate complete plans and elevations into their design considerations. There were too many differences socially and culturally for such a mimetic practice to work. Even if the scale matched the relatively modest requirements of a Chesapeake planter, English house plans diverged from local practices, making them more difficult to copy. For example, Virginians held onto ground-floor bedchambers long after gentry in England had moved upstairs. Nevertheless, a working familiarity with such books distinguished builders as men of taste, a cut above the leather-aproned local artisans.

In the absence of account books, letters, and design drawings, the careers and work of professional undertakers such as Mourning Richards, John Moore, Daniel French, and James Skelton can never be fully analyzed. What can be discovered about the activities of a successful contractor in the Northern Neck in the 1740s, William Walker of Stafford County, may serve to dispel certain misconceptions about the role of master builders in colonial Virginia and provide a general overview of the range of work practiced by regional undertakers. His career over two decades can be pierced together from information in county court records.

William Walker began his career in the building trades at a propitious moment. Born in 1707 in Westmoreland County, he came to maturity in the late 1720s when the Virginia gentry initiated the construction of a number of large dwelling houses, sizable churches, and brick courthouses, which required the talents of entrepreneurial craftsmen capable of incorporating popular Georgian elements into local practices. Like most Virginia craftsmen, Walker probably learned the joiner's trade as an apprentice to a local man and started his own practice in neighboring Stafford County in the late 1720s. As his reputation developed with practice in the next decade, he came to the attention of local magnates, doing small repairs for the lawyer John Mercer at Marlborough and unspecified work for Thomas Lee at Stratford.[67] By the late 1730s Walker was

FIGURE 137. Stratford, Westmoreland County, 1738–39. Prerestoration photograph, c. 1930.

deeply involved in the construction of Lee's great house on the Potomac, perhaps acting as its undertaker (fig. 137). Whether he was involved in the design of this unusual structure is unknown.

Walker started his career with certain advantages. He possessed enough capital to have two slave craftsmen laboring for him while he was in his mid-twenties.[68] Although there is little evidence as to the nature of his work, he probably contracted to build houses and outbuildings and make repairs across Stafford County, perhaps expanding the range of his work into neighboring counties and augmenting his workforce with convict laborers when necessary.

Walker benefited from the patronage of important men. He enhanced these social connections in 1731 when he married Elizabeth Netherton, daughter of Henry Netherton, a gentlemen and former surveyor in Westmoreland County. By the time he was thirty, Walker was in a position to take on public building projects beyond the confines of his own community.[69] His reputation allowed him to compete successfully against local builders for the choice jobs offered by parish vestries and county courts. In 1739 with the endorsement of the Reverend Patrick Henry, the vestry of St. Paul's Parish, Hanover County, accepted Walker's design and specifications for a brick glebe house and contracted him to build it for £220. During the next year Walker spent considerable time traveling about eastern Virginia, bidding on contracts and supervising projects under construction. In April 1740 he submitted a plan for the addition of a brick steeple and vestry room for St. Peter's Church, New Kent County, and won the contract to undertake the work for £130 (fig. 138). Perhaps a recommendation from the Reverend Mr. Henry, the minister in the neighboring parish and Walker's security for the project, helped the Stafford County builder win this new project. While he was in the area, Walker may have visited Henry in Hanover to observe the progress on the glebe house and leave instructions with William Frazer, the bricklayer whom he had subcontracted to build the walls.[70]

Public contracts also kept Walker busy in his native region of the Northern Neck. In July 1740 the Stafford County "undertaker and Arthiteck" agreed with Landon Carter on behalf of the Richmond County court to build two "good and substantial" wooden bridges over Rappahannock and Totuskey Creeks. A few years later he undertook similar engineering projects with the construction of a bridge across Maddox Creek in Westmoreland County and a fairly substantial one costing £130 across the Pamunkey River from Newcastle in Hanover County to King William County. In 1745 Walker received a contract in his own county to build a new 60-foot-square brick church for Overwharton Parish, perhaps through the influence of John Mercer and other personal friends on the vestry. Walker was to receive 153,920 pounds of tobacco for his labors.[71] Magistrates also hired him to design and construct frame prisons in King George and Westmoreland Counties. Walker undoubtedly received the latter contract through the influence of Colonel Thomas Lee of Stratford. Suspecting that Robert Caula had overcharged the county for repairs made to the prison, Lee had Walker appointed to view Caula's work. After examining the repairs, Walker agreed with Lee, and the court requested the attorney general to prosecute Caula in the General Court. With the prison still in need of substantial repairs, the court decided to construct two new wooden buildings to house felons and debtors. In January 1749, with little discussion, the court accepted Walker's plan and specifications for two frame structures.[72]

At the same time that he was undertaking public works, Walker was engaged in the construction of two large houses for his gentry friends. In 1747 the builder finished work on Cleve, a brick house trimmed in stone on the Rappahannock River, for Landon Carter's brother Charles (fig. 139).[73] Working with brickmaker David Minitree of Williamsburg, Walker directed the construction of a new brick house at Marlborough for his old friend and legal counsel John Mercer, who had argued Walker's case in the General Court against the Hanover County magistrates for the fees he earned building a bridge across the Pamunkey River. With Marlborough nearing completion in early 1749, Walker reached the summit of his career. The close connections that Walker had developed with the Carters, Lees, and Mercer landed the builder with the contract

FIGURE 138. St. Peter's Church, New Kent County. The body of the church dates to 1701–3.

for one of the most prestigious projects in the colony, the reconstruction of the Capitol in Williamsburg, which had burned in 1747. In March 1749 he contracted to undertake the work for £2,600, one of the most expensive building projects in the colony. However, in February 1750 Walker died before the men and materials he had procured in London and other parts of Great Britain had arrived to begin work, leaving unfinished the Capitol and "many buildings on hand" spread across the colony.[74]

A significant rise in social and economic status matched Walker's growing success in the building industry. Trained as a carpenter and joiner, Walker spent his early career taking what work he could find in Stafford County. Much of his

FIGURE 139. Cleve, King George County, c. 1747. The original hipped roof was replaced at a later date. The house burned in 1917. (Courtesy of The Library of Virginia)

time was spent at Stafford courthouse where on court day he could bid on small public jobs and negotiate for work among the scores of farmers and planters who showed up for the county's business. At one such gathering at the beginning of his career in the late 1720s, Walker made the mistake of getting into a quarrel with Robert Carter Jr., the son of Robert "King" Carter and older brother of Charles and Landon. Fearing that the indignation of the Carter family would cause his career to suffer severely, Walker wrote a supplicatory letter to King Carter in hopes that it would ease tensions. Apparently this unfortunate incident did not retard his attempt to gain gentry patronage and respect in his trade, for by the end of the next decade, Walker began to be referred to by his contemporaries as "Mr." Somewhat later he was referred to as "Major" or "Gent.," titles of courtesy given to men of sizable means and status. In the early 1740s his now well-established role of entrepreneur and supervisor of crews of artisans earned him the title of "master builder," "undertaker," and occasionally, "architect."[75] In recognition of his rising status, Walker was nominated by Stafford County magistrates to become a member of the local bench. With the wealth gained from building, Walker invested in land, purchasing tracts in

Prince William and Fairfax Counties and expanding his holding in Stafford County. He also purchased more slaves for building operations and to tend his plantation, Pasbytanzy in Overwharton Parish, where he entertained clients, neighbors, and friends with the hospitality expected of a Virginia gentleman.[76]

The symbiotic relationship that the undertaker had with the planters of the Northern Neck reached beyond building matters. When Walker died in 1750, he left his plantation along with the "many workmen many tools and many materials" for continuing unfinished building projects in the hands of his executors and "worthy Friends the Honble Thomas Lee Esq., Charles Carter, John Tayloe, Nathaniel Harrison, & Philip Lee Esq." His will clearly demonstrates that he looked upon his gentry friends to care for his family once he was dead. Thomas Lee and Nathaniel Harrison were left with the task of sorting out his business affairs and personal estate. Because Walker left no grown children to inherit the trade, his business came to a complete halt. A practice built on personal reputation and patronage could not survive the death of its principal. The contract for the Capitol quickly passed to James Skelton of Hanover County; the construction of the brick church in Walker's own parish of Overwharton was taken over by Mourning Richards of King and Queen County. Many of the skilled slaves and indentured workmen in Walker's possession were sold to other craftsmen.[77] Although his professional career lasted less than a quarter century, the Stafford County builder achieved a measure of success that few craftsmen would have thought possible earlier in the century when little else but small, impermanent buildings dominated the Virginia landscape.

PUNISHMENT
AND PRISONS

Introduction

CRIME PLAGUED COLONIAL Virginia. The menace of petty thefts led many to lock their valuables in trunks and closets and fasten their doors against thieves within and without their shops and houses. The fear of felonious assaults walked with many who ventured out at night into the dark and poorly patrolled streets in towns such as Norfolk, Alexandria, and Fredericksburg, which contained transient populations of seamen and poor laborers as well as numerous slaves. Virginians responded to perceived and real threats to their security and well-being by building prisons and erecting instruments of punishment. Arrayed around the courthouse grounds and in the possession of the sheriff and his constables were a series of devices for punishing those found guilty of a variety of offenses. Stocks, pillories, gallows, gibbets, whipping posts, ducking stools, restraining irons of all types, branding irons, and other instruments were none too subtle reminders of the many ways in which those who fell afoul of the law could be physically punished. In addition to this arsenal of weapons that could destroy a life, maim a leg, or scar a face, magistrates could also inflict economic distress by imposing fines for certain types of offenses.

Prisons also served as rude reminders of the fate of those who overstepped the legal boundaries of Virginia society. Shabby in appearance, foul smelling, and dangerous to the health of their inhabitants, they were indispensable instruments of the judicial system. Yet few functioned well. In 1747 Norfolk city officials decided to supplement the county prison by building one for the municipality—a 20-by-15-foot structure with a brick chimney—to house those awaiting trial in the hustings court.[1] Two years later the new jail proved no match for a hardened criminal like Thomas Seale, alias John Hill, who had been incarcerated to await his trial for robbery. Seale climbed up the chimney stack to escape his imprisonment, whereupon he burgled a store and then "cunningly got into prison again, to prevent his being suspected of the robbery."[2] In response to this and other incidents, Norfolk City Council members voted to build a stronger prison in 1753.[3] The quest for less porous lockups shaped most aspects of prison design in the eighteenth century. Cunning criminals such as Thomas Seale led magistrates to devise ever more elaborate structural systems and barriers to keep the truly desperate behind thick bars. In addition, the changing nature of the prison population in the eighteenth century forced authorities to consider new arrangements for incarceration.

The Nature of Crime

Like the English squires they sought to emulate in many ways, the Virginia planters who met in the House of Burgesses and filled the county court benches viewed the law as a powerful instrument for preserving and maintaining their dominant position in Virginia society. In 1755 Governor Robert Dinwiddie spoke of the law as the bulwark "of our most happy Constitut'n, but if those Laws are not put in due and proper Execut'n, they become of no Effect, but rather an Encouragem't to the dissolute, profane, and abandon'd Part of our People."[4] Dinwiddie's sentiments would have received full approbation among those charged with establishing and executing the rule of law in colonial Virginia. Magistrates strove hard to instill into the general populace an appreciation for the role of the law in their lives. They believed that people in a well-ordered society readily understood the limits of acceptable behavior. In fact, most white Virginians rarely challenged the moral authority of the common law and General Assembly statutes, which defined or determined the boundaries of criminal behavior, or even the right of local or provincial authorities to regulate their conduct. Those who committed criminal acts were seen to do so out of human weaknesses: greed, envy, anger, or malice. The preservation of social harmony required the punishment of those who transgressed these accepted laws. The power to punish was vested in the local county courts. With authority granted them by their commissions of the peace, the members of the wealthy oligarchy that rose to dominate the county magistracy wielded extensive power. In one way or the other, they heard all criminal cases that arose within their jurisdiction; passed judgment on friends, neighbors, strangers, and slaves; and weighed the degree of punishment to be meted out to the guilty.[5]

This control of local society could not rest solely on the threat of punishment; fear alone could not maintain the power of the gentry. After all, the county magistrates exercised their authority without anything resembling a police force. Much of the work of the court depended upon the cooperation of scores of small farmers and freeholders who filled minor offices such as constable or undersheriff. The power to coerce, therefore, depended to a large degree upon the willingness of the local populace to accept the legitimacy of the magistrates' authority. If a massive loss of confidence in those who governed occurred, as it did, for example, during Bacon's Rebellion in the 1670s, then the elaborate facade of power could easily be damaged or collapse. Magistrates were acutely aware that their authority depended on the widespread belief in the justice of their rule, and for the most part people obeyed their county officials. This deferential attitude did not prevent disturbances or challenges to their command. Sometimes magistrates had to consider popular sentiments on divisive issues or incidents. Thus at times severe punishment had to be waived or reduced to meet commonly accepted ideas of justice and to prevent popular indignation or petty incidents from turning into outright insubordination. In 1666 the magistrates of Lancaster County court learned this lesson almost too late. When the Lancaster court sentenced Stephen Chilton to sit in the stocks, two of his friends, Simon East and William Busbee, prevented the high sheriff from executing the order and so threatened the court that the magistrates "thought it not safe to sitt any Longer, and being in a manner forced to adjourne, & did thereupon adjourne for the preventon of any further trouble, which then in all probability was likely to follow."[6] The aim of magistrates above all was to avoid exposing to the public any weaknesses in the law and issues that would call into question the appropriateness of their authority.

If most white Virginians accepted the rule of the gentry by the late seventeenth century, they also helped define the nature of criminal behavior. Several times a year the court called together two dozen freeholders to sit as a grand jury and inquire into "everything that has a tendency to promote Irreligion, to Corrupt the Morals of the people, to disturb the Publick Peace," and "all breaches of the Penal Laws." From this broad charge the grand jury was asked specifically to indict "all disturbers of Religious Worship & Sabbath breakers, all prophane Swearers in common conversation, or false swearers when called upon to give evidence, Drunkeness, all Petit Larceny's, Buyers & receivers of Stolen goods . . . all forceable Entrys & detainers by force of Lands & Tenements, all Riotts, Routs & unlawful Assemblys, Affrays, Assaults, Battery's & in General all breakers of the Peace."[7]

Most presentments by the grand jury and other cases brought before the court docket divided into two types: offenses against the laws of the church and offenses against property, which were treated quite differently. Moral offenses were not viewed as crimes even though they may have constituted disruptive antisocial behavior. They were deemed to be sins: offenses against God, not man. As such, sin lacked the strictly criminal element of deliberate and malicious intent against another person. In the absence of separate ecclesiastical courts, the county justices were charged with caring for the poor and disciplining moral miscreants for misdemeanors such as swearing, drunkenness, fornication, and failure to attend church. From the seventeenth century through the first years of the eighteenth, county courts vigorously prosecuted even the most minor, nonthreatening deviation from moral norms. The justices had an interest in the economic consequences of morally proscribed behavior. Courts went to great lengths to learn the names of fathers of bastards born to servants and indigent women in order to make these men assume responsibility for the children's upbringing rather than to have them thrust upon the care of the parish. But courts also took an active interest in regulating private behavior that had little economic consequence. Sabbath breaking, nonattendance at church, adultery, fornication, and profane swearing were serious offenses that were subject to pecuniary penalties and public punishment. Henry Charleton, a man who called his minister William Cotton "a black cotted raskoll" and refused to attend church, was forced by Northampton County court to build a pair of stocks in front of the parish church and then sit in them for three consecutive Sundays during services.[8] Adulterers were often forced to stand in the parish church dressed in a white sheet and ask the entire congregation for forgiveness.

Prosecution of premarital sexual unions grew steadily in the late seventeenth century and peaked in most tidewater counties in the 1720s and 1730s.[9] Justices exacted fines, bonds for good behavior, and occasional whippings for convicted transgressors. However, after this time the number of grand jury presentments for such offenses gradually decreased. It was not that men and women got a sudden dose of remorseful guilt or an early case of Victorian propriety. In more ways than one the nature of colonial society was changing, making some traditional laws irrelevant. For example, prosecution of individuals for nonattendance at their Anglican parish church became increasingly unusual as settlement moved west, for in some piedmont and Shenandoah Valley counties the populace included magistrates and leading planters whose religious persuasions leaned toward dissenting denominations.[10] Other issues that had once demanded the attention of court officials no longer seemed as threatening, perhaps suggesting a greater tolerance for human frailties. A general statute of 1744 admitted that after a century of legislating against immorality, the old laws had done little to curb promiscuity.[11] The passage of additional statutes indicated that the breakdown of sexual mores continued to spread even though the men and women presented for these offenses came into court and paid their fines. The concomitant decline in the number of prosecutions suggests that the court had turned its attention elsewhere. People's behavior had not changed, but the type of morality proscribed and prosecuted by the court had. By the end of the century, only the more serious and threatening sexual offenses ended up in the court docket. By and large, the courts left the regulation of morality to other institutions such as the church and the family.

Recent historians of the Chesapeake have seen the years between the 1680s and the 1720s as the critical period when the planter class finally emerged as the dominant force in colonial society. The planters' power and wealth stemmed from their ability to control vast estates and a large labor force of black slaves to cultivate tobacco. By the second quarter of the eighteenth century, great planters began to build brick houses and invest their money in fine things such as costly furniture, ceramics, and other consumer goods that English industries were manufacturing by the shipload. Amid this rising tide of personal wealth and material goods, Virginia magistrates began to defend property rights vigorously. Late seventeenth-century English jurisprudence provided Virginians with the philosophical basis they needed to attack those who would ignore or undermine the sanctity of property. The Glorious Revolution of 1688 established the freedom, not of men, but men of property. Its apologist John Locke transformed old arguments of natural law to justify the liberation of property from old burdens. In writings that were extremely popular in America, he concluded that the laws of nature sanctioned the security of property: money, goods, and land. Henceforth, the triumphant landed aristocracy and the growing bourgeoisie made little pretense that the law was concerned with equal justice or charity. Locke declared that "the great and chief end" of men "putting themselves under government is the preservation of their property."[12]

Once property had become sanctified in the legal commentaries of Blackstone and others, it became the measure of all things. In England in the eighteenth century, the gentry continued to redefine the nature of crime against property through the enactment of an ever-increasing number of laws proscribing hitherto innocent or venial activities such as poaching, wood theft, and smuggling. The number of capital statutes there grew from 50 to well over 200 between 1688 and 1820. Almost all these concerned offenses against property. Virginians did not follow the English in the introduction of draconian measures such as the game laws for relatively minor property offenses, although crimes against property filled Virginia court dockets in much greater numbers in the eighteenth century.[13] Yet most felonious crimes against property in the colony were reduced in the severity of their punishment. Coupled with a very liberal application of the benefit of the clergy, many first-time offenders and those who showed signs of contrition escaped with relatively light sentences from their county magistrates.

What may have been a more lenient attitude in Virginia toward white felons proved just the opposite for the growing number of black slaves. Virginians became increasingly concerned with the regulation of slave activities. By the late seventeenth century, black bondsmen had suffered a steady decline in their legal status as they were reduced from servants to chattel slaves. The slave court act of 1692 put all ambiguities about legal rights for slaves to rest. This act allowed commissions of oyer and terminer to be given to all justices of the peace to dispose of serious crimes charged against slaves in the county where the offense occurred. It gave to the local bench greater power than was possessed by the king's criminal courts in England. Unlike whites, who could only be tried for capital cases in the provincial court at Williamsburg, slaves now had to face local magistrates who proceeded without indictments by a grand jury or verdicts by a petit jury. To minimize the attention surrounding slave crimes, trials did not take place on regular court days but when the need arose at specially called courts. Little legal recourse stood between a slave and the gallows. Accused slaves enjoyed few rights and rarely had a sympathetic ear from the presiding justices, who were not their peers but often masters, owners of other slaves who had an inherent interest in preserving their subservience. Like white felons, most slaves stood before the special oyer and terminer court sessions to face charges concerning property: breaking and entering and the theft of goods.[14] After preliminary hearings in the county court, whites accused of a serious crime were sent to Williamsburg for a proper felony trial; all cases involving slaves were summarily disposed of at oyer and terminer courts.

While many convicted slaves had their sentences reduced or were pardoned, a small number were punished with savage harshness. Thus when slaves were convicted of murdering their masters, mere hanging was not enough. Peter, a slave in Orange County, pleaded guilty in 1737 to murdering his master, John Riddle. The justices ordered that he be hanged at the next court day between the hours of ten and noon; his head was then to be cut off and stuck "on a pole near the courthouse to deter others from doing the like."[15] The brutality of the punishment reflected slave owners' fear of losing control over their servile labor force, which in some counties amounted to more than half the population by the late colonial period. With the growth of slavery, the county justices increased their efforts to control their black population, vigorously prosecuting slaves for any incidents or crimes that threatened the social order.[16] Vigilant wariness sometimes turned to outright paranoia in some courts at certain times as magistrates let fear overcome sound judgment and experience. A legal system that by necessity tolerated the application of systematic violence and the occasional miscarriage of justice was part of the price white Virginians paid for investing their fortunes in a servile labor force.

Punishment

The type of punishment and the manner in which it was carried out depended upon the nature of the crime and the status, record, and behavior of the individual. Convicted murderers frequently paid for their crimes with their life, habitual hog stealers lost their earlobes, planters who swore and slandered in a drunken rage paid a sobering fine, and contrite first-time petty thieves sometimes received a pardon. Virginians believed that punishment should be tailored to the individual and the circumstances surrounding the infraction or crime. Alcohol, for example, was an integral part of the social and legal spectacle known as court day. Public drunkenness was tolerated generally when its effects resulted in harmless amusement. An inoffensive comment by a drunken spectator in the courtroom might be met with mirth. However, when rum and punch loosened tongues and fired a mean-spirited attack upon the panoply of power, contempt of court was severely punished. As Emanuel Cleve of Richmond County learned, disruption of court proceedings and the open and direct questioning of judicial authority could prove ruinous. Upset over the court's decision to put him in the stocks for his drunken behavior, Cleve uttered, "God dam the Court and the Justices if they shall put me in the stocks, I will fire the Court house about their ears." Richmond County magistrates promptly threw him in the county prison, from which he immediately escaped. After he was recaptured, he was convicted of assault and forced to stand in the pillory with his ear nailed against the headboard.[17] Although other incorrigible rogues can be found in Virginia court order books, what is surprising is how little people directly challenged judicial authority whether drunk or sober.

With minor crimes that did not directly challenge or threaten the authority of the established order, justices exercised a far greater flexibility in their sentencings. They clearly recognized that different crimes deserved different punishments. No man convicted of stealing goods valued at five shillings would receive the same punishment as a man convicted of felonious housebreaking. Those convicted of petty theft were often sentenced to stand at the whipping post and have anywhere from ten to thirty-nine lashes "well laid on" his or her bare back. However, thirty-nine lashes could be softly applied in privacy to those who had committed their first offense or had showed signs of repentance during their trial. Servant Samuel Cox was brought before Orange County court in 1749 for stealing one of Justice George Taylor's handkerchiefs. The servant readily confessed his guilt, and the court ordered that he receive only ten lashes at "the common whipping post." In contrast, another servant, Milo Cain, brought before Westmoreland County court in 1745 for stealing "several trifling things," only exacerbated his plight by "molesting" court officers when he attempted to flee apprehension. What might have been a petty offense cost Cain twenty-five lashes "well laid on" for his impudent affront of the law.[18]

Habitual offenders or those who showed no sign of contrition probably were subjected to a particularly vicious whipping, slowly done, in front of a loud and taunting crowd. If the crowd was hostile, then the pain of punishment increased immeasurably; its hostility might also encourage the undersheriff or constable to lay on the whip with a vengeance. In 1737 the *Virginia Gazette* reported that a free black man had been tried and convicted in the Isle of Wight

County court for attempting to ravish a seven-year-old white girl. The justices sentenced him "to stand in the Pillory an Hour" and "to have 29 lashes well laid on his bare Back, and to be sold for the Payment of his Fees." The paper noted with some satisfaction that while he stood in the pillory, the man was vigorously pelted by a sizable crowd that had gathered to witness the execution of the sentence. The rough and humiliating treatment the prisoner received from the crowd was not an isolated incident of mob behavior in colonial Virginia but an integral part of that culture's system of punishment. Far from discouraging the boisterous behavior of the court-day crowd, the magistrates who passed judgment on the convicted man welcomed their active participation. They fully believed this exposure to public ridicule served as a powerful deterrent to those who contemplated similar actions. In fact, those who tried to mitigate the severity of punishment often found themselves in trouble. Mary Cole of Accomack County tried to loosen one the nails fastened to the ear of Michael Wardell as he stood in the pillory in 1688. The justices reckoned that by her actions the woman had shown contempt for their authority in "a most notorious & insolent manner" and ordered that she stand for two hours with her back against the pillory facing the courthouse with "a Paper fastened to her breast written in Capital letters viz. *for her contempt of authority.*"[19]

A man or woman who stood in the pillory for an hour suffered far more than the temporary pain of a well-placed cabbage. Many had one of their ears nailed against the headboard. After the sentence was carried out, part of their ear was cut off as a mark of villainy. As soon as felons descended the pillory, they became ostracized individuals of "evil fame," making it extremely difficult for them to resume their place in the local community. Branding was another form of punishment that created momentary pain and long-lasting shame. Those branded in the hand for hog stealing, forgery, or counterfeiting carried their punishment with them for the rest of their lives. As one antebellum Georgian observed of those who had been branded, "The mark of their infamy is fixed and visible to all—let them remove from the scenes of their past crimes, go where they will, they are regarded, shunned, and pointed at as villains, excluded forever from society."[20] Small wonder that the many rough pugilists who lost their ears in drunken fights at the courthouse, rather than by decree of the court, were quick to have recorded by the court the exact circumstances of their mishap, as did Owen Wynn of Westmoreland County in 1741 and Dennis Doyle of Louisa County in 1744.[21]

The principal purpose of most physical punishments in the seventeenth and early eighteenth centuries was to prevent crime in the future by disabling particular offenders and terrifying others into obeying the laws. Through the pain of corporal punishment such as whipping, sitting in the stocks, standing

FIGURE 140. Whipping. English engraving, late seventeenth century.

in the pillory, and branding, the various sentences carried out by the courts were intended to have a deterrent effect. Shaming and maiming punishments were most effective in relatively close-knit, stable communities. Although sitting in the stocks was a mild discomfiture, the lasting punishment came from the ridicule of friends and neighbors and the loss of honor and reputation.

Magistrates also considered who the offender was when deciding the proper punishment. Rich men paid fines rather than lose honor by being subjected to shaming corporal punishments. A drunken planter who interrupted the court's deliberations would be fined for his actions; a drunken servant would be thrown in the stocks. Because it was associated with the punishment of slaves by the beginning of the eighteenth century, whipping was a particularly humiliating form of punishment for whites, especially when it was done in public in front of a crowd that included slaves (fig. 140). White servants were much more likely to find themselves before the whipping posts than planters or other men of substance. The loss of honor that the latter would incur would be greater punishment than the law intended.

Instruments of Punishment

Long before there were courthouses and courthouse grounds, Virginians erected traditional English instruments of punishment in public and common places. In the early and mid-seventeenth century, flagrant violators of Christian morality were forced to erect stocks outside of churches and sit in them during services. A law in 1662 made the courthouse grounds the locus for exacting public punishments with "a pillory, a pair of stocks, and whipping post," but it specified that the counties were to continue to erect "a ducking stoole in such place as they shall think convenient." Built to punish shrewish or difficult women by immersing them in water, ducking stools were sited at a convenient water source. Though required by law, they seem to have been used very rarely. In Richmond County in 1754, the magistrates selected the ferry at Totuskey Creek as the best location for its ducking stool. Neighboring Northumberland County magistrates erected theirs in 1748 at a shipyard, while in King George County the magistrates ordered a ducking stool to be built on a wharf in Falmouth in 1767. Similarly, although most counties erected their gallows and gibbets on the courthouse grounds, a few elected to hang or place the bodies of executed slaves in other prominent locations. In 1756 Bedford County judges ordered the quartered remains of a slave hung at a crossroads, while Augusta magistrates decided in 1793 to erect their gallows at a fork in the road opposite a slaughterhouse.[22]

Although some components of corporal punishment occasionally appeared in distant parts of the county, the courthouse grounds were home to most instruments used to shame, maim, and execute those convicted of petty offenses or capital crimes. In some instances corporal punishment took place inside the courtroom itself. Some individuals, especially slaves convicted of theft, were burned in the hand at the bar (fig. 141). A deputy sheriff or constable heated a branding iron in the fireplace of a jury room and brought the red-hot implement, whose end may have been shaped to form the letter F for felon or to spell the name of the county as did some English irons, into the courtroom.[23] Just as he applied the iron to the flesh, the convicted felon would call out "God save the King." Soon after the last colonial governor, John Murray, fourth earl of Dunmore, promised freedom for slaves who fled their masters and supported the king in early 1776, a court in Lancaster County found a slave guilty of sheep stealing and sentenced him to be burned in the hand. The *Virginia Gazette* reported that "instead of saying, God save the King (as is usual upon such occasions) he roared out, with the greatest seeming sincerity, 'God d—n the K—g and the Governor too,'" apparently to the approval of the assembled spectators.[24]

The three most common implements of punishment were the stocks, pillory, and whipping post. When the General Assembly required in 1662 that every county have these items erected "neere the courthouse," it meant, in practice, somewhere on the two acres of public ground. Sometimes these three fixtures stood side by side outside the courthouse door. At other times they were placed prominently next to the main thoroughfare, and yet again, they occasionally were tucked discreetly in one corner of the grounds, perhaps near the prison. In Northampton County in 1724, the stocks and pillory were situated off to one side of the courthouse close to the main road through Eastville and next to the log prison (see fig. 50).[25] In contrast to this public display, the stocks and gallows in Lancaster County in 1809 were set well away from the courthouse, tavern, and clerk's office that lined the principal road. They stood in one corner of the grounds just in front of the public necessary house (fig. 142).

Stocks, pillories, whipping posts, and gallows were constructed of wood with a few pieces of ironwork to secure braces, crossbars, and locks and to constrain individuals. Stocks consisted of one or two posts that were set directly in the ground without benefit of raised foundations. In an effort to forestall decay, the posts in Surry County's stocks in 1685 were made of cedar. In between these posts or fastened to a central one were two boards that were hinged to open on

FIGURE 141. Branding in the hand in the New Sessions House, London. Engraving, c. 1770. (Guildhall Library, Corporation of London)

one or both ends (fig. 143). At the juncture of the two boards, holes were cut to secure the legs of offenders. A pointed rail seat was erected nearby for the offenders to sit upon, with an edge of the square rail upward rather than a flat side, making it an uncomfortable arrangement that was exacerbated by the taunting of bystanders. Some miscreants were ordered to sit for only five to fifteen minutes, more as a symbolic chastisement. Others suffered severe pain, being forced to sit from anywhere from an hour to the length of the day. In 1773 Phil

Malone so "misbehaved in [the] presence of the court" that Charlotte County magistrates ordered the sheriff to put him in the stocks until the court adjourned. The stocks were the most benign and most common form of physical punishment. In 1691 the stocks in Stafford County were to be used "for the Punishment of Drunkards Rioters and Tumultuous Persons Swearers profaners of the Lords name and all other offenders as the Law directs." The stocks were also used for those who insulted the court or interfered with court officials. After Edward Adcock had "insistently taxed one of the members" of the Rappahannock County court in 1684, he was laid fast in the stocks for an hour.[26] Although recreational fighting was common sport on court day, those individuals whose quarrels erupted in violent fighting on the courthouse grounds found themselves placed in the stocks to cool down.[27]

If petty offenders and nuisance makers were put in the stocks, those convicted of more severe crimes were made to stand in the pillory. Rapists, hog thieves, forgers, counterfeiters, and housebreakers were pilloried. The instrument consisted of a single post to which was attached a headboard about chest high. The headboard was divided in two and hinged at one end. In the center

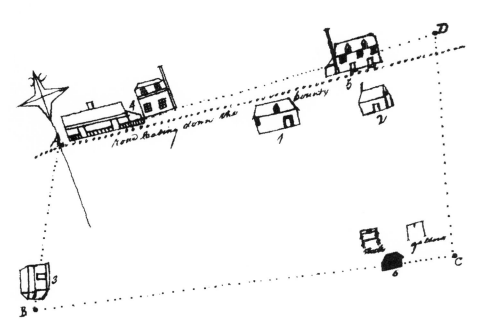

FIGURE 142. Lancaster County prison bounds, 1809. The instruments of punishment (stocks and gallows) are located in a corner of the prison bounds near the necessary house. *1:* courthouse; *2:* clerk's office; *3:* prison; *4:* ordinary occupied by Thomas West; *5:* storehouse occupied by Mr. Adam; *6:* necessary house. (Lancaster County Appeals and Land Causes Book, 1793–1823, 112, Sept. 30, 1809, The Library of Virginia)

was a large hole between the two boards for the head, with two smaller ones next to it for the hands (fig. 144). What made the pillory so effective was the disfigurement suffered by the convicted. The felon had one or both ears nailed against the headboard, the pain of which was only increased by a hostile court-day crowd that taunted or abused the convicted. Release from the pillory meant severing all or part of the ear, thus effectively marking the person as a convicted felon.[28]

Of equal ferocity was the whipping post. Some counties had a single wooden post standing in the grounds to which convicted criminals were tied and whipped on their bare backs. As some surviving English examples suggest, the whipping post may have been integrated into the pillory or stocks. Their posts, if convenient, were used to fasten an offender. Whippings were sometimes administered in conjunction with the pillory. A slave convicted of housebreaking and theft in Northumberland County in 1756 was ordered to receive thirty-nine lashes "on his bare back well laid on" as well as having his ears "nailed to the pillory and cut loose."[29]

The device most fraught with the symbolic power of the magistrates was the gallows. While whites were tried in Williamsburg at the General Court for capital offenses, slaves were tried at the county court and, if convicted, sentenced to die at the county gallows for crimes such as murder. Some counties decided to erect their gallows away from the courthouse, but others elected to construct them on the public grounds, as Essex did in 1759 and Lancaster in 1809. Although some gallows may have consisted of a tall single post with a braced horizontal member, others may have had two or three posts secured at the top by plates and braces. The image of the gallows in the 1809 plat of the courthouse grounds in Lancaster depicts two posts (see fig. 142). All these forms appear in English prints of the eighteenth century, but little is known of their form in colonial Virginia. About a mile north of Williamsburg on Capitol Landing Road, archaeologists excavated the site of the gallows used by the General Court of the colony to hang convicted white criminals and by James City County to hang slaves. Patterned after the famous gallows on Tyburn Hill in London, the Williamsburg gallows consisted of three large posts, approximately 10 inches square, set 11 feet apart from one another to form an equilateral triangle (fig. 145). The posts sat several feet in the ground and extended 10 to 15 feet in height, tall enough for the condemned to stand in a cart before execution. On top of these posts were fastened stout crossbeams, which may have had some upbraces for support.[30]

Not content merely to hang a slave, magistrates sometimes sought to make the dead person's body an example of the fate of those who would contemplate challenging the system. Peter, the Orange County slave who was convicted of murdering his master John Riddle in 1737, was not the only slave to have his

FIGURE 143. Stocks, in *Hudibras in Temptation,* by William Hogarth, 1726

FIGURE 144. Crowds taunting men standing in a four-person pillory. From W. H. Pyne,
The Costume of Great Britain (London, 1808).

FIGURE 145. Gallows, in
*The Idle 'Prentice Executed
at Tyburn,* by William
Hogarth, 1747

head severed and stuck on a pike near the court-house as a reminder to those who passed nearby. In 1730 James, a slave of Christopher Petty of Richmond County, died in prison before he was tried for the murder of Petty's daughter Mary. Nonetheless, the magistrates ordered the sheriff to take his body and "cutt it into four Quarters and hang [a] Quarter up at Potoskey [Totuskey?] Ferry, and [a] Quarter at Captain Newtons Mill, and [a] quarter at Moratico Mill and the other Quarter in William Griffins old Field and Stick his head on a pole at the Court house."[31] Other courts ordered that executed slaves be gibbeted, that is, hanged in or on a metal or wooden cage for a period of several hours or days, often coinciding with court day. The Virginia gibbets must have been wooden affairs with some ironwork; the Essex County court paid carpenter Henry Boughan a modest 200 pounds of tobacco for making a gibbet in 1707. Sometimes the distinction between the gallows and gibbet was negligible, as when the slave James Bland was hanged on the Lancaster County gibbet in 1764. At the end of the century, an English traveler in Virginia repeated the tale of a slave in the Rappahannock River valley who "was hanged alive upon a gibbet" for murdering his master. The punishment became sadistic for it was the middle of the summer and the sun beat down upon the condemned man, "who lolled out his tongue, his eyes seemed starting from their sockets, and for three long days his only cry was Water! Water! Water!"[32]

Prisons

At times an inconspicuous presence on the courthouse grounds, the county prison was an ignominious reminder of the frailties of human behavior and the realities of slave society. During the colonial period the name used for these lockups varied, the most common being *prison,* followed by the nearly synonymous *gaol.* Occasionally, Virginians called them *bridewells* or *marshalseas.* At the end of the colonial period, they began to Americanize the spelling of *gaol,* and *jail* overtook *prison* as the most common term for such a building by the early nineteenth century.[33] Whatever they were called, the scores of humble and rudely built structures erected in the seventeenth, eighteenth, and early nineteenth centuries have disappeared (fig. 146). Only a fragment of the provincial prison in Williamsburg suggests the form and scale of the best of them. The earliest surviving county prisons date from about 1800–1820, when new ideas about the treatment and incarceration of inmates led to the construction of more durable and substantial structures (fig. 147).

The origins of the first prisons are obscure, shrouded by the fact that few county records survive from the second quarter of the seventeenth century, a period when local courts began to deal with petty criminal matters far beyond Jamestown in the ever-expanding areas of settlement. Like so many building types, early prisons were scarcely distinguishable from the rest of the earthfast structures constructed by colonists to house their crops, animals, servants, and families. Although counties were required by law to construct places to confine lawbreakers as early as 1643, many were very slow in complying, choosing either to ignore the order or make do with the most casual arrangements.[34]

Eventually, security became an issue as desperate men easily punctured flimsy walls to make their escapes. Beginning in the late seventeenth century, courts began to take precautions, endeavoring to incorporate special features such as close studding, double- and triple-lined walls, iron bars, stronger locks, and perimeter walls as physical deterrents. Concern about the propriety of mixing the dangerous and dissolute, slave and free, and men and women together in a single space gradually led in the late colonial period to the construction of separate buildings for debtors and criminals or the fabrication of several cells within a single building. At the end of the eighteenth century, the state of Virginia reformed its criminal code to reflect enlightenment ideas about punishment. The immediate result of this new attitude was the construction of a penitentiary in Richmond, but it also signaled the demise of corporal punishment (except for slaves) and the increasing acceptance of incarceration as a form of punishment. By the antebellum period large brick and stone prisons enclosed behind perimeter walls became an ominous presence just beyond the main walks of the public square in many of Virginia's courthouse towns.

Prisons were constructed for the short-term accommodation of runaway servants and slaves, prisoners awaiting trial and sentencing, and debtors. Colonial Virginians never considered long-term incarceration as an alternative to shaming or pecuniary punishments, and as a result, transient prison populations found themselves in poorly constructed and inadequately maintained buildings. Essex County built perhaps as many as eight prisons between 1704 and 1788, nearly all of them as shoddy as the previous one. County officials also balked at the idea of having to pay for feeding, guarding, and clothing prisoners consigned for any length of time. For example, in 1645 in Lower Norfolk County, the court compensated Sheriff Thomas Tooker 40 pounds of tobacco

FIGURE 146. Nineteenth-century jail, Charles City, in a June 13, 1864, photograph. (Library of Congress)

FIGURE 147. Gloucester County debtors' prison, c. 1820

for imprisoning the "suspicious" John Ball but paid 420 pounds for detaining him for two weeks in the "prison house" before his trial in Jamestown. At times the bill could be extraordinary, as in the case of George Mason, the high sheriff of Stafford County, who presented the magistrates with an account amounting to 20,000 pounds of tobacco for maintaining "Six Strange Indians wch were taken and brought into this Countrey." Their imprisonment lasted for 106 days during which Mason was forced to keep "a guard over them at all time." At a time when a new county prison cost between 6,000 and 8,000 pounds of tobacco, Mason's bill must have seemed extraordinarily high.[35]

Many if not most of the earliest prisons were not purpose-built structures but merely dwellings, storehouses, and other buildings requisitioned or leased by county authorities.[36] On the Eastern Shore in 1664, Captain William Jones rented to the Northampton County court his "new store" next to his dwelling house as a prison for the sum of 600 pounds of tobacco per year. Similar offers appeared throughout the century, especially from tavern keepers and prominent citizens who saw that they could earn extra income with little or no effort. The magistrates found these temporary quarters satisfactory because they were often accessory to the buildings where the courts were held. Lancaster tavern keeper William Theriott, host of the county court for a number of years, was paid 1,500 pounds of tobacco for the use of one of his buildings as a prison in 1664. In nearby Middlesex County the public-spirited justice Richard Robinson not only spirited away large annual payments for the use of his dwelling as a court venue but in 1678 offered "to keep this County Prison" for ten years for the yearly sum of two thousand pounds of tobacco.[37]

Although magistrates recognized the need for secure prisons, the expense of building them acted as a deterrent for many years. Some counties were only prompted to build or appropriate better accommodations when threatened with the liability of damages and expenses incurred from prisoners who escaped from a prison not deemed "sufficient" by the sheriff. Perhaps as a means of turning the tables on any sheriff who might contemplate pursuing this legal action, some counties put the onus for security squarely on their chief enforcement officer. In 1667 Accomack County sheriff John West petitioned the court for a secure prison. The justices decided to designate one of the houses at the sheriff's plantation as the county prison, leaving Captain West with the problem of making the building safe. The same situation occurred in Northumberland County in 1681 when the county ordered that "any house belonging to the Sheriff shall be accounted a prison until such time that the County Prison be erected."[38]

For the next century the sheriff and the bench conducted an almost annual ritual in many counties. Upon taking office, the sheriff would lodge a formal complaint. In 1730, for example, Sheriff Tarlton Fleming of Goochland protested "against the Justices of this County for all damages, costs, and sums of money or tobacco that shall or may be recorded against him by reason of the escape of any Prisoner or Prisoners . . . out of the Goal of this County the said Goal not being sufficient as he thinks." Edward Stott was appointed to view the old prison and reported later that a new one should be erected, whereupon he was then selected to undertake the construction of the new one. Fifteen months later Sheriff Fleming protested the sufficiency of this new building. A county bench's first response to a sheriff's complaint usually was to order repairs "att the cheapest rate."[39] The story was repeated countless times, sometimes with immediate results but more often than not with halfhearted measures that only delayed the necessity to expend larger amounts of public money when major disasters such as a fire or an embarrassing escape forced the magistrates to act.

These temporary and makeshift prisons must have been as secure as a secret in an alehouse. Seventeenth-century court records often read as if the entire criminal population was on the lam. Escape took no clever stratagem, just determination and the right moment. Imprisoned at Jamestown in 1683, John Haley "took the opportunity of the Guards being gone to supper" to break the walls and "though well loaded with Irons made his escape from the said Goale."[40] In 1685 Thomas Holmes bolted from the Henrico prison after only two days and made his way out of the county "not withstanding speedy & earnest pursuit."[41]

A few years later the lax security at the same prison proved too much of a temptation for Thomas Chamberlayne, who knocked off a few exterior clapboards and tried to slip through the space between the wall studs. Although apprehended by the subsheriff who was standing guard, Chamberlayne was undeterred and soon successfully escaped through the much-abused walls. Westmoreland prison, too, was notorious for its sievelike qualities. By 1696 it was in such a ruinous and decayed condition that "prisoners therein put frequently make their escapes." Lord Culpeper, the governor, summed up the general state of affairs in the late seventeenth century when he asserted that "there are in effect no prisons, but what are soe easily broken."[42]

Culpeper's assessment only confirmed what Virginians had long taken for granted. As early as 1647 and once again in 1662, the General Assembly recognized that the scarcity of ironwork for locks, grates, bars, straps, and hinges hindered "our ability . . . to build stronger" prisons." It therefore declared that one "built according to the forme of Virginia houses, from which noe escape can be made without breaking or forcing some part of the prison house," would henceforth be deemed "sufficient." County courts would be released from any liability "imposed upon them by any such escapes or by neglect of the sheriffs." These statutes also put inmates on notice that breaking out of these porous buildings would be considered a felonious offense.[43]

TABLE 4   Early prison specifications

Date	County	Size	Height	Building features
1674	Accomack	10×15		Posts with groundsills; chimney
1678	Northampton	15×15		Chimney
1680	Lancaster	15×20		Ground posts; close studded; interior chimney
1681	Northumberland		10	Posts with groundsills; close studded
1683	Henrico	15×15		Posts with groundsills; chimney
1685	Rappahannock	15×20	7½	Close studded
1689	Norfolk	15×15		Brick
1690	Northampton			Log; same dimensions as Accomack
1691	Middlesex	15×20		Posts in the ground; close studded; interior chimney
1692	Princess Anne	15×15		Log; close joists
1692	Stafford	12×12	8	Posts & studs in the ground; interior lined
1693	Surry			New posts repaired; close studded
1698	Lancaster	12×16	8	Brick ends; internal chimney; close joists
1706	Northumberland	16×16	10	Brick foundations & ends
1711	Westmoreland	10×20	9	Brick with partition; close joists
1719	Northampton	16×16	7	Sawn logs dovetailed; block foundations

"Virginia house" was the name given by contemporaries to post-in-the-ground wooden buildings whose simplified framing system could be constructed with an economy of labor and materials. Prison specifications from the late seventeenth and early eighteenth centuries vary little from the size, materials, framing techniques, and finishes of other buildings. From the 1670s through the 1720s, prisons were one-room lockups, measuring no more than 300 square feet in size (table 4). Most were far smaller, being no more than one-third to one-half the size of contemporaneous courthouses. The 1674 prison in Accomack County stood 10 by 15 feet, while Stafford County's 1692 gaol was 12-by-12 feet square, a space that must have seemed particularly cramped if the prison population rose above one occupant.[44]

The framing system of most "Virginia houses" by the second half of the seventeenth century consisted of a series of bays defined by major posts located at

FIGURE 148. Interior, Northampton County prison, Eastville, c. 1815

either 8- or 10-foot intervals. The posts measured up to 12-by-12 inches in width and were embedded 2 to 4 feet in the ground. Atop the posts sat the wall plates, which carried the ceiling joists and the roof framing members. The 8- or 10-foot space between the posts was filled with secondary uprights or studs, usually placed between 18 inches and 2 feet apart. Carpenters sheathed the exterior with 4- or 5-foot long clapboards, depending upon the spacing of the major posts. Although some dwellings may have been plastered or sheathed on the inside, most structures had unfinished interiors with exposed framing members. Early prisons no doubt followed this practice, so it was very easy for criminals such as Thomas Chamberlayne to wreck a building through a series of violent blows against the clapboards and escape through the gap between the widely spaced framing members.

To restrain the enthusiasm of prison breakers, builders increased the size of the framing members, mortised rather than lapped studs to plates, and placed upright members a few inches apart. Close studding appeared in the 1680 Lancaster County prison. The main posts sat 3½ feet in the ground. The studs measured 6 inches square, stood buried 2 feet in the ground, and were spaced 3 inches apart. To reduce the risk of escape through the roof, the ceiling joists were laid within 6 inches of each other and were covered with "substantial rived boards." The roof frame had double the number of normal rafters. Other counties adopted similar measures. The studs in the 1685 Rappahannock County prison were spaced 6 inches apart. The 1691 specifications for the Middlesex prison required the framing members to be within 3 inches of one another with the posts set 4 feet in the ground. Surry magistrates improved the strength of their prison in 1693 by inserting five studs for each length of 4- or 5-foot clapboards and nailing the clapboards to the top of the studs on the inside to prevent the weakening of the joint between the studs and wallplate.[45] This practice of "double framing" or increasing the size and number of framing members in county prisons also became a common building practice in the Chesapeake in the late seventeenth century as a means of providing additional structural support or security for other buildings such as tobacco houses and smokehouses.

In the next century builders tried additional measures to strengthen the security of county prisons. Perhaps the most important innovation was to line the inside of the prison cell with thick planks (fig. 148). Interior sheathing spiked and pegged into the wall frame prevented prisoners from tampering and undermining the joints of the frame and provided greater rigidity to the walls. To counteract the weakness of the walls of the Westmoreland County prison, 2-inch-thick white oak planks were installed in the cell in 1715. The new prison in Princess Anne County in 1726 was "Double Studded with good oak Studds," and the exterior weatherboarded with pine plank while the interior walls were sheathed with riven clapboards. Lancaster prison in 1750 was "close sealed" with 2-inch oak planks spiked into the walls, a practice that became standard after midcentury.[46]

The search for strength and reliability lead county magistrates to explore alternatives to frame construction. In the last quarter of the seventeenth century, log and brick prisons made their first appearance. The horizontal stacking of logs secured by corner joints was not a traditional English building method but was employed by North European settlers in the Delaware Valley and adapted to the frontier conditions of the Chesapeake by the 1650s. Subject to various degrees of workmanship, from loosely stacked, unhewn timbers to tightly jointed and close-fitting planks, well-fabricated log buildings provided a high degree of security and reduced the need for nails, a shortage of which plagued a number of Chesapeake builders through the late seventeenth century. A brick building also could be far more durable than a frame one, especially if the bricks and mortar were well made and laid. However, brick building was a far more expensive enterprise, and most officials choose to build for the moment rather than for the future.

Although log prisons may already have appeared in Virginia by the 1670s, the earliest documented one was built farther south in the Albemarle region of North Carolina. In 1677 during disturbances known as Culpeper's Rebellion, Thomas Miller was taken as a prisoner "to the uppr end of Pasquotank River . . . and enclosed in a Logghouse about 10 or 11 foot square purposely built for him."[47] The earliest known Virginia ones were those erected on the Eastern Shore. Accomack County had a log gaol by 1690, for in that year the magistrates in neighboring Northampton cited it as the precedent for their new prison. On the southern perimeter of the bay, magistrates in the newly formed county of Princess Anne ordered the construction of a 15-foot-square prison built of good strong logs in 1692. This prison was also to have "joists soe thick that no man can get through between" and was to be covered with "good strong clapboards."[48] Unfortunately, none of these early specifications describe the preparation of the materials, whether the logs, for example, were carefully sawn or hewn, or how the corners were secured.[49]

The full range of log building techniques may be seen in the specifications for later prisons. After wearing out the 1690 log gaol, Northampton magistrates ordered a new one built in 1719. Thomas Griffin undertook to erect a 16-foot-square structure made of sawn oak logs. Standing on wooden blocks 2 feet above the ground, the log walls measured 5 inches in thickness and were secured at the corners with dovetail joints. Added precautions included having the 4-inch-thick oak floorboards pinned with wooden treenails to 6-inch-thick sleepers rather than nailed. The ceiling joists were pinned as well to the top logs of the walls.[50]

Of similar construction were the prisons erected by undertaker William Walker for King George County in 1746 and Westmoreland County in 1749. The one in King George and the two in Westmoreland represent a high level of craftsmanship. All three prisons sat on masonry rather than wood foundations, which ensured a measure of durability over earthfast structures. King George prison was 12 feet square and 8 feet in height from floor to ceiling. The criminals' prison in Westmoreland had the same dimensions and stood on 18-inch-high brick foundations. The debtors' prison was slightly larger, measuring 14 feet square. Walker fabricated all three prisons out of sawn white oak logs, 6 inches thick, 12 inches in height, and laid "as Close as they can be jointed with an axe." The inside walls were lined with 1¼- and 1½-inch-thick oak plank "well nailed with spikes and Trunnels," while the outer face of the logs was covered with 1-inch boards. The weatherboards were pine at King George and poplar at Westmoreland; the latter were also "plained, beaded and . . . dovetailed at the corners and dowel'd in two parts at an end" to provide an extra measure of protection.[51] With triple-thick walls secured by strong dovetailed and pinned joints, these prisons were built to withstand the most ingenious and protracted assaults upon their fabric.

Not all log buildings were so impenetrable as the Northern Neck dovetailed plank examples. At the other end of the scale were those structures hastily or cheaply erected with round or roughly hewn logs and poorly detailed corner joints. The 12-foot-square Prince Edward prison had clapboards nailed along the outside joints of the hewn logs to provide additional structural support and security. In newly formed Botetourt County, a 12-by-16-foot "log cabin" served as the first prison in 1770. In general, the term *cabin* was used describe a building of simple or crude construction, and the Botetourt structure must have been fabricated with minimum preparation. The Augusta prison, by contrast, suffered from poor workmanship. Built in the late 1740s, it was so filled with holes, many of them nearly a foot in size, and the square logs were so poorly dovetailed at the corners, that a committee appointed to view it decided "that it would be a very easy matter to pull it all down."[52] Counties in the piedmont, Shenandoah Valley, and western mountains were rife with buildings of such dubious quality in the late colonial and early national periods.

If rough log construction provided the cheapest way to build a prison, then masonry was the most expensive. Most seventeenth-century county magistrates considered brick a luxury, a material that was used sparingly in domestic architecture and rarely in public buildings except for foundations and chimneys. Even Jamestown offered few precedents for prison architecture. In the 1660s and early 1670s, prisoners brought to Jamestown to stand trial found themselves incarcerated in a brick building located within yards of the statehouse. The provincial gaol was an end unit of a series of four two-story dwelling houses probably erected in the mid-1660s in response to the town act of 1662 and known since the site was excavated in the 1930s as structure 115. Measuring 20 feet in width and 40 feet in length with a central chimney dividing the space into two equal-sized rooms, this lobby-entrance dwelling at the eastern end of the row was built with public money in an effort to foster cohabitation and increase Jamestown's urban prospect. Despite the undertaking, the row apparently had few tenants, and in 1668 James City County magistrates petitioned the House of Burgesses for the right to use "one of the Countrie Brick houses" for its gaol. The county was given a seven-year lease and permission to fit the building out as a prison at its own charge.[53] The building was then probably used for about eight years before being torched by Nathaniel Bacon and his followers when they burned Jamestown in 1676. A lease in 1680 described this structure "now lying in ruins" as "that house where the gaole was kept." Compared to others of the period, the James City County prison contained spacious quarters with at least four heated rooms and a number of windows. Nothing is known of any additional measures that local authorities may have taken to convert this dwelling into a more secure lockup. Because of the fragmentary nature of the records, there is little evidence of any other prisons purposely built either before or after the temporary home at structure 115. Archaeological excavations at Jamestown in the 1930s and once again in the 1950s failed to locate any foundations that could be identified as a county or provincial prison. In 1693 James City County representatives to the House of Burgesses petitioned that body on behalf of the county magistrates to be reimbursed for the use of the county prison by the provincial government, which suggests that there was not at this time, if ever, a provincial prison.[54]

In a landscape of poorly built wooden structures, brick implied permanence and, in the case of prisons, solidity. In a few of the wealthier and more populous counties that had relatively stable boundaries and a cohesive bench, brick prisons began to appear by the last years of the century. The county of Norfolk demonstrated its commitment to the development of the eponymous new town on the north shore of the Elizabeth River when the magistrates agreed to locate a brick courthouse and prison there in 1689. Other than its 15-foot-square dimensions and the material of its walls, little else is known about the construction of this early brick prison.[55] Norfolk flourished and became the most important seaport in Virginia.

Another planned town with similar beginnings, Queenstown in Lancaster County, failed. Established near the mouth of the Rappahannock River in the early 1690s, Queenstown received a significant boost when the county seat was established there in 1698. In that year planter Robert "King" Carter, one of the most powerful and most wealthy men in the colony, undertook the construction of a brick courthouse and a 12-by-16-foot prison. The gable ends of the gaol, one of which contained an inside chimney, were built of brick, while the long walls were frame.[56] Despite these public buildings, the town never grew beyond a village, and by the time Town Creek silted up in the middle of the eighteenth century, the county had moved its business to the present-day town of Lancaster where new buildings were erected including a brick prison. Constructed in 1740, this 12-by-20-foot prison displayed little difference in form from other brick buildings. The foundation walls were three bricks thick, or approximately 2 feet in breadth. From the surface of the ground to the plate, the walls narrowed to two bricks, or approximately 1 foot 8 inches. These thicknesses were typical of most brick structures erected in the region. Only the composition of the mortar showed any variations from standard practice.[57] Consisting of three-quarters lime to one-quarter sand, the mortar was rock hard, creating a bond resistant to degradation by weather or by design. Most colonial mortars were much softer, with a higher percentage of sand to lime, up to one-half to three-fifths of the mixture. The strong mortar joints were matched on the inside by walls lined with 1½-inch oak planks that were nailed to wooden bond timbers with tenpenny nails.[58]

Two late colonial projects capitalized on the strength and fire-resistant qualities of masonry. In 1764 Stafford magistrates ordered the construction of a brick gaol whose walls were to be 3 feet thick and whose ceiling was "to be arched over with brick, to prevent being set on fire." The specifications also called for the exterior to be "well covered with stucco, to keep out the weather."[59] In the following year the justices in Orange County reached the paranoid level of prison design (fig. 149). Although their specifications did not call for brick walls as thick as the Stafford ones, wrapped inside the brick core was to be an internal wall of 6-inch-thick sawn logs that were dovetailed at the corners and tenoned into large doorposts. Builder Zachariah Burnley was to sheath the logs with 1½-inch oak planks laid vertically and spiked every 2 feet with large twenty-penny nails. The exterior brick walls were to be enclosed by yet another wall of 6-inch sawn oak logs, dovetailed at the corners and windows, doweled with 2-inch pins, and tenoned into the doorposts. Over this log wall Burnley was to nail tarred weatherboards.

As solid and bunkerlike as the walls, the Orange roof was to start with a series of 12-inch-square ceiling joists laid side by side. On top of these would stand a solid core of bricks, laid six courses high around the edges and rising to 2 feet in the center to form a hip roof. This mass of brickwork was to be laid in hard lime mortar with tar and sand placed over it to help seal it. Finally, a tarred clapboarded roof would cover the brickwork and add further sealing against the elements. Burnley was to receive 12,800 pounds of tobacco for his labors, which seem to have been successful because there were no recorded escapes.[60]

In the last half of the eighteenth century, a small number of counties outside of the tidewater considered stone to be a suitable building material not just for foundations or chimneys but for entire walls. Where it was available as fieldstone or easily quarried, stone presented an attractive alternative to wood and even brick because of its bulk strength and durability. When William Byrd observed Spotsylvania's new stone prison in Fredericksburg in 1732, he declared the walls of native white stone were strong enough to withstand the efforts of Jack Sheppard, a notorious English highwayman known for his legendary escapes from custody.[61] Working against the widespread use of building stone, however, was its absence in the older and wealthier counties in the southeast,

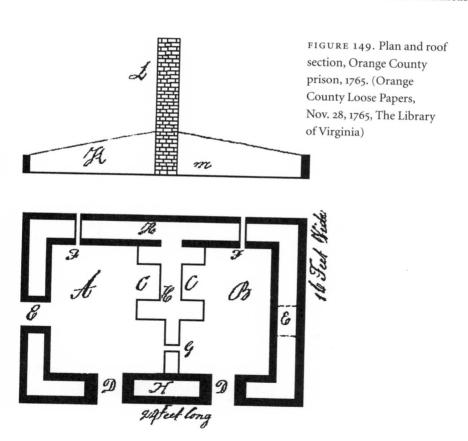

FIGURE 149. Plan and roof section, Orange County prison, 1765. (Orange County Loose Papers, Nov. 28, 1765, The Library of Virginia)

the difficulty of transporting the material to the building site, and the limited availability and high cost of skilled masons.

One of the earliest descriptions of a stone jail appeared in the Loudoun County records in 1767. The magistrates ordered the construction of a two-story prison measuring 16 by 24 feet. Perhaps worried about possible under-mining, the justices wanted the building's foundations at least 4 feet in the ground and 4 feet above the surface. The walls of the first story were to be 4 feet thick and those of the second 2 feet. The whole was to be laid in hard lime mortar. Another county whose security was to be set in stone was Prince William, whose justices decided to build a two-story structure in the town of Dumfries in 1788. The plan and elevation drawn by Edward Vieller for the 32-by-38-foot building called for the foundations to stand 2½ feet deep and 2½ feet wide. After stepping in 6 inches at the water table, the first- and second-story walls were to be 2 feet thick and "laid in Regular courses on the outside and well and sufficiently bound with stones to go through the walls." The mortar was to consist of "two thirds good stone or shell lime and one third of good clean sand," a recipe that ensured solid bonding. The cost of the undertaking came to the substantial sum of £785, far more than many counties were willing to spend on their courthouses.[62]

Prisons were the weakest where there were holes; apertures were therefore kept to an absolute minimum. All that was really necessary was a single entrance into the cell, and it is reasonable to assume that the earliest prisons rarely had additional openings. The 1692 Stafford prison probably was made a little more bearable by the presence of a small barred window that let in some light, and the 1698 prison in Lancaster County also had a window "with Iron grates."[63] However, such a feature was still unusual. Light, ventilation, and sanitation were not important considerations. Early prison specifications seldom mention any apertures other than a door, which suggests that concern about escape routes and the scarcity of ironwork combined to make most cells dark and putrid. George Wilson, a Quaker tossed into the "nasty, stinking prison" at Jamestown in 1662, complained that "we have not had the benefit to do what nature requireth, nor so much as air, to blow in, at a window, but close made up with brick and lime, so that there is no air to take away the smell [of] our dung and p——."[64]

Good prison doors were smaller and stouter than those found on other buildings (fig. 150). The doorway to the 1756 Northumberland prison, for example, measured 2½ by 5 feet. The Orange prison doorway was 2 feet wide and 5½ feet tall. Most doors were double sheathed, containing an outer layer of 1¼- to 2-inch oak boards running in one direction, backed by an inner layer applied in the opposite direction or in a diagonal or chevron pattern. The two layers were secured together with large nails or spikes that were clinched at their tips to prevent easy extraction. The 4-inch-thick Orange prison door was "nailed thick with 30d nails, or large spikes to clinch." Builders commonly reinforced the doors with iron strapwork, either with a series of bands or a grid of horizontal and vertical straps. The Norfolk (1733), Westmoreland (1749), Northumberland (1756), Surry (1756), and Prince Edward (1760) jails are midcentury examples of doors plated with ironwork.[65] The grated ironwork of the Middlesex prison door was not to exceed a weave of 6 inches square. The first prison erected in Madison County in 1793 had a set of two doors to secure its opening. The inner door consisted of a gridiron of flat 2-inch-wide iron bars spaced 2 inches apart. A wooden double door enclosed the outside of this 2½-by-5-foot opening. The outer iron door at the nineteenth-century Spotsylvania jail had a wider weave with similar broad, flat bars (fig. 151). These and other prison doors required good, large iron hinges. Most were secured with two or more strap hinges; the early nineteenth-century prison in Northampton County has three hinges. The Surry prison door was hung with cross garnets. Locks were essential, and the most common type was a padlock, which had to

FIGURE 150. Door, Northampton County prison, Eastville, c. 1815

withstand the force of culprits within and accomplices without. In an attempted escape Westmoreland prisoner Stephen Peacock burned the lock of the gaol door, a desperate act repeated countless times throughout the colony. Men like Peacock kept local blacksmiths in business. County accounts record many payments for the repair or fabrication of prison locks. In an effort to double the difficulty, some counties such as York and King George put two padlocks on their prisons.[66]

Prison windows required iron bars or grates and were deliberately made small to prevent prisoners from squeezing through them or people on the outside passing objects through to inmates. The danger was real, for accomplices of William Towe handed him a spike, gimlet, and chisel through the open window of the Suffolk prison, and he proceeded to use them to bore his way through the floorboards, sleepers, and brick underpinnings and fled one night despite being fettered.[67] From the late seventeenth century onward, one of the criteria by which a sheriff deemed a prison sufficient was if these apertures were enclosed by either a series of vertical or horizontal bars or cross-woven grates.

FIGURE 151. Iron exterior door, Spotsylvania County jail, in a late nineteenth-century photograph. (Virginia Historical Society)

The ends of the iron bars or grates sometimes were deeply embedded in the frame or brickwork to ensure better structural integrity.[68] Generally, there was only one window per cell, though some prisons had an additional grated opening in the door. Each of the 1749 Westmoreland prisons had a grated window in the upper part of its door coupled with a window on the opposite wall "for air." At their most considerate, some Virginia prison builders allowed debtors' cells to be lit by larger apertures or two windows compared to miserly provisions for criminals' cells. Such was the case in the 1756 Northumberland prison where the debtors' room contained "two large windows" 2½ feet long by 1½ feet in height.[69] The early nineteenth-century prison in Northampton, which may have been erected to house debtors, has a generously sized window measuring 1½ feet in width by 3 feet in height in each of the gable ends (fig. 152).

Prisons were miserable structures for a number of reasons, not the least of which was the fact that a closed environment did little for a prisoner's health, as the Quaker Wilson learned after six months in his "dirty dungeon" at Jamestown.[70] Combined with bad air circulation, poor sanitation aggravated the risk of catching a disease under stressful circumstances. Some prisons may have had chamber pots, others not. A few contained built-in features to take care of bodily waste. As early as 1691 the builder of the Middlesex gaol erected "a place of Easmt.," perhaps some sort of closestool.[71] Other prisons had lead pipes or lead-lined wooden troughs set into the walls "for conveying the filth" out of the cell.[72] The 1749 Westmoreland prisons had "a conveniency to ease Nature with," primarily a "lead pipe thro' the wall to carry off excrement" and a "stool or cistern" which was lined with lead.[73] The remnants of a convenience survive in the southeast corner of the debtors' prison in Gloucester where a 6-by-9-inch hole was cut through the interior plank sheathing and brick wall about 1½ feet above the floor. A 10-by-16-inch collection box once enclosed a wooden or lead funnel that drained downward to a hole in the exterior wall. Despite these amenities, a few prisoners perished from a variety of diseases before they could be hanged for their crimes.[74]

Chimneys were a great liability in early prisons, but they were a necessity. The absence of a chimney in the debtors' room of the Richmond prison in 1783 caused its jailer to plead for the construction of one. He lamented "those who may unfortunately be thrown into it, in the winter seasons suffer a punishment beyond the intention of the Laws or the wishes of the most Sanguinary Creditors." The justices of Westmoreland County made an important distinction between the prisons built for its debtors and its criminals. They insisted that the former have a chimney, while it was unnecessary for the latter.[75] Although not every prison had one, those that did had either an internal chimney or an external gable-end chimney. One-room prisons had end chimneys, and those with two rooms generally had a central chimney. Fireplaces warmed the prisoners on cold evenings, provided a place to cook or warm meals, and mitigated the dampness that developed in the long humid months of summer. A constant fire also helped retard the growth of rot and the spread of termites, an important consideration in the humid climate of Virginia.

Yet chimneys proved to be a security threat. The source of warmth also proved the means of escape for a number of prisoners. Sometimes a prison accidentally caught on fire, as was the case in Northampton County in 1703 and Charlotte County in 1773. The Amherst County prison proved too secure for debtor Richard Fletcher Gregory, who perished after the prison caught fire on

FIGURE 152. Window, Northampton County prison, Eastville, c. 1815

the evening of December 4, 1768.[76] More often than not, fires that got out of hand were ones deliberately set by inmates seeking their freedom. In some instances the ploy worked, and the prison arsonists fled amidst the confusion. Committed to the Chesterfield jail, robber Benjamin Jones, alias Edward Davis, burned the prison and made his escape. At other times the calculated risked backfired, as a debtor imprisoned in Brunswick County discovered when he failed to get out of the conflagration with his life. Chimney stacks and flues provided another means of escape. In 1748 part of the chimney in the Augusta prison fell down, leaving an area open to the roof "which a man might easily break with his foot or hands." The sheriff of Amelia County was so concerned about the insufficiency of his prison's chimney that the court ordered that it be taken down "and rebuilt in such a manner as no Person should be able to escape that way." Some prison builders inserted barriers in the flue to prevent such daring escapes. In 1698 the Lancaster prison had iron bars located "three foot down the funnell," while the specifications for the felons' prison in Westmoreland County in 1749 took into account accidental and maliciously set fires. They called for "an Iron stove fireplace for the greater security against burning" and an "iron grate where the chimney goes through the upper floor to prevent prisoners making their escape thro' the chimney." The Fauquier prison in 1759 had 1½-inch-square bars spaced within 4 inches of each other in the funnel of the stack and tied into the frame of the building.[77]

Besides considerations of security, Virginians became increasingly concerned about the propriety of incarcerating the evil-minded with the unfortunate. In many places through much of the colonial era, county prisons contained an indiscriminate host of men and women—from debtors, runaway slaves, Indians, English convicts deported to the Chesapeake and on the run to rogues, swindlers, and murderers—who all shared the same single-cell quarters. During the first decades of the county judicial system, the prison population was primarily composed of servants and small freeholders awaiting trial for criminal activities. However, by the end of the seventeenth century, the profile of the prison population began to change. Among the most disturbing of the new faces were English convicts who had been transported to the Chesapeake, much to the annoyance of tobacco planters who blamed upsurges in criminal activity and unruliness among servants on their presence and influence. With Virginia "endangered by the great number of fellons and other desperate villaines sent hither from the several prisons in England," the council in 1670 prohibited the importation of "any jaile birds or such others, who for notorious offenses have deserved to dye in England." Not only did they cause grave mischief, but their presence sullied the reputation of the colony, causing people to think of it as "a place onely fitt to receive such base and lewd persons."[78] The provision did little to stem the dumping of convicts, though those

English criminals who were deported to the Chesapeake colonies never formed a permanent class of lawless bandits as the council feared.

The last quarter of the seventeenth century also saw the number of blacks in Virginia's population swell as the large-scale importation of African slaves began in earnest.[79] By the beginning of the eighteenth century, Virginia's tobacco planters were fully committed to slave labor. The establishment of oyer and terminer slave courts in 1692 and the codification of slave laws in 1705 put new demands on the local legal system. More and more slaves ended up at the county gaol, which now became their first and last place of incarceration. No longer sent to Jamestown to stand trial in the General Court like whites accused of a felony, black slaves came before the county magistrates and were punished, if convicted, on the courthouse grounds. Thus prisons began to house increasing numbers of slaves awaiting trial or punishment. They also served as lockups for slaves who ran away from their masters' employment and for free or enslaved blacks who could not provide an acceptable account of their status or business.

One last group of individuals found in small but increasing numbers in county prisons was debtors, those unfortunates at the extreme end of a debt-ridden society. In the absence of banks in the colony, credit was often obtained through Scottish merchants or London and Glasgow tobacco factors. In Virginia large planters extended credit to small freeholders and tenants in the neighborhood. Because planter justices were just as likely to be indebted to Scottish and English merchants for the goods they purchased against the value of their yearly tobacco crop as small farmers were to be strapped for cash to buy necessities from local store owners, Virginians treated debt rather gingerly.[80] For the most part the courts provided a buffer for indebted colonists of all classes, as lenders suing for repayment of formal contractual arrangements and informal agreements encountered a web of procedures that only prolonged the process. In his published survey of the colony in 1722, Hugh Jones observed that "the laws [are] so favourable for debtors, that some esteem them too indulgent."[81]

Despite these propitious circumstances, some Virginians wound up imprisoned for debt. Empowered by a writ of *capias ad satisfaciendum*, a sheriff seized a debtor and locked him in prison to satisfy the creditor for his judgment and costs. This policy survived with little change until 1819 when the code was revised to make it possible for a debtor to swear to an affidavit of insolvency and be released from prison. However, he had to surrender all his property except necessary clothes and tools of his trade. Some who went to prison for debt were simply incorrigibles whose appetite for luxury outstripped their means of procuring it. Perhaps the most famous was Light-Horse Harry Lee, who misspent the fortunes of two heiresses at Stratford and spent time in Westmoreland prison in the early nineteenth century. Others who found themselves imprisoned for debt were small planters who overextended their capacities or individuals who simply suffered from bad luck or misfortune with the fluctuation of the tobacco trade. Whatever their circumstances, those who landed in prison had hit bottom. A few recovered, others did not. When Richard Fletcher Gregory realized he could not escape the accidental fire while he was incarcerated in Amherst prison in 1768, he took his clothes off and threw them out the window as his "only legacy" to his family.[82]

The practice of commingling all these different groups in single-cell prisons began to change at the beginning of the eighteenth century. Virginians recognized that debtors deserved slightly better prison accommodations than suspected or convicted criminals in part because they often became long-term residents. Deprivations of heat, air, and exercise along with disease took their toll on those incarcerated for months in small, shared spaces. The provision of chimneys, larger windows, and exercise grounds alleviated some of the misery suffered by debtors, but more importantly, public officials accepted the idea of segregating criminals from debtors. Eventually this policy gradually came to be applied to other groups of prisoners, so that by the end of the eighteenth century, some county prisons divided men from women and blacks from whites. Early, hesitant steps to segregate prisoners due to concerns for health eventually developed into a moral imperative as public officials worried about the corruptive influence of the debauched on fellow inmates. A committee of gentlemen called on to inspect the conditions of the public jail in Richmond in 1787 were shocked to learn that overcrowding forced the jailer to lodge criminals among debtors. The committee observed that "in several Instances single Women confined for Debt have been stowed—without Regard to that Decency their Sex entitles them to—among the most profligate and abandoned of mankind."[83]

The first multiple-cell prisons probably appeared in the last decade of the seventeenth century—Westmoreland prison had two rooms in 1699, for example—but it was the construction of the public gaol in Williamsburg in 1701–3 that provided the model for prison architecture for the next generation of county prisons (figs. 153, 154).[84] In August 1701 the General Assembly passed a law authorizing the construction of a

> substantiall Brick Prison, thirty foot long in the clear and twenty foot wide in the clear three rooms on the lower floor, vizt. One with the Chambers above for the goalers or prison keepers owne use and for confinement of small offenders, and the other two smaler on the lower floor for goals for the criminals of both sexes . . . and that at one end

thereof there be walled in with a substantiall wall tenn foot high, twenty foot square of ground for the prisoners to be let into to aire them as occasion shall require for preservation of their life and health till tryall.[85]

Built just north of the Capitol by the same undertaker, Henry Cary, the public gaol was finished by the end of 1703 and received its first prisoners in time for the spring session of the General Court in 1704.[86] Like so many other public buildings in the new capital, the brick prison combined familiar design elements with new ones. The brick walls and reinforced foundations were part of familiar efforts to make prisons more secure. The floors and ceilings of the cells were covered with thick planks to which iron bars were extensively fastened. The specifications also offered several new features. On the east the principal room of the resident gaoler measured approximately 16 by 20 feet with a stairway to the garret chambers. To the west the two cells, one for female criminals and the other for males, each measured approximately 12 by 9½ feet and contained one small window. A door in the west wall of each of these cells led out to the walled communal exercise yard.

Having a prison keeper residing permanently on the premises promised greater security and a reduction in "the charge which necessarily accrews in each county by keeping continuall guards."[87] Gaolers could detect inappropriate activities among the incarcerated and check improper contact between inmates and outsiders. Another innovation, the division of the prison into separate cells for men and women, offered a certain amount of protection to the latter and deterred inappropriate behavior among prisoners. To deal with sanitation problems, each cell was provided with a closed stool connected to a cesspit below. Finally, the exercise yard recognized that prisoners, often incarcerated for several months "till tryall," needed a place to get fresh air and exercise. The 10-foot-high walls ensured that the space was relatively secure from escape. Compared to the dark dungeon of Jamestown, the "strong sweet prison" in Williamsburg with its exercise yard provided a modicum of improvement over its predecessor in preserving prisoners' health.[88] It generally kept prisoners alive to stand trial or face execution, but the absence of heated cells caused tremendous hardship for the incarcerated. A slave acquitted of a felonious charge nevertheless "by long confinement in prison, became so exceedingly Frost-bitten, that a Mortification ensued, whereof he died."[89] In 1711 the fear of escape may have led to the bricking up of the small windows that initially lit the cells, plunging those inside in the winter into a cold, fetid darkness.[90]

In the same year that the criminal cells may have been darkened, the General Assembly passed an act for "Building a Prison for Debtors." The necessity

FIGURE 153. Restored and reconstructed provincial gaol, Williamsburg, 1701–3, with 1711, 1722 additions

of such a structure arose from the fact that defendants in debt cases brought "in custody from several remote and distant parts of this colony to the general court" had no means to keep themselves out of prison either before their trial or after judgment was obtained against them. Far from home and with no means of paying the usual prison fees, some debtors prosecuted in the provincial court became wards of the state. Reluctant to toss them in with criminals, the General Assembly decided to build a separate brick structure for their reception measuring 32 by 20 feet. It appointed the sheriff of York County as the keeper and allowed him sixpence per day for "the relief and subsistence of such poor prisoners."[91]

Provincial officials decided to attach this new debtors' prison to the west end of the exercise yard of the criminal prison. The overall length of the new prison was reduced from 32 to 20 feet (inside measurement), which was subdivided into two rooms of roughly 9½ feet by 20 feet and covered by an unusual flat roof. Debtors entered their cells through openings in the old west wall of the exercise yard. Sheathed with thick planks and probably lit by a single window in each room, the cells were unheated, and thus of no real improvement over the criminal cells across the yard.

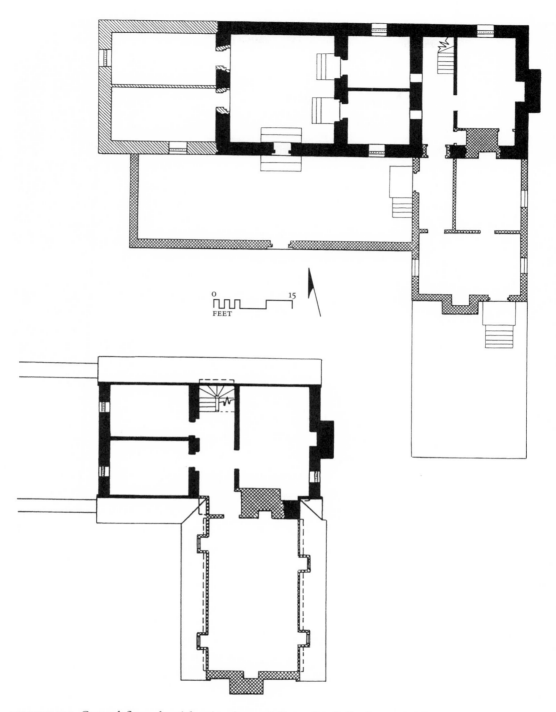

FIGURE 154. Ground-floor plan *(above)* and second-floor plan *(below)*, provincial gaol,
Williamsburg. The extent of the 1772 addition to the south is outlined but not drawn.

The new addition failed to meet the expectations of provincial officials. Within a decade they realized that there were too few debtors in prison to warrant the use of so much space. They decided to reorganize the prison to make it more commodious for its long-term inmates. In 1722 the General Assembly passed a bill to make "the Public Prisons in Williamsburg more convenient and for building a House for the Keeper."[92] The debtors were moved from the west end of the prison to the east room of the original section, which had been formerly the main room of the gaoler. This move provided the debtors with two heated rooms, one large one on the ground floor and a smaller one on the second floor. The two unheated cells in the 1711 addition were given over to the increased criminal population. Officials built a new one-story brick gaoler's house, which was attached to the south wall of the original section. These accommodations consisted of two heated ground-floor rooms and at least two rooms above that were possibly heated as well. In addition to the keeper's house, a new exercise yard enclosed by a tall brick wall was built on the south side of the building. The new yard provided greater segregation between criminals and debtors. Entrance from the outside into this 18-by-52-foot space was through a central doorway on the south side. Criminals proceeded from the new yard through the old doorway in the original exercise yard, into which their four cells opened, while debtors exited the new yard through a doorway on the east side and passed through another door into the original portion of the building to reach their new accommodations. Criminals took their exercise in the old yard, and debtors refreshed themselves in the new one.

These additions must have served the needs of the colony fairly well, for only minor changes were made to the prison over the next fifty years. Escapes continued to happen, and even though it was more commodious than county gaols, prisoners nevertheless continued to complain of overcrowding, and criminals still suffered in their unheated spaces. Yet despite these shortcomings, the Williamsburg gaol set the precedent for prison development in Virginia for the next century. A number of counties followed its practice of segregating prisoners, a few accommodated their prison keepers on or near the site of their gaols, and a handful began to erect perimeter walls in an attempt to make them more secure.

In the county penal system, the physical segregation of prisoners occurred in two ways. Some prisons were built with multiple apartments or cells for the different classes of prisoners. Alternatively, a few counties erected separate buildings, one for criminals and another for debtors. Counties that had two separate prisons included Brunswick (1748), Westmoreland (1749), Surry (1756), Caroline (1764), Dinwiddie (1769), Gloucester (1769), King William (1774), Chesterfield (1777), and Madison (by 1806). In 1751 Norfolk County added a small wooden prison behind its principal one as a way of segregating

TABLE 5 Two-celled prisons erected, 1726–40

Date	County	Size	Height	Special features
1726	Princess Anne	12×16		frame walls
1728	Essex	14×24	7 ft.	
1733	Norfolk	16×30	2-story	
1736	Middlesex	22×26	8 ft. 9 in.	brick walls
1739	Brunswick	12×20		
1740	Lancaster	12×20	7 ft.	brick walls

its prisoners and constructed a brick perimeter wall around both to prevent escapes from either one.[93] A few counties continued to erect two prisons well into the early nineteenth century, but most favored a single structure. Both strategies had their advantages. It was more economical to construct a single structure than to build two separate buildings, and prisoners clustered together beneath a single roof required less surveillance than two buildings standing many feet if not yards apart. Yet two separate structures guaranteed the separation of debtors from criminals. The construction of two buildings allowed officials greater flexibility in improving the accommodations of debtors, thereby expressing distinctions in status between criminals and debtors. Debtors' prisons were generally larger than criminal ones: the new debtors' prison erected in Westmoreland County in 1749 was 14 feet square, while the felons' prison measured but 12 feet square. Similarly, specifications for the two Surry prisons in 1756 called for the debtors' prison to be 18 by 12 feet and the criminal prison only 14 by 12 feet.[94] Besides a few extra square feet, debtors almost always had warm cells and an extra window while many criminal prisons remained unheated and dimly lit.

Most of the older, well-established, and populous tidewater counties erected multiple-cell prisons in the second and third quarters of the eighteenth century though they were modest in size (table 5). By midcentury, Elizabeth City and Northumberland Counties had three-room prisons. Each had a cell for criminals and another slightly larger and better-lit one for debtors.[95] How the third room was used in these two prisons is unknown. It may have served to house additional prisoners regardless of their status, or it may have been reserved for female prisoners or for slaves. If the latter, these would be among the first prisons in Virginia to segregate prisoners by either sex or race. The Elizabeth City prison was 30 by 18 feet, and the Northumberland one was only 26 by 12 feet. The relatively small size of the three-room structures makes it unlikely that the third room housed the gaoler or a deputy watchman.

In the last decade of the colonial period, some counties undertook the construction of larger and more complex prisons. In 1767 Thomas Pritchard built a large stone prison for Loudoun County. Measuring 24 by 16 feet, the building stood two stories. The ground-floor walls were 4 feet in thickness while those on the second floor were reduced to 2 feet. A partition divided the building into two chambers on each floor, both sides of which were heated by fireplaces. Four years later Albemarle County advertised in the *Virginia Gazette* for workmen to undertake the construction of a two-story brick prison that was to be divided into four rooms. This building's plan was devised by a committee that included Thomas Jefferson.[96] Neither project described how the rooms were to be arranged other than the traditional division of space for criminals and debtors. It seems quite likely that separate rooms for female prisoners or slaves may have been envisioned in these plans.

It is just as likely that the Loudoun and Albemarle prisons provided accommodations for a prisoner keeper, as had been the case in the provincial prison in Williamsburg at the beginning of the century. The vulnerability of many exposed prisons led some counties to improve their surveillance by accommodating jailers and their deputies in apartments in the prison itself or in a house nearby. Augusta magistrates made one of the earliest and most elaborate efforts to improve their prison's security. In 1762 they ordered the construction of a 23½-by-17-foot stone residence for the jailer near the prison. The builder was William Hyde. Divided into a hall and chamber plan with heated rooms on both floors, plastered walls, paneled doors, and glass in the sash windows, the dwelling was in many ways far superior to the rude housing inhabited by most of the county's residents. Its fine finish was in part an enticement for a trustworthy person willing to take on the responsibilities of prison keeper. The dwelling stood a few feet away from the prison and was joined to it by a 10-foot-high wall enclosing a yard 10 feet square. This space provided an exercise yard for prisoners but, more importantly, prevented immediate entrance into the prison from the outside. The placement of sharp spikes in the 2½-foot-thick walls at 6-inch intervals thwarted ideas of escape over the yard wall, and a stout double-sheathed door in the opening leading from the jailer's house to the yard discouraged mischief in that direction.[97] One wall of Northampton County's similar exercise yard still stands (fig. 155).

A few other counties followed the example set by the Augusta magistrates, sometimes in an effort to restore the dignity of the punishment system. Fauquier County built a jailer's house by 1772 but could not find a resident. In 1789 a committee in Northumberland County recommended that a wall be erected around the rather flimsy log prisons on the courthouse grounds. Such a barrier, the members argued, would prevent the "immediate communication between the Friend or Confederate of the Prisoners which now takes place, and

FIGURE 155. Wall of Northampton County prison yard, Eastville, c. 1815. The prison is on the left and the slightly earlier clerk's office is on the right. The wall was part of an enclosed exercise yard in front of the prison.

by which the latter are furnished with proper instruments for making their way out, so that a debtor is seldom confined longer than a day." As a result of such lax security, imprisonment had "become rather a ludicrous affair, than a source of awe & subjection to the Laws—the authority & respectability of the Court has proportionably declined." In a similar vein Accomack County justices recognized the increasing fragility of their prison and in 1782 recommended that "a suitable wall made of Brick" be built "around the gaol at a convenient distance" and "that there ought to be a small house built . . . adjoining the said wall for the residence of the jailor without which . . . prisoners cannot be kept in perfect security." Within a couple of years, Selby Simpson had completed a 33-by-22-foot brick jailer's house (fig. 156). Like the Augusta one, the Accomack house contained two heated rooms on the ground floor with a pair of garret rooms abovestairs. The residence stood in the southwest corner of an approximately 80-foot-square prison yard; the tall brick walls of the yard were integrally bonded into those of the house. The north wall of the residence facing into the prison yard originally had no apertures. The central door and windows now on the facade were later additions made first in the early nineteenth century and improved in 1824 when the residence was converted permanently into a debtors' prison.[98]

FIGURE 156. Accomack County debtors' prison, formerly the jailer's house, Accomac, 1783, reworked 1824. (Courtesy of The Library of Virginia)

Some keepers complained that detached jailers' residences did little to maintain order and keep the peace among prisoners. William Rose, keeper of the public jail in the city of Richmond at the end of the Revolution, found that his residence was too far away from the prison "to prevent Escapes and preserve order." Rose believed that "prisoners should be taught to love and fear their Keeper: this constituted his and their safety. He should on this account live under the same roof with them, as a schoolmaster should with his scholars." Only a very few counties had tried incorporating a jailer's apartment within the body of the prison. One of the first was Botetourt County, which in 1770 authorized the construction of a 16-by-12 foot "addition at the end of" its log-cabin prison to be "the Goalers house." Some jails had a room at the entrance, which probably served more as an office than a residence. Others contained a ground-floor office with a stair leading to a second-floor chamber. No doubt this is what was intended for the new prison in Southampton County in 1773, which was to have "apartments for debtors, criminals, and the gaoler's family therein."[99]

The architect John Hawks's 1773 design for a new prison in Edenton, North Carolina, incorporated rooms for the jailer within a double-pile, two-story prison (fig. 157). Surrounded on three sides by a 10-foot-high perimeter wall standing 10 feet from the body of the building, the prison's principal entrance on the front led directly into a heated room that provided access to all the other spaces in the prison. This central circulation space was the jailer's office. A door opposite the front one led into an inner yard that was to be used by criminals for exercise and contained a privy in one corner. Two vaulted, unheated criminal cells opened off this yard. A heated debtors' room stood next to the jailer's office and opened into it. Opposite the fireplace wall in the office, a stair rose along the partition wall to the second-floor rooms that either served as additional quarters for the jailer or could be used as overflow accommodations for

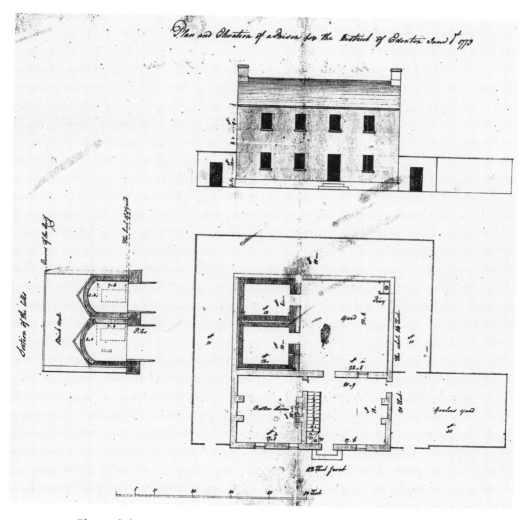

FIGURE 157. Plan and elevation, Chowan County prison, Edenton, N.C. Drawing by John Hawks, architect, 1773. (From "References to Edenton Prison," John Hawks Papers, no. 3530, Southern Historical Collection, Wilson Library, University of North Carolina at Chapel Hill)

debtors.[100] The Edenton prison plan was as elaborate and expensive as any colonial prison project in Virginia. It incorporated the latest thinking about security with perimeter walls and a jailer's apartment, combined with such earlier features as triple-lined walls, close studding, vaulted roofs, and riveted and plated doors. These were the ideals in prison design at the end of the colonial era, yet few counties achieved these measures. Even the Edenton design remained a paper project, for the magistrates of Chowan County never raised the money to undertake such an ambitious building. It was not until the nineteenth century that most counties built jails of modest comfort and maximum security.

The Prison Bounds

Cognizant of the fact that lengthy incarceration could be tantamount to a death sentence, the General Assembly in 1647 and again in 1684 authorized magistrates to lay off prison boundaries in each of their counties. Within an area designated as the prison bounds, prisoners who posted a security bond and were not incarcerated on treason or felony charges were allowed to wander freely during the day in order to breathe fresh air and exercise. So long as they stayed within the prescribed area, prisoners were permitted to enter and leave their cells at their own pleasure.[101] For the most part the prison "rules" applied to debtors who faced long periods of imprisonment, providing them with a means of surviving their financial destitution. Even though the law was again renewed in 1705, 1726, and 1748, some counties were slow in implementing its provisions. In 1701 the debtors lodged in the York County "marshallcy or goale" had to petition the magistrates to release them from close confinement and reminded them of their responsibility to have prison bounds laid out for their benefit. Similar petitions from debtors occurred in Middlesex County in 1707 and again in 1738.[102]

Most counties established an area ranging from two to ten acres of land that incorporated the prison and a number of other public buildings on the courthouse grounds. Those bounds that were recorded in plats in county record books indicate that they could be laid out in the most imaginative or the most mundane fashion. On the dull side were the nine acres laid out in the form of a square by George West for Loudoun County in 1758.[103] Equally routine was the work of Travers Daniel in Stafford County, who platted a perfect square of ten acres in 1765 (fig. 158). The prison stood along the county road, while the courthouse was located in a corner of the prison bounds. In Augusta and Shenandoah Counties the magistrates ordered that prison bounds be marked off with the courthouse in the very center, and in Accomack County in 1789 ten acres were to be laid out parallel to the sides and ends of the courthouse.[104]

Other counties considered topographical or cultural features by taking into

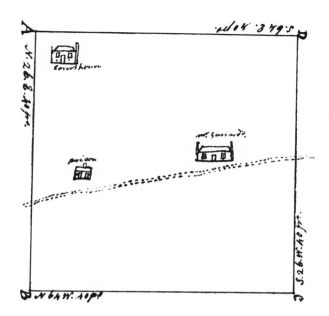

FIGURE 158. Plat of the Stafford County prison bounds, 1765. (Stafford County Loose Papers, Oct. 31, 1765, The Library of Virginia)

account the location of streams, taverns, the courthouse, and roads in drawing their boundaries, creating exaggerated shapes or ones of exceeding complexity.[105] In Northumberland County in 1657, prisoners could venture down to the local creek and then wander through a half mile of woods before returning to James Magregor's house where court was kept. Somewhere within this generous space stood the prison. As in Northumberland, springs and creeks were often included within the bounds, providing prisoners with sources of fresh water.[106] Courthouses, taverns, residences, and shops that stood within the bounds provided prisoners with opportunities to maintain contact with their neighbors and friends, while away the hours, and engage in a variety of pursuits. Yet these encounters were also fraught with liabilities for debtors and their creditors. Some creditors feared that debtors would incur further debts from gaming, drinking, or shopping. On hearing an argument by James Wood that the inclusion of the town of Winchester within the prison bounds was "detrimental to the creditor," the magistrates of Frederick County ordered them changed to encompass a less developed section of the town. Similarly, magistrates in Accomack in 1789 sought to limit the unencumbered movement of debtors within their prison bounds. Prisoners could frequent neighboring taverns, but they were forbidden to enter rooms that contained billiards tables.[107]

Complicated boundaries defining the legal extent of a bonded prisoner's wanderings required clear designation. Many counties began marking the prison bounds, first with wooden posts, then by stones and other visible symbols. In 1711 Westmoreland's prison rules were delineated by locust posts set up at each turn and corner of the grounds. Trees marked by a series of chops and blazes were used to indicate the limits of the grounds in Louisa County in 1745. In 1773 these were replaced by posts, features that also marked the prison boundaries in Caroline, Fauquier, and Bedford Counties. Farther west in Henry County, magistrates ordered in 1806 that the county prison bounds be set off by a series of large stones fifty yards apart. They were to be sunk at least 12 inches into the earth and to stand at least 6 inches above ground.[108] Only the most myopic of prisoners could have inadvertently ventured beyond this henge of stone.

Penal Reform

Critics in England and Virginia began to question the deterrent value of the old punishments in the fourth quarter of the eighteenth century. Motivated by Enlightenment ideas about individual dignity, they saw the shaming punishments as inhumane and degrading and not suitable for miscreants who were expected to reenter society and lead useful lives. The old punishments offered no pretense of reforming the offender and were only effective, if they succeeded at all, when they brought scorn and ridicule of the culprit by friends and neighbors. With the growth of Norfolk, Richmond, Alexandria, Portsmouth, and Fredericksburg in the years following the Revolution, new city governments had to police a growing population filled with many transients, wage laborers, and slaves. The old shaming punishments were less effective in anonymous urban communities where ostracism meant little.

Advocates of penal reform believed that the old punishments failed to curb crime and wasted human potential. English reformers John Howard and Jeremy Bentham argued that imprisonment offered a way to reshape the mind of the miscreant and redeem his value to society. They thought that a prison system that provided solitude and hard work would give an inmate the chance to reflect upon the errors of his ways in order to mend them, so that upon leaving prison at the end of his term, he would take up a normal life. Instead of the physical terror of the old ways, it was the psychological terror of the penitentiary that offered the best hope for dealing with crime. Howard believed that locking a man up was "the more rational plan for softening the mind in order for its amendment."[109] As one member of the Virginia legislature optimistically put it, "A dead man is forever useless but the very worst living man . . . may be turned to some account."[110]

These late eighteenth-century reformers recognized that the old prisons and bridewells were far from ideal places for the criminal to contemplate past mistakes. On the contrary, they saw them as the breeding grounds for further vice and corruption. The prisoners kept in the Richmond gaol in the 1780s found temptation all around them. They were "surrounded by tippling houses, liquor is conveyed to them by the guards, by disorderly people plying round the Picketts" of the perimeter fence. They drank "frequently to excess and immediately the Prison is all riot and confusion." More than once, the life of the prison keeper, William Rose, had been in danger when he tried to quell the tumult of those "unhappy wretches committed for murder and robbery."[111]

An entirely new type of structure was needed in order to create the type of environment conducive to reflective solitude. John Howard documented the failure of haphazard controls and communal cells that did little but promote the spread of disease. A new perspective arose that emphasized the reformation of the incarcerated through the application of discipline and obedience.[112] A number of English prisons were designed and built in the 1780s and 1790s that segregated one prisoner from another in physical isolation. Perhaps the most famous, Jeremy Bentham's Panopticon, featured a series of private cells stretching out in a series of blocks from a central core much like spokes in a wheel. From the center of the wheel, the gaolers kept a watchful eye on the prisoners, who followed an unvarying daily routine of silent labor interspersed by hours of solitary confinement. Workshops and exercise yards were arranged around a central observation post that provided an optimum viewing area from which to monitor and regulate activities.[113]

In the years following the American Revolution, the belief that architecture could help reform social problems was slowly gaining adherents in Virginia. Even before the war the idea of locking people away in order that they might be cured of their disorders had been instituted at the Public Hospital in Williamsburg, where the insane were accorded some measure of treatment. Advocates of penal reform gained a significant victory in 1796 when the General Assembly revised the criminal code. It drastically reduced several capital offenses punishable by death to only one, murder. Robbery and horse theft became punishable by imprisonment, and corporal punishment was severely limited, generally to those who broke out of jail or disregarded prison rules. The act also called for the construction of "a gaol and penitentiary house" to contain the white felons convicted under the revised code.[114]

The state hired English immigrant architect Benjamin Henry Latrobe to devise plans for a massive masonry prison for Richmond (figs. 159, 160). While not copying Bentham's Panopticon or even the design of the new penitentiary house built at the Walnut Street Gaol in Philadelphia (1790–91), his plans of 1797 reflect the characteristic elements of the reformed plan: a semiradial plan for the efficient supervision of the inmates and dozens of private cells for the their confinement. Interspersed among the curving, arcaded corridors were workshops and a chapel, essential elements of the prisoners' contemplative world. Private vaulted cells and workshops were arrayed around the semicircular block three stories in height, which enclosed a large exercise yard. Keeping

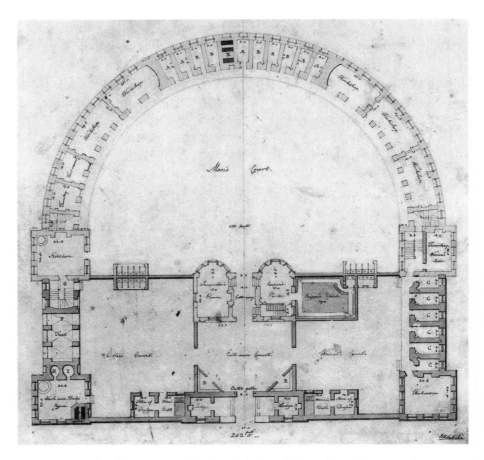

FIGURE 159. First-floor plan, penitentiary, Richmond. Drawing by B. H. Latrobe, architect, 1797. (Courtesy of The Library of Virginia)

in mind the movement to segregate the sexes, women had their own quarters, workshop, and yard in the east range of the great horseshoe-shaped complex. The penitentiary also had a cellar that contained storage rooms, vaulted solitary cells, and a washhouse. The Reverend Jesse Lee, a chaplain who ministered to the needs of the inmates, had high hopes for the spiritual reform of his flock. Not long after the prison opened, he noted that the inmates "frequently engaged in singing psalms, hymns, and spiritual songs, as well as praying, until the whole circular building was made to resound with high praises of God." Despite what Lee observed, a true reform spirit failed to take root. Monumental in conception, expensive in execution, the Richmond penitentiary disappointed all those who expected an immediate and lasting reform of Virginia's troubled prison population. Small prisoners' cells made for a dismal solitary existence, providing little chance to improve the attitudes of those who managed to sur-

FIGURE 160. Gatehouse, penitentiary, Richmond. Drawing by B. H. Latrobe, architect, 1797. (Courtesy of The Library of Virginia)

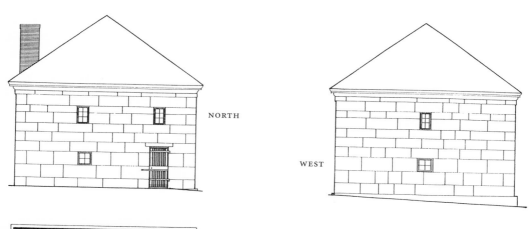

NORTH

WEST

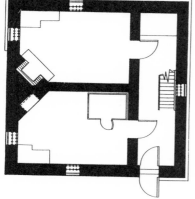

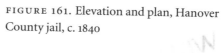

FIGURE 161. Elevation and plan, Hanover County jail, c. 1840

vive their incarceration. During the first years of its existence, many prisoners died, a number escaped, and the workshops failed to turn a profit. Martin Mims, the prison keeper, admitted that most prisoners were "insensible to favour and admonition."[115]

The Richmond penitentiary siphoned off the most desperate of Virginia's white criminal population in the first decades of the nineteenth century, but it did little to transform prison building in the counties. Although the reform of the penal system eventually made the stocks and pillory things of the past, there was no surge in prison building in the early federal period. Some counties improved older structures and added additional rooms or new structures to separate men from women, blacks from whites, debtors from criminals. The one-room brick prison in Northampton County on the Eastern Shore probably dates to c. 1815. In scale, materials, and security, it epitomizes the best of prison building at the beginning of the century (see figs. 148, 152, 155). The fact that it was devoted to a single class of prisoners and had an exercise yard enclosed by a 10-foot-high brick wall signifies the penetration of colonial and newer reform ideas and security measures to many localities. The scale of prisons increased in the following decades. In the 1820s and 1830s, many of the old colonial buildings were replaced by larger masonry structures. Antebellum stone jails such as those that survive in Hanover, Goochland, Fauquier, Charlotte, and Fluvanna Counties incorporated multiple cells, jailer's rooms, perimeter walls, and other features that were envisioned and tried in places but never fully implemented in the colonial era (fig. 161). Many of these served their jurisdictions well into the twentieth century.

6

TAVERNS AND
CLERKS' OFFICES

A Most Convivial Delight: The Courthouse Tavern

IN 1732 ON ONE OF HIS many perambulations around the colony, William Byrd II of Westover stopped at the courthouse village in Caroline County. Though the county had only been established five years previously, the seat of government had developed rapidly. Byrd, who detested rum's harmful effects, noted that two local planters, Colonel Henry Armistead and Colonel William Beverley, had each "erected an ordinary well supplied with wine and other polite liquors for the worshipful bench. Besides these, there is a rum ordinary for persons of a more vulgar taste. Such liberal supplies of strong drink often make Justice nod and drop the scales out of her hands."[1] Finding a drink at Madison County courthouse in the early nineteenth century was never a problem either. Three taverns operated within staggering distance of the courthouse (fig. 162). Not all county courts were as well supplied with taverns as Caroline and Madison Counties were, but as Byrd wryly observed, court day could not have functioned without such an establishment somewhere near the temple of Justice. Whether a private dwelling with a public license or a purpose-built structure, the courthouse tavern provided rooms to accommodate travelers, served meals and spirituous beverages to guests, acted as a business exchange, and was the venue for polite and raucous public entertainments such as assemblies, theatricals, lectures, gambling, and sporting activities (fig. 163).[2] From the seventeenth century through the end of the colonial period, the term *ordinary* was commonly used to describe a tippling house in the Chesapeake. By the middle decades of the eighteenth century, *tavern* supplanted *ordinary* as the name of a better establishment. An Englishman traveling through Virginia in the early 1780s remarked that "there is no distinction here between inns, taverns, ordinaries, and public-houses; they are all in one, and are known by the appellation of taverns"; he found them "all very indifferent indeed."[3] Finally, in the last decade of the eighteenth century, *hotel* came into general use to designate the places with superior accommodations to separate them from the poorer sort that often gave public hostelries a bad name among travelers.[4] The

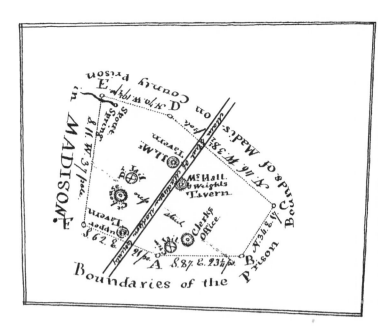

FIGURE 162. Madison County prison bounds, 1806, encompassing three taverns in addition to the official buildings. (Plat Book 2, 435, Oct. 3, 1806, Clerk's Office, Madison County)

FIGURE 163. Tavern, Charles City. From Benson J. Lossing, *The Pictorial Field Book of the Revolution* (New York, 1860), 2:238. (Courtesy of The Library of Virginia)

English terms *inn* and *public house* appeared infrequently throughout the colonial and early national periods.

Whatever they were called, alehouses were essential for court-day proceedings, for tavern keepers not only provided food, small beer, and lodgings for court officials and the public but also were the only licensed purveyors of spirits for the multitude that flocked to the courthouse. Throughout the seventeenth and eighteenth centuries, the General Assembly passed legislation regulating the activities of taverns. In the 1630s it set the prices that tavern keepers could charge for beer and food, and in 1655 it granted the county courts the power to license taverns. Fifty years later, a comprehensive law once again set regulatory standards in laying out procedures for obtaining a license, stating the penalties for retailing without one, prohibiting unlawful gaming, and granting the county court the right to set annually the maximum prices for lodging, liquor, food, pasturage, and fodder. For example, the Northumberland County court granted in 1711 a license to James Moulder after he posted a bond guaranteeing that he would "provide in his ordinary good wholesome & cleanly Lodging & dyett for Travellers and Stablage fodder & provender or pasturage . . . and shall not suffer or permitt any unlawfull gaming in his house nor on the Sabbath day suffer any person to Tipple or drink more than is necessary."[5] In the same year the York County magistrates set the following rates that were to be charged at ordinaries within their jurisdiction:

Each dyett	0-1-0
Lodgeing for each person	0-0-7½
Stableroom & fodder for each horse per night	0-0-7½
Stableroom & fodder sufficient for each horse 24 hours	0-0-11¼
Each gallon of corn	0-0-7½
Wine of Va produce per quart	0-5-0
Canary & sherry per quart	0-4-4½
Red & white Lisbon per quart	0-3-1½
Western Island wine per quart	0-1-10½
French brandy per quart	0-4-0
French brandy punch or French brandy flip per quart	0-1-3
Rum & Va brandy per quart	0-2-0
Rum punch & rum flip per quart	0-0-7½
Va Midling Bear [beer] & cyder per quart	0-0-3¾
Pa bear & Rogers's best Virg Aile per quart	0-0-6
English bear per quart	0-1-0[6]

This regulatory oversight on the part of the county court was done to prevent unscrupulous hostelers from taking advantage of travelers as well as to discourage unfair competition and deter the creation of indiscriminate drinking houses that might foster the gathering of seamen, apprentices, servants, slaves, and others whose leisure activities warranted close scrutiny. Those who sold spirituous drinks without a license were hauled before the court and forced to pay a fine in an effort to suppress the proliferation of bawdy houses out of fear that such unregulated gatherings would lead beyond merely drunken disorderly conduct. York County magistrates were disturbed by people in Yorktown retailing liquor in small quantities without a license "not only to the meaner sort of people, but even to servants and slaves, often adulterating or mixing the same with water, whereby they can afford to sell it the cheaper." In response, in 1736 the General Assembly passed an act prohibiting the selling of any strong liquors in Yorktown in any quantity less than two gallons at any one time.[7]

Not that a licensed tavern alleviated the threat of boisterous behavior, for public drunkenness was a common phenomenon in colonial America, and nowhere was this more evident than on court day. Although the bureaucratic routine of the court docket served as the primary focus of court day, tavern hospitality offered a convivial counterbalance (fig. 164). Large crowds mingled in the taproom, conversed on the piazza, or gathered outside the tavern door. Even

FIGURE 164. *The Country Club* (London, 1788). English satirical print depicting a club of gentlemen wits gathering for a meeting in a private room of a tavern whose entertainments included a bowl of rum punch and a sumptuous dinner.

after the court closed its doors for the day, many remained in the tavern well into the evening, sharing a bowl of punch and recounting the day's course of events. "There were upwards of an hundred people in and about the ordinary" at Sussex one summer court-day evening in 1768 when lightning struck and killed two horses and three hogs standing nearby.[8]

Tavern keepers fought hard to keep unlicensed entrepreneurs from plying their refreshments anywhere near the courthouse, since they cut into a very lucrative franchise. To stem the tide of outside vendors who drove their carts and carriages into the courthouse yard and set up stands to sell their illegal alcohol, Accomack County magistrates in 1786 ordered that none but licensed residents could do business within a quarter mile of the courthouse. Anyone else would be summarily brought before the tribunal in contempt of court. Three-quarters of a century earlier the Accomack court had ordered "that no person shall come to this court to sell liquor or other things . . . [or] shall bring or sell the same any nearer this Courthouse then the Road." The sheriff of Loudoun County was ordered in 1814 to "remove from the public lot all persons that may be found thereon selling or offering for sale Liquor, Cyder, Cakes, etc." In Augusta County a vendor was prosecuted in 1747 for selling liquors without a license from a stall at the courthouse.[9]

With several hundred customers on hand for the better part of one or two days, the effort by the magistrates on behalf of the tavern keepers was well worth the public ire it may have provoked. For as one English traveler observed of the Essex County court in Tappahannock, judicial proceedings usually became spirituous affairs: "It being court day the town is very full, though what they come for God only knows, excepting its to get drunk. No other business seems to be going on."[10] Court day in Goochland County attracted great "numbers of idle people who come less from a desire to learn what is going forwards than to drink together."[11] This was certainly the case for more than a half dozen men in Talbot County, Maryland, who went on a four-day drinking binge during the February 1692 court session. Taking lodgings in Salter's Tavern where the court convened, the inebriates hurled insults at the justices during the day and continued their "drinking all night." Deep into their cups, some rode their horses through the courtroom, while others "in their frolicks . . . put themselves into the Pillory and there they Drank [the following] Day at the Point they were so drunk that they fell together by the Ears."[12] For many obliging tavern keepers such as Salter, who must have made a tidy sum selling food and drink to this gang of revelers, obtaining and maintaining the exclusive right to "swill the planters with bumbo," or rum, promised to be the road to "genteel Fortunes."[13]

Not surprisingly, some Virginians felt troubled by the amount of alcohol consumed at court day and the effects that it had on the populace. Tired of the "disorders misrules and riots" provoked by alcohol-sodden crowds, Stafford County magistrates decreed in 1691 "that no person of what degree condition or Quality whatsoever shall sell any Sort of Liquor whatever to any manner of Person or Persons whatsoever upon a Court day whilest their Majesties Justices of the peace Sitting without first Leave being Prayed for and granted by the Court," no doubt to little effect.[14] Governor Dinwiddie thought it important "to discourage Gaming, Swearing, and immoderate Drinking, particularly at the County Courts," and urged members of the General Assembly to set an example of temperance for "the lower Class of our People." Leading by example was not enough for a small minority who saw the road to ruination running through the courthouse tavern. Ministers and the high-minded railed against ordinaries as "Nurseries of Vice" that had been "perverted from their original Intention, and proper Use; viz. the Reception, Accommodation, and Refreshment of the weary and benighted Traveller." Taverns had become "the common Receptacle, and Rendezvous of the very Dreggs of the People . . . where only Time and Money are vainly and unprofitably squandered" on games, sports, and pastimes including "Cards, Dice, Horse-racing, and Cock-fighting." They gave rise to "Drunkeness, Swearing, Cursing, Perjury, Blasphemy, Cheating, Lying, and Fighting." A lure for "Satan's Service," taverns ensnared not only the weak and dangerous but nearly all segments of the white male population of colonial Virginia.[15]

Sources of degradation or not, taverns provided one of the few venues where men of many classes could meet to discuss business, religion, or politics in a more relaxed setting, not free of but certainly loosened from the normal restraints of a status-conscious hierarchical society. Magistrates regularly adjourned to the comforts of a private dining room for their court-day dinners or executive sessions where important issues were discussed over a variety of liquid refreshments. On occasion, the warmth of a tavern fire prompted justices to conduct some of their business in a more convivial setting rather than from the cold hard benches of the courtroom.[16] Others gathered in the more public taprooms where politics, commerce, and gossip dominated conversations. The generous consumption of cider, brandy, and beer turned public gatherings such as court day and militia musters into festive diversions from the routine of rural life.

Sometimes liquor trumped conviviality, and insolent words provoked violent reactions. After a court-day dinner in Richmond County in 1775, magistrate Landon Carter tried to reconcile a long-standing feud with Dr. Nicholas Flood because both were in poor health near the end of their lives. After drinking several toasts that did nothing but stir the hostility the doctor held for the planter, they parted the tavern with harsh words. Dr. Flood threatened to kill Carter. The magistrate "bid him use his tongue and not touch his sword, for if he did I would then be through his sword." Carter noted in his diary, "Thus did a scandalous affair end," in heated drunken words but at least nothing more sinister.[17]

A brawl in Benjamin Mosby's tavern at Cumberland a few years earlier ended in bloodshed. In the summer of 1766 Colonel John Chiswell of Williamsburg became embroiled in an argument with Robert Routlidge, a merchant living in neighboring Prince Edward County. Routlidge, who had been drinking much of the day, took offense at some of the foul language Chiswell had been using, whereupon the colonel called the merchant "a fugitive rebel, a villain who came to Virginia to cheat and defraud men of their property, and a Presbyterian fellow." Routlidge doused Chiswell with wine, and the colonel tried to strike back first with a bowl of toddy, then with a candlestick, and finally with a pair of fire tongs. Prevented by those around him from throwing objects at hand, Chiswell then called for his servant to bring him his sword and "swore that he would run any man through the body who should dare to come near him." After another exchange in which Chiswell reiterated the words "Presbyterian fellow," Routlidge tried to leave the room. Before a friend could get him to the door, Chiswell lunged across a table that separated the two combatants and stabbed Routlidge "through the heart" with his sword (fig.

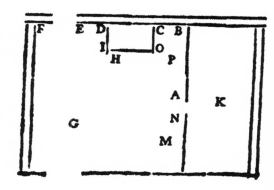

FIGURE 165. A diagram in the *Virginia Gazette* (Purdie and Dixon, July 18, 1766) depicting the interior of Benjamin Mosby's tavern in Cumberland County where John Chiswell murdered Robert Routlidge on June 3, 1766. The tavern had a back shed room *(K)* where Chiswell was handed his sword by his servant. The main public room had a corner fireplace *(M)* and a few chairs and a table at one end where Chiswell stabbed Routlidge with his sword. Nearby was a doorway leading out of the room *(EF)*.

165). With Routlidge dead on the floor, Chiswell ordered a bowl of toddy, which he "drank very freely," until he was arrested by a Cumberland County magistrate who had been summoned to the tavern. Released on bail to await his trial in Williamsburg before the General Court, Chiswell died suddenly, perhaps by his own hand, before his appearance in court that fall.[18] This tragic incident was unusual in the trivial nature of the slights that set the two men at one another. Courthouse taverns did have their share of violent behavior, especially where men's passions, fueled by alcohol, overcame gentlemanly decorum. Few of the tavern arguments were settled by the sword, but the possibility of conflict was always present in a plantation society that was accustomed to the use of violence as a means of maintaining social order.

Circuit lawyers such as John Mercer who followed court day from one county to the next, foreign and American visitors, and others who traveled through Virginia on business or for pleasure found a range of hospitality and accommodations, some pleasurable, others execrable. A few taverns, especially those in towns like Norfolk, Alexandria, and Williamsburg and along the main roads, had well-appointed accommodations in sizable structures with many specialized rooms, good food, and a well-stocked bar and hosted a variety of genteel activities. Though much altered and raised to two full stories in the late nineteenth century, the tavern still standing on the main street in Smithfield provided those who attended Isle of Wight County court with commodious and genteel accommodations during the late colonial and early federal periods. Erected in 1752 and purchased four years later by William Rand, the builder of the courthouse, the tavern was described in 1766 as "a spacious brick house, upwards of fifty feet in length, with four rooms below and three above and a good cellar under the same in three apartments, together with a store house and counting room under the same roof and many other convenient houses adjoining the court house." When the county court vacated Smithfield in the early nineteenth century for a more central location to the south at Boykin's Tavern, it was not for lack of hospitality at the old tavern. Rand's successor had furnished the Smithfield tavern with eight tables of all sizes, eighteen Windsor chairs, twelve of which were painted green, three armchairs, a writing desk, thirty-two framed pictures, eight beds and their furniture, and numerous bottles, glasses, pewter, and suitable crockery to keep customers satiated and slumbering. Besides this structure, the brick store and countinghouse between the tavern and the courthouse had been converted into public entertaining rooms for gaming and billiards.[19]

Similarly well supplied were the inhabitants of Mecklenburg County. An early nineteenth-century proprietor of Boyd's Tavern at the courthouse boasted that a guest could dine from "a table amply supplied with all the meats raised in this part of the Country and a cellar furnished with the liquors of Europe, Africa, and America." The imposing two-story frame tavern measured "nearly one hundred and fifty feet in length with fourteen rooms and twelve fire places for their accommodations, with stables as good as any in the state" (fig. 166). One of the best taverns in Virginia stood in Leeds, a small community in West-moreland County on the north side of the Rappahannock River. "The House and Furniture," observed an English traveler in 1755, "has as elegant an appear-ance, as any I have seen in the country, Mr. Finnays [Raleigh Tavern] or Wether-bernes in Williamsburg not excepted. The chairs, Tables, &c. of the Room I was conducted into, was all of Mahogany, and so stuft with fine large glazed Cop-per Plate Prints: That I almost fancied myself in Jeffriess' or some other elegant Print Shop" in London.[20]

FIGURE 166. Boyd's Tavern, Boydton, Mecklenburg County. Though the building was remodeled and much expanded in the antebellum period, its core dates from the early nineteenth century.

Even among the best taverns in Virginia, privacy was rare. The sociable thrived and the aloof suffered. The Richmond tavern where the German traveler Johann David Schoepf lodged

> contained but two large rooms on the ground-floor, and two of the same size above, the apartments under the roof furnished with numerous beds standing close together, both rooms and chambers standing open to every person throughout the day. Here, no less than in most other public-houses in America, it is expected that rooms are to be used only as places for sleeping, eating and drinking. The whole day long, therefore, one is compelled to be among all sorts of company and at night to sleep in like manner; thus travellers almost anywhere in America, must renounce the pleasure of withdrawing apart, (for their own convenience or their own affairs), from the noisy, disturbing, or curious crowd.

Schoepf found peculiar the "custom of having so many beds together in one room . . . since elsewhere in America there is much store set by decorum and neatness, which by such arrangement as this must often be dispensed with."[21]

Other travelers were also struck by the indiscriminate mixing of social classes in taverns. In the 1790s Englishman Francis Baily observed that "during meals a general conversation is commenced, which is continued without reserve; and in this manner, two strangers, who had never seen one another before will be come as intimate as if they had known each other for years." He noted that the Eagle Tavern in Norfolk had "four beds in a room crowded pretty close together; these beds laid on a kind of frame without any curtains, and the room itself without any ornament, save the bare white wall." The architect Benjamin Henry Latrobe complained of the lodgings he found at the Surry courthouse tavern in June 1797. He and his companions "were miserably off for beds. Six of us slept in a miserable, low, hot Garret. Several Gentlemen went to the Court house opposite to the inn, and slept on the Ground." The pattern of crowding people together within a room and within the same bed was not just a Virginia habit but one encountered throughout colonial America (fig. 167). One travel-weary Englishman observed that "after you have been some time in bed, a stranger of any condition (for there is little distinction), comes into the room, pulls off his clothes, and places himself, without ceremony, between your sheets."[22]

The absence of privacy in the best taverns was matched and exacerbated by questionable hospitality at many country ordinaries, those rural taverns in the tidewater and the piedmont located off the main roads, at ferry crossings, and even at a few courthouses. These were generally small one- or two-room build-

FIGURE 167. Bedchamber with two beds, Wetherburn's Tavern, Williamsburg, c. 1740

ings that seldom provided more than rudimentary provisions. Travelers found their food and drink indifferent at best and often meager, few beds and many bedbugs, and seldom any provision for stabling or feeding animals. In 1777 Ebenezer Hazard lodged at Seton's Tavern in the courthouse town of Dumfries in Prince William County, "an ill-furnished, dirty House; very little in or about it for either Man or Beast; I could not get even clean Sheets to sleep in, & the dirty ones were very ragged." The marquis de Chastellux and his travel companions found that Powhatan's county seat in the early 1780s consisted "of a plain wooden structure that serves as a courthouse, and another which does for an inn, but which was barely ready for travelers." Despite its appearance, they were able to obtain "a good supper and good beds, but our horses were obliged to do without forage." Roane's Ordinary in King and Queen County had "a mean look, standing naked upon a common, without any inclosure (not so much as a Garden) about it." The forlorn appearance outside was matched by a spareness within. Instead of "a Chicken, Eggs, Milk, or such things which I presume few Houses in the Country could well do without," a visitor discovered that the only thing available to eat was "a piece of broiled rust Bacon and an Indian Hoe Cake." Southern's Tavern on the Rappahannock River in Essex County "was no more than a mere Hut, full of rude, mean people, . . . every one, as well as the Land Lord, inflamed with Liquor and exceeding turbulent and noisy."[23]

Despite a recommendation from Thomas Jefferson, the marquis found Mrs. Teaze's tavern in Waynesboro to be "one of the worst lodging places in all of America. Mrs. Teaze, the mistress of the house, was some time ago bereft by the death of her husband, and I verily believe that she was also bereft of all her furniture, for I have never seen a more badly furnished house. A poor tin vessel was the only 'bowl' used for the family, our servants, and ourselves; I dare not say for what other use it was offered to us when we went to bed." To accommodate them "the hostess and her family were obliged to give up their bed" to the party of five travelers. Another candidate for the title of the most wretched accommodation in Virginia was the tavern at Louisa. Appalled by what he encountered at this ordinary run by the former militia officer Paul Johnson, Baron Ludwig von Closen, one of General Rochambeau's aides, declared that he "had never seen a dirtier, more shocking, and more stinking barracks than that of this major, who, himself, was the greatest pig that the earth had produced. . . . None of us could shut an eye throughout the night. The general, who alone could have a bed, was eaten by vermin, and we, who slept on straw, had our ears tickled by rats."[24]

Taverns often dominated the rural crossroad villages that slowly grew up around the public buildings. In many counties one or two individuals possessed the land surrounding the two or so acres of public ground on which the courthouse stood. Sterling Clack owned "350 acres whereon is the Courthouse [and] Ordinary" of Brunswick County in 1752. In Prince Edward County in 1754 Charles Anderson advertised the sale of "3000 Acres, whereon is the Court-House of the said County, with all necessary Buildings, Store-Houses, &c. Orchards, garden, Pastures, and plantable Land cleared and fenced; There is now a Store kept on the Premises and a well accustomed Ordinary." The courthouse and ordinary in Charles City County in 1773 stood on a 200-acre tract, as did the tavern at Orange courthouse. In 1799 the courthouse tavern in Spotsylvania County was on a 143-acre tract.[25] As a result, there were few other buildings except the courthouse plantation with its tavern and perhaps an associated store or workshop. Grouped around the courthouse tavern were the occasional free-standing billiards rooms, stables, kitchens, smokehouses, dairies, granaries, and other domestic outbuildings, wells, and pumps (fig. 168). Standing near the immediate work yard were vegetable gardens enclosed by wooden pales where much of the tavern food was grown as well as fields for pasturing horses and apple, cherry, and peach orchards whose distilled fruits contributed to the variety of beverages sold in the public room. A few taverns even featured formal gardens for pleasure walks and open-air entertainments. One tavern at Bowling Green in Caroline County boasted an extensive public garden "in a high state of cultivation, with Summer houses, and bowers for the accommodation of company: on this well improved Lot is also erected—Shuffle Boards, Ten-Pin Alleys, and a Ball Battery, for the accommodation and exercise of gentlemen."[26]

Caroline County courthouse had at least three taverns nestled around it, one of which was owned by Colonel William Beverley, who also owned 200 acres of the surrounding land.[27] During the colonial period a landowner sometimes enticed the county government to a site with the promise of donating land or materials for the public buildings, often with an eye toward enhancing existing tavern trade or establishing a lucrative new one. Some of these landowners, particularly in the seventeenth century, operated the courthouse tavern as their principal business and became wedded to the court-day trade. In the eighteenth century many owners turned over the business to a tenant who paid an annual rent. The cantankerous Daniel Fisher, who had met little success as a tavern keeper in Williamsburg in the early 1750s, noted that it was a common practice "in the Country" when the owner of a tavern was either a member of the county court or an important planter or merchant for him to lease his tavern in order to avoid any opprobrium associated with his interest in the business. The owner thus avoided "the Reproach of being deemed an Ordinary keeper, and the scandal of what is then transacted; yet he reaps the greatest share of the Profits." The annual rent of a courthouse tavern varied significantly, from £50 in Bedford County and £45 in Culpeper County in 1768 to £170 per annum in 1773 in King William County, where the tavern was on a

FIGURE 168. An early nineteenth-century tavern with its complement of outbuildings at Bowling Green, the new seat of local government in Caroline County. Watercolor. (Courtesy of W. Brown Morton Jr.)

main road.[28] Given the right location and some initiative, the keeper could make a good wage catering to the monthly court-day crowds and the steady stream of passing travelers, especially if the tavern was on a main road or in a populous county. Yet in other counties there was too little tavern trade to make a steady wage so that hostelers were often forced to supplement their income through agriculture.

The tavern at King William provided a good living on both accounts. It was a principal landmark on the busy road leading northwest out of Williamsburg, and it was the only establishment at the courthouse. A popular retreat for court-day participants, the tavern also had a constant clientele of travelers. At one time it had gotten a bad reputation as being "disorderly and ill kept," but a new keeper revived its fortunes by providing "the best of tables and liquors" and good "stablage and pasturage" for horses. He tried to set the proper tone for his establishment by sponsoring a subscription "CONCERT of INSTRU-MENTAL MUSIC, by Gentlemen of note," which was followed by a ball. Whether or not these genteel aspirations overcame previous practices, the tavern had all the advantages to make it a success. John Quarles, a late colonial owner, boasted that "no place in this country is better calculated for a tavern than this, and none more frequented, trade has flourished here for many years, it being very convenient to navigation." The property was well equipped to handle this trade with many buildings, including a "public house, which is 72 feet by 20 with a portico the whole length, there are 4 rooms below and 4 above, with 4 closets on a floor." In addition to the tavern, there was "another dwelling house 36 by 18 with 2 rooms above and 2 below, a passage and 2 closets; a large store house 40 by 16; a counting house 28 by 12, with 2 rooms; a private dwelling house 40 by 16, with 2 rooms below and 1 above; a large kitchen 28 by 20, with 2 rooms; stables, corn houses, a large fertile garden, and every other conveniency requisite for publick or private houses." Accompanying these appurtenances were over 500 acres of land capable of producing "tobacco, corn, and wheat exceedingly well." Good money was made from the crops produced in the fields that surrounded the courthouse grounds. Part of the corn and wheat harvest went back into domestic consumption in the tavern kitchen, stable, coops, and pens. The tobacco crop and surplus wheat were transported to a landing for shipment to outside markets. Between the tavern facilities and the fertile fields, Quarles calculated that the owner of the plantation at King William was guaranteed an income of between £1,000 and £1,500 a year, a tidy sum for an enterprising businessman.[29]

By the end of the colonial period, the best courthouse taverns such as the one in King William County were sizable buildings that contained first- and second-floor bedchambers and large ground-floor entertaining rooms for eating, drinking, card playing, billiards, and dancing. Most, however, were far more domestic in scale and plan and were indistinguishable from private dwellings. Other than the occasional sign that announced the name of the inn and public notices nailed to the door and plastered to the walls, there were few outward indications of a tavern's public function.[30] Reduced to the basic essentials, a tavern only needed a bed for sleeping, a hearth to cook meals, and a place to eat and drink. The most rudimentary dwelling required the same accoutrements and spaces. Dwellings frequently became taverns, and taverns reverted to domestic use. Scotchtown, a large frame house in Hanover County previously inhabited by Patrick Henry, was offered for sale in 1782 and described as being "extremely convenient either for a tavern, merchant, or private gentleman."[31]

The domestic origins of the colonial tavern appear in the plans of surviving eighteenth- and early nineteenth-century buildings that once served as courthouse ordinaries.[32] Hanover Tavern at Hanover and Boykin's Tavern at Isle of Wight started life as dwelling houses and later were converted into taverns. Boyd's Tavern in Boydton, the county seat of Mecklenburg County; the Smithfield Tavern in Smithfield, the county seat of Isle of Wight in the last half of the eighteenth century; the Eastville Inn in Northampton County; Hughlett's Tavern in Heathsville, Northumberland County; and the tavern at New Kent were all built as taverns from the beginning. Yet all of these structures originally had typical domestic plans characteristic of the late colonial and early national periods.

Hughlett's Tavern was built in the last quarter of the eighteenth century specifically to cater to the Northumberland courthouse trade. Though it is now a sprawling structure extending more than 100 feet in length with additions dating from the 1830s through the 1930s, the original section of the two-story frame tavern measures only 32 by 16 feet (figs. 169, 170). Except for the fact that it was built two full stories in an era when one-story structures predominated and had a brick chimney at each end (one of them has long since been demolished), there is nothing remarkable about the building to suggest its original function. In plan, the tavern started as a typical hall-chamber building. The central entrance opened directly into the larger room, which was the hall or entertaining space. Gable-end fireplaces heated this room and the smaller inner room to the south. There is no indication in the much-altered fabric to suggest that there was a separate stair passage, so the stair probably rose in one corner of the larger room. The plan abovestairs repeated the pattern below with two heated bedchambers, again a step above most dwellings of the period, especially ones of such modest dimensions.[33]

Built as a private residence in 1791, the original section of Hanover Tavern has twice the square footage as Hughlett's Tavern and provided slightly more space for travelers when it was converted into an ordinary in the early nineteenth century (figs. 171, 172). It replaced an older one-story structure that had been run by the Thilman family in the late colonial period. Located directly in front of the arcaded brick courthouse, the original section of this frame build-

FIGURE 169. Hughlett's Tavern, Heathsville, Northumberland County, late eighteenth century with nineteenth- and early twentieth-century additions

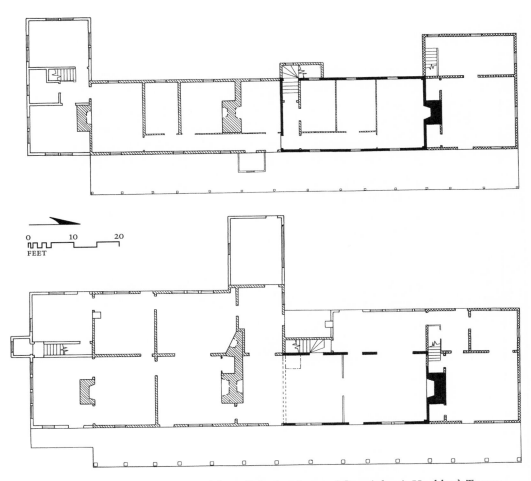

FIGURE 170. Plan, ground floor (*below*) and second floor (*above*), Hughlett's Tavern, Heathsville, Northumberland County

ing is 50 by 22 feet and has a central stair passage dividing two heated ground-floor rooms. On the second floor there were originally two heated bedchambers and a smaller pair of unheated ones at the top of the stairs. Standing two full stories, the original plan of Hanover Tavern matched a domestic form that would gain widespread popularity throughout Virginia and much of the country in the nineteenth century. A subsequent addition in 1822, which more than doubled the size of the building, transformed the domestic plan into a form that expressed its public nature, with spacious public entertaining rooms, including a ballroom and dining room. This expansion was probably done when the dwelling was converted into the principal tavern for the courthouse community.[34]

A third courthouse tavern that reflected a domestic plan when first built is

FIGURE 171. Hanover Tavern, Hanover, 1791 with 1822 and 1832 additions, in a c. 1899 photograph

the two-story frame Eastville Inn in Northampton County (fig. 173). Like Hughlett's Tavern, the Eastville Inn was purposely built as a tavern sometime after the Revolution by James Taylor to replace a series of earlier ordinaries that had served this Eastern Shore courthouse village since the 1690s. Slightly larger than Hanover Tavern, the original section of the Eastville Inn extended 46 feet in length and was 25½ feet in width (fig. 174). It too had a center stair passage. The extra depth of the building allowed for the creation of two rooms on the south side of the passage, each of which was heated by a corner fireplace. To the north of the passage was a large entertaining room. Because the plan has been so altered in subsequent renovations, the exact number of second-floor bed-chambers is uncertain. There may have been at least three heated ones with perhaps one or two more unheated spaces providing extra accommodations for guests.

Successful taverns expanded to accommodate growing numbers of travelers and court-day guests. Most replicated standard domestic patterns. One of the most common methods was the addition of shed rooms to the rear or sides of the building. These provided extra workrooms, entertaining rooms, lodging chambers, or additional domestic space for the tavern keeper and his family, who often lived alongside their guests. Another method was to build a wing at

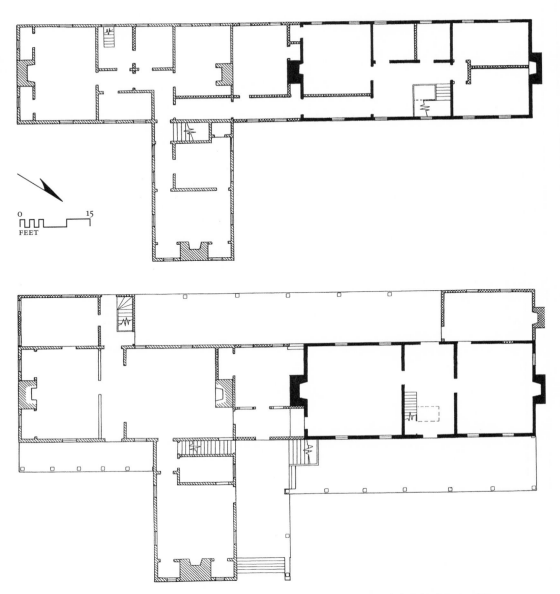

FIGURE 172. Plan, ground floor (*below*) and second floor (*above*), Hanover Tavern, Hanover

right angles to the original section, which often provided a private apartment for the keeper or additional public rooms and lodging rooms. A third option was the construction of an entirely new house attached to one of the gable ends of the original building. This was the way John Marot expanded his ordinary located near the Capitol on the Duke of Gloucester Street in Williamsburg. Marot purchased a two-room, hall-chamber dwelling in the early eighteenth century and by 1708 had acquired a tavern license in order to cater to the growing crowd of people who flocked to the new Capitol during the meetings of the General Court and General Assembly. With increased patronage, he enlarged the tavern by more than doubling its original size (fig. 175). The keeper constructed a second two-room structure to the east and replaced the old east chimney with a new one that was shared by both sections. He also constructed a series of smaller rooms in a shed addition that spanned the back of both the new and old sections. On the outside, Marot's Ordinary appeared to be two sep-

FIGURE 173. Eastville Inn, Northampton County, late eighteenth century with nineteenth- and early twentieth-century additions. Photograph by Peter Sandbeck

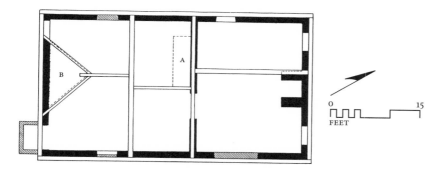

FIGURE 174. Reflected cellar plan of the original section of the Eastville Inn, Northampton County. *A:* position of cellar stair; *B:* original chimney stack removed.

FIGURE 175. Shields Tavern, Williamsburg, c. 1708 with later eighteenth-century additions, reconstructed 1954

arate two-room houses. Significantly, the inventory made of the property on the death of James Shields, its mid-eighteenth-century proprietor, identified the function of the main ground-floor rooms in domestic terms: the hall, parlor, kitchen, and chamber. Yet the contents of the rooms enumerated by the inventory reveal a growing specialization of tavern objects. There were far more chairs, tables, beds, sheets, cooking implements, dining equipage, and drinking vessels than would have been found in a domestic household of comparable size. Even though the internal arrangement and exterior appearance suggested a domestic function, the fittings and the presence of a space known as "the Barr," which was filled with carboys, bottles, pots, and money scales, suggest the beginnings of a tavern as a distinctive building type.[35]

These new taverns first appeared in cities such as Williamsburg and Norfolk by the 1750s and eventually spread to the courthouse villages in the hinterland in the half century following the American Revolution. As the travel accounts of French officers during the Revolution attest, the process of improving public accommodations had scarcely affected much of Virginia by the early 1780s. Yet when the marquis de Lafayette returned to Virginia in 1824 to visit the scenes of his youthful exploits, a grateful citizenry toasted this old hero of the Revolution with sumptuous banquets held in the finest public assembly rooms and hotels across the state. Old taverns had shed their domestic appearance and assumed certain characteristic features. By the early nineteenth century, the typical courthouse tavern had grown in size, and almost all of them were two stories in height and had a long piazza stretching across the front range. Inside, these taverns, or hotels as many were now called, were divided into a series of specialized rooms that included bars, assembly rooms, semiprivate dining rooms, billiards rooms, and private bedrooms. The reconfiguration of tavern architecture responded to changing customs and forms of sociability among the Virginia elite, and substantive upgrades signaled tavern keepers' bids for respectability and the patronage of a more genteel clientele.

The emergence of the tavern as a distinct building type parallels a similar transformation of house interiors in the late colonial period. In the second and third quarters of the eighteenth century, Virginians created a variety of new domestic spaces that segregated people and partitioned household activities into a series of increasingly specific categories. They reordered the manner in which they worked, slept, dined, and socialized in their dwellings and constructed passages, saloons, dining rooms, dressing rooms, and libraries to respond to an ever-growing demand for specialized domestic spaces. This refashioning of domestic architecture was motivated by the adoption of a new set of rules, manners, and behaviors that had formed English and European ideas of gentility and had gained broad currency in the American colonies in the late seventeenth and early eighteenth centuries.[36] Gentility sought to improve or beautify many aspects of human existence and to exclude all that was coarse or vulgar, whether things or people. As historian Richard Bushman has observed, "whether in dress, personal manners, or architecture," the chief traits of gentility were "harmony, smoothness, polish, gradual rather than abrupt variation, [and] the subduing of harsh emotions." People who accepted this elaborate code of polite behavior made it a standard by which they could shape and judge their personal lives, the interactions with their family, friends, and strangers, and their material possessions.[37] It even created an attitude toward ordinary occurrences at tavern tables. For example, in material terms gentility affected the selection and preparation of food, the setting for the meal, and the manner in which it was served and consumed. In short, food moved beyond a daily necessity to a marker of social status.

Gentility also affected architecture. Perhaps the most significant change in domestic architecture in Virginia in the first half of the eighteenth century was the introduction of a center stair passage.[38] It facilitated the reordering of household activities by providing the means for family members, servants, and visitors to move between rooms and floors without having to pass through one room to enter another, allowing for certain rooms to be set aside for specific functions. The passage created a physical and social barrier, preventing the indiscriminate intrusion into spaces and activities that were now considered to be

FIGURE 176. Gentlemen smoking. English engraving, mid-eighteenth century. Though smoking and drinking had been commonplace activities since the beginning of colonial period, tavern owners erected special rooms filled with fashionable accoutrements where gentlemen could meet as members of private clubs or in more informal gatherings to socialize.

more private and less communal. Where the houses of the better sort had once contained a few multipurpose rooms, they now increased in size to include a number of rooms reserved for a few discrete activities. A growing tendency to entertain guests away from daily chores of housework led to the setting aside of rooms that opened off the entrance passage for the reception of visitors. These rooms contained specialized implements for entertainment such as new forms of seating furniture, tea sets, and fashionable tableware, which allowed the host and invited company to display their refined tastes in social intercourse and show off the material goods that signaled their understanding of the role of specialized objects in genteel society. To underscore the social importance of these entertaining spaces, dining rooms, drawing rooms, and parlors received the best architectural finishes, having carved chimneypieces, paneled wainscoting, paperhangings, and built-in buffets in which to display costly ceramics and glass. Across the colony planters, merchants, and professionals upgraded and remodeled the public arena of their domestic lives to accord with metropolitan-inspired ideals of gentility.

Savvy tavern keepers soon created such spaces as public extensions of domestic gentility. Richard Bushman has asserted that "gentility did not introduce its own peculiar activities into the world of public entertainment. Instead it elevated the commonplace. Cards, dancing, eating, music, writing, conversing, and plays all took on new meaning when carried out in refined environments and in polished forms to suit delicate and tasteful minds."[39] The better urban taverns could advertise fashionable, well-appointed new rooms for public and private entertainments and boast of spaces dedicated to specific functions (fig. 176). One of the most specialized of these new spaces was the bar. It was a small room or semienclosed area secured by grillwork in a corner of a room where tavern keepers stored and dispensed their valuable serving stock of liquors. At Ishmael Moody's death an inventory of his estate taken in 1748 listed items in the "Bar Room" at his tavern next to the courthouse in Yorktown that clearly defined the nature of the space: "5 3 Qt. China Bowles £3, 2

Gallon Do. 26/, 1 Qt. Do. 10/; 1 large Case with 16 two Gallon Bottles; 1 Less Do. With 9 Gallon Bottles filled with Arrack; 2 smaller Do. With 16 two Qt. Bottles; 10 earthen Bowls & 2 old waiters; 2 Bottle Sliders, Candle Box and Tobo. Box; 1 pr. Large Money Scales, 2 old Tables, 1 Powder Horn Shotbag; 1 Tobo. Sive, 2 Pewter Inkstands."[40] Shields Tavern in Williamsburg also had a bar by 1751, and bars became increasingly commonplace after this time though they had little effect on the planning of taverns or their exterior appearance.

Some tavern owners created small, well-appointed semiprivate rooms that allowed patrons willing to pay an extra fee to dine on better fare in more select company. Located near the courthouse in Alexandria, the George featured "a dining room 26 Feet by 18, with a Room above of the same Dimensions, in which is a Fire-Place and a very good LONDON BILLIARD-TABLE" (fig. 177).[41] Perhaps most noticeable were large, well-finished rooms that were built to provide the appropriate setting for large public entertainments such as balls, assemblies, and concerts that catered to a clientele composed of both sexes (fig. 178). These assembly rooms or long rooms, as they were sometimes called, often rivaled the furnishings in the parlors and withdrawing rooms of the best gentry houses in the quality of their appointments. As travelers found at the Leeds tavern in Westmoreland County or any number of the finest establishments on the Duke of Gloucester Street in Williamsburg, the best of these rooms had

FIGURE 177. *Billiards in Hanover Town.* Drawing by B. H. Latrobe, 1797. (The Maryland Historical Society, Baltimore)

FIGURE 178. *The Village Assembly,* English engraving, London, 1776.

mahogany tables, chairs, copperplate prints hanging on the walls, fashionable tableware and glasses, and stone chimneypieces. Free of unpleasant things and people, they became the public stage for polite society to act out its version of refinement.

To match the growing emphasis on privacy and decorum, Virginians finally stopped sleeping indiscriminately in communal beds. Richard Charlton offered "Private Lodgings . . . for seven or eight Gentlemen, during the Assembly, at the Coffeehouse near the Capitol" in Williamsburg, a proposition that was taken up by a number of burgesses including George Washington who lodged there a number of times in the late 1760s and early 1770s.[42] Toward the end of the century, relatively few private bedchambers were available for women and elite gentlemen in the best hotels in Virginia. However, by the beginning of the second quarter of the nineteenth century, few fashionable hotels could do without some private rooms.

Finally, piazzas became nearly universal features of late colonial and early federal-period taverns (fig. 179). Stretching across the front of buildings, these open porches were used as a sitting area, a place to gather and converse. Many piazzas were finished in a manner that suggested they were perceived as an outdoor room. Paul Thilman's tavern, which preceded the present structure at Hanover, was noted for its "very large hall and a covered portico" that was used "to receive people" who assembled for court day.[43] Frame structures such as the

FIGURE 179. Tavern, New Kent

Rising Sun Tavern in Fredericksburg often had flush board sheathing, normally associated with interior wall coverings, instead of weatherboards. The piazzas of other taverns, like many dwellings, were finished with wainscoting, chair boards, and bases, interior architectural features that attest to the roomlike quality of the open space.

The addition of special dining rooms and large assembly rooms naturally increased the size of many taverns. At the Raleigh Tavern in the early 1750s, Alexander Finnie added a rear wing to an earlier standard domestic plan to create two substantial entertaining spaces—the Apollo and Daphne Rooms—replicating the type of spaces now found in the best houses. These rooms immediately became places of fashionable resort, especially during public times in Williamsburg when the General Court and General Assembly met, which brought scores of planters from across the colony to the capital. George Washington noted that on November 13, 1772, he "went to a Ball at the Apollo in the Evening." Following the pattern established at the Raleigh, Henry Wetherburn added around 1752 a "Great Room," an elaborately finished entertaining room replete with a marble chimneypiece just to the west of the double-pile original section (fig. 180). Suited for large-scale entertaining, Wetherburn's great room, measuring 25 by 25 feet, soon rivaled the Raleigh as a center for subscription balls, private dinners, lectures, and concerts (fig. 181).[44] The public rooms at Wetherburn's and at the Raleigh, like others that were built across the

FIGURE 180. Wetherburn's Tavern, Williamsburg, c. 1730s with c. 1752 addition. Entrance to the Great Room addition is through the door to the right of the tavern sign.

FIGURE 181. Great Room, Wetherburn's Tavern, Williamsburg, c. 1752

colony, had separate entrances, which meant that men and women—who now became a part of these genteel functions—could enter these spaces without passing through the main body of the tavern.

Perhaps one of the most impressive courthouse taverns to survive from the colonial period is a brick structure erected around 1770 at Gloucester (fig. 182). Standing less than 100 feet to the southeast of the 1766 brick courthouse, the Botetourt Hotel, as it is now called, was one of several ordinaries erected in the colonial period to serve the county seat. Despite numerous alterations during its long use as a hotel in the nineteenth and twentieth centuries, the surviving parts of original plan reveal that its builder incorporated many of the distinctive features found in late colonial taverns (fig. 183). Measuring 77 feet in length and 23 feet in width, the two-story walls of the tavern are laid in Flemish bond above a high cellar. Stretching the full length of the six-bay front facade is a one-story (rebuilt) piazza that would have served as a popular gathering spot for court-day revelers and weary travelers. Four doorways from this piazza led into a series of ground-floor entertaining spaces that probably consisted of one or two dining rooms, a billiards room, and a taproom.[45] In the rear yard stood a full complement of service buildings including a large stable, all of which have now been demolished (figs. 184, 185).

The two easternmost front doors contain transom lights, while the west doors do not, suggesting that the former were the primary entries into the building. In the eastern rooms the doorways and window openings were

FIGURE 182. Botetourt Hotel, Gloucester, early 1770s

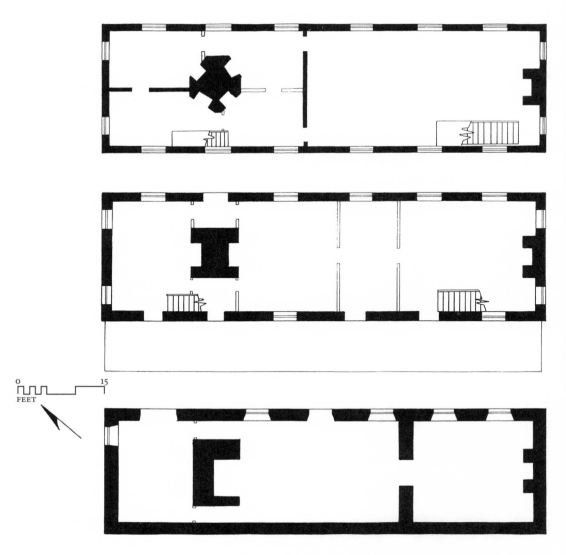

FIGURE 183. Plan, cellar (*below*), ground floor (*center*), and second floor (*above*), Botetourt Hotel, Gloucester

trimmed with double architraves, while the western doorways are finished with single architraves and the window apertures have only beaded boards and no architraves on their interior surfaces. These differences in the trim on the ground floor imply the western rooms were less formal than those to the east. The easternmost room was clearly an important public room, perhaps the principal drinking room. Original partitions in the eastern part of this floor do not survive, but the presence of two doorways suggests that there were at least

FIGURE 184. Stable, Botetourt Hotel, Gloucester, in an early 1930s photograph.

FIGURE 185. Stall in the stable, Botetourt Hotel, Gloucester, in an early 1930s photograph

one and probably two internal partitions. If the latter, then the second door from the east would have led into a passage, forestalling direct access from the outside into the room to the west, which was heated by the internal western chimney. This arrangement is consistent with other late eighteenth-century Virginia tavern plans and would suggest that the inner room served as a more private heated parlor because it had a more restricted access. Equally complex was the original circulation at the western end of the tavern. The far western front door entered directly into the western heated room. A partially rebuilt staircase rises from this room to the second floor. The second door from the west created a lobby entrance with access to the inner parlor room to the east and perhaps to the western room as well. At the back of the building, another lobby entrance on the other side of the western, internal chimney gave access to the inner parlor and the western room. This rear entrance provided the easiest access to the spaces below in the cellar. Evidence for a bar, if there was one, has disappeared.

The cellar, divided into three rooms, ran the full length of the building. The large central room probably served as a kitchen. It had direct exterior access at the back of the building and contained an extremely large fireplace opening measuring 7 feet in width, 4½ feet in depth, and nearly 5 feet in height. An un-heated room with a separate exterior doorway was on the west, and a heated room to the east was entered through the kitchen. The former room may have served as a storage space, while the latter perhaps was used as a work space for servants.

The second floor contained a block of small rooms and one large one. In the western end of the building, four heated rooms cluster around a central chimney. They are modestly finished with two-part door architraves and beaded board jambs without architraves for the window openings. At least three of these rooms probably were used as chambers, but how they communicated with one another is not entirely clear. A stair in the south central room descended to one of the public rooms immediately below it. It also has an early hatch leading to the unfinished attic that appears to have been unlit, unheated, and unused.

The eastern half of the second floor contained a large public assembly or ballroom. From the eastern ground-floor entertaining room, a stair rose to the southeast corner of this second-floor space. The western partition of this large room contains two doors that led to separate chambers. During public assemblies, one or both of these rooms may have been used as secondary spaces for cards or for taking refreshments, a pattern that can be seen in other assembly rooms such the ones in the early brick market house in Fredericksburg and in the second story of the courthouse in Edenton, North Carolina (fig. 186). A visitor to Fredericksburg described its colonial market house as "entirely devoted

FIGURE 186. Second-floor Assembly Room, Chowan County courthouse, Edenton, N.C., 1767–68

to Dissipation. It is of Brick (not elegant) & contains a Room for Dancing & two for retirement & Cards."[46] As the largest and best space in the Gloucester tavern, the assembly room contained the most elaborate finishes. All woodwork on the chimney breast in the east end is modern, but a symmetrical surbase, beaded base, beaded peg strip for hanging cloaks and hats, operable internal window shutters, and part of the cornice survive, suggesting that this space was fairly well appointed in the colonial period.

The Botetourt Hotel with its piazza, billiards table, fancy furnishings, private dining rooms, and large ballroom suitable for polite entertainments set the standards that would eventually transform other courthouse taverns in the decades following the Revolution. It dominated the Gloucester County courthouse grounds. Its two-story height and 80-foot length made it by far the most imposing structure in the little crossroads village that grew up around the new courthouse in the last decade before the Revolution. The long piazza and multiple doors announced a complex arrangement of public entertaining rooms and chambers within. The plan reflected the effort of a style-conscious owner to separate activities into discrete areas and embellish reception spaces to rival the most refined domestic rooms. The large cellar kitchen and associated rooms were the work spaces of a staff of slaves and servants who circulated throughout the building to perform their many tasks. On court days they spent much of their time in the kitchen, bar, public room, and piazza catering to a boisterous male crowd intent on draining bottles of wine, kegs of beer, and bowls of punch. On special occasions they worked in other spaces such as the private dining room, cardroom, billiards room, and ballroom. Here they ministered to the thirst and appetites of genteel folk—men and women—who now came to the large brick structure to be entertained on a scale and in a manner unknown in the past.

Preservation of Their Patrimony: The Clerk's Office

Clerks' offices served as the repository of deed, will, inventory, and order books whose written instruments legitimized the claims of landowners and legatees and served as a collective record of local law and custom. The collection and storage of Virginia's legal records evolved in a haphazard manner. English custom offered some precedent for the safekeeping of public records. Civil and ecclesiastical courts kept records of their transactions and deposited these in muniment rooms in public buildings. In Virginia the county court amalgamated many of the duties of various English courts of record, taking the responsibility of ecclesiastical courts in recording probate inventories, for example, and providing a record of civil and criminal cases as did quarter-sessional courts. The county court also became the custodian of land records, a function that had not been a part of the custom in England, where deeds were held in private hands. As in the other American colonies, it was only natural for Virginia's courts to assume this function. Whereas in England the knowledge of land ownership often stretched back for centuries, giving fields and forests in every parish a well-known genealogy, no such common memory of the possession of land in Virginia existed. Thus publicly recorded deeds provided the proof of ownership acceptable to all in a place where cultural markers were weak or nonexistent.

Virginians suffered the destruction of their legal documents through neglect, vandalism, and fires. Scholars have frequently bemoaned the warehouse fire in Richmond on April 3, 1865, that destroyed the court records from a number of the oldest tidewater counties as a substantial blow to the writing of Virginia's early history. However, the burning of those papers at the end of the Civil War was only the most dramatic in a series of unfortunate incidents and practices that diminished the legal legacy from the colonial and early national eras. Perhaps the greatest detriment was the fact that the idea of well-kept archives, housed in fireproof storage and cared for by the county clerk, was not fully developed until the end of the eighteenth century. In fact, the record for most of the colonial period was dismal in many places. Dampness harmed the seventeenth-century York County record books, and rats destroyed many of the early court records in Surry County. Justices purged old legal papers considered "to be of no use" that were contained in two old bookpresses in the Northumberland County courthouse. Accidental fires destroyed the records of Northumberland County in 1710, Nansemond County in 1734, King William County in 1788, and Monongalia County (now in West Virginia) in 1796, while an arsonist burned the clerk's office in New Kent County in 1787.[47] These incidents and many more that followed in the nineteenth century left few records in any county fully intact.

Each county clerk accumulated thousands of sheets of loose papers and dozens of bound record books, published laws, and judicial handbooks. The indifferent attitude that most county officials displayed toward this patrimony is evident in the arrangements they made for storage and preservation. Rarely were records kept in a single place. Rather, they were often dispersed in several locations: in jury rooms, lofts, and private dwellings, including the homes of the clerks. Until the early eighteenth century, loose papers and record books were stored in chests, trunks, boxes, and loose volumes.[48] For example, in 1707 the Middlesex justices stored a chest filled with court books in the jury room. An inventory of York County records made in 1692 suggests the size and condition of court materials that had accumulated over a sixty-year period and the manner in which they were stowed. Housed in a room in the courthouse were "Thirteen Record Bookes bound, five of them dampnifyed in some respect in the Covers and paper . . . five more Record bookes dapnifyed being unbound and very old . . . The Statues att large, a Collection of the Statutes att large, Daltons Justice of peace also a bound written booke of the lawes of Virga writt pr Mr. Job Howes . . . A deal box of papers ould & nailed up . . . An old Dansick Case of papers since the time of Coll Edmund Jennings being first Clarke heare together with a p[ar]cell of loose papers." The clerk removed these items from the courthouse for safekeeping and placed them in his dwelling.[49]

By the second decade of the eighteenth century, bookpresses began to replace chests for the storage of papers. In 1711 York County paid its clerk, Philip Lightfoot, 1,161 pounds of tobacco for a lock and press "to preserve the papers in."[50] Most presses, built of pine or walnut, contained a series of pigeonholes for loose papers and tall thin partitions for storing books and were partially or fully enclosed with folding doors secured by locks. An early eighteenth-century hanging press with doors found in the attic of the Colony House in Newport, Rhode Island, consists of a series of boards nailed together with the dates of court terms (1728–31) inscribed in pencil on the front of five of the eight pigeonholes (fig. 187). When Princess Anne County officials wanted a bookcase "to preserve the Records from being obliterated by the various changes of the Weather, and to Keep them free from Dust," carpenter James Williamson estimated that such a case could not be built for less than the sizable cost of

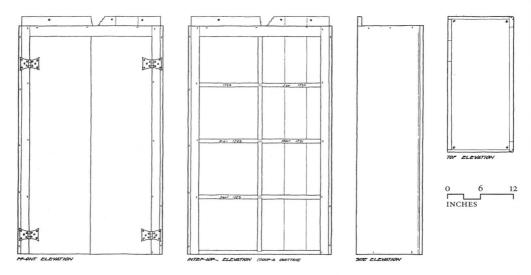

FIGURE 187. Elevation and plan, documents press, Colony House, Newport, R.I., c. 1730s. This simple bookpress consists of several sawn boards nailed together. Similar presses first began to appear in Virginia after 1700.

FIGURE 188. Front and side elevations of a bookpress added c. 1750–75 to the Northampton County courthouse of 1731, Eastville

£10 given the intricacy of the internal partitions and the "number of Locks and Handles [that] will be required." In 1743 Louisa and Middlesex Counties each paid the low sum of 500 pounds of tobacco for a bookpress. The surviving bookpress in Northampton County with its solid panel doors and multiple internal partitions must have been typical of the dozens constructed by local joiners for county clerks in the late colonial period; it was used as a model for reproducing a bookpress for the Williamsburg–James City County courthouse (figs. 188, 189).[51]

Court business required a place where people could record their legal instruments. On court day transactions often took place in one of the all-purpose side rooms, often known as jury rooms, where the clerk and his assistant set up shop. Individuals entered into contracts, posted bonds, got their cases on the docket, and returned court papers in these spaces. More unusual were rooms specifically allocated to the clerk. In 1678 the Westmoreland County clerk had a heated room in the garret of the courthouse dedicated to his business. The clerk in the courthouse in Charles City County in the late 1680s had "a fair closett or office" with a large window to aid his work on dark days. In 1720 the Elizabeth City County court instructed its clerk to build an office inside the courthouse and move all the records there within three months. Whether the clerk took over one of the jury rooms or space above the courtroom is unknown, but clearly the

FIGURE 189. Court books and legal papers inside a bookpress, Williamsburg–James City County courthouse. The design of the press was based on the eighteenth-century one in Northampton County. Books, papers, and press reproduced, 1990–91.

stacks of paper continued to grow. In 1736 the sheriff was ordered to get shelves made in the clerk's office. In 1742 the clerk was requested to get another press "for the Preservation of the Records." If he used it full time, rather than only on "rules day" before the court sat, the room needed a fireplace to warm the clerk as well as to keep the papers dry in summer and the ink liquid in winter. A few other counties followed Elizabeth City County in setting up a clerk's office in the courthouse. Henrico had an office in its courthouse by 1720 though the absence of bookpresses, tables, and window shutters made it "neither safe nor convenient for keeping records." After York County built a new courthouse in 1732, the clerk kept an office in one of the ground-floor rooms of this arcaded structure. By the end of the Revolution, the space had a number of presses and desks for its active records and nearly a century and a half of accumulated "dead papers."[52]

A few counties chose to build a separate clerk's office on the courthouse grounds. In 1707 when the York County court ordered Clerk William Tunley to return the county records to the courthouse, he refused, alleging that they in part belonged to him. The magistrates sent the sheriff to Tunley's residence to seize the public records. When they were examined at the courthouse, they revealed that Tunley had misappropriated public funds. In response, the York court obtained a new clerk, the Yorktown merchant Philip Lightfoot, and decided the following year to build a 16-foot-square frame office on the courthouse lot in Yorktown. The office was conveniently located for Lightfoot just a few paces up the street from his residence. In 1734 Brunswick County paid William Poole 1,000 pounds of tobacco to build a clerk's office, enough for a small frame structure. Orange County court granted Clerk Henry Willis leave to build an office on the courthouse grounds in 1737. The clerk had permission to fell any timber on the grounds for that purpose, but there is no indication that he was paid for his effort. Willis also was responsible for erecting the first county courthouse at the same time, for which he was paid. The desire to have the court's papers close at hand led the Cumberland County magistrates to order the construction of a 16-by-12-foot brick or stone office on the public land in 1749. A few months later the court ordered that a press be made for its papers. Prince Edward County raised money in 1767 to build a clerk's office at the courthouse.[53]

These and other examples indicate that the practice of erecting a central records repository and office for the clerk on the courthouse grounds grew steadily in the eighteenth century, though it was by no means prevalent. Courts sometimes wanted reassurance that records were stored safely and kept up-to-date and dispatched a delegation of their members to these offices to inspect their contents. Often they were pleased to find things in good order, though there were instances when they were extremely dismayed.[54] The Middlesex County justices who inspected their clerk's office in 1767 found the place to be "in great disorder."[55]

Even with the advantage of having all the records together in one place in a clerk's office on the courthouse grounds, the most common place in the colonial period to keep court record books and papers was at the clerk's own house. Even when there was an office in the courthouse or on the public grounds, the clerk sometimes made little use of it. In 1692 the York County justices granted the newly appointed clerk, William Sedgwicke, permission to remove all the books and papers in the office in the courthouse to Undersheriff John Myhill's plantation where he was then residing.[56]

As in the case of Sedgwicke, most clerks chose not to live at the tiny cluster of buildings that made up the county seat but often resided several miles from the courthouse. In the 1750s, for example, the Hanover clerk lived within a mile of Page's warehouse rather than at the courthouse. In the early 1770s George Seaton, the clerk of Amherst County, resided eight miles from the courthouse on a plantation owned by Gabriel Penn. He lived and worked in a frame house measuring 20 by 16 feet. Penn's plantation was not isolated but was located along the main road to North Carolina and had evolved into a thriving community in the late colonial period with a large commodious tavern, two stores, a blacksmith's shop, and a tailor's shop, all laid out "in Lines and Squares, so as to resemble a Town." The clerk of Prince George County kept his office in the town of Blandford in 1779 rather than at Prince George, the rural county seat several miles away.[57] In 1787 many of the court records of New Kent resided with the clerk two miles from the courthouse.[58] For many years in the 1780s, the deputy clerk of Accomack County kept the court records at his house in the port of Onancock instead of the county seat of Accomac two miles to the east.[59]

Although a county clerkship provided a good income for its incumbents, most clerks aspired to own land, slaves, and the accoutrements that would establish them in the middle to upper level of Virginia society. William Byrd observed that Major Benjamin Robinson of Caroline County, whose fortunes had sunk through "gaming and idleness," had reformed and on being appointed "to a clerk's place in a quarrelsome county will soon be able to clear his old scores."[60] Often the sons of planters, they inherited or purchased plantations in order to maintain or enhance their status and spent much of their time overseeing their holdings. Except for the two or three days of the month when court was in session, the clerk kept his office at his plantation, and those who wanted to do business out of session traveled to his home. There, either in a room in his dwelling or in a small heated building on the grounds, the clerk transacted public business. In 1755 the *Virginia Gazette* advertised for sale a plantation of 150 acres in Hanover County containing a "good dwelling house," several outhouses, and "a small house with a brick chimney, which was formerly the clerk's office." The Berkeley County clerk's office was constructed of stone, as were the dwelling, kitchen, dairy, springhouse, and stable on the 850-acre plantation.[61]

In 1772 James Steptoe was appointed clerk of Bedford County court, an office he held for the next fifty-four years (fig. 190). When he first entered the position, the county court met in the town of New London, and Steptoe probably lived in the vicinity. In 1781 Campbell County was formed from the eastern part of Bedford, leaving the old county seat near the dividing line between the two counties. Although Bedford magistrates moved the court of the truncated county westward to a more central location called Liberty (now Bedford), the county clerk did not move. In the late eighteenth century, the clerk erected an

FIGURE 190. James
Steptoe (1750–1826), clerk
of Bedford County Court,
1772–1826. (Clerk's Office,
Circuit Court of Bedford
County; photograph, The
Library of Virginia)

imposing three-part frame dwelling called Federal Hill about a half mile north of New London in Campbell County. On his plantation Steptoe built a one-story wooden clerk's office that he used until his death in 1826 (fig. 191). The building was heated by a fireplace on one gable end and was lined with shelves for the books and papers that accumulated during his long tenure.[62]

Inconveniently located in another county, Bedford citizens had to travel to the mountain of paperwork at Steptoe's plantation rather than move that mountain to the county seat because the clerk jealously guarded his prerogatives. Acutely aware of the precarious situation in which many county records were kept, the General Assembly passed a law in 1792 that required county officials to preserve their books and papers. The law called for the construction of a fireproof clerk's office on the courthouse grounds of every county. It also required that each clerk should reside within the county or corporation in which he held office and that he should keep his office at the courthouse or another convenient place designated by the court. However, the law exempted those clerks who had been appointed to their positions before June 4, 1776, when Virginia was still a royal colony.[63] Steptoe, appointed in 1772, obviously believed he had no need to comply with the law and preferred to conduct his business from the convenience of his own plantation. With little legal recourse, Bedford magistrates respected his wishes.

When other county courts attempted to follow the law, they met with stiff opposition from entrenched clerks. Loudoun County magistrates ordered the construction of a clerk's office in Leesburg in 1800, but the clerk, Charles Binns, objected to moving his affairs to the new building, arguing that he had been grandfathered in by the 1792 law. Binns was the eponymous son of the previous clerk who had served for forty years in the office, from 1756 to 1796. However, the court pointed out that the son took office after the passage of the law and was thus not legally entitled to a waiver of its provision. Although Charles Binns Jr. remained in office until 1837, surpassing the length of his father's tenure by a year, he was obliged to conduct the county's business in a two-story brick clerk's office constructed on the courthouse grounds by 1805, which was replaced by another one at the end of the decade.[64]

FIGURE 191. James Steptoe's office, Federal Hill, Campbell County. (Virginia Department of Historic Resources)

When the Caroline court established Bowling Green as the new seat of government in 1801, the magistrates ordered the clerk to move his operations to the new venue as soon as an office was constructed. William Nelson, clerk of the court for thirty-five years, pointed out that his length of service, which began before June 4, 1776, exempted him from moving. He argued that the 1792 law allowed him the "priviledge of keeping his office at any place in the County as was practiced through the state, and accordingly by this county from its first establishment." Besides, Nelson made it clear that he could not possibly move to Bowling Green because the county had not purchased land on which to build him a dwelling, outhouses, and a garden "for the use and residence of the Clerk." The court refused to build Nelson a dwelling with public money and allowed him to continue in his old office, knowing full well that time was on their side. The dispute did no lasting harm between the clerk and the bench. In December 1807 twenty-three magistrates, an unusually full complement of members, gathered in the courthouse in Bowling Green to pay tribute to the recently deceased clerk. The magistrates and officers of the court resolved to "wear crape around their left arm for three months, as a testimonial of the high re-spect and esteem which they had for Col. William Nelson."[65]

Respect for conscientious officeholders, longevity of service, tradition, and tenacity retarded the implementation of the 1792 law. Some counties preferred to keep their clerks happy and allowed them to maintain their offices away from the courthouse nearly thirty years after the passage of the act. Like Colonel Nelson of Caroline and James Steptoe of Bedford, old age caught up with many of the colonial appointees in the first decades of the nineteenth century, and their successors did not have the prestige or loopholes in the law to operate their offices on their own terms. Yet, some new appointees, for a variety of reasons, managed to follow the old ways and delay moving to the county seat. The clerks of Mecklenburg County kept the court's papers in private offices on various plantations until 1815 when an office was built at the courthouse in Boydton. William Miller, clerk of the Goochland County court, served from 1791 to 1846 and was allowed to maintain his office two miles from the courthouse until 1826 when Dabney Cosby built a new office and courthouse. Amelia County's clerk, too, kept his office at his home more than two miles from the courthouse as late as 1820.[66]

Even though the 1792 law aimed at reforming public record keeping in Virginia was not an immediate and universal success, it did have an eventual impact on the way in which county officials treated their documents. In the 1790s a few counties actually complied with one of the provisions in the act and built fireproof structures on their courthouse grounds. Between 1795 and 1798 Lancaster County built an office measuring 22 by 16 feet a few dozen yards east of its 1740 courthouse (figs. 192, 193). In 1796 Powhatan County began construction on a 24-by-20-foot office on the public grounds (figs. 194, 195). In 1799 Isle of Wight County completed a 16-by-22-foot office with a gable-end entrance next to its 1750 courthouse in Smithfield. All three of these surviving brick buildings contained a single room heated by a gable-end chimney, a plan that was followed in many counties. The number of new buildings increased dramatically in the first and second decades of the new century, and many of them still survive. Isle of Wight's building in Smithfield was only used for a short time as the county office. In 1800 the court moved to a new location eight miles to the southwest, and a year later the magistrates ordered the construction of a new clerk's office there "on the same plan of the same dimensions and similar as the one now in Smithfield." Some of the counties' new offices were larger than the earlier structures, containing two or more rooms on one or two floors that included an office or work space for the clerk as well as a storage room for dead records.[67]

A fireproof office in the 1790s and 1800s had few exposed surfaces of flammable materials. This meant that offices had masonry walls, mainly brick but

FIGURE 192. Lancaster County clerk's office, 1795–98. An early nineteenth-century addition is on the right.

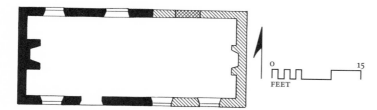

FIGURE 193. Plan, Lancaster County clerk's office

occasionally stone in regions where it was readily available. Following the language of the 1792 law, most counties required their buildings to have masonry floors made of flagstones, bricks, or tiles. The specifications for the 1794 Accomack clerk's office called for the building to be laid with flagstones, but four years later an order substituted tile. In neighboring Northampton County the early nineteenth-century office floor contains large paving stones (figs. 196, 197). Charles City County's clerk's office, a small brick building located a few feet to the east of the courthouse and demolished after the Civil War, had a flagstone floor until 1824 when the stones were taken out and sold.[68]

The law also stipulated that roofs be covered with tile, slate, or lead. If the first two materials were costly but increasingly available across the state, the

FIGURE 194. Powhatan County clerk's office, 1796. The rear wing was built in 1833–34. The woodwork of the windows and the porch are late nineteenth century.

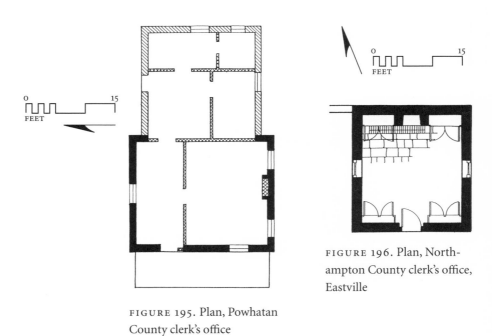

FIGURE 195. Plan, Powhatan County clerk's office

FIGURE 196. Plan, Northampton County clerk's office, Eastville

FIGURE 197. Northampton County clerk's office, Eastville, early nineteenth century

latter had to be imported and was considered prohibitively expensive. Faced with the cost of such materials, a number of counties chose to ignore the law and use wooden shingles.[69] Some offices also had arched masonry ceilings as an added measure against the spread of fire. The Accomack court specified such a feature for its clerk's office in 1794, as did the Orange County court in 1802, and the Spotsylvania justices in 1806.[70] The vaulting of the ceiling in the early nineteenth-century clerk's office in Northampton County springs 10 feet above the paved floor and forms a segmental arch that reaches 13½ feet at the apex (fig. 198).

On the inside, wooden trim was kept to a minimum. Rarely did these offices have bases, chair boards, cornices, architraves, wainscoting, or mantels, and stout, double-sheathed doors and metal or double-sheathed wooden shutters provided a measure of security against fire and vandals. The Northumberland clerk's office of 1796 was to have windows with iron grates. In 1802 the magistrates of Orange County went even further in their fire precautions, specifying that their new clerk's office have iron sashes and stone window frames. The King George County clerk's office had a stone doorsill and steps.[71]

Even with bare plaster walls, clerks' offices were filled with wooden benches, tables, chairs, writing desks, shelves with pigeonholes, and bookpresses. The record room in the Culpeper clerk's office received "shelves pigeon

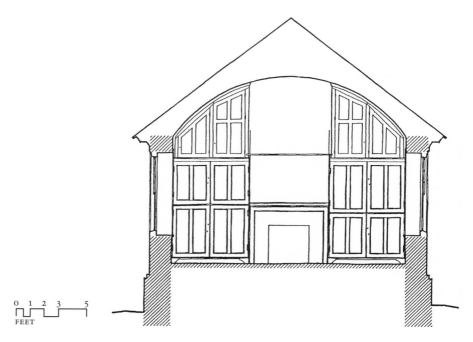

FIGURE 198. Section, Northampton County clerk's office, Eastville.
A: mid-nineteenth-century bookpresses; *B:* original bookpresses.

FIGURE 199. Sussex County courthouse, 1828, in a c. 1912 photograph

holes and sliding doors" in 1802. Powhatan justices ordered a large table and an unspecified number of "chears" for their clerk's new office in 1798, while the clerk in Accomack County received a set of six Windsor chairs in 1802.[72] Built-in presses line the two gable-end walls of the Northampton County clerk's office in Eastville. In some offices presses were often built in the space between the fireplace jambs and side walls in one of the gable ends, while freestanding ones occupied space along the long walls. Cases were built next to the chimney in the King George clerk's office in 1809 and inserted in the Powhatan clerk's office in 1821.[73]

Freestanding clerks' offices soon found competition with another scheme whereby subsidiary public functions were housed together under one roof. By the second and third decades of the nineteenth century, county magistrates experimented with a number of new courthouse plans. One type consisted of a central one- or two-story block with attached office wings. A second plan featured a large rectangular two-story structure where office and courtroom spaces were on separate floors. The winged courthouse design usually consisted of a T-shaped plan, with the clerk's office and sheriff's office or treasurer's office flanking a central courtroom. The plan was similar in configuration to the colonial T-shaped courthouses, though they functioned in a slightly different manner. Among the earliest of these new T-shaped courthouses were the ones completed in Patrick County in 1822, Sussex County in 1828, and Mathews County in the early 1830s, which contained offices on either side of the courtroom on the ground floor with jury rooms located on the second floor. The arcaded Sussex courthouse had three doors along the long front facade with the central one leading to the courtroom while the two flanking doors opened directly into the separate offices (fig. 199).[74] The Mathews design originally had only one door, which lead into the courtroom, but at a later date the front windows lighting the two side offices were converted into doorways to provide direct access to these spaces (figs. 200, 201). In 1833 the Rappahannock County public building commissioners debated the merits of constructing a freestanding clerk's office as opposed to having the office contiguous to the courthouse. They believed that "by attaching the clerk's office or rather clerks' offices to the courthouse a more comfortable, more convenient, & a building of better appearance can be built for a less sum of money." They recommended the construction of a courthouse similar to one that neighboring Page County had just begun at Luray. The Rappahannock courthouse was to be "40 feet square with an office on each side of the front end of the Courthouse 20 feet long, 15 feet wide, forming a front of 80 feet with an arcade 10 feet wide, the whole length of the front."[75]

Another way to incorporate the clerk's office within the courthouse was to build a large rectangular structure (sometimes enhanced by a front pedimented

FIGURE 200. Mathews County courthouse, c. 1835

FIGURE 201. Plan, Mathews
County courthouse

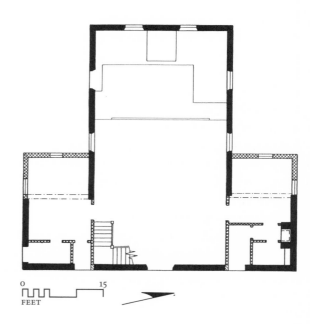

FIGURE 202. Lunenburg County courthouse, 1823–27

portico), with vaulted, fireproof offices located on either side of a central corridor on the ground floor. The courtroom was located on the second story with either exterior or interior stairs leading to it, a plan that revived a practice that had appeared in the late seventeenth and early eighteenth centuries but reversed the position of the components. This plan became popular across much of the nation in the early nineteenth century, especially in South Carolina where Robert Mills used it in the design for a number of county courthouses in the 1820s. It appeared in Virginia by the second quarter of the nineteenth century.[76] The Lunenburg courthouse, first built in 1823–27 with a two-story courtroom space with a gallery and jury rooms on the second floor, was rearranged in 1857 to conform to the Mills plan (figs. 202, 203). A full second floor was installed in the courthouse. Stairs were erected in the front portico to provide access to the second-floor courtroom, while the lower floor was reconfigured to contain vaulted rooms for the clerk and other offices.[77]

By the end of the nineteenth century, both these courthouse types—the winged plan and the two-story block with first-floor offices and central corridor and second-story courtroom—no longer satisfied the increasing demands for space. Clerks in particular needed more room to house the expanding col-

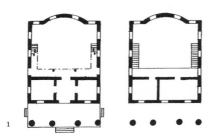

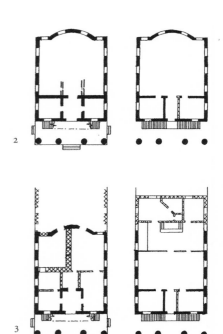

FIGURE 203. Sequential plans, Lunenburg County courthouse. *1:* 1823, two-story courtroom; *2:* 1853, full second floor created with courtroom upstairs and offices below (configuration unknown), exterior staircase added; *3:* post-1939 alterations and rear addition (addition partially omitted).

FIGURE 204. Gloucester County clerk's office, 1896, built by B. F. Smith Company of Washington, D.C.

lection of books and loose papers that had accumulated over time. In the 1890s, a century after the General Assembly had first addressed the need for fireproof clerks' offices, there was a renewed spate of building. New brick offices, most of which were built by the B. F. Smith Fireproof Company of Washington, D.C., between the 1890s and the First World War, rose on the courthouse grounds next to or in place of the first generation of late eighteenth- and early nineteenth-century buildings (fig. 204). Equipped with metal shelves, vaulted floors and ceilings, and other fire-resistant features, many of these offices still serve the same function as those first repositories erected on the courthouse grounds in the colonial period, a place where legal documents are recorded and stored for public inspection.

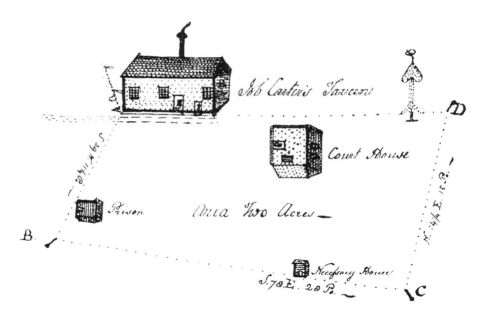

FIGURE 205. Plat of the Lancaster County courthouse grounds, 1784. (Lancaster County Deed Book, 1782–93, The Library of Virginia)

FIGURE 206. Chesterfield County courthouse grounds with dirt paths, in an early twentieth-century photograph. The 1749 courthouse was demolished in 1917. (Valentine Richmond History Center)

EPILOGUE:
COURTHOUSE GROUNDS
TO CIVIC SQUARE

Courthouse Grounds

A S VITAL AS THE COURTHOUSE and its associated public and private buildings were to the orderly functioning of colonial society, the courthouse grounds rarely presented an orderly appearance. In many counties only the courthouse exhibited any degree of architectural pretension; the rest of the buildings seldom rose above utilitarian adequacy. If magistrates erected imposing brick courthouses as symbols of the power of the law and their authority, the effect was diminished by the shabbiness of the surroundings in which they stood. Built with public money on the cheap, stables, wells, stocks and pillories, and necessary houses were habitually in disrepair with decaying posts, broken windows, and peeling paint. These and other public buildings such as the prison and the clerk's office as well as private taverns, stores, and shops were haphazardly strewn about the two acres that comprised the courthouse grounds (fig. 205). In rural settings few buildings stood in any formal relationship to the courthouse. Dirt, brickbat, and oyster-shell paths marked the informal circulation routes between tavern, courthouse, prison, clerk's office, and necessary (fig. 206).

Public grounds attracted private interests mainly by the promise of commercial gains to be had at court-day gatherings. A few commercial, industrial, and domestic structures grew up around the public buildings. Some taverns, stores, and shops encroached upon public land, which was seldom delineated visually like the prison bounds. A few of these commercial establishments appeared with permission of the authorities; others simply occupied odd corners and marginal areas where few were willing to contest the private annexation of public space. In 1749 carpenter Severn Guthrey of Accomack County received permission to construct a shop on 50 square feet of the courthouse land in return for an annual rent of four shillings; it was only a few years later that he won the contract to construct the new brick courthouse. Others were simply given public land to build upon and occupy without charge as long as they provided a socially or commercially useful service. In 1762 Northumberland magistrates

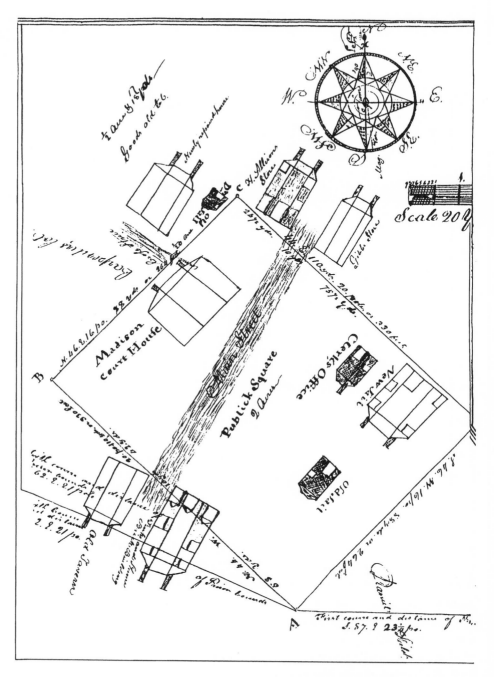

FIGURE 207. Plat of the Madison County courthouse grounds, 1824. Within thirty years of the county's establishment, a village of taverns, stores, and dwellings had grown up along the periphery of the public square. (Plat Book 2, Clerk's Office, Madison County)

FIGURE 208. New Kent in 1862. *Left to right:* tavern, factory, clerk's office, courthouse, and ruins of the jail. From Robert Johnson and Clarence Buel, eds., *Battles and Leaders of the Civil War,* 4 vols. (New York, 1884–87), 2:176.

granted James Craine permission to build an ordinary on the courthouse land. Three years later they allowed fellow justice Spence Ball liberty to build a store-house there.[1]

A number of rural courthouse grounds grew into small villages where commercial establishments hitched their fortunes to court-day business (fig. 207). As late as the second quarter of the nineteenth century, however, few rural courthouses in the tidewater attracted anything more than a handful of dwellings, one or two stores, a blacksmith's shop, and a tavern. In 1835 New Kent had a population of 41 and contained ten dwellings, six stores, and a tavern located across the road from the courthouse (fig. 208). Because many of these rural communities were devoid of a public place of worship, citizens gathered in the courthouse for divine services. Nearby, Hanover was dominated by its "very large and commodious tavern" but also had a store and blacksmith shop. Among the 50 residents were a boot and shoe maker and an attorney. King and Queen Courthouse had two stores, a tavern, a magazine, and a tanyard, but the village of 54 people (14 whites, including one attorney, and 40 blacks) was considered unhealthy because it was surrounded by marshes (fig. 209). In contrast to the old colonial heartland, many piedmont and Southside county seats prospered during the Jacksonian era. Palmyra was described as "a thriving village." Gathered around the newly erected Fluvanna County courthouse were fourteen dwellings, a tavern, a store, and a factory. In Charlotte County the citizens of Marysville were quite proud of their courthouse with its pedimented Tuscan portico "built on a plan furnished by Mr. Jefferson." The village had grown to 475 inhabitants by 1835, among whom were "mechanics, wagon makers, several

FIGURE 209. King and Queen County courthouse grounds

house carpenters and bricklayers, [and] 4 attorneys." Marysville (later renamed Charlotte Courthouse) had "2 well kept taverns, 5 stores, [and] 40 dwellings."[2]

In many of these crossroads communities, commercial growth and settlement spread randomly on the periphery of the courthouse grounds. The core also showed few signs of careful planning until the late eighteenth century. Efforts to unify and beautify public spaces seldom aspired beyond basic maintenance. In 1695 Essex County magistrates ordered the felling of trees and the removal of brush around the courthouse yard, perhaps as much out of fear of damage or fire as from any concern for appearances.[3] After the construction of a new courthouse in Tappahannock in 1730, Essex justices insisted that the area around the building be leveled and the building rubbish removed. Fairfax justices in 1756 ordered that the public lot be leveled, while in Accomack County in 1800, the justices wanted a workman to smooth out "the low places of the yard in front of the courthouse."[4]

In a few counties post-and-rail fences enclosed the courthouse grounds. As in the case of Anglican churchyards, these fences were less an attempt to distinguish the significance of the site than an effort to keep livestock and other nuisances from ruining or fouling the buildings and grounds. Cattle and hogs turned loose to forage constantly plagued rural churchyards, fields, gardens, and town streets.[5] Such must have been the concern of provincial officials at Jamestown in 1691 when the "Genll Court house" or statehouse was to be railed in "to keep it from those indecencies it is now exposed." More than a century later, the same consideration prompted district court officials at Haymarket in Prince William County to enclose the courthouse lot "to prevent stock from harbouring in the portico and damaging the pavement thereof." In 1846 Goochland magistrates ordered that "the public square around the courthouse be kept in good order and that animals and beasts were to be kept out of the same."[6] The fence built in Richmond County in 1750 after the erection of the new double-arcaded courthouse by Landon Carter was typical of the size and form of these early enclosures. Erected at a distance of 20 feet from each of the four corners of the courthouse, the 5-foot-high fence was composed of locust posts set at regular intervals with "sawn white oak rails spaced within three inches of one another." The magistrates also ordered the fabrication of four benches to be placed beneath the windows in the two arcades, an unusual gesture of convenience for members of the public who normally stood long hours in and outside of the courthouse. Nearly twenty years later when the fence was renewed, an unspecified number of gates with locks were to be built, making the immediate precincts of the courthouse off-limits not only to animals but to people when court was not in session. Following the Revolution, the Richmond County magistrates decided to mark the entrances into the fenced area formally by planting two locust trees on each side of each gate.[7] Placing the building out of bounds when court was not in session followed the precedent established by Anglican parish churches whereby the churchyard gates were locked when there were no services. Locked gates added a measure of protection to structures standing in relatively isolated surroundings.

By the beginning of the nineteenth century, a few counties had begun to follow the lead of Richmond County magistrates, establishing the precedent for formal landscaping that turned these amorphous public spaces into civic greens. In the 1820s the magistrates of Goochland County went to great lengths to improve the setting of their new two-story courthouse. A post-and-rail fence with handsome gates went up around the courthouse yard, and ornamental trees were planted within the square. The new public buildings in Bowling Green, the seat of Caroline County, were described in 1835 as being "on a beautiful level green, ornamented with fine trees." In the same year the courthouse, clerk's office, and two jails at King William were "handsomely inclosed with an iron railing. The lot is beautifully set with grass and shaded with a grove of locust trees."[8] During the antebellum period the Spotsylvania County courthouse acquired a low coped brick wall, entrance gates, and shade trees to ornament its grounds (fig. 210).

Even with these initiatives, the majority of the courthouse grounds in Vir-

FIGURE 210. Spotsylvania County courthouse, 1839, in an 1860s photograph. (Library of Congress)

ginia retained their untidy and jumbled appearance. Antebellum novelist John Pendleton Kennedy described the courthouse complex in Surry County in terms that were strikingly true of most places:

> The court-house is a low square building, entirely unadorned, occupying the middle of a large area. It has an official appearance given to it by a huge door of a dingy exterior, and ample windows covered with dust and cobwebs. An humble and modest little building, of the same material, stands on one corner of the area, and by the well worn path leading hence to the temple of Themis, it may be seen that this is the only depository of the county records. At a distance further off, a somewhat larger edifice claims a public character, which is denoted by one or two of the windows being grated. A few small forest trees have been set in the soil of this space, which, by their feeble growth and shelterless condition, as well as by the formal and graceless precision with which they have been distributed, show that the public functionaries have at times had one or two

abortive inspirations of a spirit of improvement, and a transient passion for beauty.[9]

Civic Square

In county towns the rectilinear grid of lots reserved for the public buildings ensured a little more regularity than in the countryside, but colonial magistrates rarely considered any formal relationship among the buildings other than aligning the principal structures with the street. The justices of Augusta County were unusually concerned for public appearances when they ordered the new courthouse in Staunton "to be built on the center of the lot."[10] Over time, courthouse lots in urban settings became crowded with additional structures such as churches, market houses, town halls, schools, fire-engine sheds, wells, and pumps. The incorporation of most sizable Virginia towns in the years following the Revolution quickened the pace of public building.[11] Granted the power to tax, hold courts, and regulate markets, self-governing towns felt increasing pressure and desire to build market houses, courthouses, prisons, and clerks' offices that were independent of the county judicial system. These structures often wound up on the old public lots that had been set aside when the towns were laid out in the colonial period.

Fredericksburg exemplified this pattern of expansion and readjustment of public structures. In the 1730s Spotsylvania County magistrates moved the courts to the new city on the Rappahannock River where two squares had been reserved for public use. An arcaded brick courthouse was built on the southernmost square at an irregular angle to the city grid and a stone prison stood nearby. To accommodate the need for a market and a place for polite society to be entertained, public and private money financed the construction of an arcaded brick market house on the northern square along the main street that later became Caroline Street. In a 1782 petition to the city council offering £235 to help defray the costs of repairing the Revolutionary War damage to the market house, the subscribers recognized "the great utility afforded the Country in general as well as the inhabitants of the town of Fredericksburg by the commodious situation of the Town House . . . which rendered accommodation, not only to polite, and numerous assemblies, by which youth were greatly benefited, but also to all sorts of ancient and modern societies of Fellowship" (fig. 211).[12] The Spotsylvania County courts moved out of Fredericksburg in the 1780s to a more central location to the southwest. The newly incorporated city inherited the old county buildings and refurbished the courthouse for meetings of the municipal hustings court.[13]

By the beginning of the nineteenth century, the two squares in Fredericksburg reserved for public use contained the old colonial courthouse, a new stone

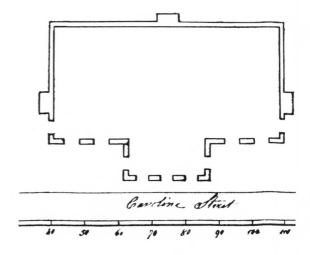

FIGURE 211. Ground-floor plan, colonial market house, Fredericksburg, 1789. (Fredericksburg City Council Minute Book, 1782–1801, The Library of Virginia)

prison that stuck out into the street several feet, a jailer's house, a clerk's office, a necessary house, stocks and pillory, a public pump near the brick market house and assembly room, hay scales, a shed for the engine, the town bell, and St. George's Episcopal Church. As early as 1776 the church sold part of the public land to raise funds, and the city followed suit several years later, selling one corner of the public land next to the market house to private investors who proceeded to erect brick stores along Caroline Street, the principal thoroughfare. The city council also set aside another corner of the courthouse lot for the construction of a "male charity school" and meeting room of the local Masonic lodge.[14] In 1814 a massive stone and brick market house and town hall rose on the western edge of the town lot along Princess Anne Street, replacing the colonial structure on Caroline Street, which was pulled down and the land sold for private development (fig. 212).[15] The pattern in Fredericksburg was repeated in towns such as Alexandria, Leesburg, Winchester, Warrenton, Lynchburg, Richmond, Petersburg, Norfolk, and Portsmouth where public buildings were renewed and rearranged on the courthouse square to fit a new image of civic architecture.[16]

The formal spatial relationships among buildings so characteristic of public squares today appeared only in the nineteenth and early twentieth centuries when changing functions and aesthetics prompted the renewal of courthouses and their ancillary structures on a larger scale and in more permanent materials. The random arrangement of colonial courthouse grounds may seem somewhat surprising considering the balanced formality between the great house and its service buildings that a number of eighteenth-century magistrates sought to achieve on their own plantations. Yet much of the built environment in the colonial period consisted of seemingly contradictory juxtapositions. In eighteenth-century towns earthfast dwellings nestled against brick mansions,

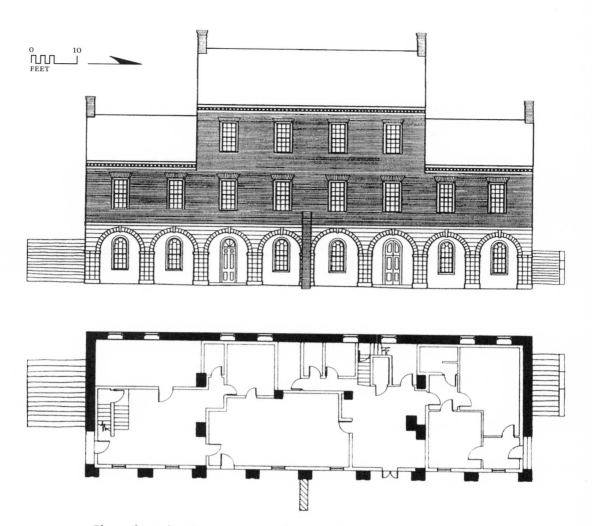

FIGURE 212. Plan and east elevation of the Fredericksburg market house and town hall, 1814–16

well-built houses supported tarred clapboard roofs, and the yards of many gentry houses were enclosed by rough-paled fences. Colonial builders easily tolerated such discrepancies, but Victorian and Colonial Revival architects, officials, and critics rarely did. Gradually the unkempt, rough-and-tumble aspect of the courthouse grounds gave way to the formal arrangement of the civic square.

A change in sensibilities made the incongruities of the earlier era intolerable. An editorial in a Richmond newspaper in 1900 spoke of past shortcomings. Virginia courthouses were "ugly and unsightly without and within, and often they are about as dirty as tobacco chewers and men with muddy boots can make them." Nothing about them or their setting was "impressive or dignified," which detracted from the "majesty and dignity of the law." The building and grounds needed to "be in keeping with the thing which it represents." Every county required a handsome courthouse in "order to make the law more impressive, and," the editorial concluded, "to make the law more impressive is to make men respect it more highly and reverence and obey it."[17] It was the duty of county officials to rid the public square of shabbiness in order to strengthen the moral fiber of the community.

The attack on the colonial legacy had begun more than half a century earlier. Antebellum critics in the Old Dominion often treated their colonial heritage with great savagery, abusing those eighteenth-century buildings that did not meet the new standards and aesthetics of the Grecian taste. Many counties replaced their old but still serviceable brick courthouses with larger two-story buildings with imposing pedimented porticoes and flanking wings. In the templed land sanctioned by Jefferson, a campaign to do away with the eighteenth-century arcaded courthouse in Fredericksburg prompted a critic in 1851 to decry its shortcomings:

> The Courthouse has been built, we should suppose one hundred years. It is a low, rough, uncouth, ill-shaped, irregular, and unsightly pile of brick and mortar of architecture established immediately after the flood—looking more like a Livery Stable or a Brewery than a place for civilized men to dispense justice. . . . It is decidedly the most uncomfortable house of the kind we have ever seen. Squat on the ground with an elevation of not one foot—it has a damp, dreary interior, better suited for the night owl or the bat than men confined, often for days successively in attending gratuitously for the public business. . . . Why a race of men should ever have been permitted to live with as mere taste as this house exhibits, is what we shall never be able to explain. Besides the outer looks . . . it is put cater-cornered to the street. Like Robin Hood's barn, you have to go all around it to get into it. It has as many corners as Solomon's temple, and yet very little larger than Diogenes' tub.[18]

Shortly after this diatribe, the Fredericksburg City Council contracted to tear down the old structure and build a new Romanesque Revival courthouse designed by architect James Renwick Jr. on its site (fig. 213).[19]

By the time of the Civil War, many courthouse towns and crossroad villages exhibited a degree of regularity where none had existed a century earlier. The systematic renewal of courthouses, jails, and clerks' offices that took place across the state in the antebellum era allowed local officials to rethink the arrangement of their public grounds. In some counties new clerks' offices built in the first and second quarters of the nineteenth century were carefully placed in relationship to the courthouse, often a few yards to one side so that they

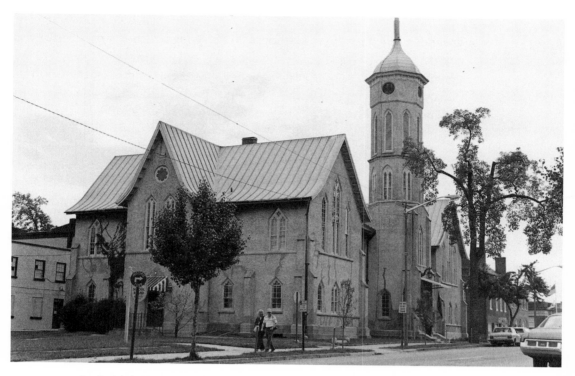

FIGURE 213. Fredericksburg courthouse, James Renwick, architect, 1851–52, altered 1870

could be matched on the other side by the construction of a treasurer's office or prison. In 1826 the magistrates of Goochland County debated the construction of two 16-by-18-foot offices on either side of the new temple-fronted court-house. To ensure a formality where none had previously existed, the buildings were to be "of similar materials and in uniformity" with the style of the court-house. As it happened, these structures were never built.[20] A similar concern for symmetry developed at Hanover where a brick clerk's office was erected at a right angle 107 feet to the northwest of the colonial courthouse with the back wall of the office in line with the front of the courthouse arcade (figs. 214, 215). Later a stone jail was erected on the south side of the grounds in the same rela-tionship to the courthouse as the clerk's office, creating a self-conscious public green where none had existed before. Because the county records were de-stroyed in the nineteenth century, their construction methods must be used to date these two buildings. The corbeled cornice and mix of 1:3 and Flemish bonding suggest that the office was built in the 1820s, and the prison has all the construction hallmarks of the 1840s. The tavern that stands across the public road nearly on center and parallel to the courthouse enhanced this formality.

In 1862 Northern visitors found a similar formality in the court structures

FIGURE 214. Hanover County courthouse grounds

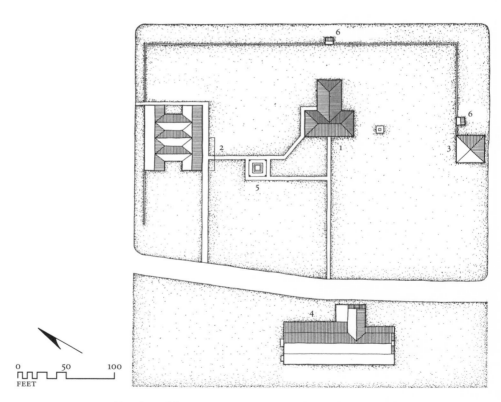

0 50 100
FEET

FIGURE 215. Site plan of the Hanover County courthouse grounds. *1:* courthouse, c. 1740; *2:* clerk's office, early nineteenth century with later additions; *3:* jail, c. 1840; *4:* tavern, 1791, 1822, and later additions; *5:* Confederate monument; *6:* privies, late nineteenth century.

in Denbigh. During the Peninsula campaign Federal troops overran the War-wick County courthouse. After a frenzied looting of the public records, a soldier from Connecticut wrote home to describe the place:

> We didn't know if Warwick was called a town or village, it took us by surprise. . . . There are two 2-story dwellings and two or three other small buildings in one side of a street & on the other side is a store . . . a brick building about the size of a smoke house which was used as a kind of County Clerk's office, the records and documents of the county were kept there, the small house is a small one story concern with no windows and a door in the side, next is the court house a brick building about the size of a carriage house up our way, the court room about the size of an office, there are two wings to the building & each have smaller rooms. . . . Next is another little smoke house with grated windows which was a jail, these buildings are all in a line, the Court house is the largest of the whole group, altogether they will perhaps cover a quarter of an acre [fig. 216].[21]

The 1810 courthouse and later clerk's office and prison all lined up to face the main street opposite private dwellings, a tavern, and stores, suggesting that the county magistrates had carefully considered the placement of their new but humble set of public buildings (fig. 217).

Arguing for greater efficiency and improved aesthetics, antebellum magistrates and late nineteenth- and twentieth-century boards of supervisors sys-

FIGURE 216. Warwick County courthouse grounds (now in Denbigh, Newport News), c. 1862. *Left to right:* dwelling (with exterior chimneys), unidentified structure, clerk's office, courthouse, and prison. From Benson J. Lossing, *Pictorial History of the Civil War* 2 (Philadelphia, 1866), 373.

tematically cleared away many small early buildings—sheds, necessary houses, stores, stables, and law offices—that stood or encroached upon the public grounds and took a more active interest in the quality and placement of new buildings. For example, in 1872 Richmond County officials ordered Durand Shackleford to remove the building adjoining the courthouse that he had been using as his personal buggy shed. In Hanover County in 1883, the board of supervisors granted R. H. Cardwell permission to erect a law office near the clerk's office if it was "neatly built so as not to be a disfigurement to the grounds."[22]

County officials also drew visual distinctions between public land and private real estate where none had existed previously. The boundaries of the courthouse precinct became marked in a formal manner with walls, gates, plantings, benches, and sidewalks that enclosed, connected, and unified the setting of the buildings. Before and after the Civil War, brick and stone walls began to replace post-and-rail fences around many court squares. Masonry walls that enclose the courthouses in Goochland, King William, and Hanover Counties, for example, date from this period. In 1835 the courthouse in Henry County was enclosed with a brick wall. Fifty years later county officials looked beyond traditional materials when they specified a cast-iron fence from the catalog of the Champion Iron Fence Company of Kenton, Ohio. The fence was to stand

FIGURE 217. Warwick County courthouse (now in Denbigh, Newport News), 1810

FIGURE 218. Gloucester County courthouse grounds, in an early twentieth-century photograph. (Loaned by Miss Caroline Sinclair, Naxera, Va., to The Library of Virginia)

3½ feet in height above a granite base and to have four gates around the square in Martinsville. Twelve years later, in another effort to create a well-regulated, parklike setting for the public buildings, the supervisors purchased several "shade trees for the courthouse yard."[23] In cities and small towns, the courthouse square took on the appearance of a well-groomed park. In order to achieve this transformation, magistrates and (after the new constitution of 1869) boards of supervisors had to set the appropriate tone for the place, which sometimes meant banning some long-standing habits and attitudes toward public property. Officials prohibited the grazing of livestock on public grounds and insisted that horses not be corralled there or tied to the fences that now ringed most public squares (fig. 218).[24] Closing down the private use of public space was also the concern of the Mathews County Board of Supervisors. In 1935 it ordered owners of chickens that had been turned loose on the courthouse grounds to remove them because they were damaging the plants and shrubs. The sheriff was ordered to destroy any fowl that ran afoul of the ordinance.[25] Such efforts preserved new plantings but removed the natural fertilizer that formerly littered the grounds.

Old pastimes associated with court day also faded or were reined in by officials wary of their disruptiveness. Perhaps most importantly, the alcoholic fumes that had once emanated from the seat of justice evaporated as new attitudes and prohibitions against public drinking severed one of the most traditional activities associated with court day. Emblematic of the change in attitude toward drinking, the magistrates of Henry County in the 1850s granted permission for the Sons of Temperance to hold their meetings in the courthouse. In the nineteenth and early twentieth centuries, temperance societies and religious denominations such as the Baptists fought hard to curb the excesses of court day and later became successful in limiting alcohol sales in many localities before national prohibition put an end to the long association of court day with drunkenness. Although fights may still have broken out on the grounds despite the decrease in alcoholic consumption, the charm of eye gouging and other rough sports had dissipated, as did the lure of the turf. In 1857 Bishop William Meade noted that the old Prince William County courthouse in Haymarket had been converted into an Episcopal church. He recalled earlier days when he preached from the magistrates' bench but could glimpse larger crowds attracted to the adjacent racetrack. He reflected, "Those times, I trust, [have] passed away forever."[26]

Public officials strove to control or curtail many other traditional activities and practices. Ordinances regulated behavior and prevented private intrusions on public space. In an effort to "stop all further deprivation and injuries to the Courthouse premises," Henry County magistrates in 1867 banned "shooting against the walls of the buildings or the trees" as well as the fence that enclosed the square in Martinsville. The courthouse grounds had traditionally served as a forum for private as well as public business. Though colonial magistrates had long tried to regulate the nature and location of court-day commerce conducted by itinerant peddlers and "country people," efforts were renewed in the nineteenth century to restrict the bazaar of temporary stands spread across the grounds. For example, in 1866 the sheriff of Charlotte County received orders "to prevent all auctioneers and tradesmen from occupying the steps leading into the courthouse square as a place for vending their goods, wares, etc. and . . . prevent all such persons from vending or selling goods within the Court House square." In 1912 the county's board of supervisors put an end to another old practice by prohibiting the "posting of all signs or advertisements in the Courthouse Grounds" (fig. 219).[27] The loss of the advertising venue may have been offset by the concurrent rise in the coverage and the readership of local newspapers.

In some counties the courthouse grounds had served as a dumping ground

FIGURE 219. Charlotte County courthouse, in a 1907 photograph. (Valentine Richmond History Center)

or potter's field for the unwanted. In 1826 Essex magistrates put an end to "the interment of the dead upon the public square" in Tappahannock.[28] If the corporal remains of paupers and criminals were not welcomed, monuments to slain heroes gained a prominent place on the squares in the closing decades of the nineteenth century. Stone and bronze statues, first to the Confederate dead and then to citizens who served in later wars, rose on the courthouse grounds and became the focus of communal commemoration. The citizens of Lancaster County erected one of the first Civil War monuments in Virginia on the grounds of a courthouse in 1872 (fig. 220). The next year a monument went up at the courthouse in Heathsville in neighboring Northumberland County. Westmoreland County added its monument in 1876. The dedications of the monuments in these three Northern Neck counties in the decade following the end of hostilities was unusually early. The great wave of commemorative Civil War statuary began in the late 1880s and reached a climax in the decade preceding the First World War. In lieu of the militia musters that had once enlivened the grounds and signaled their martial spirit, white Virginians marked the collective sacrifice of a community of fallen comrades, the heroes that had marched off to battles and perished defending native soil. Where space

FIGURE 220. (left) Confederate
monument, Lancaster, 1872

FIGURE 221. Confederate monument in front of the Amelia County courthouse, in a
1920s photograph. (Courtesy of The Library of Virginia)

FIGURE 222. Gloucester County courthouse grounds, with the debtors' prison on the far left

allowed, these monuments were placed in very prominent positions on the courthouse grounds, often centered on the courthouse itself or at the corner of two streets (fig. 221). In 1916 the Charlotte County Board of Supervisors granted the H. A. Carrington Camp of Confederate Veterans permission "to move the monument in front of the Court House to the triangle in the street" where it would be more prominent.[29]

In a rural state like Virginia, the process of transforming the courthouse grounds into a civic square took more than a century in some places. On the eve of the Second World War, some local governments could still fit comfortably within buildings erected in the colonial era in rural backwaters such as Gloucester and King William Counties. Yet even in these places paved sidewalks and brick perimeter walls created a more formal ensemble. In 1933 the Gloucester County Board of Supervisors replaced the wooden fence around the public buildings with a brick wall inspired by the reconstructed one erected at the Capitol in Williamsburg by the restoration architects of the Colonial Williamsburg Foundation (figs. 222, 223). Public officials added new buildings in the Colonial Revival style, self-consciously appropriating the architectural language of an earlier era even as the legacies of colonial institutions were being

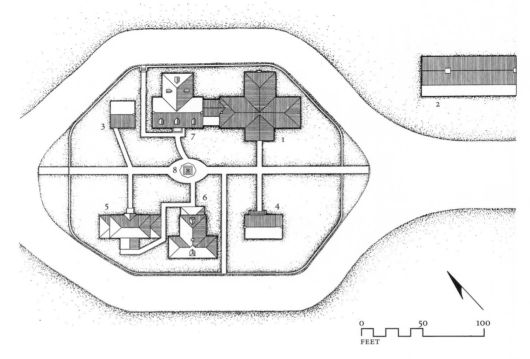

FIGURE 223. Site plan of the Gloucester County courthouse grounds. *1:* courthouse, 1766; *2:* Botetourt Hotel, early 1770s; *3:* debtors' prison, c. 1820; *4:* clerk's office, 1823; *5:* jail, 1873; *6:* clerk's office, 1896; *7:* clerk's office, 1956; *8:* Confederate monument, 1889.

FIGURE 224. United States Post Office and Courthouse, 1932, Alexandria. Photograph by John O. Peters. (Courtesy of The Virginia Bar Association)

FIGURE 225. Halifax County courthouse, 1838, in a 1920s photograph. (Courtesy of The Library of Virginia)

eclipsed. Massive federal courthouse complexes in cities such as Norfolk, Alexandria, and Danville heralded a shift in the scale and locus of judicial authority (fig. 224). In the 1930s rural electrification, radios, newspapers, paved roads, and automobiles opened the world beyond the county courthouse, diminishing the significance of the county seat and court day as sources of information and entertainment (fig. 225). After nearly three centuries court day as a political and social event disappeared from the cultural landscape, and Virginia lost one of the most important ties that had bound its communities together.

APPENDIX:
A CHECKLIST OF PUBLIC BUILDINGS
IN EARLY VIRGINIA

THIS LIST PROVIDES a summary of public building activity in most of the Virginia counties that were formed in the seventeenth and eighteenth centuries. Because of the loss of early court records in many locations, information from some counties is meager. This list includes all documented courthouses proposed for construction or actually built during this time as well as the handful of clerk's offices constructed in the eighteenth century and the first fifteen years of the nineteenth century. A full listing of the scores of prisons erected during the colonial and early national periods has been omitted for the sake of brevity, though a few early ones that do survive have been included. For the history of later nineteenth- and twentieth-century courthouses, see the series of articles on public buildings in various counties published in the *Virginia Cavalcade* in the 1960s and 1970s as well as Mary Kegley Bucklen and Larrie L. Bucklen, *County Courthouses of Virginia, Old and New* (1988) and John O. and Margaret T. Peters, *Virginia's Historic Courthouses* (1995).

Accomack County (1663)

1677: In the 1660s and early 1670s, county magistrates held court in various taverns including John Cole's ordinary. In 1677 Cole offered to build a courthouse on his land. If built, it was used for only a short period as the court met in Onancock and then Matomkin (Accomac) in the last two decades of the seventeenth century.

1705: Justices ordered a new wooden courthouse with brick underpinnings to be built. Specifications revised the following year called for a 40-by-20-foot structure with 10-foot-pitch walls. At one end was to be a room with a brick chimney and a chamber overhead. The courtroom was to have two bars with balusters and seats and a table for the magistrates.

1710: Courthouse finished by builder Delight Shield.

1754: The court ordered the construction of a brick courthouse.

1758: Local builder Severn Guthrey completed a rectangular brick courthouse measuring 25 by 45 feet with entrances into the courtroom from the center of each of the long sides.

1783: Selby Simpson built a one-story brick jailer's house. County officials converted this 33-by-22-foot structure into a debtors' prison in 1824. Much altered, the building survives on the courthouse grounds in Accomac.

1794: In response to a new state law requiring fireproof offices, the justices ordered the construction of a brick clerk's office on the courthouse grounds.

1798: Justice Thomas Custis completed a brick clerk's office.

1899: The B. F. Smith Fireproof Construction Company of Washington, D.C., erected the present courthouse.

Albemarle County (1744)

1745: Samuel Scott undertook the construction of the county's first courthouse. The building was patterned after the one in the parent county of Goochland.

1762: William Cabell signed a contract to build a new courthouse "the exact size and model" of the one in Henrico County. The next year he sublet the construction of the courthouse to John Moore, John Fry, and John Lewis.

1803: A new two-story rectangular brick courthouse was built. Though much altered, this building exists as the rear wing of the present county courthouse.

Amelia County (1734)

1735: Court officials ordered the construction of a courthouse on the lands of Colonel Benjamin Harrison.

1766: Justices made plans to erect a framed courthouse. Specifications called for it to be 40 by 20 feet with a 12-foot pitch. It was to have a heated jury room at one end.

1767: Christopher Ford undertook the construction of the new courthouse with some alterations to the plan. The building was 10 feet longer, 4 feet wider, and a foot taller than the previous agreement specified. It was to have two jury rooms at one end, a curved justices' bench, and two benches for the lawyers' bar.

1791: Justices ordered the construction of a T-shaped building with jury rooms flanking the central courtroom. The building was erected at Pincham's Cool Springs and served the county for the next half century.

1850: A new brick courthouse was built with a pedimented portico. This building survived until it was replaced in 1924 by the present structure.

Amherst County (1761)

1761: Justices decided to erect the first county courthouse on the land of Lunsford Lomax.

1808: A new courthouse was built after Nelson County was split off from Amherst.

1872: The firm of Kirkpatrick and Smith erected a two-story brick courthouse that is still in use. Additions to the building were made in the early 1930s and 1962.

Augusta County (1738)

1745: After county government was established in 1745, the court met in a log house.

1748: A log courthouse measuring 38 by 18 feet was built on land that would become the town of Staunton.

1753: Justices ordered the construction of a new log courthouse. The building was finished in 1755.

1788: Anthony Mustoe contracted to build a two-story stone courthouse.

1835: A new courthouse with a two-story central block and one-story wings was constructed. The courtroom was situated on the second floor.

1901: T. J. Collins designed the present courthouse, which was completed in 1901. In 1939 an addition was made to the rear of the building.

Bath County (1790)

1796: Anthony Mustoe built a stone courthouse and a clerk's office.

1843: A two-story brick courthouse with one-story wings replaced the earlier courthouse. The building and the two-story jail survive and have been converted into an inn.

1908: A new courthouse designed by Frank Milburn was erected some distance from the earlier courthouse in Warm Springs. This building burned in 1912 and was replaced in 1915 by the present building designed by Samuel Collins.

Bedford County (1753)

1754: William Callaway and others erected the first courthouse in New London.

1766: Justices ordered the construction of a new wooden courthouse 36 by 24 feet with a 12-foot pitch. The building was to have two 12-foot-square jury rooms with chimneys.

1768: Alterations to the courthouse "now building" added 14 feet to the west end. John Murphy finished the building in 1771.

1782: Magistrates ordered the construction of a new courthouse after the county was divided. In 1789 a brick courthouse and other public buildings were completed.

1833: A new brick courthouse was built with a central pedimented portico. The courtroom stood in the center of the upper floor above the raised basement. This building was replaced in turn by the present structure, which was erected in 1930.

Berkeley County (1772) (now West Virginia)

1773: The magistrates ordered the construction of a two-story arcaded court-house. Before construction began on this T-shaped structure, the design of the magistrates' end of the courtroom was altered to be apsidal. William Brown undertook the construction of the building, which was finished in 1778 by James McCalister.

Botetourt County (1769)

1770: A 24-by-20-foot log cabin was built for the first courthouse. It had two small sheds, one at each end for jury rooms. James McGavock, a justice and tavern keeper, completed the building in 1773. In the late 1790s the county erected a clerk's office (fig. A1).

1818: Justices requested a design for a new courthouse from Thomas Jefferson. There is no evidence of Jefferson's design or whether the magistrates followed his recommendations. The building erected apparently had a two-story central block with a dome and two flanking one-story wings.

1848: A new two-story courthouse with a pedimented portico and flanking two-story wings was constructed. This building was altered in the early twentieth century, burned in 1970, and later was restored to its mid-nineteenth-century appearance.

Brunswick County (1720)

1732: After a boundary dispute with North Carolina was settled in 1728 and the county government was organized in 1732, the magistrates built a court-house.

1746: With the division of the county, a new courthouse was ordered to be built of the same dimensions as the one erected in Prince George County in 1726, but it was to be of wood rather than brick. Sterling Clack gave the land and undertook the construction of the courthouse.

1783: A new courthouse was to be built on Jones Williams's land. Williams agreed to construct a 44-by-24-foot wooden building with a 14-foot pitch and brick chimney.

1854: Robert Kirkland and E. R. Turnbull erected the present two-story brick courthouse. The building has a Greek Doric pedimented portico. An addition was made to the building in 1939.

Buckingham County (1761)

1761: The first county courthouse was to be established on land of Samuel Glover, considered to be the "most centrical and commodious."

1777: Magistrates ordered the construction of a T-shaped brick courthouse.

1821: At the request of the building commissioners, Thomas Jefferson submit-

FIGURE A1. Botetourt County clerk's office, Fincastle, 1790s with later addition.
(Botetourt County Historical Museum)

ted a plan for a two-story porticoed courthouse. The building was destroyed
by fire in 1869. An archaeological examination of the building site in 2003
suggests the building had some fidelity to the Jefferson design.

1869: The county erected the present two-story courthouse with Doric pedimented portico near the site of the previous one.

Campbell County (1781)

1785: Patrick Gibson built a courthouse on the land of Jeremiah Rust in what
would become the county seat of Rustburg.

1848: John Wills built the present two-story brick courthouse. Like many mid-
nineteenth-century buildings, the courtroom occupies the center of the
second floor with a flight of exterior steps leading to a central raised, pedimented portico.

Caroline County (1727)

1732: The first courthouse, of unknown size and materials, was built by this year.
In 1740 artist Charles Bridges was paid for painting the king's arms for the
courtroom. In 1742 the building was damaged by fire.

1760: Justices ordered the construction of a new courthouse of the same dimensions as the T-shaped brick one in King and Queen County. John Wily finished the building by 1766.

1794: The magistrates ordered the county seat to be moved to Bowling Green.

1808: John Hoomes completed the courthouse in Bowling Green.

1835: The present two-story arcaded brick courthouse was built about this time. An addition and extensive alterations were made to the building in 1970.

Charles City County (1634)

1659: During its earliest years the county stretched across both sides of the James River, and the court was peripatetic, rotating venues. In 1659 the magistrates ordered Edward Hill and John Stith to finish the courthouse at Westover.

1665: A new earthfast courthouse was built at Westover.

1687: William Bernard and John Baxter undertook the construction of a framed courthouse measuring 35 by 20 feet.

1757: In the late 1740s justices levied money for the construction of a new courthouse. Richard Bland completed the present T-shaped, arcaded brick courthouse in 1757. Damaged slightly during the Civil War, the courthouse was repaired and reoriented as the arcade was enclosed and the entrance moved

FIGURE A2. Charles City County courthouse and clerk's office, in a June 13, 1864, photograph. From Alexander Gardner, *Gardner's Photographic Sketch Book of the War* 2 (Washington, D.C., 1865–66), 168. (Courtesy of The Library of Virginia)

to the lower end of the building in the last quarter of the nineteenth century (figs. A2, A3, A4).

1901: In the late nineteenth century, the old clerk's office next to the courthouse was torn down, and the present fireproof office erected by the B. F. Smith Company took its place.

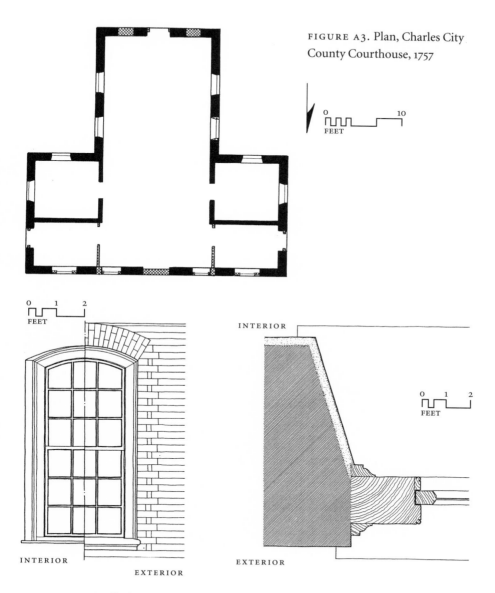

FIGURE A3. Plan, Charles City County Courthouse, 1757

FIGURE A4. Detail of north window and jamb of the east jury room, Charles City County courthouse. This window frame and sash are rare survivors from the mid-1750s.

Charlotte County (1764)

1765: Clement Read contracted to build a 30-by-22-foot courthouse on the magazine land. After Read's death, his son finished the project. In 1784 some "evil disposed person" set fire to the building.

1785: Pines Ingram agreed to construct a new wooden courthouse. It was T-shaped, 32 by 24 feet, with jury room on each side measuring 12 by 14 feet. Work on the courthouse was finished around 1790. In 1798 the magistrates ordered the construction of a piazza in front of the courthouse.

1823: John Percival constructed the present two-story brick courthouse with a pedimented portico after designs provided by Thomas Jefferson. The magistrates' end of the courthouse was originally faceted as shown in Jefferson's plan.

Chesterfield County (1749)

1749: John Booker undertook the construction of the county's first courthouse, designed to be the same dimensions and materials as the one in Henrico County. The brick building was rectangular with segmental arched openings and glazed header brickwork.

1781: The courthouse was burned by the British and later repaired.

1805: A wing was added at right angles to the courthouse creating a T-shaped configuration. The courtroom was reoriented. The courthouse was demolished in 1917 after efforts to preserve it failed.

1918: Architect J. T. Skinner of Petersburg designed a new T-shaped brick courthouse with a Roman Doric portico and an octagonal cupola.

Culpeper County (1749)

1749: The county justices recommended Robert Coleman's land as the most convenient on which to erect a courthouse.

1763: A porch was to be added to the courthouse.

1800: The magistrates ordered the construction of a brick clerk's office measuring 44 by 21 feet. The building was completed in 1802.

1807: After the old courthouse became too ruinous to meet in, the judges decided to build a brick one that would be two stories and the same dimensions of the previous one. This building was completed by 1809, and an arcaded tower was added sometime later (fig. A5).

1874: The present courthouse was erected under the supervision of Samuel Proctor.

Cumberland County (1749)

1749: A brick clerk's office measuring 16 by 12 feet was erected on the courthouse grounds.

FIGURE A5. Culpeper County courthouse, 1809, tower later, in an 1860s photograph.
(Library of Congress)

1752: Benjamin Mosby finished the county courthouse. He was paid for additional repairs to the building through the 1760s.

1778: Justice Maurice Langhorne agreed to build a new courthouse of the same dimensions and materials as the old one.

1818: William A. Howard undertook the construction of the present courthouse, a one-story T-shaped brick building with a pedimented portico in the Tuscan order.

Dinwiddie County (1752)

1753: The county courthouse was to be built on Anthony Haynes's land.

1773: An arsonist destroyed the courthouse.

1851: The present brick courthouse was built. The building was remodeled in the late 1850s, and the Doric portico was added in 1939.

Elizabeth City County (1634) (now part of the city of Hampton)

1715: The loss of the early records of the county has obliterated the history of its early courthouses. In 1715 Samuel Sweny built a courthouse in Hampton.

1876: The core of the present courthouse was built. In 1910 it was remodeled and

FIGURE A6. Essex County courthouse, Tappahannock, 1729

given a pedimented portico. The building was reworked in 1939, and wings were added in 1962 and 1975.

Essex County (1692)

1693: The magistrates specified the construction of a framed courthouse. The building was to be 25 by 20 feet with a raised platform for the magistrates. In 1695 Daniel Diskins was paid for building the courthouse.

1702: Larkin Chew agreed to build a framed courthouse 45 by 22 feet with a 10-foot pitch. The building was to be finished according to "the exact dimensions and proportions of King and Queen Court House in every particular both within and without." In 1712 Francis Meriwether made repairs and alterations to the building.

1726: Arguments arose between residents in the upper and lower ends of the county over the location of the court. James Broughan agreed to erect a temporary 24-by-20-foot clapboarded courthouse at Ward's Old Field. In 1727 animosities among members of the bench continue to linger after the "late courthouse was burnt." Specifications for a 30-by-20-foot clapboard courthouse were made, but the building may have not been executed.

1728: John Moore agreed to build a 40-by-20-foot brick courthouse in Tappahannock and have it finished by the following year. Three exterior walls of this glazed-header structure survive despite a fire in 1814 and numerous alterations and additions. In the middle of the nineteenth century, it was converted into a warehouse after a new courthouse was built. In 1875 the building was transformed into a church (figs. A6, A7, A8).

1847: Construction began on the present two-story brick courthouse. This building was remodeled in 1926, burned in 1965, and repaired in 1967.

Fairfax County (1742)

1742: Justices ordered the construction of the first courthouse at Spring Fields.

1752: The county court moved to Alexandria.

1790: The upper part of the market house in Alexandria was fitted as a courtroom after controversy arose over the location of the county court.

1799: A two-story arcaded brick courthouse was undertaken at Fairfax and finished the following year. Several additions were made to the building in

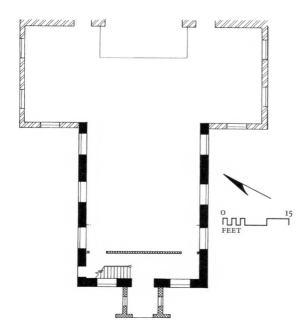

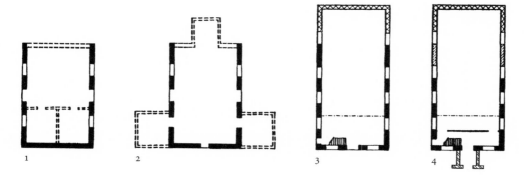

1 2 3 4

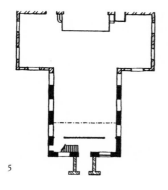

5

FIGURE A8. Sequential plans, Essex County court-house, Tappahannock. *1:* 1729, configuration of jury rooms uncertain; *2:* c. 1815, rebuilt after fire with side jury rooms and rear room, perhaps for magistrates; converted to a warehouse c. 1850 and to a church in 1875; *3:* c. 1880, building extended 20 feet to the northeast, door inserted in northwest corner, windows added in southwest facade, and original side doors converted into windows; *4:* post-1894, tower added; *5:* 1926, church enlarged with wings and Sunday school building to the northeast.

APPENDIX: PUBLIC BUILDINGS IN EARLY VIRGINIA   347

FIGURE A9. Fairfax County courthouse, 1799–1800

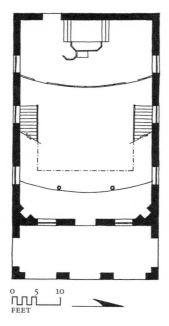

0   5   10
FEET

FIGURE A10. Plan, Fairfax County courthouse

1929 and the 1950s. In 1982 a massive new building reflecting the growth of the suburbs of Washington, D.C., was built in the vicinity (figs. A9, A10).

Fauquier County (1759)

1760: Justices ordered the construction of a temporary wooden courthouse measuring 24 by 16 feet on lands belonging to Richard Henry Lee. They later agree with John Bell to construct a 36-by-20-foot brick courthouse with an 18-foot pitch modeled after the 1740 Lancaster courthouse.

1770: Construction began on a 24-by-16-foot building adjacent to the courthouse that was to house a justices' meeting room below and a jury room above.

1790: Justices order the erection of a brick courthouse measuring 52 by 30 feet with two rooms at one end of the building and two jury rooms abovestairs. The building was finished in 1795.

1808: A two-story brick prison was completed. In 1822 the county completed a stone addition behind the older building. Both buildings survive in Warrenton.

1818: David Kline built a new courthouse that was destroyed by fire in 1853.

1854: A porticoed courthouse replaced the burned building. This structure was also consumed by fire in 1879, and the present building, which resembles the 1854 structure, was erected on the site in 1890.

Fluvanna County (1777)

1778: John Beckley agreed to build a 24-by-18-foot framed courthouse with an inside chimney.

1802: Magistrates devised a plan for a 24-by-36-foot framed courthouse (figs. A11, A12).

1832: John Hartwell Cocke undertook the construction of the present two-story temple-fronted courthouse in Palmyra (fig. A13). An inscription on the stone lintel above the front door reads: "The maxim held sacred by every free people / Obey the laws."

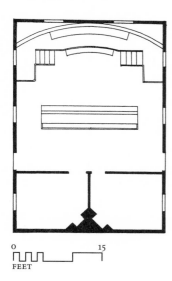

0   15
FEET

FIGURE A11. Plan, old Fluvanna County courthouse, 1802, redrawn from the original. (Loose Papers, Mar. 24, 1802, box 36A, Fluvanna County Historical Society, County Jail, Palmyra)

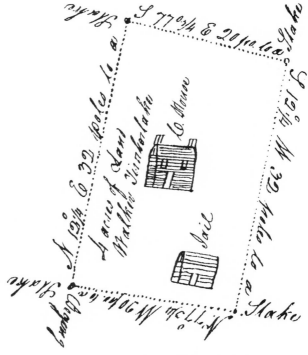

FIGURE A12. Plat of the old Fluvanna County courthouse bounds, 1828. Loose Papers, Fluvanna County Historical Society, County Jail, Palmyra)

FIGURE A13. Fluvanna County courthouse, Palmyra, 1832

Franklin County (1785)

1786: The first sessions of the court met in a building erected in Rocky Mount.

1831: A new courthouse was erected with a pedimented two-story central block flanked by single-story wings. The building was replaced by a much larger structure in 1910.

Frederick County (1738)

1745: After county government was established in 1743, the magistrates proceed to erect a framed courthouse in Winchester. John Hardin finished the fittings and interior woodwork by 1751.

1785: County magistrates ordered the construction of a two-story courthouse measuring 50 by 40 feet.

1840: Baltimore architect Robert Cary Long Jr. designed a two-story brick courthouse with a pedimented front portico and cupola. In 1984 a large judicial center was constructed nearby.

Gloucester County (1651)

1685: A brick courthouse had been "lately" built (fig. A14).

1766: The present one-story T-shaped brick building was erected (figs. A15, A16). The pedimented front porch was added in 1907 along with a number of windows on the side of the building. In 1956 the county built an addition to one side of the colonial building. Outgrowing this addition thirty years later, the courts moved to a judicial complex north of the court green.

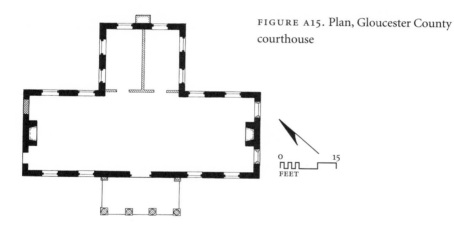

FIGURE A14. Plat of the prison bounds, Gloucester, 1754. (Surveyor's Book, 1733–1810, Clerk's Office, Gloucester County)

FIGURE A15. Plan, Gloucester County courthouse

FIGURE A16. Gloucester County courthouse, 1766; portico, 1907

APPENDIX: PUBLIC BUILDINGS IN EARLY VIRGINIA   351

c. 1820: A small one-room brick debtors' prison was erected on the courthouse grounds. This building survives and preserves its interior sheathing.

Goochland County (1727)

1730: James Skelton, who was later to build the second Capitol in Williamsburg in the early 1750s, agreed to build a courthouse for the county. It was completed by 1737.

1755: John Payne agreed to build a 45-by-20-foot courthouse with partitions at one end for jury rooms.

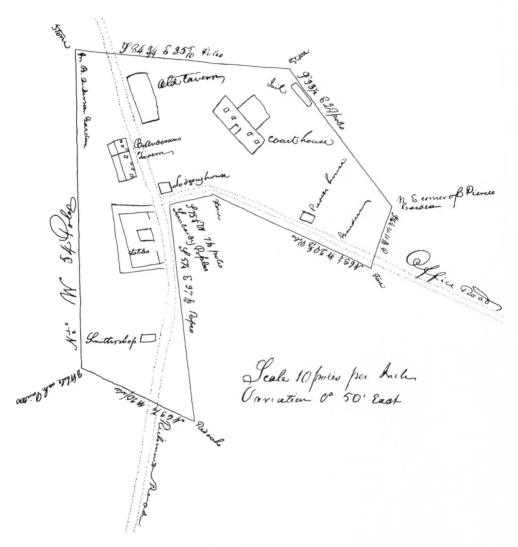

FIGURE A17. Plat of the Goochland County prison bounds, 1822. (Deed Book, 1821–24, Clerk's Office, Goochland County)

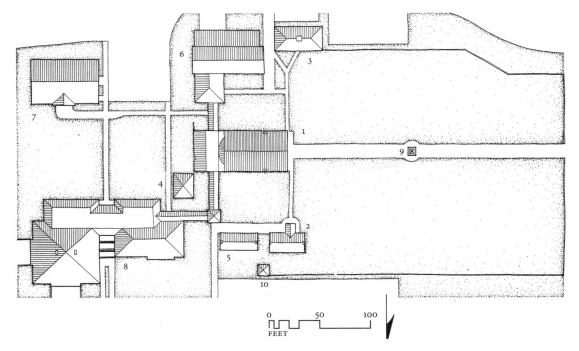

FIGURE A18. Site plan of the Goochland County courthouse grounds. *1:* courthouse, 1826; *2:* clerk's office, 1847; *3:* jail, rebuilt 1857; *4:* former law office, 1839; *5:* county agent, 1906; *6:* administration building, 1967; *7:* health department; *8:* county offices, 1979; *9:* Confederate monument, *10:* storehouse.

1763: The county court moved to the land of Alexander Baine on Beaverdam Creek. The courthouse built in this new location had been altered into a T-shaped structure by 1822 (fig. A17).

1826: Dabney Cosby and Valentine Parrish undertook the construction of the present two-story brick courthouse with pedimented front portico. In the twentieth century the county expanded the judicial and administrative functions into several buildings adjoining the rear of the courthouse (fig. A18).

Halifax County (1752)

1752: Clerk of Court George Currie agreed to erect a courthouse the same size as the one in Lunenburg County.

1774: After the division of the county and continuing disagreements over where to locate the county seat, the court ordered the construction of a 44-by-20-foot framed courthouse. This may not have been erected until a few years later in 1777 when the county finally settled on John Bouram's land south of the Banister River.

1802: The magistrates ordered the construction of a wooden courthouse measuring 52 by 28 feet. Thomas Stone and David Hunt completed the building the following year.

1838: Dabney Cosby, the builder of earlier courthouses in Goochland County and Sussex County, erected the present two-story brick courthouse. The T-shaped building features an Ionic pedimented portico across the central three bays. In subsequent years numerous alterations and additions were made to the building.

Hanover County (1720)

1735: The county justices ordered the construction of a brick courthouse despite protests from inhabitants in the upper part of the county who thought that the old one was still usable. In 1737 the council ruled against those who challenged the construction of a new building. The erection of the present T-shaped arcaded courthouse began around this time (fig. A19). Numerous alterations were made to the building through the nineteenth century, culminating in the addition of a bay at the rear of the building (fig A20). In 1954–55 the building was restored and refurbished in a manner that destroyed much of the early fabric and later alterations.

1976: The county erected two new court buildings behind the colonial structure.

Henrico County (1634)

1634–1680s: During the early years of its existence, the county court followed a peripatetic course, meeting in numerous dwellings and taverns including the home of William Byrd I.

1688: Sometime in the early 1680s, the county constructed an earthfast courthouse at Varina. The posts of this building required substantial repairs in 1688 to keep it from collapsing.

1690: A tavern keeper rented the upper floor of the courthouse as lodgings.

1750: The magistrates moved the court venue to the new city of Richmond and in the following year ordered the construction of a courthouse. In 1782 chimneys were to be built to the jury rooms of the courthouse.

1814: Architect Robert Mills designed a new courthouse for the county. After much discussion over four or five years, the decision to build was rescinded.

1825: William Street and William Allen built a courthouse designed by Samuel Sublett. The building was moved a few yards in 1840, damaged during the Civil War, and repaired. After a fire in 1894, the building was pulled down and replaced by a Romanesque structure in 1896. In 1974 this building was in turn replaced by a sprawling new structure.

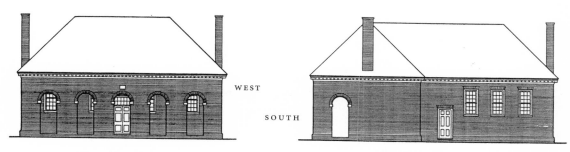

WEST

SOUTH

FIGURE A19. Elevations, Hanover County courthouse, c. 1740 with later additions

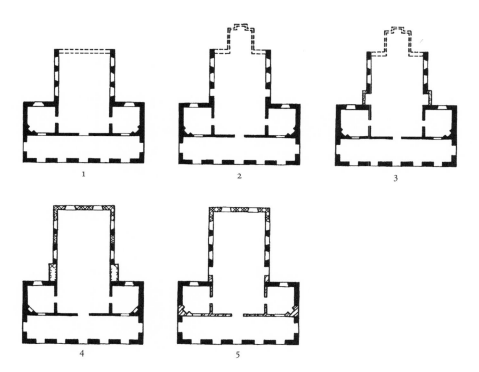

1

2

3

4

5

FIGURE A20. Sequential plans, Hanover County courthouse. *1:* c. 1740, fenestration of back wall uncertain; *2:* 1825–50, justices' bench or chamber at the northeast end, doors inserted in sides of courtroom; *3:* c. 1850, chimneys added to sides of courtroom; *4:* 1875–1900, courtroom extended one bay to the northeast, two courtroom windows and fireplaces blocked; *5:* 1954, internal partition walls and front wall of courthouse rebuilt, last bay of courtroom and rear wall refaced, chimneys removed, and doors re-created in the side walls.

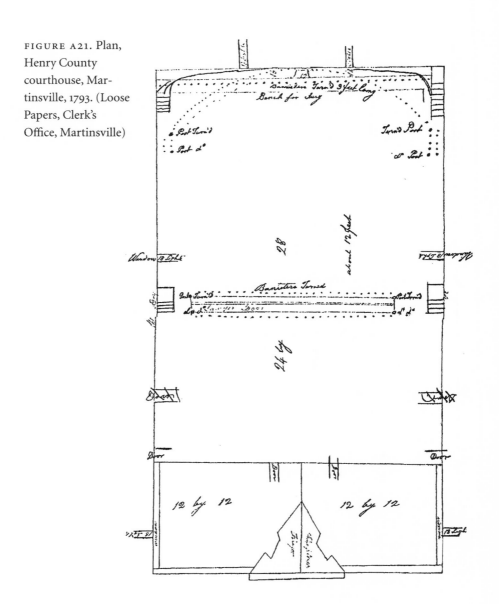

FIGURE A21. Plan, Henry County courthouse, Martinsville, 1793. (Loose Papers, Clerk's Office, Martinsville)

Henry County (1776)

1778: The court ordered the construction of a log courthouse measuring 24 by 20 feet at Fort Trail. This structure probably was not built immediately for the magistrates repeated their order for a log building of the same dimensions in 1780.

1793: Richard Stockton agreed to build a courthouse in Martinsville modeled after the one built in Franklin County in 1786 (fig. A21). With some modifications to the original plan, the courthouse was completed two years later.

1823: George Tucker designed the present two-story brick courthouse, which was built the following year by Samuel Taliaferro. Additions to the building were made in 1929 and 1940 to accommodate the growing needs of the legal system.

Isle of Wight County (1634)

1655: County courts met in alternating locations in two different parishes. The venues for these gatherings varied between taverns and private dwellings. By the 1690s a building specifically set aside for court business was standing.

1750: After the creation of Southampton County, justices decided to build a courthouse in Smithfield. They hired William Rand to construct the surviving T-shaped arcaded building with an apsidal end. The courthouse was completed the following year and used by the county for the next half century (fig. A22). After the county seat moved in 1800, the old courthouse in Smithfield was converted into a private residence in the early nineteenth century. Lawrence Kocher supervised the restoration of its courthouse form for the Association for the Preservation of Virginia Antiquities (APVA) in 1960. In 2001 most of the early courtroom fittings were reconstructed. Nearby

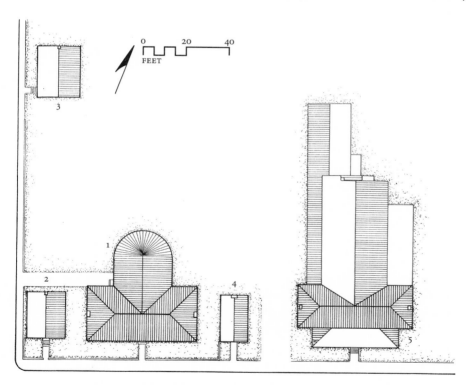

FIGURE A22. Site plan of the old Isle of Wight County courthouse grounds, Smithfield. *1:* courthouse, 1750–51; *2:* clerk's office, 1799; *3:* jail, c. 1799; *4:* store, late eighteenth century; *5:* tavern, 1750s with later additions.

stand a tavern built just after the courthouse, a brick store, a two-story prison from the late eighteenth century, and a one-story clerk's office erected in 1799.

1800: The county government moved eight miles south of Smithfield to its present location at Isle of Wight where a courthouse was built. Much altered and expanded in the nineteenth and twentieth centuries, this structure still houses the local court.

James City County (1634)

1652: Although the county encompassed the south side of the river until this time, it is likely that the court sat in Jamestown in these early years. The court probably met in taverns and dwellings rather than a purpose-built structure. When a statehouse was built in Jamestown in the late 1660s, the General Court gave permission for the county to use its courtroom for meetings of the local magistrates.

1676: Rebel soldiers burned the statehouse during Bacon's Rebellion, and for the next fifteen years the county court convened in a separate unknown structure in Jamestown.

1691: The county court met once again in the statehouse until it was destroyed again by fire in 1698.

1715: The James City County court remained at Jamestown until 1715 when Governor Alexander Spotswood granted permission for it to move to the new capital of Williamsburg. By 1721 the county had erected a courthouse on the southwest corner of England and Francis Streets.

1770: The city of Williamsburg and James City County joined together to erect the surviving T-shaped brick courthouse on Market Square. The building was completed in late 1770 or early 1771 and served as the venue for city and county government for the next century and a half. In 1911 the building was severely damaged by a fire. In 1932 the exterior of the building was restored to its colonial appearance and converted into an archaeological museum by the Colonial Williamsburg Foundation. In 1991 the museum restored the eighteenth-century courtroom fittings.

1932: A new courthouse was built on the site of the early eighteenth-century courthouse on the corner of England and Francis Streets. It was replaced by a modern facility behind the Eastern State Hospital in 1969. Thirty years later in 1999 the present courthouse was built on the edge of Williamsburg. Both the 1932 and 1969 courthouses were demolished.

King and Queen County (1691)

1702: A rectangular wooden courthouse existed by this time, for the magistrates in Essex County ordered the construction of their new building after the form of the one in King and Queen.

FIGURE A23. King and Queen County courthouse

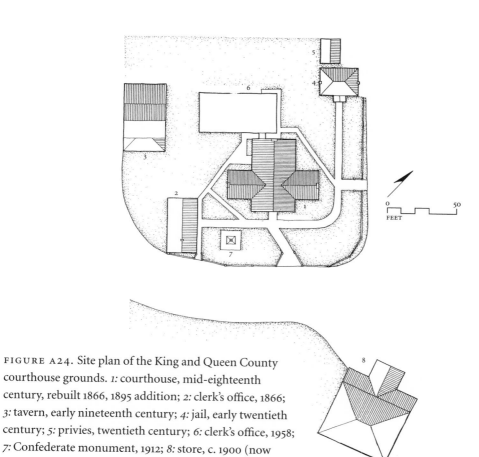

FIGURE A24. Site plan of the King and Queen County
courthouse grounds. *1:* courthouse, mid-eighteenth
century, rebuilt 1866, 1895 addition; *2:* clerk's office, 1866;
3: tavern, early nineteenth century; *4:* jail, early twentieth
century; *5:* privies, twentieth century; *6:* clerk's office, 1958;
7: Confederate monument, 1912; *8:* store, c. 1900 (now
destroyed).

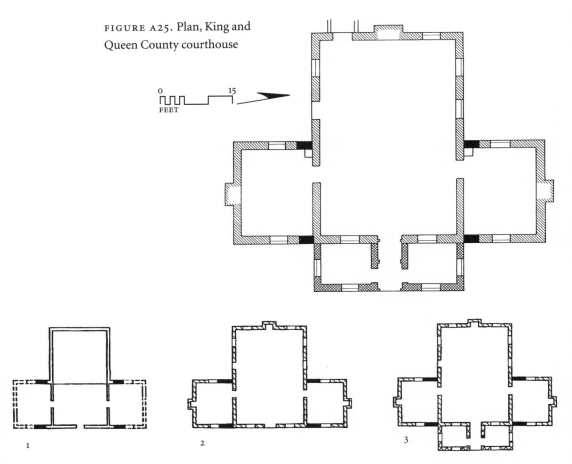

FIGURE A25. Plan, King and Queen County courthouse

0 ... 15 FEET

FIGURE A26. Sequential plans, King and Queen County courthouse. *1:* Mid-eighteenth century, fenestration of courtroom unknown; *2:* 1866, rebuilt after destruction by Federal troops during the Civil War; *3:* 1895, offices added to front.

1760: A T-shaped brick courthouse had been built by this time, for in 1760 the magistrates of Caroline County wanted their building patterned after the one in King and Queen. Fragments of this midcentury courthouse survive and are incorporated into the present structure that was erected in 1866 after Federal troops, known in the county records as the "public enemy," burned the colonial building in 1864 (figs. A23, A24, A25, A26). The building was altered again in the early 1890s with additions to the front.

King George County (1720)

1725: Hugh Roberts completed a framed courthouse.

1792: Justice Peter Jett undertook the construction of a new courthouse, which was completed two years later.

1809: Magistrates advertised the construction of a fireproof brick clerk's office measuring 30 by 20 feet.

1923: The present one-story brick courthouse with a central pedimented portico was completed. In 1974 additions were made to the courthouse.

King William County (1701)

1722: With the old courthouse in ruinous condition, the magistrates sought permission of the provincial government to construct a new building. A year later the court was still in its old location on land that had been donated by Henry Fox and Richard Littlepage. Probably within the next decade, the present T-shaped, arcaded brick courthouse was constructed (figs. A27, A28).

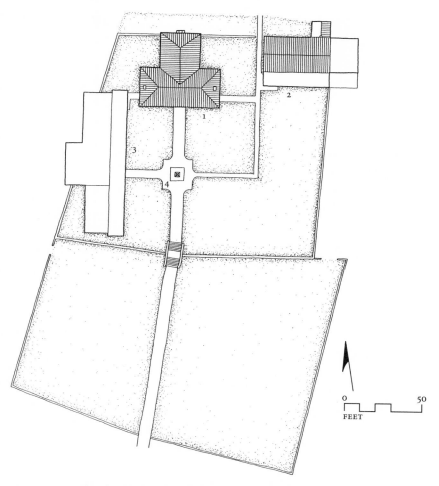

FIGURE A27. Site plan of the King William County courthouse grounds. *1:* courthouse, second quarter of the eighteenth century; *2:* jail, offices, 1890, c. 1940; *3:* clerk's office, rebuilt 1897, 1928; *4:* Confederate monument, 1904.

FIGURE A28. King William County courthouse

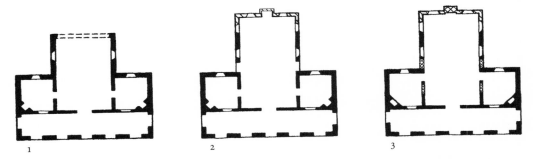

FIGURE A29. Sequential plans, King William County courthouse. *1*: original c. 1730 plan, fenestration of rear courtroom wall unknown; *2*: early nineteenth century, courtroom extended a bay to the north including a fireplace, doors to the east and west walls of the courtroom inserted; *3*: c. 1925, second-period doors blocked, jury room doors shifted, fireplaces closed, courtroom windows widened and lengthened.

In 1777 it was described as a "neat brick building" surrounded by outbuildings including two prisons. In the early nineteenth century, a one-bay addition was made at the back of the building to provide more space for courtroom fittings, probably to incorporate an expanded lawyers' bar (figs. A29, A30, A31). In 1979 a new building was constructed behind the colonial building to house additional courtrooms and administrative offices. Four years later the colonial courthouse was thoroughly renovated.

1788: A fire in the clerk's office destroyed the early court records.

1885: The clerk's office and county records perished in a fire.

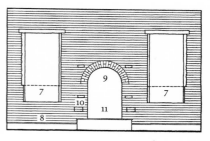

FIGURE A30. West and north courtroom wall elevations stripped of plaster, King William County courthouse, 1983. *1:* putlog holes used during original construction; *2:* pocket for unknown purpose corresponding to one found in the east wall in the same position; *3:* location of original jury room doorway; *4:* early nineteenth-century doorway, blocked c. 1925; *5:* nailing blocks for early nineteenth-century newel posts for platform; *6:* early nineteenth-century joist pockets for magistrates' platform; *7:* original height of window sills, lowered c. 1925; *8:* c. 1925 judge's platform, removed 1983; *9:* relieving arch, c. 1925; *10:* nailers for early nineteenth-century mantel; *11:* early nineteenth-century fireplace, blocked, c. 1925.

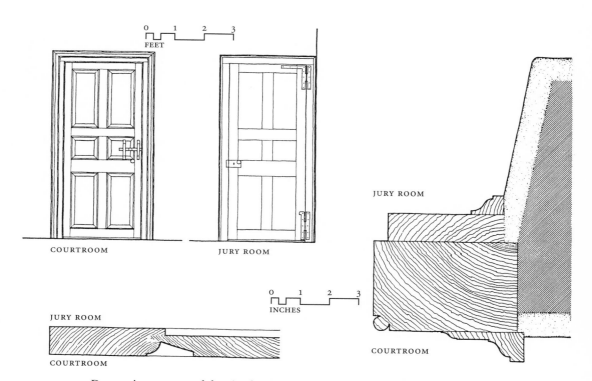

FIGURE A31. Door to jury room and doorjamb, King William County courthouse, c. 1730. Though these original jury room doors and jambs had been moved in the nineteenth century, they survived until 1983.

Lancaster County (1651)

1655: The county magistrates ordered the construction of two courthouses. John Carter agreed to build one at Corotoman, and William Neasham signed the contract to build a second courthouse for the upper part of the county. Both buildings may not have been constructed, for in 1657 the courts met at the home of Dominic Theriott. Over the next few decades the Theriott family continued to host the monthly court meetings.

1698: Robert Carter undertook the construction of a brick courthouse at the newly platted port of Queenstown. Completed in 1701, the building measured 33 by 23 feet and had a 10-foot-square porch.

1738: Queenstown had failed to become a major entrepôt. Complaints arose that the location of the courthouse was "inaccessible to most inhabitants except by water."

1740: Bricklayer James Jones of King George County built a courthouse at the present county seat of Lancaster. The building measured 38 by 25 feet and was apsidal at the magistrates' end. Jones also built the first prison at the site.

1795: Following the passage of a state law requiring the construction of fireproof clerks' offices, the county ordered the construction of one measuring 22 by 18 feet. William Palmer built the present structure, completed in 1798. An addition was made in the early nineteenth century.

1819: The southern part of the present two-story jail was built. Four years later the north addition was constructed.

1860: The present courthouse was constructed. In 1937 it was remodeled, and the portico and a new clerk's office were built.

Loudoun County (1757)

1758: Sheriff Aneas Campbell undertook the construction of a 40-by-28-foot brick courthouse in Leesburg. Daniel French agreed to build the county's first prison.

1800: A brick clerk's office was ordered built on the courthouse grounds.

1809: County magistrates decided to build a new courthouse, clerk's office, and jail. The courthouse was finished around 1811 and was one of the first temple forms with a two-story pedimented portico erected in Virginia. Benjamin Henry Latrobe noted in 1815 that the entablature was incorrectly detailed (fig. A32).

1895: The present brick courthouse with pilastered walls, pedimented portico, compass-headed windows, and cupola was completed.

Louisa County (1742)

1743: The court ordered the construction of a courthouse patterned after the T-shaped arcaded one in neighboring Hanover County. A debate over the lo-

FIGURE A32. Loudoun County courthouse, Leesburg, 1811. Drawing by B. H. Latrobe, May 10, 1815. (The Maryland Historical Society, Baltimore)

cation of the county seat may have delayed or prevented the execution of this plan.

1768: Money was raised to pay Thomas Montague on the completion of the county courthouse.

1818: Samuel Ragland built a new courthouse with a gable-fronted central courtroom block flanked by lower wings containing offices and jury rooms.

1905: Designed by D. Wiley Anderson of Richmond, the present two-story courthouse with its central dome and Ionic pedimented portico replaced the early nineteenth-century building.

Lunenburg County (1745)

1746: Because of its large size and its constant division to create new counties, Lunenburg County had no settled court venue during its first twenty years.

1765: Robert Estes agreed to build a courthouse on his property at Bluestone Creek with the same dimensions as the 1753 Dinwiddie courthouse. Estes completed the structure three years later.

1782: The court moved to its present location. By the end of the decade, a courthouse had been constructed.

1823: The present two-story temple-fronted courthouse was ordered constructed. Completed by William Howard in 1827, the building was modeled after the Jefferson-designed courthouse in Charlotte County with some slight differences. The Lunenburg courthouse has a shallow apsidal end whereas the Charlotte courthouse was originally faceted at the magistrates' end.

1857: Alterations were made to the courthouse as the courtroom was moved upstairs, offices were created on the ground floor, and an exterior stair was erected in the pedimented portico. A rear extension was made in 1939 to provide more room for the clerk's office.

Madison County (1792)

1793: A 42-by-24-foot wooden courthouse was ordered constructed.

1797: The magistrates ordered the building of a brick clerk's office 16 feet square.

1828: Malcolm Crawford and William B. Phillips, craftsmen who had earlier worked on the buildings at the University of Virginia, submitted proposals to build a two-story arcaded courthouse. The magistrates accepted the offer, and the present structure was completed by 1830.

Mathews County (1791)

1792: The first county courthouse was erected.

c. 1835: Sometime in the early 1830s the present one-story T-shaped courthouse was constructed at the edge of the public square in Mathews (fig. A33). The jury rooms were originally located in the garret and offices in the ground-floor wings. A jail was built sometime in the early nineteenth century (fig. A34).

1858–59: William Brown built a one-story clerk's office just south of the courthouse.

Mecklenburg County (1764)

1768: Matthew Mills undertook the construction of a 40-by-24-foot wooden courthouse with jury rooms located at one end of the building opposite the magistrates' bench. Mills finished this building in 1770.

1838: The county hired William Howard, builder of the Lunenburg County and Cumberland County courthouses, to construct the present two-story temple-fronted courthouse with its pedimented portico of six columns. Originally the building contained a two-story courtroom, but it was later subdivided into two floors. The courtroom was moved to the second floor as in the Lunenburg courthouse. An addition was made to the rear of the building in the early twentieth century.

Middlesex County (1669)

1685: Through the 1680s the court rented rooms in a dwelling. In 1685 the county ordered the construction of a brick courthouse the same dimensions as the Gloucester courthouse. This probably was not executed.

1691: James Curtis and John Hipkins agreed to build "a good strong substantial

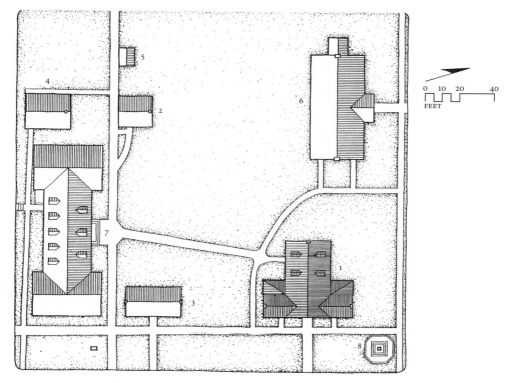

FIGURE A33. Site plan of the Mathews County courthouse grounds. *1:* courthouse, early 1830s; *2:* jail, early nineteenth century; *3:* clerk's office, 1858–59; *4:* jail, c. 1900; *5:* privies, mid-twentieth century; *6:* sheriff's office, 1930; *7:* county offices, 1957; *8:* Confederate monument, c. 1900.

FIGURE A34. Jail, Mathews, early nineteenth century, in a 1930s photograph

FIGURE A35. Old Middlesex County courthouse, Urbanna, 1759

FIGURE A36. Plan, old
Middlesex County court-
house, Urbanna

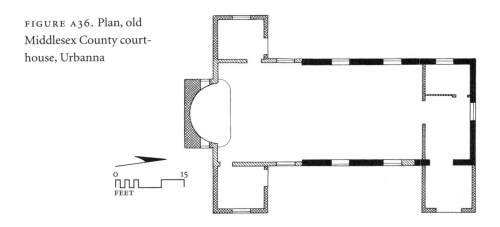

Virginia-built house for a courthouse" that was to be 30 by 20 feet. This
building was not constructed, and the court continued to meet in rented
quarters.

1704: John Hipkins signed a contract to build "a good English frame" courthouse 32 by 20 feet on George Wortham's land. This building was completed
by 1706 and served the county until 1748 when the court moved to Urbanna.

1759: A one-story brick courthouse was finally finished in Urbanna (figs. A35,
A36). The court ordered a 24-foot addition to be made to it. This building
survives and was converted into an Episcopal church in the early nineteenth
century.

1799: Elry Burroughs agreed to build a brick clerk's office 26 by 16 feet. The structure was completed by 1803.

1852: The county seat moved to Saluda in 1849, and John P. Hill erected the present two-story arcaded courthouse. A wing was added in 1965.

Nansemond County (1646) (now part of the city of Suffolk)

1723: In 1723 a fire destroyed the county records that were housed in Clerk Christopher Jackson's dwelling. As a result, little is known of the location and form of this county's early courthouses.

1777: A small brick courthouse was located in Suffolk. British soldiers burned the building in 1779.

1837: A fire destroyed the county courthouse. The present two-story temple-fronted courthouse was built following this fire. In 1958 an addition was made to the rear of the building.

Nelson County (1807)

1809: Justices debated the plan of the new county courthouse, finally deciding upon a two-story arcaded structure. George Varnum supervised the construction of the present building, which was completed the following year (fig. A37). The county made additions to the rear of the building in 1940 and remodeled it in 1968.

New Kent County (1654)

1688: County courts were held in two locations. Three years later King and Queen County was formed, and the New Kent court settled upon the present location for holding its monthly meetings.

1695: A brick courthouse was built by this time and was used until it was destroyed by fire in 1753.

1775: Fire destroyed the courthouse, which was rebuilt shortly afterward.

1787: An arsonist destroyed the prison and the clerk's office with all the county records.

1862: The courthouse was seriously damaged during the Civil War but was repaired in the years following.

1909: The B. F. Smith Fireproof Company of Washington, D.C., erected the present one-story courthouse. The building was later expanded.

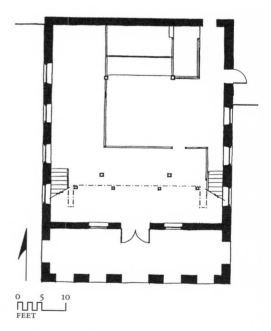

0 5 10
FEET

FIGURE A37. Plan, Nelson County courthouse, Lovingston, 1809

Norfolk County (1636) (now part of the city of Chesapeake)

1689: As in many counties in the seventeenth century, the Norfolk court was peripatetic in its early decades, meeting in taverns and dwellings. After the port of Norfolk was platted in the late seventeenth century, the magistrates decided to establish a courthouse in the new town. In 1689 they ordered the construction of two courthouses, a rectangular brick one measuring 35 by 20 in Norfolk and a smaller wooden structure at Lynnhaven. The Norfolk building was later changed to a post-in-the-ground wooden structure measuring 40 by 20 feet.

1726: Peter Malbone agreed to build a brick courthouse 32 by 20 feet with an apsidal end in Norfolk. The interior was modeled after the fittings in the "General Courthouse" in Williamsburg.

1788: William Hobday and Lemuel Carter built a two-story brick courthouse capped by a cupola that was finished the following year.

1790: The county court moved out of the city of Norfolk to a new location farther south at Washington where James Matthews erected a brick courthouse. This was completed in 1792.

1801: The county court moved to Portsmouth where a building was erected shortly thereafter.

1846: William Singleton designed a two-story porticoed courthouse across the street from the earlier courthouse. This building was remodeled following the Civil War.

Northampton County (1634)

1655: The court sat in two different locations. By 1659 the court met at Thomas Selby's house.

1664: Justice William Waters erected a wooden courthouse 25 by 20 feet in Town Fields.

1688: Tavern keeper Joseph Godwin built a courthouse 25 feet in length in the present town of Eastville. It was completed in 1690.

1715: William Rabyshaw built a 30-by-20-foot wooden courthouse to replace the earlier structure.

1731: John Marshall undertook the construction of a one-story brick courthouse. Though truncated and severely altered, the building survives. It was moved to its present location on the courthouse grounds and partially restored in 1913.

1795: A rectangular one-story brick courthouse was built.

c. 1815: The county erected a one-room, one-story brick prison, which survives along with a fragment of a perimeter wall that enclosed an exercise yard. The neighboring clerk's office was built slightly earlier.

1899: The present two-story courthouse was constructed by the B. F. Smith Fireproof Construction Company.

Northumberland County (1648)

1679: After meeting for many years in various houses, the court ordered the construction of a wooden courthouse at Hughlett's Indian Field in what is now the county seat of Heathsville. Two years later John Hughlett undertook the construction of a 35-by-20-foot earthfast courthouse.

1693: Richard Haynie agreed to build a 12-by-12-foot jury house.

1703: Joseph Humphrey began construction of a courthouse that was finished in 1706.

1744: The magistrates ordered the building of an 18-by-16-foot brick addition to the courthouse for the convenience of the justices and jury.

1796: George Astin agreed to build a brick clerk's office 16 by 18 feet in size, which he completed three years later.

1851: John Donohoe built a new courthouse in Heathsville.

1900: The B. F. Smith Fireproof Company erected the present two-story brick courthouse.

Nottoway County (1788)

1789: The magistrates settled upon the present location on which to build the first courthouse. This building was a framed structure that was completed by 1793.

1841: Branch Ellington contracted to build the present brick courthouse, a structure featuring a tall central courtroom block with a Tuscan portico flanked by lower wings.

Orange County (1734)

1737: After some debate about where to construct the county courthouse, Thomas Jones agreed to build a structure on John Braham's land. In 1739 Henry Willis was paid to finish the courthouse.

1749: Upon the creation of Culpeper County, Orange County magistrates moved court sessions to Timothy Crosthwait's house in the present town of Orange. The following year Charles Curtis contracted to build a courthouse that was finished in 1752.

1754: The magistrates ordered the construction of a 20-foot addition to the south end of the courthouse. James Walker may have completed this in 1761.

1803: Dudley Ellis and Robert King undertook the construction of a courthouse and clerk's office.

1859: The present Italianate courthouse was built. The arcade was enclosed in 1949 to create more office space. In 2003 an addition was built, and the arcade was reopened.

Pittsylvania County (1766)

1767: James Roberts built the first courthouse, modeled after the one in Halifax County.

1777: On the division of the county, plans were made to construct a 32-by-24-foot courthouse.

1783: At the end of the Revolution, David Hunt agreed to build a courthouse on land owned by James Johnson, which now forms the present town of Chatham.

1812: A one-story brick clerk's office was built in Chatham for Clerk William Tunstall. Though made redundant with the construction of a new courthouse in 1853, the building survives.

1853: L. A. Shumaker designed and constructed the present two-story courthouse.

Powhatan County (1777)

1778: The justices ordered the construction of a 50-by-20-foot brick courthouse of the same size and plan as the Buckingham courthouse. Building was delayed by the exigencies of war.

1783: Following the Revolution, the magistrates returned to the issue of building a permanent courthouse in the village of Scottsville, the present county seat, now known as Powhatan. John Cox may have undertaken the construction of the building, which was finished in 1786.

1796: William Hickman finished work on the present clerk's office. In 1832 Thomas Dorsett completed an addition to the building.

1822: Richard Bass completed a large two-story brick tavern across the street from the courthouse square. The brick section was added to an early nineteenth-century one-story framed building, forming a sizable hotel.

1849: The present one-story Greek Revival courthouse, designed by A. J. Davis, was erected. In 1992 a rear addition was made to the building.

Prince Edward County (1753)

1754: Tavern keeper Charles Anderson erected a rectangular wooden courthouse on his property in what is now the village of Worsham. In 1767 the courthouse underwent major repairs including the addition of a number of windows and underpinning the building with brick.

1773: Christopher Ford, the builder of the Amelia County courthouse, contracted to build a 46-by-24-foot wooden courthouse. Work on the building dragged on for more than a decade.

1810: A brick clerk's office was ordered built. This was replaced by another clerk's office in 1855, which still survives in Worsham along with a log structure said to be an early prison.

1832: A brick courthouse, designed by William A. Howard, replaced the colonial framed structure.

1872: After the county seat moved to Farmville, a two-story brick building was erected to house the county court and town council.

1939: The present two-story brick courthouse was completed.

Prince George County (1702)

1781: The destruction of many of the county's record books makes it impossible to trace the history of the earliest county buildings. In 1779 the clerk of the court moved his office to the town of Blandford though the courthouse stood outside of town four miles from the James River. In 1781 the courthouse was "almost entirely destroyed" by British soldiers during the Revolutionary War.

1785: A courthouse was built a few miles east of Petersburg.

1810: Another courthouse replaced the late eighteenth-century structure. The building burned during the Civil War.

1884: The present two-story courthouse was built at Prince George. The arcade was added in 1929.

Princess Anne County (1691) (now part of the city of Virginia Beach)

1692: Magistrates order the construction of an earthfast courthouse measuring 35 by 20 feet to be built on the eastern shore of the Lynnhaven River. Benjamin Burrough and William Moseley completed the building and a prison by 1696.

1728: Money was raised to pay for a new courthouse to be built by James Langley. Whether this building was completed is unknown.

1758: The court moved farther south to New Town.

1778: The magistrates decided to move their venue to Kempsville where a building was later erected to hold sessions.

1824: Once again the court moved its business to a more convenient location at Cross Roads, later named Princess Anne, near the center of the county. A brick courthouse was built shortly thereafter.

Prince William County (1730)

1731: The first county courthouse was erected on land owned by George Mason III on the south side of the Occoquan River.

1743: Following the creation of Fairfax County, the court moved to Brent Town where new buildings were erected.

1762: Under pressure from merchants in Dumfries and the division of Fauquier County from Prince William, the court moved to the port town. Influenced by the designs of William Buckland in consultation with town trustee

George Mason IV, the county magistrates erected a one-story brick building with an apsidal end, side loggias, and front entry. The building included sandstone quoins.

1822: The court moved to a more central location at Brentsville where William Claytor built the two-story brick building that survives and was restored in 2003–4.

1892: The town of Manassas managed to have the county seat removed from Brentsville to the prosperous rail junction. In 1894 the county court moved into a two-story structure designed by James C. Teague and Philip Thornton Mayre.

1984: All the county offices and court functions moved out of Manassas to a new judicial center.

Richmond County (1692)

1692: James Orchard agreed with county officials to build a wooden building to house judicial proceedings on his property. The building was to be 20 feet square.

1703: Thomas Bradley constructed a 20-by-16-foot room adjoining the courthouse as a place for the justices and jury to deliberate.

1721: Money was raised to build a new courthouse. Whether this was executed is unknown.

1735: The magistrates order the construction of a room adjoining the courthouse to be built of brick measuring 33 by 16 feet.

1749–50: Justice Landon Carter built the present one-story brick courthouse. The building originally had two side arcades, but these were enclosed in 1877 when the plan was severely altered (fig. A38).

1816: John Tayloe undertook the construction of the surviving one-story clerk's office. The building was completed two years later.

1971: A new county office building was constructed to house offices and records that had been located in the old courthouse and clerk's office.

Rockbridge County (1778)

1778: The court authorized the construction in Lexington of a temporary wooden courthouse that measured 20 by 16 feet.

1779: The magistrates approved a plan for a T-shaped brick courthouse. Modified slightly in size and plan, the building was not constructed until after the Revolution by William Brice who finished it in 1787 or 1788. In 1796 a fire destroyed the courthouse.

1803: A two-story brick courthouse was built.

1897: William McDowell designed the present brick courthouse.

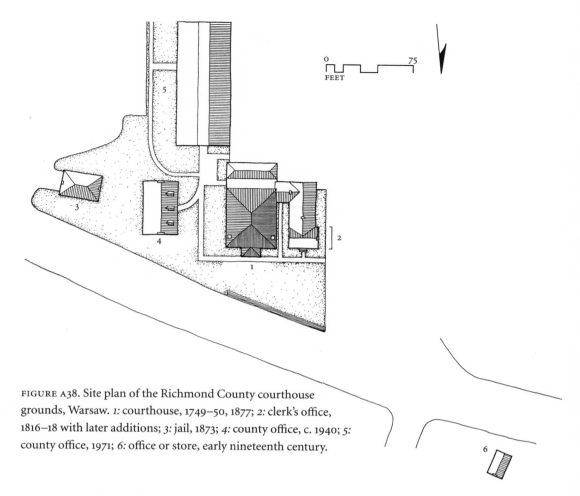

FIGURE A38. Site plan of the Richmond County courthouse grounds, Warsaw. *1:* courthouse, 1749–50, 1877; *2:* clerk's office, 1816–18 with later additions; *3:* jail, 1873; *4:* county office, c. 1940; *5:* county office, 1971; *6:* office or store, early nineteenth century.

Rockingham County (1778)

1779: Robert Campbell undertook the construction of a 30-by-20-foot log courthouse on Thomas Harrison's land.

1791: Tavern keeper Brewer Reeves supervised the construction of a two-story stone courthouse measuring 32 by 26 feet.

1834: Isaac Pennybacker constructed a 50-by-40-foot brick courthouse.

1874: The firm of Holmes and Rust erected a larger brick courthouse in Harrisonburg.

1897: The present three-story stone courthouse designed by T. J. Collins was completed.

Russell County (1786)

1787: Court clerk Henry Dickenson built a 24-by-20-foot log courthouse on his land.

1799: A two-story 36-by-26-foot stone courthouse was erected for county business near Dickensonville. The building still survives, incorporated as a wing into a larger early nineteenth-century farmhouse.

1816: After the county seat moved to Lebanon, the magistrates ordered the construction of a new brick courthouse. John Toneray completed the new building two years later.

1852: A two-story brick courthouse with a portico in front and capped by a cupola was completed.

1874: After fire destroyed the previous courthouse, a larger two-story structure was erected. In the early twentieth century, the building was expanded and remodeled several times.

Shenandoah County (1772)

1772: The county was named after Lord Dunmore, the last royal governor of Virginia, but it was renamed Shenandoah County in 1778. In 1772 a dwelling was moved to the public lots in Woodstock and fitted up as a courthouse.

1795: Construction of the present two-story stone courthouse began. The building was completed two years later. Additions were made to the rear of the building in 1840 and 1880. In 1929 the two-story pedimented portico was built.

Southampton County (1749)

1749: The justices order the construction of 40-by-24-foot courthouse on Elizabeth Exum's land near Flower's Bridge. Three years later Arthur Williamson completed the building.

1767: The courthouse was set on fire "by some wicked and malicious incendiary." The following year William Wills built a replacement.

1804: John Crichlow built a new courthouse.

1834: Jeremiah Cobb and Clements Rochelle undertook the construction of the present two-story brick courthouse. In 1924 the columned portico was added. The building was remodeled in 1960.

Spotsylvania County (1720)

1721: The first court met at Germanna, the home of Governor Alexander Spotswood. In the next few years, Spotswood built a courthouse and prison for the county.

1732: The court moved from Germanna to the town of Fredericksburg.

1736: Henry Willis contracted to build an arcaded brick courthouse measuring 48 by 34 feet with a 34-by-12-foot side building. Willis completed the building two years later.

1779: The county court left Fredericksburg for a more central location on the north side of the Poe River. Thomas Pritchett built a courthouse that was ready for use in 1781.

1798: The magistrates ordered the construction of a new courthouse based on the design of the old Fredericksburg building except without a piazza. The building was completed by 1801.

1805: County officials ordered the building of a brick clerk's office.

1839: The courts moved to the present location. Malcolm Crawford, builder of the Madison County courthouse, erected a two-story brick building. Fighting during the Civil War damaged the courthouse.

1901: The B. F. Smith Fireproof Construction Company rebuilt the courthouse.

Stafford County (1664)

1665: The justices order the construction of a courthouse whose location is unknown.

1691: After the establishment of the county seat at the town of Marlborough on Potomac Creek, the county magistrates contracted with Sampson Darrell to construct a wooden courthouse. Darrell subcontracted the work to Ambrose Bayly who probably completed the building in 1692 or 1693.

1720: The courthouse had become ruinous.

1731: A new courthouse was built. It burned in 1744.

1749: Nathaniel Harrison and Hugh Adie contracted to build a brick courthouse for the county. Before it could be completed, it was "feloniously" burned. The building was reconstructed. Archaeological excavation of the site revealed that it was a T-shaped building measuring 52 by 26 feet (fig. A39).

1776: An act was passed establishing a new place to hold court on land donated by William Fitzhugh and William Gerrard at what is now the county seat.

c. 1791: A one-story T-shaped courthouse was erected (fig. A40). Within a

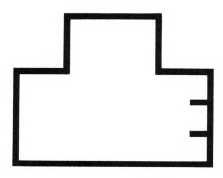

FIGURE A39. Archaeological plan of the c. 1749 Stafford County courthouse, Marlborough. After C. Malcolm Watkins, *The Cultural History of Marlborough, Virginia* (Washington, D.C., 1968), 118.

0   15
FEET

FIGURE A40. Stafford County's T-shaped courthouse at Stafford, possibly 1791 with alterations in second quarter of the nineteenth century, demolished early twentieth century

FIGURE A41. Early nineteenth-century Stafford County clerk's office; demolished early twentieth century

couple of decades the county had built a one-story brick clerk's office (fig. A41).

1922: Construction began on the present courthouse.

Surry County (1652)

1650 and 1660s: During its first decades the county court met at Southwark, east of Gray's Creek.

1681: William Blackbonne agreed to build a courthouse, but the following year the court noted that he had not completed the building.

1702: The justices believed it necessary to have a courthouse built.

1711: The court paid Nathaniel Harrison for finishing the courthouse.

1728: The magistrates ordered the construction of a courthouse on the north side of Blackwater Swamp.

1756: The partition of Sussex County necessitated the construction of a new courthouse. William Clinch agreed to build a wooden one at Troopers. Two years later Clinch asked for further time to complete the building. After he failed to execute the contract, the court looked into bringing a suit to recover money given for the work. The building may have been completed by 1763. However, two years later "some ill disposed person" burned it down.

1765: Robert Watkins undertook the construction of a brick courthouse 44 by 23 feet.

1795: After the county seat moved to Cross Roads, Robert McIntosh built a brick courthouse slightly larger than the old one at Troopers. It was completed two years later.

1895: A brick courthouse replaced the late eighteenth-century building. This structure burned in 1906.

1907: A two-story brick courthouse with a large portico was built. This structure also burned.

1923: The present courthouse with its front portico of Ionic columns, designed by G. R. Berryman and modeled after the 1907 structure, was erected.

Sussex County (1753)

1754: The magistrates ordered the construction of a courthouse the same size as the one in Southampton County, which measured 40 by 24 feet. The wooden structure was completed two years later.

1810: The court looked into the possibility of raising the courthouse to two stories.

1814: The county justices ordered the construction of a 20-foot-square brick clerk's office. Finished in 1817, the one-story building stands across the road from the present courthouse.

1828: Dabney Cosby, builder of the Goochland County courthouse, completed construction of the present two-story courthouse, which features a central three-bay arcade. The structure was renovated in 1877, and in 1954 a rear wing was added.

Warwick County (1634) (now part of Newport News)

1691: The loss of early records makes it impossible to trace the history of the early courthouses in the county. By 1691 a brick structure existed that was repaired ten years later.

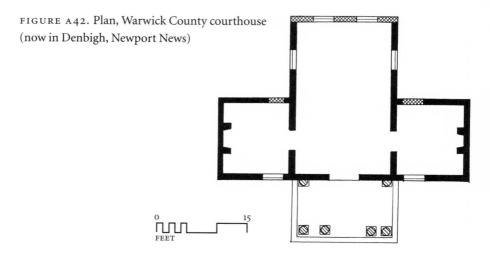

FIGURE A42. Plan, Warwick County courthouse (now in Denbigh, Newport News)

1810: T. Sandy undertook the construction of a small one-story T-shaped courthouse in the present town of Denbigh (fig. A42). The building survives, and its interior was restored in 1989.

1884: A larger courthouse was erected next door to the older one.

Westmoreland County (1653)

1673: The early courts met in various locations. By 1669 a courthouse existed. In 1673 John Lee agreed to build a wooden courthouse 35 by 20 feet. This building was unexecuted because Lee died shortly after signing the contract.

1678: The magistrates specified the building of a wooden courthouse measuring 46 by 24 feet. The building was not started until 1683 and remained unfinished three years later. By 1691 it had grown ruinous and out of repair.

1707: John Gardner built a brick courthouse at Vaulx Quarter measuring 36 by 22 feet with a 10-foot-square entrance porch.

1735: Nicholas Minor erected a small chamber adjoining the courthouse for the magistrates' deliberations.

1799: The justices ordered the construction of a clerk's office.

1818: Ethelwald Sanford undertook the construction of a two-story brick courthouse at Montross.

1900: The B. F. Smith Fireproof Construction Company rebuilt the courthouse. In 1930 it was substantially remodeled with a pedimented front portico added. Further alterations occurred in 1964.

York County (1634)

1680: Until the 1680s the court moved around, holding sessions at various houses and taverns. In 1680 a courthouse was established at the French Ordinary. This earthfast structure was repaired several times in the 1680s and early 1690s.

1697: Henry Cary built a wooden courthouse in Yorktown. In 1708 William Buckner added a 16-foot-square office and a 7-foot-square porch to the courthouse.

1731: Robert Ballard began construction of an arcaded, T-shaped brick courthouse measuring 59 feet across the front by 52 feet deep. The interior of the courthouse was severely damaged during the siege of the town in 1781 and was rebuilt following the war. In 1814 the courthouse burned along with many other buildings in the town.

1808: Elry Burroughs, builder of the 1803 clerk's office in Middlesex County, undertook the construction of a clerk's office.

1816: Robert Garrett began construction of a two-story brick courthouse that was completed two years later. Federal ammunition stored in the courthouse exploded in 1863, and the subsequent fire destroyed the building, the clerk's office, and the jail that stood nearby.

1876: A two-story brick courthouse replaced the one destroyed during the Civil War. In 1940 this building was also destroyed by fire.

1955: A new courthouse resembling the general form of the 1730s one was constructed on the site of the colonial building.

NOTES

Abbreviations

COUNTY AND VESTRY RECORDS

Unless otherwise noted, all county and vestry records are either on microfilm at the Library of Virginia and or in the clerk's office in the respective county or municipality.

AB	Account Book	MB	Minute Book
ALCB	Appeals and Land Causes Book	OB	Order Book
BSMB	Board of Supervisors Minute Book	OJB	Order and Judgment Book
		OWB	Order and Will Book
CB	Court Book	PB	Plat Book
DB	Deed Book	RB	Record Book
DOWB	Deed, Order, and Will Book	SB	Survey Book
DPB	Deed and Patent Book	VB	Vestry Book
IB	Inventory Book	WB	Will Book
JB	Judgment Book	WDB	Will and Deed Book
LB	Ledger Book	WIB	Will and Inventory Book
LRB	Land Record Book		

JOURNALS AND NEWSPAPERS

AHR	*American Historical Review*
JSAH	*Journal of the Society of Architectural Historians*
Md. Gaz.	*Maryland Gazette*
Va. Gaz.	*Virginia Gazette*
VC	*Virginia Cavalcade*
VMHB	*Virginia Magazine of History and Biography*
WMQ	*William and Mary Quarterly*

PUBLISHED DOCUMENTS

CVS	William Palmer, ed., *Calendar of Virginia State Papers,* 11 vols. (Richmond, 1875–93).
EJC	H. R. McIlwaine et al., eds., *Executive Journals of the Council of Colonial Virginia,* 6 vols. (Richmond, 1925–66).

Hening,   William Waller Hening, *The Statutes at Large; Being a Collection of All the Laws*
    Statutes   *of Virginia,* 13 vols. (New York, Philadelphia, 1823).

JHB   H. R. McIlwaine et al., eds., *Journals of the House of Burgesses,* 13 vols. (Richmond, 1905–14).

LJC   H. R. McIlwaine, ed., *Legislative Journals of the Council of Colonial Virginia,* 3 vols. (Richmond, 1918–19).

REPOSITORIES

CWF   Colonial Williamsburg Foundation Library, Williamsburg, Va.
LVA   Library of Virginia, Richmond
UVA   University of Virginia Library, Charlottesville
VHS   Virginia Historical Society, Richmond

Introduction: The Structure of Justice

1. Westmoreland Co. OB 1690–98, 10a, Feb. 25, 1691. For the "hundreds of horses" and "multitude" of people at Charlotte County court day in 1827, see James W. Alexander, *Forty Years' Familiar Letters of James W. Alexander, D.D.,* ed. John Hall, 2 vols. (New York, 1860), 1:100.

2. Maria G. Carr, *Recollections of Rocktown, Now Known as Harrisonburg, from 1817–1820* (Harrisonburg, Va., n.d.), 11. I am grateful to Mark R. Wenger for bringing this reference to my attention.

3. For another good description of court day in Virginia in the early nineteenth century by an unnamed lawyer recalling his first experience in his new profession, see *Southern Literary Messenger* 1 (July 1835): 645.

4. Alexander, *Forty Years* 1:100.

5. Richard R. Beeman, ed., "Trade and Travel in Post-Revolutionary Virginia: A Diary of an Itinerant Peddler, 1807–1808," *VMHB* 84 (Apr. 1976): 183.

6. Accomack Co. OB 1703–9, 164, Feb. 10, 1710.

7. *Va. Gaz.* (R), Apr. 26, 1770, 1:3.

8. Goochland Co. OB 1728–30, 115, June 17, 1729.

9. An itinerant peddler working through the Southside of the state in the early nineteenth century observed that the December court day at the Pittsylvania County courthouse coincided with several days of horse racing. Beeman, "Trade and Travel in Post-Revolutionary Virginia," 183.

10. Frederick Co. OB 1745–48, 311, Aug. 7, 1747.

11. For the cultural implication of violent brawling, see Elliott J. Gorn, "'Gouge and Bite, Pull Hair and Scratch': The Social Significance of Fighting in the Southern Backcountry," *AHR* 90 (1985): 18–43.

12. Westmoreland Co. OB 1739–43, 93, Apr. 1, 1741; Beeman, "Trade and Travel in Post-Revolutionary Virginia," 181.

13. *Va. Gaz.* (P), Apr. 19, 1776, 2:2; Accomack Co. OB 1753–63, 568, June 2, 1763; Westmoreland Co. OB 1790–95, 121–22, June 4, 1791.

14. Philip A. Bruce, *Institutional History of Virginia in the Seventeenth Century* (New York, 1910); Charles Sydnor, *Gentlemen Freeholders: Political Practices in Washington's Virginia* (Chapel Hill, 1952); Rhys Isaac, *The Transformation of Virginia, 1740–1790* (Chapel Hill,

N.C., 1982), 92; A. G. Roeber, *Faithful Magistrates and Republican Lawyers* (Chapel Hill, N.C., 1981), 74.

15. See David Konig, "A Summary View of the Law of British America," *WMQ*, 3d ser., 50 (Jan. 1993): 44–46. For recent scholarship in early American legal history, see Cornelia Hughes Dayton, "Turning Points and the Relevance of Colonial Legal History," ibid., 7–17; and Terri L. Snyder, "Legal History of the Colonial South: Assessment and Suggestions," ibid., 18–27.

16. Dell Upton, *Holy Things and Profane: Anglican Parish Churches in Colonial Virginia* (Cambridge, Mass., 1986), xix.

17. Ibid., 160; Cary Carson, "The Consumer Revolution in Colonial British America: Why Demand?" in *Of Consuming Interests: The Style of Life in the Eighteenth Century*, ed. Cary Carson, Ronald Hoffman, and Peter Albert (Charlottesville, Va., 1994), 619–42.

18. Roeber, *Faithful Magistrates and Republican Lawyers*, xvii.

19. Waterman, *Mansions of Virginia*, 243–48. For a reassessment of Ariss's career, see Carl Lounsbury, "John Ariss," in *Dictionary of Virginia Biography* 1, ed. John Kneebone et al. (Richmond, 1998), 199–201. The chimerical quest for the self-conscious professional architect traveling the roads of colonial Virginia armed with a portfolio of designs continues. For trends in architectural historiography, see Dell Upton, "New Views of the Virginia Landscape," *VMHB* 96 (Oct. 1988): 407–70; Camille Wells, "The Multi-Storied House: Twentieth-Century Encounters with Domestic Architecture of Colonial Virginia," ibid., 106 (Oct. 1998): 353–418.

20. Dell Upton reached this same perspective in his study of Anglican parish churches, in part because many of the individuals and circumstances of the building process were the same. Upton, *Holy Things and Profane*, 11–34. See also Catherine Bishir et al., *Architects and Builders in North Carolina: A History of the Practice of Building* (Chapel Hill, N.C., 1990), 1–129; Catherine Bishir, "Good and Sufficient Language for Building," in *Perspectives in Vernacular Architecture* 4, ed. Thomas Carter and Bernard Herman (Columbia, S.C., 1991), 43–52; Carl Lounsbury, "The Dynamics of Architectural Design in Eighteenth-Century Charleston and the Lowcountry," in *Exploring Everyday Landscapes: Perspectives in Vernacular Architecture* 7, ed. Annmarie Adams and Sally McMurry (Knoxville, Tenn., 1997), 58–72.

21. See, for example, Alan Macfarlane, *The Justice and the Mare's Ale: Law and Disorder in Seventeenth-Century England* (New York, 1981); Sharon Salinger, *Taverns and Drinking in Early America* (Baltimore, 2002); David Conroy, *In Public Houses: Drink and the Revolution of Authority in Colonial Massachusetts* (Chapel Hill, N.C., 1995); Peter Thompson, *Rum Punch and Revolution: Taverngoing and Public Life in Eighteenth-Century Philadelphia* (Philadelphia, 1999).

22. For the effects of gentility on architecture and landscape, see Richard Bushman, *The Refinement of America: Persons, Houses, Cities* (New York, 1992), 100–180.

1. The County Court in Early Virginia

1. Landon Carter, "Speech to the Grand Jury," Carter Family Papers, CWF; *Va. Gaz.*, Oct. 3, 1745, 1:1.

2. Susan M. Kingsbury, ed., *Records of the Virginia Company of London*, 4 vols. (Washington, D.C., 1906–35), 1:14; Bernard Bailyn, *The Ideological Origins of the American Revolu-*

tion (Cambridge, Mass., 1967), 56–57; John Locke, *The Second Treatise of Government*, ed. Thomas Peardon (New York, 1952), 71; "Agreement among the Settlers (Exeter, New Hampshire, 1639)," in *Remarkable Providences, 1600–1760*, ed. John Demos (New York, 1972), 192; David Thomas Konig, *Law and Society in Puritan Massachusetts: Essex County, 1629–1682* (Chapel Hill, N.C., 1979), 3.

3. Carter, "Speech to the Grand Jury."

4. Benjamin Leigh, ed., *The Revised Code of the Laws of Virginia*, 2 vols. (Richmond, 1819), 1:244n.

5. York Co. DOWB 1657–62, 175, Oct. 24, 1662.

6. Prince William Co. Legislative Petition, Oct. 14, 1779, LVA; Henrico Co. OB 1710–14, 239, June 1713; Goochland Co. OB 1728–30, 82–83, Mar. 19, 1729.

7. York Co. DOWB 1722–27, 283, 287, 294, 301, June 15, July 24, Aug. 17, Sept. 21, 1724; Richmond Co. OB 1711–16, 377, Feb. 1, 1716; Westmoreland County Co. OB 1705–21, 276a, Mar. 26, 1716.

8. I would like to thank Lori Cousins Macintire and Betty Leviner for summarizing the careers of the York County justices from information compiled by the Research Department of the Colonial Williamsburg Foundation from the York County Records.

9. York Co. DOWB 1729–32.

10. The wording of the commission of the peace is from the instructions from Lieutenant Governor Francis Nicholson to the justices of Northampton County, May 21, 1691. Northampton Co. OB 1689–98, 97–99, May 28, 1691.

11. Ibid.

12. York Co. DOWB 1721–29, 342, June 21, 1725; DOWB 1733–37, 219, Aug. 18, 1735.

13. Ibid., 158, Nov. 6, 1734.

14. For the discretionary role of constables and other minor law enforcement officers in the English judicial system, see Keith Wrightson, "Two Concepts of Order: Justices, Constables, and Jurymen in Seventeenth-Century England," in *An Ungovernable People*, ed. John Brewer and John Styles (New Brunswick, N.J., 1980), 21–46.

15. York Co. DOWB 1729–32, 138, 179, 245, 252, 296, Jan. 18, June 21, Dec. 20, 1731, Jan. 17, July 17, 1732.

16. Northampton Co. OB 1689–98, 97–99, May 28, 1691.

17. *WMQ*, 1st ser., 17 (Oct. 1908): 122–23; York Co. DOWB 1721–29, 148, July 16, 1722; David Thomas Konig, "The Williamsburg Courthouse: A Research Report and Interpretive Guide" (research report, CWF, 1987), 130. Quote in the *Va. Gaz.*, Oct. 3, 1745, 1:1, cited by Konig.

18. Accomack Co. OB 1703–9, 74, Aug. 6, 1706; Lancaster Co. OB 1729–43, 152, Oct. 13, 1736; Amelia Co. OB 1735–46, 66, Apr. 20, 1739; Orange Co. OB 1743–46, 230, Nov. 23, 1744; Brunswick Co. OB 1757–59, 403, Oct. 22, 1759; Prince William Co. OB 1766–69, 47, June 4, 1767; Loudoun Co. OB 1767–70, 134, Oct. 11, 1768; Bedford Co. OB 1795–99, 67, Feb. 23, 1796.

19. On market regulations, see Fredericksburg City Council MB 1801–29, 126–29, June 10, 1809; Staunton City Council MB 1813–34, 17–20, July 24, 1813.

20. York Co. DOWB 1729–32, 192, July 19, 1731.

21. Arthur Middleton, *Tobacco Coast: A Maritime History of Chesapeake Bay in the Colonial Era* (Baltimore, 1984), 487.

22. Charles E. Hatch Jr., *"York under the Hill": Yorktown's Waterfront* (Denver, 1973), 2–7.

23. The two principal merchants in the port of Yorktown, Philip Lightfoot and Thomas Nelson, "preferred Bristol and Liverpool to London for many staple articles." *WMQ*, 1st ser., 11 (Jan. 1903): 154.

24. Charles E. Hatch Jr., *Yorktown's Main Street* (Denver, 1974), 35.

25. "Journal of a French Traveler in the Colonies, 1765," *AHR* 26 (July 1921): 741.

26. "Observations in Several Voyages and Travels in America in the Year 1736," *WMQ*, 1st ser., 15 (Apr. 1907): 222.

27. Ibid., 11 (Jan. 1903): 154.

28. Edward Riley, "The Founding and Development of Yorktown 1691–1781" (Ph.D. diss., Univ. of Southern California, 1942), 78–80.

29. Hatch, *Yorktown's Main Street*, 79–82, 13–15.

30. Thomas Hunt, "The Plan of the Parlour Floor of a House now building by The Honble. Thos. Nelson Esqr. in York Town Virginia," in "Original architectural plans [Thomas] Hunt 1765," f. 29r (which includes fig. 13 and descriptive text), RIBA Library Drawings Collection, London. I would like to thank John Harris for bringing this plan to my attention.

31. Marquis de Chastellux, *Travels in North America in the Years 1780, 1781, and 1782*, ed. and trans. Howard C. Rice, 2 vols. (Chapel Hill, N.C., 1963), 1:25–26.

32. In 1732 William Hugh Grove, an English visitor, noted that Yorktown had "about 10 good houses, not above 4 of Brick, the rest of Timber, viz. Pine Planks Covered with shingles of Cypress. They are not Contiguous but Seperated 40, 50, or 100 Yards from Each other, for the town is divided into Lotts, each of which contains about 100 yds. square, and the streets [are] about 50 feet Wide." Grove, "Virginia in 1732: The Travel Journal of William Hugh Grove," ed. Gregory Stiverson and Patrick H. Butler III, *VMHB* 85 (1977): 22.

33. For the function of stores in colonial Virginia, see Ann Smart Martin, "Commercial Space as Consumption Arena: Retail Stores in Early Virginia," in *People, Power, Places: Perspectives in Vernacular Architecture* 8, ed. Sally McMurry and Annmarie Adams (Knoxville, Tenn., 2000), 201–18.

34. *WMQ*, 1st ser., 15 (Apr. 1907): 222.

35. For these lots, see Hatch, *Yorktown's Main Street*, 24–60.

36. Inventory of the Estate of Edward Powers, York Co. DOWB 1716–20, 464–66, July 4, 1719.

37. Inventory of the Estate of Ishmael Moody, York Co. WIB 1745–59, 134–38, Jan. 16, 1748.

38. For a comparison, see the reconstruction of the events surrounding the meeting of the Court of General Sessions of the Peace for York County, Maine, in July 1725, in Neal W. Allen Jr., "Law and Authority to the Eastward: Maine Courts, Magistrates, and Lawyers, 1690–1730," in *Law in Colonial Massachusetts, 1630–1800* (Boston, 1984), 290–312.

39. York Co. DOWB 1694–98, 486, Nov. 24, 1697.

40. No archaeological evidence for this first building appeared during excavations on the courthouse lot in 1941 by the National Park Service. Edward M. Riley, "The Colonial Courthouses of York County, Virginia," *WMQ*, 2d ser., 22 (1942): 401.

41. York Co. DOWB 1708–10, 21, 181–82, Feb. 25, 1708, Dec. 24, 1708; DOWB 1709–16, 46, 294, Jan. 16, 1711, Dec. 21, 1713.

42. Ibid., 1721–29, 553, Nov. 18, 1728; DOWB 1729–32, 123, Nov. 17, 1730.

43. Ibid., 1729–32, 124, Dec. 21, 1730.

44. Ibid., 151, Feb. 15, 1731.

45. Ibid., 158, Mar. 15, 1731.

46. Grove, "Virginia in 1732," 22.

47. Marcus Whiffen has suggested that the first James City County courthouse built in Williamsburg sometime after 1715 at the southwest corner of England and Francis Streets may have been arcaded. Marcus Whiffen, "The Early Courthouses of Virginia," *JSAH* 18 (Mar. 1959): 4.

48. The approximate equivalent of £1,022 Virginia currency would have been £837 sterling. York Co. DOWB 1729–32, 243, 334, Nov. 15, 1731, Nov. 23, 1732; WIB 1732–40, 60, 69, July 16, Sept. 15, 1733. For the comparative monetary values, see John J. McCusker, *Money and Exchange in Europe and America, 1600–1775* (Chapel Hill, N.C., 1978), 210.

49. York Co. WIB 1732–40, 503, July 18, 1739.

50. For the cost of English public buildings, see Christopher Chalkin, *English Counties and Public Building, 1650–1830* (London, 1998), 133–47.

51. Keith Kissack, *Monmouth: The Making of a County Town* (London, 1975), 295; John Newman, *Gwent/Monmouthshire: The Buildings of Wales* (Cardiff, 2000), 401.

52. *WMQ*, 1st ser., 15 (Apr. 1907): 222.

2. The Early Courthouses, 1650–1725

1. John Smith, *A Map of Virginia. With a Description of the Countrey, the Commodities, People, Government and Religion* (1612) in *The Complete Works of Captain John Smith*, ed. Philip L. Barbour, 3 vols. (Chapel Hill, N.C., 1986), 1:159.

2. The term *burgess*, used to denote a representative in the General Assembly, was by 1700 another reminder of the difference between intentions and reality.

3. Robert Beverley, *The History and Present State of Virginia* (London, 1705), ed. Louis B. Wright (1947; reprint, Charlottesville, Va., 1968), 319.

4. Henry Hartwell, James Blair, and Edward Chilton, *The Present State of Virginia and the College* (London, 1727), ed. Hunter Farish (1943; reprint, Charlottesville, Va., 1964), 4.

5. Ibid., 7.

6. Kingsbury, *Records of the Va. Company* 4:259.

7. Beverley, *History,* 253; Kevin Kelly, "'In dispers'd Country Plantations': Settlement Patterns in Seventeenth-Century Surry County, Virginia," in *The Chesapeake in the Seventeenth Century,* ed. Thad Tate and David Ammerman (New York, 1979), 183–205.

8. Shortly after Wolstenholme Towne, the principal seat of the particular plantation of Martin's Hundred, was destroyed in the massacre of 1622, it was abandoned as a nucleated settlement. Ivor Noël Hume, *Martin's Hundred* (New York, 1982), 41–43.

9. *VMHB* 14 (Apr. 1907): 364; ibid., 25 (Apr. 1917): 144.

10. Francis Makemie, "A Plain and Friendly Perswasive to the Inhabitants of Virginia and Maryland for Promoting Towns and Cohabitation (1705)," ibid., 4 (Jan. 1897): 255–71; John W. Reps, *Tidewater Towns: City Planning in Colonial Virginia and Maryland* (Williamsburg, Va., 1972), 65–91.

11. On English urban housing in the seventeenth century, see A. F. Kelsall, "The London House Plan in the Later 17th Century," *Post-Medieval Archaeology* 8 (1974): 80–91; Alan Thompson, Francis Grew, and John Schofield, "Excavations at Aldgate, 1974," ibid., 18 (1984): 1–33; Alison Maguire and Howard Colvin, "A Collection of Seventeenth-Century Architectural Plans," *Architectural History* 35 (1992): 140–69.

12. For the literature on town functions in the seventeenth-century Chesapeake, see Peter Bergstrom and Kevin Kelly, "'Well Built Towns, Convenient Ports and Markets': The Begin-

nings of Yorktown," paper presented at the Southern Historical Association annual meeting, Atlanta, Nov. 13, 1980. See also Joseph B. Thomas, "Settlement, Community, and Economy: The Development of Towns on Maryland's Lower Eastern Shore, 1660–1775" (Ph.D. diss., Univ. of Maryland, 1994). For urban development in eighteenth-century Virginia, see Carville Earle and Ronald Hoffman, "Urban Development in the Eighteenth Century South," *Perspectives in American History* 10 (1976): 7–80; James O'Mara, *An Historical Geography of Urban System Development: Tidewater Virginia in the 18th Century,* Geographical Monographs, no. 13 (Downsview, Ont., 1983); Joseph A. Ernst and H. Roy Merrens, "'Camden's Turrets Pierce the Skies!': The Urban Process in the Southern Colonies during the Eighteenth Century," *WMQ,* 3d ser., 30 (Oct. 1973): 549–74.

13. *EJC* 4:167–68, Mar. 6, 1728, Surry Co., Isle of Wight Co., 5:422, Apr. 28, 1753, Dinwiddie Co., 6:195, June 29, 1761, Amherst Co., 6:202, Nov. 6, 1761, Buckingham Co.

14. See, for example, Sussex Co. OB 1754–56, 14, Apr. 8, 1754; Henry Co. OB 1777–78, 26, Mar. 16, 1778.

15. D. W. Meinig, *Atlantic America, 1492–1800* (New Haven, 1986), 155–56; Reps, *Tidewater Towns,* 297.

16. For the literature on this debate over the stability of society and local institutions in the seventeenth-century Chesapeake, see Jon Kukla, "Order and Chaos in Early America: Political and Social Stability in Pre-Restoration Virginia," *AHR* 90 (Apr. 1985): 275–98; Anita Rutman, "Still Planting the Seeds of Hope: The Recent Literature of the Early Chesapeake Region," *VMHB* 95 (Jan. 1987): 3–24.

17. For a contemporary assertion of this prerogative, see Northampton Co. OB 1689–98, 97, May 28, 1691.

18. Hening, *Statutes* 1:426, 497; Charles City Co. OB 1672–73, 505, 532, Feb. 4, 1673.

19. See *Merriam Webster's Collegiate Dictionary.*

20. Accomack Co. OB 1666–70, 97, Dec. 20, 1677.

21. Darrett B. and Anita H. Rutman, *A Place in Time: Middlesex County, Virginia, 1650–1750* (New York, 1984), 87–89; Middlesex Co. OB 1680–94.

22. York Co. DOWB 1633–57.

23. Riley, "Colonial Courthouses of York County," 399; York Co. DOWB 1657–62.

24. York Co. DOWB 1677–84, 9, Apr. 24, 1677; Riley, "Colonial Courthouses of York County," 400.

25. Henrico Co. OB 1678–93, 144, July 17 and Aug. 1683; Northumberland Co. OB 1652–65, 70, 188, July 20, 1657, Nov. 22, 1658; OB 1678–98, 51, 89, 110, Nov. 19, 1679, Mar. 3, Dec. 2, 1681.

26. Norfolk Co. DB 1637–46, Aug. 15, 1642.

27. Hening, *Statutes* 1:76, 98, 335–36, 424; Lancaster Co. OB 1652–55, 212, 233, Oct. 25, Dec. 7, 1655; Rappahannock Co. OB 1683–86, 130–131, May 7, 1685; OB 1686–92, 289, Apr. 1, 1691.

28. Through much of the seventeenth century the quarter session courts for Gloucestershire alternated irregularly between Gloucester, Cirencester, and Tetbury. In Surrey meetings were held at Southwark, Reigate, Guildford, and Kingston. After the Restoration the quarter sessions in Wiltshire followed an annual route of Salisbury (Hilary term), Devizes (Easter term), Warminster (Trinity term), and Marlborough (Michaelmas term). Chalkin, *English Counties and Public Building,* 27–28; I. E. Gray, ed., *Gloucestershire Quarter Session Archives, 1660–1889* (Gloucester, Eng., 1958), viii–ix; J. M. Beattie, *Crime and the Courts of England, 1660–1800* (Princeton, N.J., 1986), 311; W. R. Ward, "County Government, 1660–

1835," in *A History of Wiltshire*, ed. R. B. Pugh and Elizabeth Crittall, The Victoria Histories of the Counties of England: Wiltshire (Oxford, Eng., 1957), 5:177.

29. Norfolk Co. DB 1686–95, 146, Sept. 17, 1689.

30. Alan Everitt, "The English Urban Inn, 1560–1760," in *Perspectives in English Urban History*, ed. Alan Everitt (London, 1973), 110–11.

31. Hening, *Statutes* 2:204. Some historians have insisted that there was a "statehouse" in Jamestown in the 1640s and 1650s that had disappeared by the early 1660s. The fragmentary evidence suggests that the first "statehouse" was simply a dwelling that had been rented by the colony and was not specifically built to house the provincial government. See Samuel Yonge, "The Site of Old 'James Towne,' 1607–1698," *VMHB* 12 (July, Oct. 1904): 46–53, 113–24; George C. Gregory, "Jamestown: First Brick State House," *VMHB* 43 (July 1935): 193–99; Henry Chandlee Forman, *Jamestown and St. Mary's: Buried Cities of Romance* (Baltimore, 1938), 102–15; John L. Cotter, *Archaeological Excavations at Jamestown* (Washington, D.C., 1958), 45–51, 165; Cary Carson, "Structure 112, Jamestown" (report for the Colonial National Park, Jamestown, Apr. 28, 2000).

By the end of the century, Virginians had come to expect that their provincial offices would be housed in a proper setting. In a short-lived reorganization of the provincial court, Governor Francis Howard, fifth Baron Howard of Effingham, created in the 1680s a Court of Chancery distinct from the General Court. Although the historian Robert Beverley disapproved of this tinkering with the judicial system, he was particularly appalled by the fact that the governor refused to allow the new court to "sit in the State-House, where all the other publick business was dispatch'd, but took the Dining-Room of a private House for that Use." Beverley, *The History and Present State of Virginia*, 97.

32. The location of this statehouse remains open to question. For much of the twentieth century, scholars thought that the eastern unit of a long row, known as structure 144 (see fig. 29), was probably built as a statehouse in the 1660s. Recent reinvestigation of the archaeological and documentary evidence at Jamestown has questioned this assumption. A plausible alternative to this site is structure 112, just west of the standing late seventeenth-century church tower. The archaeological evidence reveals that this large rectangular building with its porch tower facing the river was reconstructed at least twice in the second half of the century. These rebuildings may have occurred in the late 1660s when structure 112 was converted into a statehouse and in the 1680s following its destruction by fire during Bacon's Rebellion. Until further excavations are undertaken at these two sites, no conclusive verdict can be made. For a preliminary reassessment of the Jamestown evidence, see Kathleen Bragdon, Edward Chappell, and William Graham, "A Scant Urbanity: Jamestown in the 17th Century," in *The Archaeology of 17th-Century Virginia*, ed. Theodore Reinhart and Dennis Pogue (Richmond, 1993), 223–49; Cary Carson et al., "Description and Analysis of Structure 144, Jamestown, Virginia" (report to the Association for the Preservation of Virginia Antiquities, Jamestown Rediscovery, Aug. 20, 2002).

33. Edmund S. Morgan, *American Slavery, American Freedom: The Ordeal of Colonial Virginia* (New York, 1975), 186–95.

34. *JHB* 2:30; Hening, *Statutes* 2:261.

35. Middlesex Co. OB 1680–94, 200–201, Feb. 3, 1685; Accomack Co. OB 1690–97, 190, June 17, 1696; Richmond Co. OB 1692–94, 20–21, July 7, 1692.

36. Lancaster Co. OB 1652–55, 201, 233, June 6, Dec. 7, 1655; Charles City Co. OB 1656–58, 114, Nov. 16, 1657.

37. The courthouse at Westover may not have been completed until the early 1660s. Charles City Co. OB 1658–61, 196, Aug. 3, 1659; OB 1664–65, 513, 608, Dec. 3, 1664, Oct. 14, 1665.

38. Northampton Co. OB 1657–64, 191a, Apr. 29, 1664; T. B. Robertson, "Courthouses of Northampton County," *WMQ,* 1st ser., 23 (July 1914): 51–52; Norfolk Co. WDB 1656–66, 385a, Nov. 17, 1663.

39. Carole Shammas, "English-Born and Creole Elites in Turn-of-the-Century Virginia," and David Jordan, "Political Stability and the Emergence of a Native Elite in Maryland," in Tate and Ammerman, *Chesapeake in the Seventeenth Century,* 243–96.

40. Rutman, *A Place in Time,* 211–17.

41. See, for example, the account of the gathering of more than a dozen freeholders at Lawnes Creek Church in Surry County in 1673 to protest high public levies. Surry Co. WDB 1671–84, 40a, Jan. 3, 1674.

42. Norfolk Co. DB 1686–95, 146, Sept. 17, Nov. 19, 1689.

43. Royal Commission on Historical Monuments, *An Inventory of the Historical Monuments in Herefordshire,* 3 vols. (London, 1931–34), 2:161; R. Gilyard-Beer, *The County Hall, Abingdon, Berkshire* (London, 1956).

44. Middlesex Co. OB 1694–1705, 546, Mar. 15, 1704; York Co. DOWB 1706–10, 121, Feb. 25, 1708.

45. See, for example, Northumberland Co. OB 1678–98, 89, Mar. 11, 1681; Charles City Co. OB 1687–95, 93, Dec. 21, 1687.

46. Essex Co. Suit Papers 1701/1702, Apr. 11, 1702, Clerk's Office, Tappahannock, Va.

47. Northumberland Co. OB 1678–98, 89, Mar. 11, 1681.

48. See Cary Carson et al., "Impermanent Architecture in the Southern American Colonies," *Winterthur Portfolio* 16 (Summer/Autumn 1981): 135–96.

49. Middlesex Co. DB 1687–1750, 10, Apr. 4, 1692; Carson et al., "Impermanent Architecture," 156–60; Middlesex Co. OB 1694–1705, 546, Mar. 15, 1704.

50. Northumberland Co. OB 1678–98, 89, Mar. 11, 1681; Norfolk Co. DB 1686–95, Nov. 19, 1689; Charles City Co. OB 1658–61, 196, Aug. 3, 1659 Henrico Co. RB 1678–93, 220, Dec. 1, 1688; RB 1688–97, 92, County Levy, 1689.

51. Middlesex Co. OB 1680–94, 200–201, Feb. 3, 1685; DB 1687–1750, 10, Apr. 4, 1692.

52. Hening, *Statutes* 3:60.

53. Lancaster Co. OB 1696–1702, 53a, Nov. 24, 1698; Reps, *Tidewater Towns,* 89.

54. Lancaster Co. OB 1696–1702, 53a, 92a, 100a, 128, Nov. 24, 1698, Nov. 9, Dec. 14, 1699, Jan. 14, 1701; OB 1702–13, 54, 258, 277, Dec. 8, 1703, Dec. 12, 1710, Feb. 13, 1712; OB 1729–43, 287, Aug. 8, 1740.

55. A fireplace in one of the gable ends of the 1674 Charles County, Maryland, courthouse heated the courtroom and the second-story lodging chamber. *Archives of Maryland,* 541 vols. to date (Baltimore, 1884–), 60:615–18, Nov. 10, 1674; see also Talbot Co., Maryland, JB 1675–82, 194–95, Mar. 16, 1680.

56. Essex Co. OB 1692–95, 159, Dec. 12, 1693; Lancaster Co. OB 1696–1702, 100a, Dec. 14, 1699.

57. Westmoreland Co. DPB 1665–77, 165a-66, Nov. 20, 1673.

58. Charles City Co. OB 1687–95, 93, Dec. 21, 1687; Westmoreland Co. OB 1690–98, 30–31, June 26, 1691.

59. Westmoreland Co. OB 1676–89, 145, Dec. 4, 1678; Northumberland Co. OB 1678–98,

89, Mar. 11, 1681; Norfolk Co. DB 1686–95, Nov. 19, 1689; York Co. DOWB 1677–84, 258, Oct. 26, 1680; DOWB 1687–91, 47, Nov. 24, 1687.

60. Richmond Co. OB 1699–1704, 261–62, June 3, 1703; Westmoreland Co. OB 1698–1705, 252a–53, Feb. 28, 1705; OB 1705–21, 48a, Mar. 28, 1707.

61. Westmoreland Co. OB 1675–89, 699, Nov. 30, 1688.

62. For early partial lists of the rules of court, see Northampton Co. OB 1657–64, 191a, Apr. 29, 1664; Lancaster Co. OB 1666–80, 208, Oct. 9, 1671; York Co. DOWB 1677–84, 254, Oct. 25, 1680; Rappahannock Co. OB 1686–92, 295, June 3, 1691.

63. Lancaster Co. OB 1666–80, 208, Oct. 9, 1671; Rappahannock Co. OB 1686–92, 295, June 3, 1691.

64. Sir Thomas Smith, *De Republica Anglorum: A Discourse on the Commonwealth of England,* ed. L. Alston (London, 1583; reprint, Cambridge, 1906), 96–97.

65. *Sandwich Guildhall, 1579–1979* (Sandwich, Eng., 1979), 15–16.

66. Rappahannock Co. OB 1683–86, 131, May 7, 1685; York Co. DOWB 1691–94, 186, Nov. 24, 1692; Charles Co., Md., LRB, K, no. 1, 19–20, Sept. 12, 1682.

67. For Virginia parish church furnishings, see Upton, *Holy Things and Profane,* 118–62.

68. Surry Co. OB 1671–91, 231, Nov. 6, 1678; Cited in Clayton Torrence, *Old Somerset on the Eastern Shore* (Richmond, 1935), 409, Nov. 14, 1688.

69. On the significance of seats of honor, see Peter Thornton, *Seventeenth-Century Interior Decoration in England, France, and Holland* (New Haven, 1978), 192–93.

70. Northumberland Co. OB 1678–98, 89, Mar. 11, 1681; Westmoreland Co. OB 1676–89, 145, Dec. 4, 1678.

71. Charles Co., Md., LRB K, no. 1, 19–20, Sept. 12, 1682; Dorchester Co., Md., LRB no. 1, 1669–83, Dec. 6, 1686; Baltimore Co., Md., LRB IS, no. B., 96–97, 1710.

72. Northumberland Co. OB 1678–98, 89, Mar. 11, 1681; Princess Anne Co. OB 1691–1709, 43, Sept. 27, 1692.

73. Northumberland Co. OB 1652–65, 214, Nov. 20, 1665; Middlesex Co. OB 1694–1705, 570, July 3, 1704; Northampton Co. OB 1710–16, 202, Apr. 19, 1715; Lancaster Co. OB 1696–1702, 100a, Dec. 14, 1699.

74. Thornton, *Seventeenth-Century Interior Decoration,* 294; Upton, *Holy Things and Profane,* 118–62.

75. Westmoreland Co. DPB 1665–77, 165a–66, Nov. 20, 1673; Northumberland Co. OB 1664–74, 110, June 27, 1671; Baltimore Co., Md., LRB IS, no. B, 96–97, 1710.

76. Torrence, *Old Somerset on the Eastern Shore,* 409; Essex Co. OB 1695–99, 41, Nov. 11, 1696; Warwick Co. OB 1699–1701, 320, Aug. 21, 1700; Middlesex Co. OB 1694–1705, 570, July 3, 1704.

77. Lancaster Co. OB 1680–86; York Co. DOWB 1677–84.

78. On the procedure of jury trials in Surrey and Sussex during this period, see Beatty, *Crime and the Courts of England,* 395–97.

79. Ibid.

80. Westmoreland Co. OB 1690–98, 30–31, June 26, 1691; Essex Co. Suit Papers 1701/1702, Apr. 11, 1702; Middlesex Co. OB 1694–1705, 570, July 3, 1704.

81. Roeber, *Faithful Magistrates and Republican Lawyers,* 48–53.

82. Beverley, *History,* 94–95.

83. Hening, *Statutes* 2:478–79, June 1680.

84. Richmond Co. OB 1704–8, 60, May 2, 1705; Middlesex Co. OB 1705–10, 262, Oct. 3, 1709; King George Co. OB 1721–23, 143, Sept. 6, 1723.

85. Lancaster Co. OB 1655–66, 369, Mar. 16, 1666.

86. Magistrates at many quarter sessions in England also sought to instill a sense of orderly decorum and professionalism into their courtrooms during the late seventeenth and early eighteenth centuries. In Norfolk, for example, justices forbade courtroom visitors from standing on tables and required all counsel to appear before the court in gowns. James M. Rosenheim, "County Governance and Elite Withdrawal in Norfolk, 1660–1720," in *The First Modern Society: Essays in English History in Honour of Lawrence Stone,* ed. A. Beier, David Cannadine, and James Rosenheim (Cambridge, 1989), 119–22.

3. Courthouses, 1725–1815

1. Beverley, *History*, 118–19.

2. One of the most persuasive arguments for a gentry-dominated landscape appears in Upton, *Holy Things and Profane*.

3. *JHB* 7:256, Oct. 27, 1748.

4. In colonies, and later in states, where local institutions were weaker, public building practices were sometimes more uniform. In contrast to Virginia, local jurisdictions in South Carolina never achieved the authority to construct their own courts of law but remained dependent upon the central legislature for money to build and repair their buildings. In a momentary burst of energy in the 1820s, the Palmetto state government undertook to rebuild or construct dozens of county courthouses and jails, many of which were designed by native architect Robert Mills, an effort which resulted in a degree of standardization unknown in Virginia. See Gene Waddell and Rhodri Windsor Liscombe, *Robert Mills's Courthouses and Jails* (Easley, S.C., 1981).

5. Thomas Jefferson, *Notes on the State of Virginia* (Paris, 1784), ed. William Peden (1955; reprint, New York, 1982), 154.

6. T. B. Robertson, "Court Houses of Northampton County," *WMQ*, 1st ser., 23 (July 1914): 51–52; William Gaines, "Courthouses of Virginia's Eastern Shore," *VC* 14 (Summer 1964): 20–27; Northampton Co. OB 1657–64, 43, 191, 191a, Jan. 29, 1659, Apr. 28, 29, 1664.

7. Robertson, "Court Houses of Northampton County," 53–55; Northampton Co. OB 1698–1710, 4, Mar. 1, 1699; OB 1710–16, 202, 233, 248, Apr. 19, Dec. 5, 1715, May 15, 1716.

8. Northampton Co. OB 1729–32, 60, Dec. 9, 1730.

9. Amelia Co. DB 1789–91, 336, Feb. 23, 1791; Halifax Co. OB 1774–79, 75, Aug. 18, 1774.

10. Essex Co. OB 1726–29, 84, May 16, 1727.

11. Johnston Co., N.C., MB 1759–66, 3, Apr. 24, 1759; . Amelia Co. Loose Papers, Plan of the New Courthouse, 1792, LVA. I would like to thank Selden Richardson for bringing the Amelia specifications to my attention.

12. Papers Relating to the Construction of the Courthouse, Nov. 28, 1766, Amelia Co. Loose Papers, Clerk's Office, Amelia, Va.

13. Carl Lounsbury, "The Development of Domestic Architecture in the Albemarle Region," *North Carolina Historical Review* 54 (Winter 1977): 22.

14. Northampton Co. OB 1689–98, 33, May 28, 1690; Princess Anne Co. OB 1691–1709, 43, Sept. 27, 1692.

15. Augusta Co. OB 1748–51, 34, May 21, 1748; Botetourt Co. OB 1770–71, 44, Apr. 11, 1770;

Boyd Crumrine, ed., *Virginia Court Records in Southwestern Pennsylvania: Records of the District of West Augusta and Ohio and Yohogania Counties, Virginia* (Baltimore, 1981), 91–92, 369.

16. Henry Co. OB 1778–82, 89, May 19, 1778; I. L. Terrell, "Courthouses of Rockingham County," *VC* 23 (Autumn 1973): 43.

17. *Va. Gaz., or the Winchester Advertiser*, Aug. 20, 1788, 3:3; Shenandoah Co. OB 1795–98, 53–54, May 15, 1795; Bath Co. OB 1791–1801, 301, 303, Nov. 8, 1796; Russell Co. OB 1799–1808, 6, June 26, 1799.

18. Ronald Brunskill and Alec Clifton-Taylor, *Brickwork* (New York, 1977); John Summerson, *Architecture in Britain, 1530 to 1830* (New York, 1970), 155–64.

19. In 1742 the vestry of Bruton Parish ordered that the "brick Ornaments of the Gavel ends to be taken down and finished with wood, answering the rest." Although the form of these ornaments is unknown, they must have stood upon parapets that could have been curvilinear or stepped. W. A. R. Goodwin, *The Record of Bruton Parish Church* (Richmond, 1941), 139.

20. Upton, *Holy Things and Profane*, 58–68.

21. "Report of Excavations Made in Jamestown in 1901 and 1902," in Cotter, *Archaeological Excavations at Jamestown, Virginia*, 224; Carl Lounsbury, Willie Graham, and Jonathan Prown, "The Architecture of 17th-Century English Catholicism: The Chapel at St. Mary's City, Maryland" (report for Historic St. Mary's City, Sept. 1993).

22. For brick building in colonial Virginia, see Upton, *Holy Things and Profane*, 103–5; Herbert A. Claiborne, *Comments on Virginia Brickwork before 1800* (Portland, Me., 1957); Calder Loth, "Notes on the Evolution of Virginia Brickwork from the Seventeenth Century to the Late Nineteenth Century," *APT Bulletin* 6 (1974): 82–120.

23. Spotsylvania Co. WB 1722–49, 276, Oct. 6, 1736; Lancaster Co. OB 1729–43, 287, Aug. 8, 1740.

24. Chesterfield Co. Miscellaneous Records, 1805–42, May 15, 1805, LVA. I am grateful to Selden Richardson and Paul Shelton for drawing my attention to this reference.

25. Hening, *Statutes* 3:214.

26. Norfolk Co. OWB 1723–34, 60, Aug. 19, 1726; Charlotte Co. OB 1786–89, 82a, May 8, 1787.

27. "An Account of Repairs to the Courthouse," c. 1789, York Co. Loose Papers, Clerk's Office, Yorktown, Va.

28. For an argument in favor of a comprehensive proportional system based upon mathematical formulas, see Marcus Whiffen, *The Public Buildings of Williamsburg* (Williamsburg, Va., 1958), 80–81, 157; for a rebuttal, see Upton, *Holy Things and Profane*, 31. On eighteenth-century English builders' use of proportion in speculative building, see Dan Cruickshank and Neil Burton, *Life in the Georgian City* (New York, 1990), 134–49.

29. Rappahannock Co. OB 1683–86, 131, May 7, 1685; Bertie County, N.C., MB 1740–62, 172, Nov. 11, 1741.

30. Henry Co. Loose Papers, Dec. 15, 1793, Clerk's Office, Martinsville, Va.; Truro Parish VB 1732–88, 115–17, Sept. 21, 1769.

31. For examples of brickwork specifications, see Spotsylvania Co. WB 1722–49, 276, Oct. 6, 1736; Lancaster Co. OB 1729–43, 287, Aug. 8, 1740; Surry Co. OB 1764–74, 51–52, Feb. 19, 1765; *Va. Gaz.* (P), May 16, 1777, 3:3.

32. Norfolk Co. OWB 1723–34, 60, Aug. 19, 1726.

33. Rockbridge Co. WB no. 1, 296, Dec. 7, 1785; Shenandoah Co. OB 1795–98, 53–54, May 15, 1795.

34. Paul Turner, *Campus, an American Planning Tradition* (Cambridge, Mass., 1984), 12–15; *The Canterbury Quadrangle, 1636–1936* (Oxford, 1936).

35. Quoted in Harold Hutchinson, *Sir Christopher Wren* (New York, 1976), 89; see also Kerry Downs, *The Architecture of Wren* (New York, 1982), 74–75.

36. For the English market house as a building type, see Mark Girouard, *The English Town: A History of Urban Life* (New Haven, 1990), 9–30; David W. Lloyd, *The Making of English Towns* (London, 1984), 196–98; Peter Borsay, *The English Urban Renaissance: Culture and Society in the Provincial Town, 1660–1770* (Oxford, 1989), 104–9.

37. For the emergence of the town hall and market house as a distinctive building type and the political and social significance of such structures in Tudor England, see Robert Tittler, *Architecture and Power: The Town Hall and the English Urban Community, c. 1500–1640* (Oxford, 1991); Clare Graham, *Ordering Laws: The Architectural and Social History of the English Law Court to 1914* (Aldershot, Eng., 2003), 35–71.

38. R. Gilyard-Beer, *The County Hall, Abingdon* (London, 1956), 2–5.

39. Whiffen, *Public Buildings of Williamsburg,* 18–33. Surprisingly, no other American college established during the colonial period incorporated an arcade in its design. Turner, *Campus,* 17–51.

40. On the possible influence and role of Governor Nicholson in the planning of the Capitol, see James D. Kornwolf, "'Doing Good to Posterity': Francis Nicholson, First Patron of Architecture, Landscape Design, and Town Planning in Virginia, Maryland, and South Carolina, 1688–1725," *VMHB* 101 (July 1993): 348–52.

41. Due to a misreading of the documentary and archaeological evidence in its rebuilding of the Capitol in the early 1930s, the firm of Perry, Shaw, and Hepburn failed to reconstruct the west porch and divided the arcade space into two north and south bays. See Carl Lounsbury, "Beaux-Arts Ideals and Colonial Reality: The Reconstruction of Williamsburg's Capitol, 1928–1934," *JSAH* 49 (Dec. 1990): 373–89.

42. Whiffen, "The Early Courthouses of Virginia," 4; "Travel Journal of William Hugh Grove," 22.

43. Spotsylvania Co. WB 1722–49, 276, Oct. 6, 1736.

44. Following a fire in September 1988, the Charles City County courthouse was stripped of its plasterwork. Investigations by members of the Architectural Research Department of the Colonial Williamsburg Foundation revealed that the wall that separated the jury rooms and front of the courtroom from the arcade was originally plastered. In contrast to the exposed brickwork elsewhere that is laid in regular Flemish bond with scribed mortar joints, this wall, like the inside of the arcade piers, was built of rough random brickwork, which argues that this space was always intended to be covered.

45. *American Architect and Building News,* June 23, 1877, 199.

46. Lancaster Co. OB 1696–1702, 100a, Dec. 14, 1699.

47. Richmond Co. OB 1739–52, 257, Aug. 6, 1750.

48. Berkeley Co. OB 1772–73, 360, Aug. 17, 1773; OB 1777–79, 64, Mar. 18, 1778.

49. Rockingham Co. OB 1791–94, 4, Jan. 25, 1791. The design plan of the building does not clearly distinguish how the 10-foot space before the front of the courtroom wall was to be treated. See Terrell, "Courthouses of Rockingham County," 44.

50. Nelson Co. OB 1808–11, 21, Oct. 24, 1808.

51. Dorchester Co., Md., LRB 1669–83, 148–49, Dec. 6, 1686; Lancaster Co. OB 1696–1702, 100a, Dec. 14, 1699.

52. *JHB* 3:272–73.

53. Jefferson, *Notes on the State of Virginia,* 152–53.

54. Latrobe, April 5, 1796, in Edward C. Carter II, ed., *Virginia Journals of Benjamin Henry Latrobe, 1795–1798,* 2 vols. (New Haven, 1977), 1:87.

55. Jefferson quoted in Fiske Kimball, *The Capitol of Virginia* (Richmond, 1989), 11; Mark R. Wenger, "Thomas Jefferson and the Virginia State Capitol," *VMHB* 101 (Jan. 1993): 97–99.

56. Prince Edward Co. OB 1771–81, 196, 477, Dec. 21, 1772, July 17, 1775; Westmoreland Co. OB 1676–89, 145, Dec. 4, 1678; Prince Edward Co. OB 1767–70, 7, May 5, 1767.

57. Only two courthouse roofs are known to have had anything other than a common-rafter truss system. The hipped roof of the c. 1730 King William County courthouse is supported by a series of slender king posts that are secured into principal rafters. Staggered butt purlins are mortised into the principal rafters. Segmented common rafters are lapped to the back side of the purlins. Before it was altered in the 1870s, the roof of the 1750 Richmond County courthouse, which spanned 41 feet, had a similar truss system. Two 8-by-8-inch white oak king posts supported principal rafters, which in turn carried 6-by-5-inch purlins. As in the King William courthouse roof, smaller 3-by-3½-inch common rafters extended in segments from purlin to purlin. For a description of the Richmond County courthouse roof, see *American Architect and Building News,* June 23, 1877, 199.

58. Westmoreland Co. OB 1731–39, 179, July 30, 1735; Richmond Co. OB 1732–39, 51, Jan. 8, 1735.

59. "Surry County Grievances," *VMHB* 2 (Oct. 1894): 172.

60. Richmond Co. OB 1699–1704, 261–62, June 3, 1703; Spotsylvania Co. OB 1738–49, 86, 105, June 3, Oct. 7, 1740; Westmoreland Co. OB 1731–38, 220–20a, Dec. 28, 1736.

61. See Neil McKendrick, John Brewer, and J. H. Plumb, eds., *The Commercialization of Eighteenth Century England* (Bloomington, Ind., 1982); Carole Shammas, *The Pre-industrial Consumer in England and America* (Oxford, 1990); and John Brewer and Roy Porter, eds., *Consumption and the World of Goods* (New York, 1993).

62. Carson, "The Consumer Revolution in Colonial British America: Why Demand?" 483–697.

63. On the significance of public building in late seventeenth-century provincial England, see Borsay, *The English Urban Renaissance,* 101–13, 325–28; Girouard, *The English Town,* 26–30, 45–56; Graham, *Ordering Law,* 58–68.

64. *JHB* 4:29.

65. Marcus Whiffen has suggested that the apsidal ends of the new Capitol, which had little precedent in English public building, may have derived from the tribune of a Roman basilica, which was used in antiquity as the seat of magistrates. Whiffen, *Public Buildings of Williamsburg,* 36–37. The use of an apsidal tribune, while unusual in English public building, was nonetheless developed by Inigo Jones in his unexecuted design for the King's Star Chamber in the Palace of Westminster in 1617. Yet few public buildings were erected in Great Britain before the Williamsburg Capitol, which had the tribune expressed as a curved exterior wall. Robert Tavernor, *Palladio and Palladianism* (London, 1991), 128–29.

66. In the 1930s limited research and an unfamiliarity with early English courtrooms led the members of the architectural firm of Perry, Shaw, and Hepburn, who designed the

courtroom in the reconstructed Capitol, to misinterpret the cryptic recommendations of 1703. They took the words "Seats of Benches" to mean individual seats of chairs rather than a fixed bench. The architects reasoned that chairs would have been more comfortable since General Court "sessions were often quite lengthy." A quick study of late seventeenth-century seating for English magistrates or even later examples from Virginia would have corrected this view. It is extremely rare to find eighteenth-century references to Virginia magistrates sitting in chairs on a raised platform.

A second and more fundamental mistake was the architects' inability to decipher the instructions for "the Circular part thereof to be rais'd from the seat up to the windows." They interpreted it as being practically meaningless; what they failed to understand about this elliptic phrase was that the word "paneling" had been omitted. The colonial committee had intended for the courtroom to be paneled only the 3½ or 4 feet between the top of the bench and the lower part of the windows. Based on a 1705 specification for the "wanscote" to be painted "Like Marble," the reconstruction architects decided to construct floor-to-ceiling raised paneling with Ionic pilasters throughout the entire courtroom. They recognized that the term *wainscot* was applied in the eighteenth century to all heights of wooden wall paneling but felt that rooms in the Capitol used by the governor and council would have been richly decorated. The splendid woodwork installed in the 1930s sadly mitigates the contrast that the colonial builders had intended between an ornamented bench and a much plainer public space. For a detailed study of the problems involved in the restoration of the Capitol by the Colonial Williamsburg Foundation, see Lounsbury, "Beaux-Arts Ideals and Colonial Reality."

67. Norfolk Co. OWB 1723–34, 60, Aug. 19, 1726; Spotsylvania Co. WB 1722–49, 276, Oct. 6, 1736.

68. Essex Co. WDB no. 10, 109, Apr. 11, 1702; Middlesex Co. OB 1694–1705, 570, July 3, 1704; Norfolk Co. OWB 1723–34, 60, Aug. 19, 1726; Amelia Co. DB 1789–91, 336–37, Feb. 23, 1791; *American Architect and Building News,* June 23, 1877, 199; Amelia Co. Loose Papers Relating to the Courthouse, May 29, 1767, Clerk's Office, Amelia, Va.; Prince George's Co., Md., CRB no. 10, 1734–35, 667–68; Lancaster Co. OB 1729–43, 287, Aug. 8, 1740.

69. Fluvanna Co. Loose Papers Relating to the Courthouse, Mar. 24, 1802, box 36A, Fluvanna County Jail, Palmyra, Va.

70. See, for example, Loudoun Co. OB 1757–62, 142–43, Aug. 9, 1758.

71. Norfolk Co. OWB 1723–34, 60, Aug. 19, 1726.

72. Richmond Co. AB 1798–1806, 155, May 7, 1806; Lancaster Co. OB 1811–18, 164, Aug. 11, 1813; Southampton Co. OB 1814–16, 269, Jan. 16, 1816.

73. Amelia Co. Loose Papers Relating to the Courthouse, May 29, 1767; DB 1789–91, 336–37, Feb. 23, 1791.

74. Lancaster Co. OB 1729–43, 287, Aug. 8, 1740; Amelia Co. DB 1789–91, 336–37, Feb. 23, 1791.

75. Fiske Kimball identified Jefferson's unnamed design as a plan for the Buckingham County courthouse. A scholar has recently suggested that the plan is instead for the courthouse in nearby Charlotte County. Fiske Kimball, *Thomas Jefferson, Architect* (Boston, 1916; reprint, New York, 1968), pls. 214–15; Delos Hughes, "The Charlotte County Courthouse: Attribution and Misattribution in Jefferson Studies," *Arris* 4 (1993): 8–18.

76. *EJC* 6:411.

77. Spotsylvania Co. WB 1722–49, 276, Oct. 1736.

78. "An Account of Repairs to the Courthouse," c. 1789, York Co. Loose Papers.

79. *JHB* 4:30; *LJC* 2:681; Richmond Co. OB 1769–73, 288, June 9, 1771; Princess Anne Co. MB 1773–82, Jan. 13, 1774.

80. Petsworth Parish in Gloucester County paid more than £103 in 1751 for importing crimson velvet ornaments with good fringe and lace for its pulpit cloth and altar hangings. Upton, *Holy Things and Profane,* 152–53. At Christ Church in Philadelphia, the pulpit was ornamented by cloth, cushion, and tassels valued at £80. Bruce Gill, "Christ Church in Philadelphia: Furnishings, the Early Years," in *Christ Church, Philadelphia: Arts, Architecture, Archives* (Philadelphia, 1981), 130–31.

81. *JHB* 1:254.

82. Lancaster Co. OB 1696–1702, 100a, Dec. 14, 1699; Westmoreland Co. OB 1705–21, 49, Mar. 28, 1707.

83. In 1740 the justices of Caroline County decided to pay Bridges "the same rate he hath been paid by other County Courts" for painting the king's arms. Caroline Co. OB 1732–40, 595, Apr. 11, 1740.

84. Carved coats of arms appeared in other provinces. For example, in the fall of 1765, Philadelphia carver Nicholas Bernard arrived in the port of Charleston and offered for a sale "the King's Coat-of-Arms carved in wood, suitable for a State House or Court-House." Apparently the provincial government purchased this handiwork from him for the council chamber of the statehouse. *South Carolina Gazette,* Oct. 12, 1765, 1:2; Journal of the [South Carolina] Commons House of Assembly, no. 37, pt. 2, 526–27, Feb. 23, 1768, South Carolina Division of Archives and History, Columbia. For the decoration of the council chamber, see Carl Lounsbury, *From Statehouse to Courthouse: An Architectural History of South Carolina's Colonial Capitol and Charleston County Courthouse* (Columbia, S.C., 2001), 38–43.

85. In 1832 a visitor to the Nelson County courthouse in Lovingston observed that on the wall above the magistrates' platform "there was emblazoned the coat of arms of the United States." John E. Semmes, *John H. B. Latrobe and His Times, 1803–1891* (Baltimore, 1917), 265.

86. Chowan Co., N.C., MB 1766–72, 371, June 21, 1768; Caroline Co., Md., MB No. 7, 1801; *Impartial Review and Cumberland Repository* (Nashville), Aug. 25, 1808, 3:2.

87. Middlesex Co. OB 1705–10, 262, Oct. 3, 1709; Lancaster Co. OB 1702–13, 258, Dec. 13, 1710; OB 1729–43, 287, Aug. 8, 1740.

88. Fluvanna Co. Loose Papers; "Specifications for the Goochland Co. Courthouse: Agreement with Dabney Cosby and Valentine Parrish," Jan. 17, 1826, John Hartwell Cocke Papers, UVA.

89. Prince Georges Co., Md., CRB 5, no. 10, 1734–35, 667–68.

90. Goochland Co. OB 1772–78, 395–96, Nov. 16, 1773; "Specifications for the Goochland Co. Courthouse," Jan. 17, 1826, Cocke Papers, UVA.

91. Middlesex Co. OB 1694–1705, 570, July 3, 1704.

92. See, for example, Westmoreland Co. OB 1739–43, 46a, Apr. 9, 1740; Louisa Co. OB 1742–48, 82, Oct. 10, 1743.

93. Spotsylvania Co. OB 1738–49, 275, Aug. 7, 1744.

94. "An Account of Repairs to the Courthouse," c. 1789, York Co. Loose Papers.

95. An 1849 specification for yet another Amelia courthouse required the box to be elevated 2 feet. "Papers Relating to the Construction of the Amelia Court House," June 16, 1849, Clerk's Office, Amelia, Va.

96. Fluvanna County Loose Papers.

97. John H. Langbein, *The Origins of Adversary Criminal Trial* (Oxford, 2003).

98. *Negrin's Directory and Almanac for the Year 1806* (Charleston, S.C., 1806).

99. William Munford, *Poems and Compositions in Prose on Several Occasions* (Richmond, 1798), 146.

100. Jack Greene, ed., *The Diary of Colonel Landon Carter* (Charlottesville, Va., 1965), 406; Roeber, *Faithful Magistrates and Republican Lawyers; Va. Gaz.* (PD), Dec. 29, 1768, 2:3.

101. George Webb, *The Office and Authority of a Justice of Peace* (Williamsburg, Va., 1736), ix; *Diary of Colonel Landon Carter,* 726–27.

102. "Observations in Several Voyages and Travels in America," *London Magazine,* July 1746, quoted in *WMQ,* 1st ser., 15 (Jan. 1907): 147; W. Hamilton Bryson, *Legal Education in Virginia, 1779–1979* (Charlottesville, Va., 1982), 1–20.

103. Essex Co. OB 1736–38, 174, Nov. 21, 1737; "An Account of Repairs to the Courthouse," c. 1789, York Co. Loose Papers; Amelia Co. DB 1789–91, 336–37, Feb. 23, 1791.

104. "Specifications for the Goochland Co. Courthouse," Jan. 17, 1826, Cocke Papers, UVA.

105. Two nineteenth-century witness stands survive in Rhode Island. One stand, dated 1841, is in the courtroom on the second floor of the Old Colony House in Newport. A slightly later one survives in the old courthouse in the town of Bristol.

106. Charles Lanman, ed., *Journal of Alfred Ely, a Prisoner of War in Richmond* (New York, 1862), 10. I am indebted to Noel Harrison for bringing this reference to my attention.

107. Articles of agreement for building the Madison County courthouse, June 1829, Malcolm Crawford Papers, LVA.

108. Besides the introduction of a prisoner's box, this plan for the first Warren County courthouse of 1836 shows other variations from the standard late colonial plan. The clerk's table was moved from its central location below the magistrates' platform and in front of the jury bench to a raised platform extending out from the magistrates' bench on the other side of the courtroom opposite the prisoner's box. The design also featured an enclosed staircase rising behind the magistrates' bench leading to two jury rooms on the second floor, which allowed the jury to "pass from their bench . . . directly to their rooms, without passing through the crowd, being then secured from any interference whatever." Warren Co. Miscellaneous Records, Historical Papers, acc. 37588, 37589, LVA. I am grateful to Selden Richardson and the staff of the Circuit Court Records Preservation Program at the Library of Virginia for bringing these drawings and specifications to my attention.

109. Richmond Co. OB 1769–73, 231, Mar. 4, 1771; Loudoun Co. OB 1767–70, 97, Aug. 9, 1768.

110. "Papers Relating to the Construction of the Amelia Court House," June 16, 1849; Goochland Co. OB 1852–62, 268, Feb. 16, 1857; Warren Co. Miscellaneous Records, LVA.

111. Richmond Co. BSMB 1870–86, 91, 93, Apr. 5, May 10, June 4, 1877; *American Architect and Building News,* June 23, 1877, 199.

4. The Public Building Process in Early Virginia

1. See, for example, letters to the constable of the town of Northfield, Hampshire County, Mass., Oct. 12, 1761, May 24, 1763, March 7, 1769, Society of the Preservation of New England Antiquities Library, Boston.

2. Accomack Co. OB 1676–78, 71, Nov. 20, 1677; Northampton Co. OB 1674–79, 203, Nov. 26, 1677; *EJC* 4:366, 396, Dec. 10, 1735, June 16, 1737.

3. Essex Co. OB 1703–8, 134–35, Dec. 11, 1704; OB 1716–23, 109, Jan. 24, 1718; OB 1726–29, 244, July 17, 1728; OB 1745–47, 3, 21, Apr. 16, May 21, 1745; OB 1747–49, 121, Nov. 17, 1747; OB 1751–52,

117, 131, Nov. 19, 1751, Jan. 21, 1752; OB 1762–63, 9, 37, Feb. 15, Mar. 17, 1762; OB 1767–70, 34, Nov. 16, 1767; OB 1770–72, 13, Nov. 19, 1770; *Va. Gaz.*, Feb. 28, 1751, 4:1; (PD), June 4, 1767, 4:1.

4. Upton, *Holy Things and Profane*, 13.

5. Martha W. Hiden, *How Justice Grew: Virginia Counties, an Abstract of Their Formation* (Charlottesville, Va., 1957), 32; Cumberland Co. OB 1774–78, 435, Mar. 23, 1778; Halifax Co. OB 1774–79, 195, Feb. 20, 1777; Lunenburg Co. OB 1777–84, 89, Sept. 4, 1782; Pittsylvania Co. OB 1777–83, 403, 416, May 21, July 17, 1782; Rockbridge Co. OB 1778–84, 77–78, Apr. 7, 1779; Spotsylvania Co. OB 1774–82, Mar. 18, 1779.

6. Frederick Co. OB 1772–78, 479, May 4, 1778; *CVS* 2:332–33, 666; *WMQ*, 1st ser., 7 (1899): 277; Chesterfield Co. Legislative Petition, Dec. 15, 1781, LVA; Chesterfield Co. OB 1774–78, 319, May 8, 1781: Riley, "Colonial Courthouses of York County," 404.

7. Quoted in William Rasmussen, "Designers, Builders, and Architectural Traditions in Colonial Virginia," *VMHB* 90 (Apr. 1982): 202.

8. See Calder Loth, "Palladio in Southside Virginia: Brandon and Battersea," and William Rasmussen, "Palladio in Tidewater Virginia: Mount Airy and Blandfield," in *Building by the Book* 1, ed. Mario di Valmarana (Charlottesville, Va., 1984), 25–46, 75–109; Gene Waddell, "The First Monticello," *JSAH* 46 (Mar. 1987): 5–29. For the architectural books that circulated in the colony in the eighteenth century, see Bennie Brown, "The Ownership of Architecture Books in Colonial Virginia," in *American Architects and Their Books to 1848*, ed. Kenneth Hafertepe and James F. O'Gorman (Amherst, Mass., 2001), 17–33.

9. John Carter to Charles Carter, Aug. 26, 1738, Plummer-Carter Letterbook, UVA. I am indebted to Mark R. Wenger for bringing this reference to my attention.

10. Richmond Co. OB 1746–52, 207, Nov. 6, 1749; Brown, "The Ownership of Architecture Books in Colonial Virginia," 18; *Diary of Colonel Landon Carter*, 457–58.

11. Charles City Co. OB 1758–62, 7, Nov. 1, 1758.

12. Chesterfield Co. OB 1774–78, 154, Dec. 5, 1777.

13. Charlotte Co. OB 1780–84, 35, Mar. 4, 1782; Powhatan Co. OB 1777–84, 53, July 16, 1778.

14. *Va. Gaz.* (R), Jan. 31, 1771, 3:1.

15. Loudoun Co. OB 1757–62, 142–43, Aug. 9, 1758; Bedford Co. OB 1763–71, 270–71, July 23, 1766; *Va. Gaz.* (PD), Aug. 8, 1766, 3:2.

16. Isle of Wight Co. OB 1746–52, 201, 239, Dec. 7, 1749, June 7, 1750.

17. Fauquier Co. OB 1759–62, 12, June 28, 1759; Westmoreland Co. OB 1747–50, 101, 102a, Nov. 30, 1748, Jan. 31, 1749.

18. Lancaster Co. OB 1729–43, 322, Aug. 14, 1741; Isle of Wight Co. OB 1746–52, 345, Aug. 1, 1751.

19. Amelia Co. OB 1760–63, 355, Nov. 26, 1762; OB 1764–65, 278–79, Oct. 25, 1764; OB 1766–69, 32, Nov. 28, 1766; Papers Relating to the Courthouse, Nov. 28, 1766, Amelia County Loose Papers.

20. Papers Relating to the Courthouse, May 29, 1767, Amelia County Loose Papers .

21. Amelia Co. OB 1765–67, 171, May 29, 1767; OB 1767–68, 328, Sept. 23, 1768.

22. Charlotte Co. OB 1784–86, 89, June 7, 1785; Spotsylvania Co. OB 1738–49, 275, Aug. 4, 1744.

23. Brunswick Co. OB 1745–49, 42, July 3, 1746; Edmund Berkeley, "New Light on Albemarle County Courthouse," *Magazine of Albemarle County History* 29 (1971): 64–66.

24. Northampton Co. OB 1689–98, 33, May 28, 1690; Caroline Co. OB 1759–63, 93, Jan. 10, 1760; Fauquier Co. OB 1759–62, 96–97, Aug. 29, 1760.

25. Louisa Co. OB 1742–48, 32, Apr. 11, 1743; Albemarle Co. OB 1744–48, 22–23, June 27, 1745; Loudoun Co. OB 1757–62, 142–43, Aug. 9, 1758; Elizabeth City Co. DOWB 1715–21, 58, Feb. 21, 1717.

26. Brunswick Co. OB 1745–49, 42, July 3, 1746; Chesterfield Co. OB 1749–54, 6, July 7, 1749; Berkeley, "Albemarle County Courthouse," 64.

27. Lancaster Co. OB 1696–1702, 53a, 100a, Nov. 24, 1698, Dec. 14, 1699; Richmond Co. OB 1746–52, 159, 207, Mar. 6, Nov. 6, 1749; For the struggle between Wormeley and the Middlesex magistrates, see Rutman, *A Place in Time*, 211–17.

28. Essex Co. Suit Papers, Apr. 11, 1702. Dell Upton has noted a similar appearance in the use of drawings for Virginia churches about the same time. Upton, *Holy Things and Profane*, 32–33.

29. Marcus Whiffen, *The Eighteenth-Century Houses of Williamsburg* (Williamsburg, Va., 1960), 30.

30. See, for example, Fauquier Co. OB 1763–67, 111, Apr. 24, 1764; Orange Co. Loose Papers, Nov. 28, 1765, LVA.

31. For a view that emphasizes the common if not ubiquitous use of plans in the design of nearly all structures no matter how humble, see Dell Upton, "Pattern Books and Professionalism: Aspects of the Transformation of Domestic Architecture in America, 1800–1860," *Winterthur Portfolio* 19 (Summer/Autumn 1984): 109.

32. *Md. Gaz.* Nov. 3, 1774, 3:2. I am indebted to Donna Ware for providing this reference.

33. Prince William Co. DB 1787–91, 101–3, Apr. 9, 1788.

34. This discussion of the Gunston Hall courthouse sketches is based on my article "'An Elegant and Commodious Building': William Buckland and the Design of the Prince William County Courthouse," *JSAH* 46 (Sept. 1987): 228–40.

35. York Co. OWB 1694–98, 350, Jan. 25, 1697.

36. Charles City Co. OB 1672–73, 505, Feb. 4, 1673; *VMHB* 3 (Oct. 1895): 143.

37. Augusta Co. Loose Papers, Court Judgments, bundle 1750 (A), May 1750, LVA. I would like to thank Turk McCleskey for this information.

38. Elizabeth City Co. OB 1731–47, 363, Dec. 22, 1743; *Va. Gaz.*, July 6, 1764, 3:2; ibid. (PD), Sept. 28, 1769, 3:2; Westmoreland Co. OB 1747–50, 102a, Jan. 31, 1749.

39. Surry Co. OB 1753–57, 366, Feb. 17, 1756; *VMHB* 8 (Jan. 1901): 257. In 1757 Clinch was expelled from the House of Burgesses for his violent behavior toward a man whom he owed a debt.

40. Bedford Co. OB 1754–58, 3–4, 190, May 27, 1754, Mar. 29, 1757; DB A, 434, Mar. 28, 1757.

41. John Tayloe III, MB 1811–12, Tayloe Family Papers, VHS; Richmond Co. OB 1816–20, 4, June 3, 1816.

42. Ralph Happel, "Stafford and King George Courthouses," *VMHB* 66 (Apr. 1958): 185–86; Berkeley, "Albemarle County Courthouse," 64–68. Moore may have been the same individual who contracted with Thomas Jefferson for landscaping in May 1768 in preparation for the construction of Monticello. Waddell, "The First Monticello," *JSAH* 46 (1987): 6; James A. Bear Jr. and Lucia C. Stanton, *Jefferson's Memorandum Books: Accounts, with Legal Records and Miscellany, 1767–1826*, 2 vols. (Princeton, N.J., 1997), 1:76.

43. Essex Co. Suit Papers, Apr. 11, 1702, LVA; VMHB 1 (Oct. 1893): 197.

44. Essex Co. OB 1726–29, 243a, 266, July 17, Sept. 18, 1728; Berkeley, "Albemarle County Courthouse," 66.

45. Accomack Co. OB 1737–44, 338, May 28, 1741; DB 1746–57, 252, Feb. 28, 1749; OB 1744–

53, 369, 455, Nov. 29, 1749, Nov. 29, 1750; DB 1746–57, 406, Jan. 31, 1752; OB 1753–63, 72, 103, 119, 140, 223, 230, 249, Dec. 16, 1754, July 30, Nov. 27, 1755, May 25, 1756, Feb. 1, Mar. 1, June 28, 1758; St. George's Parish VB 1763–87, 2, 15, 24, Apr. 4, 1763, Mar. 10, 1767, Mar. 24, 1768; Accomack Co. OB 1767–68, 397, Jan. 27, 1768; DB 1770–77, 283, Sept. 20, 1773; OB 1774–77, 253, July 29, 1774; DB 1777–83, 13, Feb. 6, 1777; WB 1772–77, 499–501, Feb. 7, 1777; OB 1774–77, 506, Mar. 25, 1777.

46. *Va. Gaz.*, May 16, 1755, 2:1; Upton, *Holy Things and Profane*, 17.

47. King George Co. OJB 1721–34, 382, 427, 466, 576, 617, 635, Oct. 7, 1727, Nov. 1, 1728, Oct. 3, 1729, Nov. 5, 1731, Nov. 3, 1732, Oct. 14, 1733, July 5, 1734; IB 1721–44, 306, July 6, 1744; OB 1735–51, 98, 173, 216, Mar. 4, 1737, Dec. 1, 1738, Nov. 2, 1739; DB 1735–44, 239–40, Mar. 2, 1738; Richmond Co. OB 1732–39, 563, Nov. 7, 1737; John Mercer LB 1725–32, Oct. 5, 1730, quoted in Malcolm Watkins, *The Cultural History of Marlborough, Virginia* (Washington, D.C., 1968), 18; Richmond Co. OB 1739–46, 306, Mar. 7, 1743.

48. King George Co. DB 1735–44, 295–97, Mar. 7, 1739; IB 1721–44, 306, July 6, 1744; Christ Church Parish VB 1739–86, 1, Nov. 26, 1739; Lancaster Co. OB 1729–43, 286–87, Aug. 8, 1740; Richmond Co. OB 1739–46, 296, 306, Feb. 8, Mar. 7, 1743.

49. Spotsylvania Co. WB 1798–1801, 303, Sept. 16, 1801.

50. See R. K. Brock, *Archibald Cary of Ampthill* (Richmond, 1937), 1–4.

51. For the rise of genteel culture in the American colonies, see Bushman, *Refinement of America.*

52. *Md. Gaz.*, May 15, 1751. It was this advertisement and other circumstantial stylistic evidence that led Thomas Waterman to believe that John Ariss was responsible for the design of many major gentry houses in northern Virginia. However, very few buildings can be firmly attributed to Ariss. Waterman, *Mansions of Virginia*, 243–48; Lounsbury, "John Ariss."

53. *Md. Gaz.*, May 15, 1751. See also *Va. Gaz.* (PD), Dec. 28, 1769, 3:1.

54. Rosamond Beirne and John Scarff, *William Buckland: Architect of Virginia and Maryland* (Baltimore, 1958), 142.

55. On the demand for skilled indentured and convict laborers in the Chesapeake, see Bernard Bailyn, *Voyagers to the West* (New York, 1986), 264–66. On the character of convicts transported to the colonies and the operation of the trade in Maryland, see Roger Ekirch, "Bound for America: A Profile of British Convicts Transported to the Colonies, 1718–1775," and Kenneth Morgan, "The Organization of the Convict Trade to Maryland: Stevenson, Randolph & Cheston, 1768–1775," *WMQ*, 3d ser., 42 (Apr. 1985): 184–227.

56. *Va. Gaz.* (PD), Mar. 3, 1774, 3:1.

57. Ibid. (R), June 15, 1769, 3:3, July 26, 1770, 2:3; *Md. Gaz.*, Sept. 23, 1773, 3:2, Dec. 16, 1773, 2:3, Mar. 17, 1774, 3:3, Apr. 3, 1774.

58. *Va. Gaz.* (PD), Dec. 21, 1769, 2:3.

59. *Alexandria Herald*, May 4, 1818, 3:1. For Sears's career and carving, see Luke Beckerdite, "William Buckland and William Bernard Sears: The Designer and the Carver," *Journal of Early Southern Decorative Arts* 8 (Nov. 1982): 7–41.

60. *Va. Gaz.*, Dec. 17, 1736, 4:2; (D), July 29, 1776, 7:1; (P), June 23, 1775, 3:1.

61. Ibid. (P), Sept. 15, 1775, 3:2, Dec. 30, 1773, 3:1, June 23, 1775, 3:1, June 9, 1738, 4:1, July 6, 1739, 4:2; *South-Carolina Gazette*, Oct. 27, 1739.

62. *Va. Gaz.* (P), Aug. 15, 1777, 3:1; (D), Aug. 15, 1777, 6:2, Dec. 11, 1779, 3:1.

63. For the influence of Palladian theories of proportion on English speculative building, see Cruickshank and Burton, *Life in the Georgian City*, 134–49.

64. For a list of these books, see Bennie Brown, "The Library of William Buckland," in *Buckland: Master Builder of the 18th Century* (Gunston Hall, Va., 1977), 27–40.

65. King George Co. IB 1721–44, July 6, 1744.

66. Virginia Gazette Day Book 1751–52, 123, CWF; *Va. Gaz.*, May 24, 1751, 3:2, Sept. 19, 1751, 3:2; (PD), July 18, 1771, 3:3, Sept. 17, 1772, 2:1.

67. Watkins, *Cultural History of Marlborough*, 25, 28; *Va. Gaz.*, July 6, 1739, 4:2.

68. John Mercer LB, 1725–32, Bucks Co. Historical Society, Doylestown, Pa., copy at LVA, 82.

69. William Walker married Elizabeth Netherton on Aug. 17, 1731, in St. Paul's Parish, Stafford County. She died six years later at the age of twenty-nine. John Bailey Calvert Nicklin, *St. Paul's Parish Register, Stafford and King George Co., Va., 1715–1798* (Baltimore, 1962), 64. Her gravestone is in the churchyard at St. Paul's Church, now in King George County after a shift in the county boundary.

70. C. G. Chamberlayne, ed., *The Vestry Book of St. Paul's Parish, Hanover County, Virginia* (Richmond, 1940), 157, 163; C. G. Chamberlayne, ed., *The Vestry Book of St. Peter's Parish, New Kent and James City Counties* (Richmond, 1937), 182.

71. Richmond Co. OB 1739–46, 96, July 7, 1740; AB 1724–83, 153, Aug. 4, 1740; Westmoreland Co. OB 1739–43, 120a, Aug. 25, 1741; RB 1723–46, 297, June 25, 1744; OB 1743–47, 35, June 26, 1744; *JHB* 7:312, 203.

72. Westmoreland Co. OB 1747–50, 37a, 102a, 157a, Sept. 29, 1747, Jan. 31, Sept. 26, 1749.

73. A nineteenth-century transcript of a receipt dated May 21, 1747, notes the payment of £200 from Charles Carter, "being the last payment due to Mr. William Walker for building and finishing Cleve House." Minor Collection-Carter Family Papers, box 8, James Monroe Law Office Museum, Fredericksburg.

74. John Mercer LB 1741–50, Bucks Co. Historical Society, copy at LVA, 9; *JHB* 7:312; Watkins, *Cultural History of Marlborough*, 34–36; Whiffen, *Public Buildings of Williamsburg*, 134–35; Ralph Fall, ed., *The Diary of Robert Rose* (Verona, Va., 1977), 73; Stafford Co. WB 1748–63, 83–84, Feb. 7, 1750.

75. Deposition of Landon Carter, Aug. 2, 1770, Carter Family Papers, 1659–97, Sabine Hall Collection, College of William and Mary, Williamsburg; *Vestry Book of St. Peter's Parish*, 182, Apr. 12, 1740; Richmond Co. OB 1739–46, 96, July 7, 1740; AB 1724–83, 153, Aug. 4, 1740; Westmoreland Co. OB 1739–43, 120a, Aug. 25, 1741; IB 1746–52, 35, Aug. 25, 1747.

76. *EJC* 5:192, 199; Gertrude Gray, ed., *Virginia Northern Neck Land Grants*, 4 vols. (Baltimore, 1987), 1:134; Stafford Co. WB 1748–63, 83–84, Feb. 7, 1750; *Va. Gaz.*, Oct. 17, 1751, 4:2; *Diary of Robert Rose*, 6; John Mercer LB B, Travel Itinerary.

77. Stafford Co. WB 1748–63, 83–84, Feb. 7, 1750; *Va. Gaz.*, Oct. 17, 1751, 4:2.

5. Punishment and Prisons

1. Norfolk Common Hall OB 1736–98, June 24, 1747.

2. Two years later Seale petitioned the court for clemency after being convicted of horse theft. Even though it was Seale's fourth appearance before the General Court, the president of the council pardoned him after "several Gentlemen of Distinction" pleaded for his life. *Md. Gaz.*, July 26, 1749; *Va. Gaz.*, Apr. 18, 1751, 2:2, May 9, 1751, 3:1, Aug. 16, 1751, 3:1.

3. Norfolk Common Hall OB 1736–98, Mar. 19, 1753.

4. Quoted in Hugh Rankin, "Criminal Trial Proceedings in the General Court of Colonial Virginia," *VMHB* 72 (Jan. 1964): 57.

5. For the administration of criminal justice in colonial Virginia, see Peter Charles Hoffer and William B. Scott, eds., *Criminal Proceedings in Colonial Virginia: [Records of] Fines, Examination of Criminals, Trials of Slaves, etc., from March 1710 [1711] to [1754, Richmond County, Virginia]* (Athens, Ga., 1984).

6. Lancaster Co. OB 1655–66, 364, 369, Mar. 16, 1666.

7. Charge to the Grand Jury, Augusta Co., Aug. Court, 1787, Cabell Family Papers, College of William and Mary, Williamsburg.

8. *County Court Records, Accomack-Northampton, Virginia, 1632–1640*, ed. Susie M. Ames (Washington, D.C., 1954), 28, Feb. 19, 1635.

9. Hoffer and Scott, *Criminal Proceedings in Colonial Virginia*, xxvii.

10. For dissenters on the county benches in the Shenandoah Valley, see Warren Hofstra, "Ethnicity and Community Formation on the Shenandoah Valley Frontier, 1730–1800," and Turk McCleskey, "The Price of Conformity: Class, Ethnicity, and Local Authority on the Colonial Frontier," in *Diversity and Accommodation: Essays on the Cultural Composition of the Virginia Frontier*, ed. Michael J. Puglisi (Knoxville, Tenn., 1997), 68–71, 219–22.

11. Hening, *Statutes* 5:225, Sept. 1744.

12. Locke, *Second Treatise of Government*, 71.

13. Arthur Scott, *Criminal Law in Colonial Virginia* (Chicago, 1930), 321.

14. Roeber, *Faithful Magistrates and Republican Lawyers*, 93.

15. Orange Co. OB 1734–39, 181, June 23, 1737.

16. Hoffer and Scott, *Criminal Proceedings in Colonial Virginia*, 1.

17. Richmond Co. OB 1704–8, 258–59, Apr. 2, 3, 1707.

18. Orange Co. OB 1747–54, 231, Nov. 23, 1749; Westmoreland Co. OB 1743–47, 67a, Apr. 30, 1745.

19. *Va. Gaz.*, Aug. 20, 1737, 4:2; Accomack Co. OWB 1682–17, 141, Sept. 20, 1688.

20. Quoted in Edward Ayers, *Vengeance and Justice: Crime and Punishment in the Nineteenth-Century American South* (New York, 1984), 43.

21. Westmoreland Co. OB 1739–43, 93, Apr. 1, 1741; Louisa Co. OB 1742–48, 124, Nov. 24, 1744. For other instances, see ibid., 249, Feb. 23, 1748, and Henry Co. OB 1792–97, Apr. 28, 1795.

22. Hening, *Statutes* 2:75, Mar. 1662; Richmond Co. OB 1721–32, 171, Aug. 6, 1724; Northumberland Co. OB 1743–49, 380, Aug. 9, 1748; King George Co. OB 1766–70, 75, Aug. 6, 1767; Bedford Co. OB 1754–58, 166, May 3, 1756; Augusta Co. OB 1791–93, 346, Oct. 15, 1793.

23. See, for example, the irons on display in the guildhall, Sandwich, Kent, Eng.

24. *Va. Gaz.* (D), Jan. 6, 1776, 3:3. For other instances of branding, see Lancaster Co. OB 1729–43, 339, Apr. 19, 1742; OB 1764–67, 31, May 8, 1764; Fredericksburg District Court MB 1791–92, Oct. 10, 1792, College of William and Mary.

25. Hening, *Statutes* 2:75, Mar. 1662; Northampton Co. WDB 1718–25, 209, June 10, 1724.

26. Surry Co. OB 1671–91, 479, May 5, 1685; Charlotte Co. OB 1772–74, Apr. 6, 1773; Stafford Co. OB 1689–93, Oct. 7, 1691; Rappahannock Co. OB 1683–86, 56, Oct. 1, 1684.

27. Richmond Co. OB 1739–46, 12, June 5, 1739.

28. See, for example, Lancaster Co. OB 1729–43, 339, Apr. 19, 1742.

29. Northumberland Co. OB 1753–56, 488, Apr. 29, 1756.

30. Essex Co. OB 1759–61, 70, Aug. 20, 1759; Lancaster Co. ALCB 1793–1823, 112, Sept. 30, 1809; Joseph Jones and Charles Downing, "Capital Punishment in Colonial Virginia: Phase

III Data Recovery for Mitigation of Adverse Effects to Site 44WB66" (Technical Report Series no. 18, William and Mary Center for Archaeological Research, Dec. 2, 1992), 68–74; see also Alfred Marks, *Tyburn Tree: Its History and Annals* (London, 1908).

31. Orange Co. OB 1734–39, 181, June 23, 1737; Hoffer and Scott, *Criminal Proceedings in Colonial Virginia*, 134.

32. Essex Co. OB 1703–8, 382, Oct. 11, 1707; Lancaster Co. OB 1764–67, 75, Nov. 8, 1764; John Davis, *Travels of Four Years and a Half in the United States of America during 1798, 1799, 1800, 1801, and 1802* (London, 1803), 380.

33. For the use of *prison* and its synonyms in Virginia, see Carl Lounsbury, ed., *An Illustrated Glossary of Early Southern Architecture and Landscape* (New York, 1994), 50, 155, 193, 226, 291.

34. Hening, *Statutes* 1:265, Mar. 1643.

35. Essex Co. OB 1703–8, 134–35, Dec. 11, 1704; OB 1716–23, 109, Jan. 24, 1718; OB 1726–29, 244, July 17, 1728; OB 1745–47, 3, Apr. 16, 1745; OB 1747–49, 121, Nov. 17, 1747; *Va. Gaz.*, Feb. 28, 1751; Essex Co. OB 1751–52, 131, Jan. 21, 1752; OB 1762–63, 9, Feb. 15, 1762; *Va. Gaz.*, June 4, 1767, 4:1; Essex Co. OB 1767–70, 370, July 16, 1770; OB 1770–72, 13, 282, Nov. 19, 1770, Apr. 22, 1772; OB 1788–90, 63, June 17, 1788; Lower Norfolk Co. MB 1637–46 (transcript), 51, June 16, 1645, LVA; Stafford Co. OB 1689–93, Mar. 11, 1692.

36. Later examples of temporary prison quarters included the former clerk's office in Accomack County in 1705, a storehouse in Prince George County in 1720, the jury room in the Northumberland County courthouse in 1748 and again in 1756, and a joiner's shop in Essex County in 1762. All of these served as prisons until the old ones had been repaired or new ones erected in their place. Accomack Co. OB 1703–9, 58a, Dec. 7, 1704; Prince George Co. OB 1714–20, 335, Sept. 13, 1720; Northumberland Co. OB 1743–49, 275, Jan. 12, 1748; OB 1756–58, 7, May 10, 1756; Essex Co. OB 1762–63, 37, Mar. 17, 1762.

37. Northampton Co. OB 1657–64, 191, Apr. 29, 1664; Lancaster Co. OB 1655–66, 301, Oct. 27, 1664; Middlesex Co. OB 1673–80, 148, Nov. 4, 1678.

38. Hening, *Statutes* 1:265, Mar. 1643; Accomack Co. OB 1666–70, 30, July 16, 1667; Northumberland Co. OB 1678–98, 96, June 15, 1681.

39. Goochland Co. OB 1728–30, 242–43, 256, May 19, May 20, 1730; OB 1730–31, 177, Aug. 17, 1731; Accomack Co. OB 1719–24, 65a, Sept. 4, 1723.

40. *WMQ*, 1st ser., 26 (July 1917): 35.

41. Henrico Co. OB 1678–93, 190, June 10, 1685.

42. Ibid., 413, Mar. 21, 1692; Westmoreland Co. OB 1690–98, 215a, July 30, 1696; "Culpeper's Report on Virginia in 1683," *VMHB* 3 (Jan. 1896): 231. Even after prison architecture had improved considerably, prison escapes were still very common. In a fifteen-year period between 1766 and 1780, the *Virginia Gazette* noted more than eighty separate instances.

43. Hening, *Statutes* 1:340–41, Nov. 1647, 2:76–77, Mar. 1662.

44. Accomack Co. DOWB 1673–76, 155, July 17, 1674; Stafford Co. OB 1689–93, Feb. 11, 1692.

45. Lancaster Co. OB 1680–86, 4, July 14, 1680; Rappahannock Co. OB 1683–86, 130, May 7, 1685; Middlesex Co. DB 1687–1750, 10, Dec. 7, 1691; Surry Co. OB 1691–1713, 95, Nov. 21, 1693.

46. Westmoreland Co. OB 1705–21, 268, May 25, 1715; Princess Anne Co. MB 1717–28, 269, Nov. 3, 1726; Lancaster Co. OB 1743–52, 220a, June 8, 1750.

47. William L. Saunders, ed., *The Colonial Records of North Carolina*, 10 vols. (Raleigh, N.C., 1886–90), 1:300. For log building in this region, see Carl Lounsbury, "The Plague of Building: Construction Practices on the Frontier, 1650–1730," in Bishir et al., *Architects and Builders in North Carolina*, 18.

48. Northampton Co. OB 1689–98, 33, May 28, 1690; Princess Anne Co. OB 1691–1709, 43, Sept. 27, 1692.

49. In 1706 the Kent County, Delaware, magistrates ordered a new 15-by-20-foot prison built in Dover. Its walls were "to be of Oak Loggs Nine inches Thick the under loggs butt into the upper Swods [Swedes?] ffashion." Kent Co., Del., RB 1703–18, 51, Jan. 1706. I would like to thank Bernard Herman for bringing this reference to my attention.

50. Northampton Co. OB 1719–22, 36–37, Sept. 17, 1719.

51. King George Co. OB 1735–51, 500, Oct. 3, 1746; Westmoreland Co. OB 1747–50, 102a, Jan. 31, 1749.

52. Prince Edward Co. OB 1754–58, 65, Dec. 9, 1755; Botetourt Co. OB 1770–71, 44, Apr. 11, 1770; Augusta Co. OB 1748–51, 34, May 21, 1748.

53. *JHB* 2:53, Sept. 17, 1668. For the archaeological and documentary evidence about this site, see Audrey Horning, "A Verie Fit Place to Erect a Great Cittie": Comparative Contextual Analysis of Archaeological Jamestown" (Ph.D. diss., Univ. of Pennsylvania, 1995), 291–95.

54. *JHB* 2:152, 438, June 8, 1680, Mar. 24, 1693.

55. Norfolk Co. DB 1686–95, 46, Sept. 17, 1689.

56. Lancaster Co. OB 1696–1702, 53a, Nov. 24, 1698. For Queenstown, see Reps, *Tidewater Towns*, 89.

57. See, for example, specifications for the 1711 Westmoreland prison and the 1765 Orange prison. Westmoreland Co. OB 1705–21, 159, Apr. 27, 1711; Orange Co. Loose Court Papers, Nov. 28, 1765, LVA.

58. Lancaster Co. OB 1729–43, 287, Aug. 8, 1740.

59. *Va. Gaz.*, July 6, 1764, 3:2.

60. Orange Co. Loose Papers, Nov. 28, 1765. In 1774 Amherst County followed the example of Orange and ordered the construction of a brick prison with 3-foot-thick walls and a brick roof. *Va. Gaz.* (R), Aug. 11, 1774, 3:3.

61. William Byrd, "A Progress to the Mines in the Year 1732," in *The Prose Works of William Byrd of Westover*, ed. Louis B. Wright (Cambridge, Mass., 1966), 368.

62. Loudoun Co. OB 1765–67, 233, Jan. 12, 1767; Prince William Co. DB 1787–91, 101–3, Apr. 9, 1788.

63. Stafford Co. OB 1689–93, Feb. 11, 1692; Lancaster Co. OB 1696–1702, 53a, Nov. 24, 1698.

64. Quoted in Edward D. Neill, *Virginia Carolorum: The Colony under the Rule of Charles the First and Second, AD 1625–AD 1685* (Albany, 1886), 285–86. Victorian sensibilities led Neill, not George Wilson, the Quaker incarcerated in the prison, to delete the vulgarism.

65. Northumberland Co. OB 1753–56, 493, Apr. 12, 1756; Orange Co. Loose Papers, Nov. 28, 1765; Norfolk Co. OW 1723–34, July 23, 1733; Westmoreland Co. OB 1747–49, 102a, Jan. 31, 1749; Northumberland Co. OB 1753–56, 493, Apr. 12, 1756; Surry Co. OB 1754–57, 376, Apr. 20, 1756; Prince Edward Co. WB 1754–84, 393, Feb. 12, 1760.

66. Middlesex Co. OB 1732–37, 63–64, Mar. 2, 1736; Madison Co. OB 1793–98, 6, June 27, 1793; Surry Co. OB 1754–57, 376, Apr. 20, 1756; Westmoreland Co. OB 1752–55, 278a, June 24, 1755; York Co. DOWB 1706–10, 181–82, Dec. 24, 1708; King George Co. OJB 1721–34, 73, Dec. 8, 1722.

67. *CVS* 5:608, June 25, 1792.

68. See, for example, the specifications for Middlesex prison in 1736. Middlesex Co. OB 1732–37, 63–64, Mar. 2, 1736.

69. Westmoreland Co. OB 1747–49, 102a, Jan. 31, 1749; Northumberland Co. OB 1753–56, 493, Apr. 12, 1756. The Fauquier prison may also have had a grated opening in the door. Fauquier Co. OB 1759–62, 20, July 26, 1759.

70. Neill, *Virginia Carolorum,* 285.

71. Middlesex Co. DB 1687–1750, 10, Dec. 7, 1691. For magistrates' purchase of a close stool for the use of the prisoners, see. Cumberland Co. OB 1772–74, 501, Dec. 28, 1773.

72. Northumberland Co. OB 1753–56, 493, Apr. 12, 1756. For other examples of waste pipes in prison cell walls, see Northampton Co. OB 1719–22, 36–37, Sept. 17, 1719; Lancaster Co. OB 1729–43, 287, Aug. 8, 1740; King George Co. OB 1735–51, 500, Oct. 3, 1746; Northumberland Co. OB 1753–56, 493, Apr. 12, 1756; Loudoun Co. OB 1757–62, 305, Nov. 14, 1759; and Orange Co. Loose Papers, Nov. 28, 1765.

73. Westmoreland Co. OB 1747–50, 102a, Jan. 31, 1749.

74. See, for example, *Va. Gaz.* (Pi), Mar. 30, 1775, 3:2.

75. *CVS* 3:538, July 10, 1783; Westmoreland Co. OB 1747–50, 102a, Jan. 31, 1749.

76. Northampton Co. OB 1698–1703, 162, Aug. 28, 1703; Charlotte Co. OB 1772–74, Dec. 6, 1773; *Va. Gaz.* (PD), Dec. 15, 1768, 2:3.

77. *Va. Gaz.* (PD), Jan. 28, 1773, 3:2, Mar. 9, 1739, 4:1; Augusta Co. OB 1748–51, 34, May 21, 1748; Amelia Co. OB 1735–45, 246, Oct. 21, 1743; Lancaster Co. OB 1696–1702, 53a, Nov. 24, 1698; Westmoreland Co. OB 1747–50, 102a, Jan. 31, 1749; Fauquier Co. OB 1759–62, 20, July 26, 1759.

78. Hening, *Statutes* 2:510.

79. Russell Menard, "From Servants to Slaves: The Transformation of the Chesapeake Labor System," *Southern Studies* 16 (1977): 360–67.

80. For the role of debt in the plantation economy, see T. H. Breen, *Tobacco Culture: The Mentality of the Great Tidewater Planters on the Eve of the Revolution* (Princeton, N.J., 1985), 84–106.

81. Hugh Jones, *The Present State of Virginia* (London, 1724), ed. Richard L. Morton (Chapel Hill, N.C., 1956), 69.

82. *Va. Gaz.* (PD), Dec. 15, 1768, 2:3.

83. *CVS* 4:368, Dec. 18, 1787.

84. The Westmoreland court ordered that "a platform about four foot wide and six foot long" for bedding be erected "in each room of the prison." This suggests that there was more than one room in the prison, but whether these were divided according to type of prisoner is unknown. Westmoreland Co. OB 1698–1705, 57a, Aug. 31, 1699.

85. Hening, *Statutes* 3:214–15, Aug. 1701.

86. Whiffen, *Public Buildings of Williamsburg,* 51–52.

87. Ibid.

88. Jones, *Present State of Virginia,* 69.

89. *JHB* 6:341, Nov. 15, 1738. Other prisoners of higher status who became deftly ill overcame "jail fever" by posting a bond and leaving prison, promising to return upon recovery. See, for example, *EJC* 4:322, May 4, 1734.

90. Because of the "Inconveniencys in having a Window on each side of the sd Goal" in Williamsburg, keeper John Broadnax was given leave to close them. However, he was in-

structed to install a window on the west wall of the cells. It is not clear if this change was made. The 10-foot-high exercise yard wall would have made this new opening less of a security risk than the two windows that opened out on the north and south exterior walls. *LJC* 1:518–19, Nov. 20, 1711.

91. Hening, *Statutes* 4:26, Nov. 1711.

92. Ibid., 114, May 1722.

93. Norfolk Co. OB 1750–53, 69a, Nov. 28, 1751.

94. Westmoreland Co. OB 1747–49, 102a, Jan. 31, 1749; Surry Co. OB 1754–57, 376, Apr. 20, 1756.

95. Elizabeth City Co. OB 1731–47, 363, 370, Dec. 22, 1743, Feb. 15, 1744; Northumberland Co. OB 1743–49, 265, Nov. 10, 1747.

96. Loudoun Co. OB 1765–67, 233, 289, Jan. 12, June 11, 1767; *Va. Gaz.* (R), Jan. 31, 1771, 3:1.

97. Augusta Co. Executive Papers, 162–63, Mar. 15, 1762, Clerk's Office, Staunton, Va. I am indebted to Turk McCleskey for this reference. William Hyde the builder of the jailer's house and wall may have been the same William Hyde who had been apprenticed to builder Benjamin Powell of Williamsburg a few years earlier. See York Co. DB 1755–63, 56–57, Dec. 5, 1755.

98. Fauquier Co. OB 1768–73, 454, Nov. 24, 1772; Northumberland Co. District Court OB 1789–95, 5, Apr. 1, 1789; Accomack Co. OB 1780–83, 211, Mar. 27, 1782; Floyd Nock, *Drummondtown, "A One Horse Town": Accomac Court House, Virginia* (Verona, Va., 1976), 194–95.

99. *CVS* 3:471, Apr. 24, 1783; Botetourt Co. OB 1770–71, 44, Apr. 11, 1770; *Va. Gaz.* (R), Sept. 2, 1773, 3:2.

100. "References to Edenton Prison," Hawks Papers, no. 3530, Southern Historical Collection, Wilson Library, University of North Carolina at Chapel Hill.

101. Hening, *Statutes* 1:341, 3:15, 4:162, Nov. 1647, Apr. 1684, May 1726.

102. York Co. DOWB 1698–1702, 382, Feb. 24, 1701; Middlesex Co. OB 1705–10, 87, Feb. 4, 1707; OB 1732–37, 94, Jan. 3, 1738.

103. Loudoun Co. OB 1757–62, 103, May 9, 1758.

104. Augusta Co. OB 1745–47, 134, Nov. 20, 1746; Shenandoah Co. OB 1785–88, 204, Feb. 28, 1788; Accomack Co. SB 1784–94, 117,)ct. 14, 1789; OB 1787–90, 465, Oct. 29, 1789.

105. Goochland Co. OB 1741–44, 161, Nov. 16, 1742; Louisa Co. OB 1742–48, 168, Sept. 29, 1745; Middlesex Co. OB 1752–58, 143, Apr. 22, 1754; Lancaster Co. OB 1770–78, 392, May 20, 1774.

106. Northumberland Co. OB 1652–65, 70, July 20, 1657; Goochland Co. OB 1741–44, 161, Nov. 16, 1742; Louisa Co. OB 1742–48, 168, Sept. 24, 1745; Frederick Co. OB 1748–51, 50, Mar. 8, 1749; Orange Co. OB 1747–54, 373, May 29, 1752; Berkeley Co. DB no. 3, 242, Feb. 24, 1775; Henry Co. OB 1782–85, 95, May 23, 1783; Bedford Co. OB 1795–99, 270, May 29, 1798; Westmoreland Co. OB 1810–13, 339–40, May 25, 1813; Gloucester Co. OB 1820–21, 371–72, Aug. 7, 1821.

107. Frederick Co. OB 1748–51, 50, Mar. 8, 1749; Accomack Co. OB 1787–89, 465, Oct. 29, 1789.

108. Westmoreland Co. OB 1705–21, 174a, Sept. 26, 1711; Louisa Co. OB 1742–48, 168; OB 1773, 43, May 11, 1773; Caroline Co. OB 1764–65, 323, Nov. 8, 1764; Fauquier Co. OB 1768–73, 434, Aug. 25, 1772; Bedford Co. OB 1784–86, 218, Nov. 28, 1785; Henry Co. OB 1804–8, 112, Oct. 29, 1806.

109. Quoted in Robin Evans, *The Fabrication of Virtue: English Prison Architecture, 1750–1840* (Cambridge, 1982), 7.

110. Quoted in Ayers, *Vengeance and Justice*, 44.

111. *CVS* 3:471, Apr. 24, 1783.

112. On prison reform in the late eighteenth and early nineteenth centuries, see, for example, David Rothman, *The Discovery of the Asylum: Social Order and Disorder in the New Republic* (Boston, 1971); Michel Foucault, *Discipline and Punish: The Birth of the Prison*, trans. Alan Sheridan (New York, 1977); Michael Ignatieff, *A Just Measure of Pain: The Penitentiary in the Industrial Revolution, 1750–1850* (New York, 1978).

113. Evans, *The Fabrication of Virtue*, 195–235.

114. Jeffrey Cohen and Charles Brownell, *The Architectural Drawing of Benjamin Henry Latrobe*, 2 vols. (New Haven, 1994), vol. 2, pt. 1, 98–112; William H. Gaines Jr., "The 'Penitentiary House,'" *VC* 6 (Summer 1956): 11–17.

115. Cohen and Brownell, *Architectural Drawings of Benjamin Henry Latrobe*, vol. 2, pt. 1, 109; Leroy M. Lee, *The Life and Times of the Reverend Jesse Lee* (Richmond, 1848), 482–84; Gaines, "The 'Penitentiary House,'" 15.

6. Taverns and Clerks' Offices

1. William Byrd, "A Progress to the Mines in the Year 1732," in *Prose Works of William Byrd*, 374; William Byrd to John Perceval, Earl of Egmont, July 12, 1736, in Marion Tinling, ed., *The Correspondence of the Three William Byrds of Westover, Virginia, 1684–1776*, 2 vols. (Charlottesville, Va., 1977), 2:488–89.

2. See Patricia Gibbs, "Taverns in Tidewater Virginia, 1700–1774" (M.A. thesis, College of William and Mary, 1968). See also Everitt, "The English Urban Inn, 1560–1760," 91–137; Peter Clark, *The English Alehouse* (New York, 1983); Kym Rice, *Early American Taverns* (Chicago, 1983); A. K. Sandoval-Strausz, "A Public House for a New Republic," in *Constructing Image, Identity, and Place: Perspectives in Vernacular Architecture* 9, ed. Alison K. Hoagland and Kenneth A. Breisch (Knoxville, Tenn., 2003), 54–70.

3. J. F. D. Smyth, *A Tour in the United States of America* (London, 1784), 49–50.

4. For the low opinion that most travelers held for the Virginia tavern, see, for example, *The Journal of Nicholas Cresswell, 1774–1777* (New York, 1928), 20; Francis Baily, *Journal of a Tour in Unsettled Parts of North America in 1796 and 1797*, ed. Jack Holmes (Carbondale, Ill., 1969), 20–21.

5. Hening, *Statutes* 1:411, 521, 3:395–400; Northumberland Co. RB 1710–13, 44, May 16, 1711.

6. York Co. DOWB 1710–16, 71–72, Mar. 19, 1711.

7. Hening, *Statutes* 4:543.

8. *Va. Gaz.* (R), Aug. 4, 1768, 2:4.

9. Accomack Co. OB 1703–9, 164, Feb. 10, 1710; OB 1785–86, 50, June 29, 1786; Loudoun Co. OB 1813–15, 347, Nov. 14, 1814; Augusta Co. OB 1745–47, 298, Sept. 17, 1747.

10. Quoted in Robert Hunter Jr., *Quebec to Carolina in 1785–1786*, ed. Louis B. Wright and Marion Tinling (San Marino, Calif., 1943), 219.

11. François, duc de La Rochefoucauld-Liancourt, *Travels Through the United States of North America, the Country of the Iroquois, and Upper Canada, in the Years 1795, 1796, and 1797*, 2 vols. (London, 1799), 2:64.

12. *Archives of Maryland* 13:288.

13. Quoted in Sydnor, *Gentlemen Freeholders*, 51. On making money out of the court-house tavern trade, see the *Va. Gaz.* (PD), Feb. 10, 1774, 3:2.

14. *VMHB* 45 (July 1937): 48–49.

15. *Va. Gaz.*, Apr. 24, 1752, 2:2; Apr. 11, 1751, Apr. 24, 1754, Sept. 18, 1766.

16. In England in the 1740s, the quarter sessional courts for Hertfordshire adjourned their sessions to the Glove and Dolphin Inn, the Bell Inn, and Dines' Coffee House in Hertford. William Le Hardy, ed., *Hertfordshire County Records: Calendar to the Sessions Books, Sessions Minute Books, and Other Sessions Records with Appendixes, 1700–1752* (Hertford, Eng., 1931), 320, 322, 349.

17. *Diary of Colonel Landon Carter*, 937–38.

18. *Va. Gaz.* (PD), July 18, 1766, 2:1–2, Oct. 17, 1766, 3:1. See also Woody Holton, *Forced Founders: Indians, Debtors, Slaves, and the Making of the American Revolution in Virginia* (Chapel Hill, N.C., 1999), 39–43.

19. *Va. Gaz.* (PD), Nov. 5, 1766, 3:1; Appraisement of the Estate of Richard Taylor who died Dec. 10, 1806, Isle of Wight Co. WB 1804–8, 492–93, Aug. 2, 1808.

20. William B. Hill, ed., *Land by the Roanoke: An Album of Mecklenburg County, Virginia* (Richmond, 1957), 29; "Narrative of George Fisher," *WMQ*, 1st ser., 17 (Jan. 1909): 170.

21. Johann David Schoepf, *Travels in the Confederation [1783–1784*, trans. and ed. Alfred J. Morrison, 2 vols. (New York, 1968), 2:49.

22. Baily, *Journal of a Tour in Unsettled Parts of North America*, 20; *The Virginia Journal of Benjamin Henry Latrobe* 2:232; George Grieve, the eighteenth-century translator of the travel diaries of the marquis de Chastellux, in Chastellux, *Travels in North America* 2:603.

23. Fred Shelley, ed., "The Journal of Ebenezer Hazard in Virginia, 1777," *VMHB* 62 (1954): 402; Chastellux, *Travels in North America* 2:167, 170, 418.

24. Chastellux, *Travels in North America* 2:402; Baron Ludwig von Closen, *Revolutionary Journal, 1780–1783*, trans. and ed. Evelyn Acomb (Chapel Hill, N.C., 1958), 181.

25. *Va. Gaz.*, Oct. 6, 1752, 3:2, Nov. 7, 1754, 4:1, Oct. 10, 1773, 3:1; *Virginia Herald and Fredericksburg Advertiser*, Aug. 8, 1788, 3:3; *Virginia Herald* (Fredericksburg), June 21, 1799, 1:1.

26. *Virginia Gazette and General Advertiser* (Petersburg), June 11, 1799, 3:3.

27. *Va. Gaz.*, Oct. 24, 1745, 4:2.

28. Daniel Fisher in *WMQ*, 1st ser., 17 (Jan. 1909): 167; *Va. Gaz.* (R), Apr. 14, 1768, 3:3; (PD), Apr. 21, 1768, 3:1; (R), Dec. 2, 1773, 3:1.

29. *Va. Gaz.* (R), Feb. 4, 1768, 3:2, Oct. 27, 1768, 2:4; (DH), Dec. 26, 1777, 1:2. See also (R), Dec. 2, 1773, 3:1.

30. The German traveler Johann David Schoepf observed that while in Virginia taverns were "easily to be identified by the great number of miscellaneous papers and advertisements with which [their] walls and doors . . . are plaistered," the taverns around Philadelphia, in contrast, were "recognizable even at a distance, by a sort of gallows arrangement which stands out over the road and exhibits the patron of the house." Schoepf, *Travels in the Confederation* 1:124; 2:30.

31. *Va. Gaz.*, May 4, 1782.

32. Much of the following discussion of tavern plans is based upon the research of my colleagues Mark R. Wenger and Willie Graham. I am grateful to them for sharing this information with me.

33. Hughlett's Tavern was converted into a modern hotel probably in the 1830s with the

addition of a double-pile wing to the south of the original two-story section and the construction of a piazza across the entire span. The old section was heavily modified by the removal of all the divisions and woodwork to create a large, fashionable entertaining room with a Greek Revival mantel at the north end, symmetrical door and window architraves, a simple chairboard, and beaded base.

Upstairs, private chambers were carved out of communal sleeping rooms, setting the tavern's expansion on the path toward recognizable modern accommodations. That the tavern was still being used well into the twentieth century with only superficial alterations testifies to the continuing suitability of this discrete arrangement of spaces into private chambers and public circulation and entertaining rooms and marks the watershed that divides the plan of the building from its colonial predecessors.

34. Until the road was changed sometime in the middle of the nineteenth century, it ran on the west side of Hanover Tavern (now the backside of the building). The tavern stood between the road and the front of the courthouse. In 1822 William Thilman, the tavern's owner, constructed a two-story, L-shaped wing south of the original building. Rather than placing this new wing against the old section, Thilman left a 16-foot space between them, an area that was enclosed ten years later in 1832–33 by a subsequent owner. As an up-to-date stagecoach inn, Hanover Tavern offered first-class accommodations to travelers, providing the heated private or semiprivate bedchambers segregated from the public rooms that travelers expected by the second quarter of the nineteenth century.

35. Inventory of the Estate of James Shields, York Co. WIB 1746–59, 198–200, Jan. 21, 1751.

36. On the impact of these new ideas on the material world of colonial Americans, see, for example, Carson, "The Consumer Revolution in Colonial British America: Why Demand?" 483–697.

37. For gentility's role in shaping the lives of early Americans, see Bushman, *Refinement of America;* quote from ibid., 98.

38. See Mark R. Wenger, "The Central Passage in Virginia: Evolution of an Eighteenth-Century Living Space," in *Perspectives in Vernacular Architecture* 2, ed. Camille Wells (Columbia, Mo., 1986), 137–49.

39. Bushman, *Refinement of America,* 185.

40. York Co. DOWB 1745–59, 134–38, Jan. 16, 1748.

41. *Md. Gaz.,* Dec. 24, 1760.

42. *Va. Gaz.* (PD), June 25, 1767, 3:1, Jan. 23, 1772, 3:3; W. W. Abbot and Dorothy Twohig, eds., *The Papers of George Washington: Colonial Series,* 10 vols. (Charlottesville, Va., 1983–94), 8:52, 82, 9:117, 190, 395; Donald Jackson and Dorothy Twohig, eds., *The Diaries of George Washington,* 6 vols. (Charlottesville, Va., 1976–79), 3:142–43.

43. Chastellux, *Travels in North America* 2:380.

44. Whiffen, *Eighteenth-Century Houses of Williamsburg,* 146–50; *Diaries of George Washington* 3:142; *Va. Gaz.,* Feb. 27, 1752, 4:1, Mar. 5, 1752, 3:2.

45. The description of the Botetourt Hotel is based on observations made by Willie Graham in January 1986. A billiard table that was advertised with the tavern in 1774 probably was located in one of these rooms. *Va. Gaz.* (PD), Feb. 10, 1774, 3:2.

46. "Journal of Ebenezer Hazard in Virginia, 1777," 403. For public assemblies and other activities at the Edenton courthouse, see Marc Brodsky, *The Courthouse at Edenton* (Edenton, N.C., 1989), 36–37.

47. York Co. OWB 1691–94, 110, Jan. 21, 1692; Surry Co. WDB 1778–83, 186–87, June 21,

1781; Northumberland Co. OB 1811–15, 110, Aug. 12, 1812; OB 1706–10, preface, 1710; Hening, *Statutes* 4:448, 526, Aug. 1734; *Columbian Herald* (Charleston, S.C.), Aug. 21, 1787, 2:4; George Reese, ed., *Journals of the Council of the State of Virginia, 1786–1788* (Richmond, 1967), 253, June 21, 1788; *Richmond and Manchester Advertiser*, Mar. 16, 1796, 3:2.

48. On storage of books and papers in trunks, see Thornton, *Seventeenth-Century Interior Decoration*, 306.

49. Middlesex Co. OB 1705–10, 96, Apr. 17, 1707; York Co. OWB 1691–94, 92, 110, Jan. 21, 25, 1692.

50. York County OWB 1709–16, 46, Jan. 16, 1711.

51. *Virginia Antiquary*, vol. 1, *Princess Anne County Loose Papers, 1700–1789*, ed. John Harvie Creecy (Richmond, 1954), 62; Louisa Co. OB 1742–48, 82, Oct. 10, 1743; Middlesex Co. OB 1740–44, 238, Dec. 6, 1743. On the bookpress in Northampton County, see James R. Melchor, Gordon Lohr, and Marilyn Melchor, *Eastern Shore, Virginia, Raised-Panel Furniture, 1730–1830* (Norfolk, Va., 1982), 71–72.

52. Westmoreland Co. OB 1676–89, 145, Dec. 4, 1678; Charles City Co. OB 1687–95, 93, Dec. 21, 1687; Elizabeth City Co. DOWB 1715–21, pt. 2, 187, May 19, 1720; OB 1731–46, 104, 294, Dec. 17, 1736, July 22, 1742; Henrico Co. OB 1719–24, 55, Dec. 5, 1720; York Co. WIB 1732–40, 248, Dec. 15, 1735; OB 1784–87, 3, 211, June 21, 1784, Aug. 16, 1785. See also Riley, "Colonial Courthouses of York," 403.

53. York Co. DOWB 1706–10, 82, 102, 121, July 24, Dec. 15, 1707, Feb. 25, 1708; Riley, "Founding and Development of Yorktown, 1691–1781," 78–80; Brunswick Co. OB 1732–41, 51, Jan. 4, 1734; Orange Co. OB 1734–39, 233, Oct. 27, 1737; Cumberland Co. OB 1749–51, 29, 39, Sept. 25, Nov. 28, 1749; Prince Edward Co. OB 1767–70, 7, May 5, 1767.

54. See, for example, Westmoreland IB 1723–46, 42a, Feb. 22, 1726; Surry Co. WDB 1778–83, 186–87, June 21, 1781.

55. Middlesex Co. OB 1767–69, 66, May 5, 1767.

56. York Co. DOWB 1691–94, 92, Jan. 25, 1692.

57. *Va. Gaz.*, Dec. 22, 1755, 4:2; ibid. (PD), Mar. 21, 1771, 3:2; ibid. (D), May 1, 1779, 3:1.

58. *Gazette of the State of Georgia* (Savannah), Sept. 6, 1787, 3:1.

59. *CVS* 4:380, Aug. 26, 1787.

60. Byrd, "Progress to the Mines in the Year 1732," 373.

61. *Va. Gaz.*, Dec. 22, 1755, 4:2; *Alexandria Gazette*, Dec. 4, 1788, 1:3.

62. Janet Shaffer, "New London," *VC* 15 (Winter 1966): 27–29.

63. Samuel Shepherd, ed., *The Statutes at Large of Virginia, 1792–1795*, 3 vols. (Richmond, 1835–36), 1:12.

64. Loudoun Co. OB 1799–1800, 309–10, 409, May 13, Aug. 12, 1800; OB 1805–6, 20–21, Apr. 11, 1805; OB 1811–12, 186, Dec. 9, 1811; Frederick Johnston, *Memorials of Old Virginia Clerks* (Lynchburg, Va., 1888), 240.

65. Caroline Co. OB 1799–1802, 395–96, Oct. 13, 1801; OB 1807–9, 1, Dec. 14, 1807.

66. Susan L. Bracey, *Life by the Roaring Roanoke: A History of Mecklenburg County, Virginia* (Mecklenburg Co., Va., 1977), 129; John Wood, "Map of Goochland County, 1820," *Map of Amelia County, 1820*, CWF; Johnston, *Memorials of Old Virginia Clerks*, 189; Goochland Co. OB 1825–31, 82.

67. Lancaster Co. OB 1792–99, 222, July 21, 1795; Powhatan Co. OB 1794–98, 240, May 20, 1796; Isle of Wight Co. OB 1801–3, 33, Aug. 6, 1801; Loudoun Co. OB 1799–1800, 309–10, May 13, 1800; Culpeper County reference in the *Virginia Herald*, July 1, 1800, 3:4; Orange Co. OB

1801–3, 213, Mar. 22, 1802; Spotsylvania Co. MB 1805–7, 142, Apr. 7, 1806; King George County reference in the *Virginia Herald,* July 19, 1809, 3:3; Henry Co. OB 1808–11, 76–77, Sept. 25, 1809.

68. Accomack Co. OB 1793–96, 180, Apr. 29, 1794; OB 1796–98, 366, Feb. 27, 1798; Charles City Co. OB 1823–29, 46, Mar. 20, 1824.

69. Accomack Co. OB 1793–96, 180, Apr. 29, 1794; Bath Co. OB 1791–1801, 378, Oct. 11, 1797; Spotsylvania Co. MB 1805–7, 142, Apr. 7, 1806.

70. Accomack Co. OB 1793–96, 180, Apr. 29, 1794; *Virginia Herald,* Apr. 2, 1802, 3:3; Spotsylvania Co. MB 1805–7, 142, Apr. 7, 1806.

71. Northumberland Co. OB 1796–97, 37, July 12, 1796; *Virginia Herald,* Apr. 2, 1802, 3:3, July 19, 1809, 3:3.

72. Culpeper Co. OB 1802–3, 68, Aug. 20, 1802; Powhatan Co. OB 1794–98, 444, Apr. 18, 1798; Accomack Co. OB 1800–1804, 235, Apr. 27, 1802.

73. *Virginia Herald,* July 19, 1809, 3:3; Powhatan Co. OB 1820–21, 497, July 19, 1821.

74. The Sussex County courthouse may have originally had two doorways leading into the courtroom from the central three-bay arcade. Specifications for its construction called for "a partition wall of brick with two doors and one . . . window in it between the Portico and Court Room." If it was built with the two doorways, the plan was altered in the 1870s when the courthouse was substantially changed to provide for two courtrooms. A single doorway now leads into the ground-floor space. *Richmond Enquirer,* July 22, 1825.

75. Rappahannock Co. DB 1833–35, 12–13, May 6, 1833.

76. See Waddell and Liscombe, *Robert Mills's Courthouses and Jails;* John Bryan, ed., *Robert Mills, Architect* (Washington, D.C., 1989), 79–83.

77. Lunenburg Co. OB 1821–23, 408, Nov. 10, 1823; OB 1856–65, 71, May 12, 1857.

Epilogue: Courthouse Grounds to Civic Square

1. Accomack Co. OB 1744–53, 369, Nov. 29, 1749; Northumberland Co. OB 1758–62, 361, Feb. 9, 1762; OB 1762–66, 564, Aug. 10, 1765.

2. Joseph Martin, *A New and Comprehensive Gazetteer of Virginia and the District of Columbia* (Charlottesville, Va., 1835), 150, 176, 186, 201, 243.

3. Essex Co. RB 1692–95, 261, Nov. 11, 1695. For a similar order, see Frederick Co. OB 1745–48, 99, May 8, 1746.

4. Essex Co. OB 1729–33, 109, Oct. 20, 1730; Fairfax Co. OB 1756–1763, 42, Nov. 11, 1756; Accomack Co. OB 1798–1800, 250, Feb. 25, 1800.

5. Roaming livestock made themselves at home in and around an early Anglican church in Chowan County, North Carolina, for with "the Key being lost the door stood open." Rev. John Urmston to the Secretary of the Society for the Propagation of the Gospel, London, July 7, 1711, *Colonial Records of North Carolina* 1:769–70.

6. *LJC* 1:151, May 20, 1691; Shepherd, *Statutes at Large of Virginia* 3:168, Jan. 5, 1805; Goochland Co. OB 1844–52, 130, May 19, 1846.

7. Richmond Co. OB 1739–52, 257, Aug. 6, 1750; OB 1769–73, 38, Aug. 9, 1769; OB 1784–86, 128–29, Apr. 6, 1784.

8. Goochland Co. OB 1825–31, 342, Mar. 17, 1829; Martin, *Gazetteer of Virginia,* 143, 205.

9. John Pendleton Kennedy, *Swallow Barn, or a Sojourn in the Old Dominion* (New York, 1851), 168.

10. Augusta Co. OB 1749–53, 455, May 18, 1753.

11. See E. Lee Shepard, "Courts in Conflict: Town-County Relations in Post-Revolutionary Virginia," *VMHB* 85 (Apr. 1977): 184–99.

12. Fredericksburg City Council MB 1782–1801, 34–35, Sept. 4, 1782.

13. Spotsylvania Co. WB 1722–49, 246, Oct. 6, 1736; MB 1774–82, Feb. 18, 1779, June 21, 1781; Fredericksburg City Council MB 1782–1801, 189, Mar. 17, 1789.

14. *Va. Gaz.* (Pi), Apr. 20, 1775, 3:2; Fredericksburg City Council MB 1782–1801, 17, 402, Apr. 20, 1782, June 26, 1797; *Virginia Herald*, Jan. 15, 1789, 3:4; Fredericksburg City Council MB 1801–29, 174, 176, 231–32, 242, Dec. 14, 1812, Feb. 6, 1813, May 10, 15, 1815, Mar. 21, 1816; *Virginia Herald*, July 8, 1803, 4:2.

15. Paula Felder, "A History of the Market Lot: How It Became the Seat of Government in Fredericksburg" (research paper, Historic Fredericksburg Foundation, 1983); Fredericksburg City Council MB 1801–29, 206, Apr. 23, 1814.

16. The accretion of structures over several decades on the public lot in the town of Leesburg was typical of this urban pattern in Virginia. See Loudoun County Co. OB 1757–62, 544, Nov. 12, 1761; OB 1776–83, 159, Apr. 13, 1779; OB 1811–12, 21, June 3, 1811; OB 1813–15, 347, 428, Nov. 14, 1814, Mar. 17, 1815; OB 1815–17, 372, June 12, 1817.

17. *Richmond Times*, Feb. 3, 1900.

18. *Fredericksburg News*, May 2, 1851, 2:4. See also an earlier article that laid out the two extremes in the argument over public building, in *Fredericksburg News*, July 20, 1849, 2:3–4.

19. Fredericksburg City Council MB 1829–51, 462–63, May 31, 1851.

20. Because the two buildings were not erected, the clerk of Goochland court was allowed to keep his office at his residence. Twenty years later, in 1847, a one-story brick clerk's office was built at right angles 64 feet to the north of the portico of the courthouse. In the 1850s a two-story stone jail was rebuilt in a similar position to the south of the courthouse. It was slightly farther from the courthouse than the clerk's office. Goochland Co. OB 1825–31, 82, Sept. 18, 1826.

21. Unsigned letter, Virginia Counties: Warwick County, box 2, folder 7, Apr. 18, 1862, College of William and Mary.

22. Richmond Co. BSMB 1870–86, 27, Mar. 28, 1872; Hanover Co. BSMB 1871–84, 402, May 16, 1883.

23. Martin, *Gazetteer of Virginia*, 195; Henry Co. Loose Papers, June 5, 1884, Clerk's Office, Martinsville, Va.; Henry Co. MB No. 15, 274, Feb. 13, 1896.

24. Goochland Co. OB 1852–62, 155, Apr. 16, 1855; Henry Co. MB 1859–64, 359, June 10, 1862; MB 1864–67, 138, June 15, 1866; New Kent Co. BSMB 1870–90, 17–18, Dec. 4, 1871; Charlotte Co. BSMB 1900–1913, 57, Dec. 9, 1902.

25. Mathews Co. BSMB No. 2, May 3, 1935.

26. Henry Co. MB 1853–58, 42, Jan. 10, 1854; MB 1859–64, 14, Mar. 14, 1859; William Meade, *Old Churches, Ministers, and Families of Virginia*, 2 vols. (Philadelphia, 1857), 2:215.

27. Henry Co. MB 1864–67, 249, July 8, 1867; Charlotte Co. OB 1863–68, 246, July 5, 1866; BSMB no. 4, 12, July 15, 1912.

28. Essex Co. OB 1823–26, 478, Aug. 21, 1826.

29. Charlotte Co. BSMB no. 4, 204, Oct. 16, 1916.

INDEX

Italicized page numbers refer to illustrations.

Bacon's Rebellion, 58, 194, 217, 358, 390 n. 32

Bailiff, 61

Baily, Francis, 274

Baine, Alexander, 353

Baldrey, Robert, 58

Ball, John, 233

Ball, Spence, 317

Ballard, Robert, 36, 41, 43, 381; house, 30

Baltimore County, Md., courthouse, 78, 79

Balustrade, 67

Banister River, Halifax County, 353

Bar, 39

Bass, Richard, 372

Bastard, John, 114

Bastard, William, 114

Bath County, 100; courthouse, 339

Battersea, Petersburg, 173

Baxter, John, 342

Bayley, Ambrose, 197

Beaverdam Creek, Goochland County, 353

Beckley, John, 349

Bedford County, 225, 302; clerk of court, 301–2; court day, 8; courthouse, *90*, 175, 196, 339; prison, 196; prison bounds, 260; tavern, 276

Bell, 49, 89

Bell, John, 348

Bentham, Jeremy, 260, 261

Berkeley, Norbonne, baron de Botetourt, 33

Berkeley, Sir William, 60

Berkeley, Charles City County, 86

Berkeley County, (now) W.Va., courthouse, 122–23, *123*, 340

Bernard, Nicholas, 398 n. 84

Bernard, William, 342

Berryman, G. R., 379

Bertie County, N.C., courthouse, 111

Beverley, Robert, 9, 81, 84–85, 91, 390 n. 31

Beverley, William, 265, 276

Beverley, East Yorkshire, guildhall, *73, 150*

Biblical law, 66

Binns, Charles, 302

Blackbonne, William, 379

Black Boy Tavern, 60

Blackstone, William, 220

Blackwater Swamp, Surry County, 379

Blair, Archibald, 20

Blair, James, 50, 82

Blair, John, 19, 20

Bland, James, 230

Bland, Richard, 342

Blandfield, Essex County, 107

Blandford, Prince George County, 301, 373

Blandford Forum, Dorset, town hall and market house, 114, 116, 141, 146, *146*, 147, *149*

Bluestone Creek, Lunenburg County, 365

Board of supervisors, county, 165, 327, 333

Botetourt County: clerk's office, 340, *341*; courthouse, 99, 340; prison, 238, 256

Botetourt Hotel, Gloucester County, 291–96, *291, 292, 293*

Boughan, Henry, 230

Bouram, John, 353

Bowling Green, Caroline County, 276, *277*, 303, 319, 342

Boyd's Tavern, Mecklenburg County, 272, *273*, 278

Boydton, Mecklenburg County, 273, 304

Boykin's Tavern, Isle of Wight County, 272, 278

Bradley, Thomas, 374

Brafferton, College of William and Mary, *85*

Braham, John, 371

Branding, 224, *226*

Branding iron, 216, 225

Brandon, Prince George County, 173

Brentsville, Prince William County, 374

Brent Town, Prince William County, 373

Brice, William, 374

Brickwork, 8, 13, 39, 40, 60, 63, 68, 100–108, 130, 237, 239, 244; bonding, 13, 100, 101, 104–6, 108, 111, 325, 395 n. 44; foundations, 67, 104; frontispiece, 101, 103; glazed headers, 13, 45, 95, 105, 108, 113, *201*; impost block, 106; jack arch, 45, 100; lime wash on, 107, 108; molded, 101–2; mortar, 88, 106, 108, 240, 242; mullion, 101, 103, 108; pilaster, 103; rubbed and gauged, 45, 105–7, *106, 107*, 108; wall height, 111–12; water table, 45, 94, 100, 104–5, *105*, 107, 111

Bridge, 174, 200, 205, 212

Bridges, Charles, 151, 341

Bristol, England, 29, 50, 208

Bristol Parish, Charles City County and Henrico County, 59

Broughan, James, 346

Brown, William, 340, 366

Bruce, Philip A., 9

Chippenham, Wiltshire, guildhall, 77

Chipping Camden, Gloucestershire, market house, *48*

Chiswell, John, 271

Chodowiecki, Daniel, 7

Chowan County, N.C., courthouse, *136*, 141, *141*, 142, *143*, 144, 145, 146, 147, 148, *148*, 152, 294, *295*; prison, 256–58, *257*

Christ Church, Lancaster County, 107, 157

Christ Church Parish, Middlesex County: Lower Church, *104*, 108; Middle Church 108

Churches, 11, *29*, 30, 39, 42, 61, 64, 86, 88, 101– 5, *102*, *103*, *104*, 107, 108–9, 111, 195, 199, 201, 204, 205, *205*, 212, *213*, 215, 219, 321, 330, 368, 394 n. 19, 398 n. 80, 401 n. 31, 413 n. 5; as precedents for courthouse design, 66–67, 77, 79, 83, 119, 131, 137, 144, 157

Churchwarden, 23, 27

Church yard, 130, 318, 319

Civic ceremonies, England, 49, *51*

Civil War, 14, 15, 47, 91, 108, 165, 296, 304, 324, 327, 354, 360, 370, 373, 377, 381; monu- ments, *96*, 331–33, *332*, *333*, 342

Clack, Sterling, 340

Claytor, William, 374

Clerk of court, 6, 18, 26, 28, 61, 71, 73, 75, 80, 134–35, 138, 151, 156, 162, 196, 300, *302*; role of, 155–56, 296; social status, 301

Clerk's office, 9, 13, 14–15, 21, 23, 31, 40, 41, 87, *96*, 107, 129, *176*, 180, 196, 296–313, *303*, *305*, *306*, *307*, *312*, 315, 324, *341*, *342*, *378*; furnish- ings, 70, 297–99, 307–9, *308*, 313; in court- house, 70, 128–29, 130, 134, 200, 299–300

Cleve, Emanuel, 222

Cleve, King George County, 212, *214*

Clinch, William, 196, 379

Coat of arms, 49, *50*, 140, 150, *150*, *151*, 398 n. 84. *See also under* Courtroom

Cobb, Jeremiah, 376

Cocke, John Hartwell, 349

Cocke, Thomas, 58

Coffeehouse, Williamsburg, 288

Cole, John, 57, 337

Cole, Mary, 223

Coleman, Robert, 344

Coleman, Robert Spilsby, 200

College of William and Mary, 42, 43, 85, *85*, 109, 116

Collins, Samuel, 339

Collins, T. J., 339, 375

Colonial Williamsburg Foundation, 333, 358

Colonnade, 63, *64*, 113

Colony House, Newport, R.I.: documents press, 297, *298*; witness stand, 399 n. 105

Columbia, Tenn., courthouse, 153

Comenius, Johann Amos, 72

Common law, 16–17, 28, 66

Confederate monument, *96*, 331–33, *332*, *333*

Constable, 18, 21, 26, 28, 80, 87, 134, 222; du- ties of, 22–23

Contractor. *See* Undertaker

Cooke, George, 151, 152, 157

Corotoman, Lancaster County, 62, 364

Cosby, Dabney, 304, 353, 354, 379

Cotton, William, 219

Council, 20, 31, 33, 55, 117, 169

County boundaries, 11, 88, 183; map of, *52*, *92*; survey of, 54

County court: authority and functions of, 9, 16–28, 66, 87, 91, 165, 217–21, 296; establish- ment of, 54; levy, 26, 39, 63, 135, 391 n. 41; meeting places, 55–60; records, 9, 14, 296– 300; study of, 9–10, 18

Court crier, 7, 71, 80

Court day, 3–8, 9, 13, 14, 34, 117, 223, 276, 277, 299; decline of, 335; drinking, 3, 5, 8, 222, 268–70, 330; fighting, 5, 8, 223; games, 7, 8, 270; horseracing, 7, 330, 384 n. 9; travel, 3; *4*, 19; vendors, 3, 5–6, *7*, 8, 15, 38, 269, 315, 330

Courthouse, 3, 7, 9, 13, 23, 61, 62–63, 70, 82, 86, 92–99, 169, 174, 178–79, 181, 185, 195, 210, 323–24; as a building type, 11, 39, 62, 65–69, 91–92, 100–101, 108, 122, 130, 324; apse, 142, 144–45, *145*, 177, 396 n. 65; arcade or piazza, 6, 13, 41, 43, *44*, 89, 90, 108, 109, 112, 119–24, 128, 131, 165–67, 183, 186–87, 191, 198, 319, 321, 324, 325, 388 n. 47, 395 n. 44; attitudes toward, 87, 91, 323–24; ceiling, 66, 69, 78, 83, 97; cupola, 95, 123, 127; decision to build, 169–71; door, 68, 93, 95, 177, *363*; entrance, 40, 41, 70–71, 95, 123, 127, 129, 131, 165; fireplace, 70, 72, 94, 129, 177, 391 n. 55; flooring, 45, 69, 78–79, 94, 101, 119–22, 183; gallery, 69, 311; garret, 68, 69, 128; plan, 40– 41, *41*, 43–45, *44*, 68–70, *71*, 87–88, 95, 123,

earthfast (post in the ground), 60, *66*, 67, 88, 92–94, 97, 234–36, 238; English frame, 97, 130; roof, 45, 66, 67, 68, 88, 93, 130, 131, 167, 185, 200, *203*, 396 n. 57

Franklin County courthouse, 350, 356

Frazer, William, 212

Frederick County, 7; courthouse, 171, 350; prison bounds, 259

Fredericksburg, 14, 89, 119, 216, 241, 260, 289, 294–95, 376; courthouse, 324, *325*, 377; market house, 321, 322, *322*, *323*; public square, 321–24

French, Daniel, 210, 364

French Ordinary, York County, 58, 380–81

Front Royal, Warren County, 165

Fry, John, 338

Fry-Jefferson map, *92*; cartouche, *27*

Gaines, Henry, 206

Gallows, 13, 200, 216, 221, 225, 228, 230, *230*

Gaol. *See* Prison

Gardner, John, 380

Garrett, Robert, 381

Gates, Sir Thomas, 17

Gauntlett, John, 29

General Assembly, 28, 60, 61, 116, 117, 170, 196, 217, 225, 234, 248, 249, 250, 252, 261, 267, 268, 283, 302, 313

General Court, 21, 24, 25, 60, 90, 117, 140, 142, 150, 159, 212, 221, 228, 247, 249, 271, 283, 358, 390 n. 31. *See also* Capitol, Williamsburg

Gentility, influence on building forms, 11–12, 285–86

Gentry, 86–87, 91, 163, 173, 196, 204, 210, 217, 219–20

Geographic centrality, and location of courthouses, 54, 56, 59–60

The George, Alexandria, 287

George III, 8; coat of arms, *151*

Germanna, Spotsylvania County, 376

Gerrard, William, 377

Ghequiere, T. Buckler, 165–67

Gibbet, 216, 230

Gibbs, James, 206

Gibson, Patrick, 341

Glasgow, 29, 208, 247

Glebe house, 211, 212

Glorious Revolution, 220

Gloucester County, 8, 57, 58; clerk's office, 312; courthouse, 62, 65, 67–68, 71, 109, 131, 291, 350–52, *351*, 366; courthouse grounds, *329*, 333, *333*, *334*; prison, 195, 232, 245, 252, 352; prison bounds, *351*; tavern, 291–96, *291*, *292*, *293*

Gloucester Point, Gloucester County, 28

Glover, Samuel, 340

Godwin, Joseph, 93, 370

Goochland County, 7, 19; clerk of court, 304; clerk's office, 324; court day, 269; courthouse, 130, 145, 155, 163, 181, 304, 319, 325, 338, 352–53, 354, 379; courthouse grounds, 319, 328, *353*, 414 n. 20; prison, 181, 233–34, 264; prison bounds, *352*

Governor, 55, 56, 117, 169

Governor's Palace, Williamsburg, 33, 85, *85*

Gray's Creek, Surry County, 378

Great Depression, 15

Gregory, Richard Fletcher, 245–46, 248

Griffin, Thomas, 238

Grove, Hugh, 41

Gunston Hall, Fairfax County, 187, *187*, 207, 208, *209*; courthouse sketches discovered at, 187–93

Guthrey, Severn, 128, 185, 200–202, 315, 337

Haley, John, 234

Halfpenny, William, 173

Halifax County courthouse, 171, *335*, 353–54

Hampton, 28, 345

Hanover County, 172, 211, 212, 278, 301; clerk of court, 301; clerk's office, 325; courthouse, *88*, 89, 104, 105, 107, *107*, 119, 131, *132*, 151, *152*, 154, 155, 157, 169, 171, 181, 198, 279, 317, 325, 354, *355*, 364; courthouse grounds, 325, *326*, 328; prison, 263, 264, 325; tavern, 278, 279–80, *281*, *282*, 288, 317, 325

Hanover Tavern, Hanover County, 278, 279–80, 281, *281*, *282*, 288, 325, 411 n. 34

Hanover Town, Hanover County, tavern, *287*

Hansford, Thomas, 58

Hardin, John, 350

Harrison, Benjamin, 338

Harrison, David, 195

Harrison, Nathaniel, 177, 215, 377, 379

Harrison, Thomas, 375

Harrisonburg, Rockingham County, *4*, 5, 8, 375

Hartwell, Henry, 50, 82
Harwood, Humphrey, 208
Hatton, William, 19
Hawkins, Thomas, 26
Hawks, John, 256–57
Haymarket, Prince William County, 319, 330
Haynes, Anthony, 345
Haynie, Richard, 371
Hayward, Francis, 20, 21
Hazard, Ebenezer, 275
Heathsville, Northumberland County, 278, 331, 371
Hedon, East Yorkshire, town hall, 75–76, *76*, 139, 141, 142, 146
Hening, William Waller, 9
Henrico, 51
Henrico County, 19, 57, 59; clerk's office, 299; courthouse, 62, 67, 183, 197, 299, 338, 354; location of court sessions, 58; prison, 234
Henry, Patrick, 151, *152*, 154, 278
Henry, Rev. Patrick, 211, 212
Henry County: courthouse, 99, 111, 356–57, *356*; courthouse grounds, 6, 328–29, 330; prison bounds, 260
Hickman, William, 372
Hill, Edward, 56, 62, 194, 342
Hill, John. *See* Seale, Thomas
Hill, John P., 369
Hipkins, John, 366, 368
Hobday, William, 370
Holloway, John, 20, 21
Holmes, Thomas, 234
Holmes and Rust, 375
Hoomes, John, 342
Hopkins, Samuel, 146
Hotel, 265, 285, 288. *See also* Tavern
House of Burgesses, 20, 21, 61, 147, 196, 199, 217, 239
Howard, Francis, fifth Baron Howard of Effingham, 390
Howard, John, 260, 261
Howard, William A., 345, 365, 366, 373
Howes, Job, 297
Hughlett, John, 58, 371
Hughlett's Indian Field, 371
Hughlett's Tavern, Northumberland County, 278, 279, *279*, 410–11 n. 33
Humphrey, Joseph, 371

Hunt, David, 354, 372
Hyde, William, 254, 408 n. 97

Indians, 84
Ingram, Pines, 344
Inns of Court, London, 24, 161
Instruments of punishments, *69*, 181, 182, 216. *See also* Gallows; Pillory; Stocks; Whipping post
Inverness, Scotland, 208
Isaac, Rhys, 9–10
Isle of Wight County, 59, 101, 200, 222–23; clerk's office, *176*, 304, 358; courthouse, 62, 119, 131, 145, *145*, 171, 175, *176*, 177, *177*, 272, 357–58; courthouse grounds, *358*; prison, *176*, 358; store, 358; tavern, 272, 278, 358

Jackson, Christopher, 369
Jail. *See* Prison
Jailer's house, 252, 254–55, *256*
James (slave), 230
James City County, 57, 101, 228, 239; courthouse, *15*, 104, 105, 108, 109, 110, 117, 119, *126*, 127, 131, *133*, *134*, 171, 299, 358, 388 n. 47; location of court sessions, 59, 358; prison, 239. *See also* Williamsburg–James City County courthouse
James River, 18, 56, 57, 59, 62, 127, 181, 207, 342, 373
Jamestown, 25, 50, 51, 53–54, 61, 119, 233, 247, 358; parish church, 101, 103, 109; prison, 234, 239, 242, 244, 249; rowhouse, *52–53*, 53–54, 239; statehouse, 60, 61, 116, 117, 150, 318, 319, 358, 390 n. 31; 390 n. 32
Jefferson, Thomas, 9, 11, 30, 161, 254, 275, 324, 401 n. 42; designs for courthouses, 146, 155, 317, 340, 344, 365–66, 397 n. 75; on architecture, 91–92, 125, 127, 173, 175
Jennings, Edward, 297
Jerdone, Francis, 31
Jett, Peter, 360
Johnson, James, 372
Johnson, Paul, 275
Johnson, Stephen, 199, 205
Johnson's Ordinary, Westmoreland County, 8
Johnson's Tavern, Louisa County, 275
Johnston County, N.C., courthouse, 98
Jones, Benjamin, 246

COLONIAL WILLIAMSBURG STUDIES IN CHESAPEAKE HISTORY AND CULTURE

Lorena S. Walsh
From Calabar to Carter's Grove: The History of a Virginia Slave Community

Carl R. Lounsbury
The Courthouses of Early Virginia: An Architectural History